THE STATE OF SOCIAL WELFARE, 1997

This volume is in memory of Brian Abel-Smith

International Studies on Social Security

Volume 4

Chief Series Editor
PETER FLORA

Series Editors
PETER BEZEMER
PHILIP R. DE JONG
JUN-YOUNG KIM
JULIAN LE GRAND
THEODORE R. MARMOR
PER-GUNNAR SVENSSON

The State of Social Welfare, 1997

International studies on social insurance and retirement, employment, family policy and health care

Edited by
PETER FLORA
PHILIP R. DE JONG
JULIAN LE GRAND
JUN-YOUNG KIM

LONDON AND NEW YORK

First published 1998 by Ashgate Publishing

Reissued 2018 by Routledge
2 Park Square, Milton Park, Abingdon, Oxon, OX14 4RN
52 Vanderbilt Avenue, New York, NY 10017

Routledge is an imprint of the Taylor & Francis Group, an informa business

Copyright © FISS 1998

All rights reserved. No part of this book may be reprinted or reproduced or utilised in any form or by any electronic, mechanical, or other means, now known or hereafter invented, including photocopying and recording, or in any information storage or retrieval system, without permission in writing from the publishers.

Notice:
Product or corporate names may be trademarks or registered trademarks, and are used only for identification and explanation without intent to infringe.

Publisher's Note
The publisher has gone to great lengths to ensure the quality of this reprint but points out that some imperfections in the original copies may be apparent.

Disclaimer
The publisher has made every effort to trace copyright holders and welcomes correspondence from those they have been unable to contact.

A Library of Congress record exists under LC control number: 98073025

ISBN 13: 978-1-138-36368-7 (hbk)
ISBN 13: 978-1-138-36372-4 (pbk)
ISBN 13: 978-0-429-43155-5 (ebk)

Contents

Preface ix
Jonathan R. Bradshaw and Han Emanuel

Introduction and overview xi
Peter Flora, Philip R. de Jong, Jun-Young Kim and
Julian Le Grand

SOCIAL SECURITY AND MACRO-ECONOMICS

Social security, macro-economics and the European 3
Union
A.B. Atkinson

PART 1: PENSIONS AND RETIREMENT

1.1 The economic impact of widowhood in the United 17
States in the 1990s: The role of social insurance and
private pensions
Karen C. Holden and Cathleen D. Zick

1.2 Old-age provision for women: Bismarck or Beveridge? 37
Christopher Prinz

1.3 Employment and retirement: Conflicting aims within 57
the welfare society
Martin Rein and Barry L. Friedman

1.4 Cross-national patterns of labor force withdrawal 83
Timothy M. Smeeding and Joseph F. Quinn

PART 2: EMPLOYMENT AND SOCIAL SECURITY

2.1 The welfare state and full employment 119
   Robert H. Haveman

2.2 Government mandates, health insurance, and the deterioration of the low-wage labor market: Are they connected? 143
   Barbara L. Wolfe, Amy Wolaver and Timothy McBride

PART 3: FAMILY POLICY AND ECONOMIC WELLBEING

3.1 Policy responses to household vulnerability: The Norwegian case in an international context 191
   Einar Overbye

3.2 The state-parent-child relationship after family breakups: Child maintenance in Norway and Britain 217
   Anne Skevik

3.3 Changes in economic well-being and income distribution in the 1980s: Different measures, different outcomes 239
   Amy D. Crews and Richard V. Burkhauser

PART 4: PRIVATIZATION OF SOCIAL INSURANCE

4.1 Dimensions of privatisation: The Swedish welfare state in transition 265
   Tor E. Eriksen and Lars Söderström

4.2 Privatization of retirement income 283
   John A. Turner and David Rajnes

4.3 Privatization of social insurance and welfare state efficiency: Evidence from the Netherlands and the United States 297
   Leo J.M. Aarts and Philip R. de Jong

PART 5: HEALTH CARE

5.1 Cautionary lessons from the West: What (not) to learn from other countries' experiences in the financing and delivery of health care 327
Theodore R. Marmor and Kieke G.H. Okma

5.2 Inter-generational equity: The concept of a 'fair innings' 351
Alan Williams

List of contributors 365

Preface

Jonathan R. Bradshaw and Han Emanuel

This volume is the fourth in a series on international studies of issues in social security. The series is published in close cooperation with the Foundation for International Studies on Social Security (FISS) which takes care of selecting, editing and formatting the texts to include.

Chief Editor of the series is Peter Flora, professor of sociology at the University of Mannheim, Germany, and Director of the Mannheimer Centre for European Social Research. Further members of the Editorial Board, appointed by the Board of Governors of FISS, are Peter Bezemer (social law, former Vice-President for Pensions of the Dutch Civil Service Pension Fund in Heerlen), Philip R. de Jong (professor of the economics of social security, Erasmus University, Rotterdam, and senior researcher, Economics Department, Faculty of Law, Leiden University), Jun-Young Kim (professor of economics, Economics Department, Sung Gyun-Kwan University, Seoul), Julian Le Grand (professor of economics and Dean of the Department for Social Policy of the London School of Economics and Political Science), Theodore R. Marmor (professor of political science, School of Organization and Management, Yale University, New Haven, Connecticut) and Per-Gunnar Svensson (professor of medical sociology at the Centre for Health Research in Karlstad, Sweden).

The series can be seen as a platform for academic discussion between researchers and scholars of different disciplines and countries. Articles included should display studies and their results on different aspects of social security or welfare and/or their relationships with other aspects of society in a cross national setting or with at least cross national relevance. Though independent and academic many of these studies will spell out the relevance of the findings for practical issues in social policy formation. The articles are selected with an eye to their novelty and thoroughness. One of the series' aims is to confront different academic approaches with each other and with public policy perspectives. Another is to give analytic reports of cross-nationally different approaches to the design and reform of welfare state programs. Articles included will mainly and in the beginning form an edited selection of papers presented at the conferences and seminars of FISS but it is not at all excluded that other articles are offered for publication and accepted.

The present volume, edited by Peter Flora, Philip R. de Jong, Julian Le Grand and Jun-Young Kim, contains a selection of articles based on papers presented at the Fourth International Research Seminar on "Issues in Social Security", held by FISS on 14-17 June 1997 in Sigtuna, Sweden and organized in cooperation with the Swedish Federation of Social Security Offices (Försäkringskasseförbundet, FKF) in Stockholm, also acting as main financial sponsor, at the latter's conference and training centre "Sjudarhöjden".

The book could not have been completed without the financial support of a number of organizations. We are grateful to the H.P.L.C. De Kruyff Fund in Amsterdam, The Netherlands, for its willingness to provide a contribution in the publication costs for a number of subsequent volumes. For this particular volume the Dutch National Insurance Institute (LISV, Landelijk Instituut voor Sociale Verzekering) in Amsterdam also expressed willingness to act as co-sponsor).

Finally, we would like to thank Ton Koekkoek at Van Diest Word Processing in The Hague, The Netherlands, and Ursula Rossi, at the chair of sociology, Faculty of Social Sciences, University of Mannheim, Germany, for providing excellent editorial assistance for this volume.

Jonathan R. Bradshaw, University of York, U.K., President of FISS
Han Emanuel, Secretary-General of FISS, Amsterdam, the Netherlands

Introduction and overview

Peter Flora, Philip R. de Jong, Jun-Young Kim and Julian Le Grand

This is the fourth volume in the series International Studies on Social Security, and the third that contains selected papers presented at the annual Research Seminar on Issues in Social Security. This volume opens with an essay by A.B. Atkinson in memory of Brian Able-Smith, the previous Chief Editor of this Series who died in 1996. As a tribute to the work of Able-Smith Atkinson pursues in his contribution the idea of a poverty target at the European level. He argues that we should adopt long-run European performance criteria to include inflation and unemployment as economic indicators, and poverty as an indicator of the social dimension.

Five sections grouping the other papers according to subject follow the opening essay. These sections cover an array as wide as the previous three volumes did together. The first section deals with pensions and retirement issues. Holden and Zick study the economic impact of widowhood in the United States using panel data from the early 1990s. They find that income from pensions and earnings are crucial factors in minimising the risk of falling into poverty after the husband's death. Prinz summarises a comprehensive simulation study on alternative pension systems for Austrian women who are discriminated against by the current pension system. He shows that both in terms of fairness and incentives the Austrian system can be strongly improved by introduction of a system that combines a universal flat rate basic pension with an actuarially fairer additional pension. Adverse cost and employment effects of non-funded early retirement schemes is the issue dealt with by Rein and Friedman. They compare data of selected Organization for Economic Coordination and Development (OECD) countries by institutional features of early retirement programs and their employment and income effects. They conclude that early retirement benefits are ill targeted and need to be cut. The fourth, and last, paper in this section is another cross-national comparison but now one regarding patterns of labor force withdrawal. It is by Smeeding and Quinn who study labor force participation rates and income sources of those aged 55 and over in seven OECD countries. They find strong differences in the extent to which people supplement their retirement income with labor market earnings. Some countries have strict earnings tests and therefore promote a transition from full-time work to complete labor force withdrawal. Other countries appear to have less restrictive rules, and older workers respond accordingly by patterns of gradual, or partial, retirement.

Section 2 has two papers on Employment and Social Security. In an essay called The Welfare State and Full Employment Haveman proposes a blueprint of an income policy that simultaneously provides income support to poor families, and encourages work effort. Through a combination of a negative (or credit) income tax to eliminate hard-core poverty, an earned income tax credit to stimulate labor force participation by disadvantaged workers, and an employment subsidy to expand the demand for services of low-wage workers. Haveman argues that such a combination of programs is needed to strike a better balance between equity and efficiency. In a very elaborate paper Wolfe, Wolaver, and McBride explore the question of whether the United States employer-based health insurance system, combined with its high cost and with regulation requiring that all full-time workers be offered coverage, is related both to a decline in coverage and to deterioration of the low-skilled labor market. After a thorough review of the impact of fringe benefits on employment a three equations model including wages, the probability of being offered a job with health insurance, and working full versus part-time. This paper serves as an excellent example of the incentive problem Haveman seeks to solve.

Section 3 combines two, largely Norwegian, pieces on family policy with one methodological study on changes in the United States income distribution in the 1980s. Overbye describes the policy response to changing household structures due increases in two-earner families, divorce, and aging, in Norway. He shows that the major strategy to cover the new risks induced by these social changes has been to redesign the social insurance system rather than to expand social assistance, regulation, or tax measures. Skevik compares child maintenance arrangements in Norway with those in Britain. Her paper specifically deals with the question of how children of lone parents are protected against poverty in these two countries. Comparison of both child support systems shows that while Norway adheres to equality in treatment of richer and poorer families, Britain has separate laws for the rich and the poor. The subject and approach of the last paper in this section differ strongly from the previous two. In their own terms, Burkhauser and Crews compare two pictures of how the distribution of (household) income in the United States has changed in the 1980s. One is obtained by using cross-sectional data, the other through longitudinal observation For the overall population the two pictures are quite resembling, showing increasing inequality. But for two vulnerable groups, households headed by someone older than 62 and younger social assistance households, the pictures strongly differ. This study shows how important it is to set the lens appropriately.

Section 4 has three papers on a highly topical subject, privatization of social insurance. Eriksen and Söderström describe recent measures that privatize parts of the Swedish social insurance system. Other parts are scrutinized on the extent to which privatization may improve their sustainability. Turner and Rajnes contribute an informative paper titled Privatization of Retirement Income. They start with taxonomy of privatization, which is followed by a description of privatized pension systems in selected Latin American countries, the United Kingdom, and Japan. Aarts and De Jong provide a micro-economic framework, which may be used to assess the potential welfare gains of private provision of social insurance. They, then, apply this framework to the Dutch disability insurance program and the United States workers compensation scheme.

The last section deals with health policy. The essay by Marmor and Okma discusses the distinguishing characteristics of national health care systems, and how and what to learn from cross-national comparison. They argue that, despite convergence in rhetoric, national systems as well as actual experiences vary widely, and are difficult to transfer to other countries. This book ends with a brilliant essay by Alan Willams about how to measure and reduce inequality in lifetime health. He proposes the concept of fair innings to cast equity in quantitative terms, and to make the trade-offs between medical expenditures for the old or the younger, and for the poor or the rich, explicit. He ends by stating that "Quantification (...) has potential for clarification, for performance measurement, for accountability, and for policy analysis and reappraisal. The quest for greater quantification of equity considerations seems worth pursuing on those grounds alone, despite the hostility it is likely to engender from those who mistakenly equate precision with lack of humanity."

SOCIAL SECURITY
AND MACRO-ECONOMICS

Social security, macro-economics and the European Union

A.B. Atkinson

Poverty and economics

This article is dedicated to the memory of Brian Abel-Smith. He was a great man who had much more influence on my intellectual development and that of countless others than perhaps he realised, and whose untimely death means that we now have no opportunity to tell him in person. My choice of topic reflects two dimensions of Brian's work in the field of social security. He is even better known for his work on health, but his contributions to social security alone mark him as one of the leading social scientists of our age.

The first dimension is quantitative, survey-based social science. Brian followed in a strong Fabian tradition, but each generation needs reminding just how important it is to 'look at the numbers' and just how much impact quantitative evidence can have on public debate. I can vividly remember reading the press coverage of *The Poor and the Poorest*, the landmark study of poverty in postwar Britain that he wrote with Peter Townsend (Abel-Smith and Townsend, 1965). It impressed me greatly as an economics student, and when I went off to MIT to begin research, it was one of the few books that I took with me. I had switched my studies from mathematics to economics because of a belief that it would combine scientific rigour with social concern. *The Poor and the Poorest* did just that. This pioneering secondary analysis of micro-data, much of it highly labourious in a primitive computer age, was rigorous, both in its care with data handling and in its conceptual framework. It was the single most important influence on my own subsequent book on *Poverty in Britain and the Reform of Social Security* (Atkinson, 1969).

But beyond its academic contribution, *The Poor and the Poorest* attracted a great deal of public notice. It provided a sober assessment of national performance, and shocked many people out of their comfortable assumptions about the success of the postwar welfare state. This was statistics in action.

The second principal theme of this chapter is the relation between social policy and economics, or, more specifically, macro-economics. Brian began his career as an economist, taking the Economics Tripos at Cambridge, and working as an economic researcher on the Enquiry into the Cost of the National Health Service. He knew economics from the inside, and spanned the two disciplines of economics and social policy. Today these disciplines seem too often to be separated by a gulf of mutual incomprehension and suspicion. In this respect, FISS is rare meeting place, and this is one reason why, I believe, Brian found it a venture worthy of support. Nowhere is the gulf between social policy and economics more apparent than in debates about the European Union, where economists are obsessed with the completion of the Internal Market and with Monetary Union, whereas social policy academics are seeking to prevent the subordination of the social dimension of Europe to economic imperatives. It is with the relation between European economic and social policy that I begin.

Social and economic performance criteria for the European Union

Contemporary debate about the European Union has been predominantly concerned with the Maastricht criteria. In order to participate in the first phase of Economic and Monetary Union, Member States must satisfy the convergence criteria laid down in the Treaty. These conditions cover exchange rate stability, price stability, interest rate convergence, and limits on public deficits and public debt as percentages of GDP. A number of these criteria are concerned with instruments of policy, rather than with ultimate policy objectives. The main final goal of macro-policy, as embodied in these criteria, is that of a low rate of inflation, both currently and expected in the future. In terms of the 'misery index' popular with journalists, which adds the inflation rate and unemployment rates in assessing economic performance (Burda and Wyplosz, 1997: 13), the Maastricht criteria give primacy to inflation: i.e. column 1 in Table 1.

There can be little doubt that the Maastricht performance criteria have influenced economic policy in the Member States. National governments have seen them as a means of achieving policy changes which appeared politically infeasible in the absence of external constraints. Wider goals are invoked by politicians in order to render palatable cuts in public spending. Some economists argue that the existence of the criteria has increased the credibility of macro-policies, and allowed interest rates to be lower.

Table 1   Performance criteria

Country	Inflation 1989-95 average % increase in consumer prices	Unemployment 1990-95 average rate	Poverty 1988 % persons below 50% mean expenditure
Netherlands	2.7	6.4	4.8
Denmark	2.1	8.5	3.9
Luxembourg	2.9	2.4	11.1
Belgium	2.6	8.2	7.4
(West) Germany	3.6	4.9	10.9
France	2.4	10.8	14.7
UK	4.4	9.1	14.8
Ireland	2.7	14.3	15.7
Italy	5.2	10.1	21.1
Portugal	8.2	5.5	24.5
Spain	5.4	20.2	16.9
Greece	14.9	n/a	18.7

Sources: Inflation from OECD, 1997, Table 8.11 (consumer prices), except West Germany from OECD, 1995, Table 8.11 (for 1989-93); unemployment from OECD, 1997, Table 2.20, except West Germany from OECD, 1995, Table 2.20 (for 1990-93); poverty from Hagenaars et al., 1994, Table 3.2.

Performance criteria have also been adopted at a national level. In the United Kingdom, after the pound left the Exchange Rate Mechanism in October 1992, the government launched a new macro-economic strategy, at the heart of which was a formal target for the rate of inflation. Although low inflation had long been an avowed objective, there had not previously been an explicit quantitative performance standard. The government now announced its intention to keep inflation within a range of 1 to 4 percent. Credibility was sought by increasing the role of the Bank of England, including the innovation of a quarterly *Inflation Report*, providing statistical evidence about inflation and its prospects, together with a commentary.

Pursuing the parallel with macro-economic policy, I have argued in the United Kingdom that we should adopt the same kind of national commitment to the reduction of poverty (Atkinson, 1996). There should be a national poverty reduction target, with a regular *Poverty Report* assessing performance. This argument has not so far persuaded the United Kingdom Government, although I am heartened by the fact that in 1997 the Irish Government adopted a National Anti-Poverty Strategy, as a follow-up to the United Nations Social Summit in Copenhagen in 1995. This set a target for poverty reduction:

> Over the period 1997-2007, the National Anti-Poverty Strategy will aim at considerably reducing the numbers of those who are 'consistently poor' from 9% to 15% to less than 5 to 10%, as measured by the ESRI (National Anti-Poverty Strategy, 1997: 9). (The ESRI is an independent research institute.)

In the present article, I would like to pursue the idea of a poverty target at the European level. The proposal which I want to take seriously, even if it may appear utopian, is that we should adopt long-run European performance criteria to include inflation (as in the Maastricht Treaty), unemployment (as an indicator of the real economy), and poverty (as an indicator of the social dimension). All three columns in Table 1 would be relevant. The table shows the poverty rates in the Europe of Twelve in the late 1980s, together with the rate of increase of consumer prices (1989-95) and the standardised rate of unemployment (averaged over 1990-95). Of course, once a variable such as poverty became a policy performance criterion, its measurement would be subject to close scrutiny, as has been that of the rate of inflation. Measurement problems are not discussed here: see, for example, Hagenaars et al. (1994), from whose work the statistics are taken, Callan and Nolan (1991), Van den Bosch (1996), Bradshaw and Chen (1996), Nolan and Whelan (1996), and Atkinson (forthcoming).

It is important to emphasise that these are long-run, rather than convergence, criteria. Whereas the Maastricht Treaty is directed at differences in inflation rates, and the sustainability of the monetary union, here I am concerned with the next stage: the long-run objectives of the European Monetary Union. What should be the guiding principles of the new central authority? How, for example, should European policymakers respond to macro-economic shocks?

The proposal is that policymakers should be concerned with inflation, unemployment and poverty. This specification of focus variables is not however enough. The way in which the three criteria are combined may be important. Following the journalists' lead we could simply add the three rates of inflation, unemployment and poverty. Summation would be arbitrary, but is nonetheless suggestive. The countries in Table 1 are listed in order of the sum (annual inflation rate + unemployment rate + poverty rate). The top five countries are Benelux, Denmark and West Germany. It turns out that these countries have the lowest poverty rates, but this is not decisive, since they also rank top on the conventional 'misery' index of inflation plus unemployment rates.

In the present instance, this means that it would not greatly change the ordering of countries if we were to adopt a quite different approach to aggregation such as a lexicographic ordering, with performance judged first on one dimension, and then ties resolved by looking at a second, or third, dimension. The aggregation could however matter. To take a hypothetical example, there may be a choice between (1) a more restrictive policy ensuring inflation of 2% but leaving poverty at 15%, or (2) a less restrictive policy leading to inflation at 5% but reducing poverty to 10%. If priority were to be given to inflation, then the former policy trumps the latter. If we add the inflation and poverty rates, then the less restrictive policy is preferred, although it would not be if the reduction in poverty were only to 12½%. Or, we could imagine two policies which have the same consequences for inflation, but where one policy emphasises jobs and the other poverty reduction. In a lexicographic approach, with inflation coming first, does poverty come next (a 'European' approach) or does unemployment (a 'United States' approach)? If there is a poverty/unemployment trade-off, in which direction should we move?

These are difficult questions. Setting explicit performance targets forces us to think about the relative weights of different objectives. Resolution is not easy, but it is better that the issue be made explicit, rather than decided by default.

Macro-economics and poverty

The discussion above assumed that policymakers are faced with a menu of alternatives. What is in fact the trade-off between the macro-economic variables and poverty? Would a poverty reduction of 5 percentage points 'cost' a rise of 3 percentage points in inflation? This question is not easily answered. Indeed it is rarely addressed. Reading a sample of macro-economic textbooks shows that poverty scarcely features in their account of policy issues. Distributional effects as a whole are largely absent, with little recognition of the conflicting interests of different groups.

If the textbooks were to address the question, how would it be answered? Old-style macro-analysis presented a menu of choices with lower inflation being traded off against higher unemployment: the Phillips curve, which Brian may well have discussed with its originator, who was his colleague at the LSE. How would different choices from this menu affect the poor? In the United States, Blank and Blinder (1986) estimated a time-series regression relating the United States poverty rate over the period 1959 to 1983 to the rates of unemployment and inflation, and to the ratio of transfers to gross national product, and to the poverty line as a proportion of mean income. They found that:

> a 1-point rise in prime-age male unemployment raises the poverty rate by 0.7 points in the same year. If the rise in unemployment were sustained, the final net effect would be a 1.1-point rise ... the effect of a 1-point rise in inflation is only one-seventh as large as that of a 1-point rise in unemployment (Blank and Blinder, 1986: 188).

(This relationship, it should be stressed, relates to the period prior to 1983; subsequently, it does not appear to hold (Blank, 1993).) If the 'misery index' is formed by adding the inflation and unemployment rates, the equal poverty rate criterion adds the unemployment rate to only one-seventh of the inflation rate.

The existence of a stable long-run trade-off between unemployment and inflation was however called into question by the macro-economics of the 1970s, so that today's textbooks tell a different story. As explained by Mankiw, the relationship described above is a short-run trade-off:

> Because people adjust their expectations of inflation over time, this tradeoff between inflation and unemployment holds only in the short run. ... Eventually expectations adapt to whatever inflation rate the policymaker chooses. In the long run, ... unemployment returns to its natural rate, and there is no trade-off between inflation and unemployment (Mankiw, 1994: 308).

The adjustment of people's expectations means, on this view, that government policy cannot permanently sustain a combination of non-accelerating prices and unemployment, other than at the so-called 'natural rate' (a term which has many interpretations; see Rogerson, 1997). This 'natural rate' can be influenced by government policy (in this respect the choice of terminology is particularly inappropriate), even if economists disagree about which measures are the most effective. These are however largely structural policies rather than the macro-economic policies on which I am concentrating here.

In place of the Phillips curve trade-off, the typical textbook account of macro-economic policy emphasises the choice of path of adjustment:

> policy makers do not choose between inflation and unemployment, but rather between *adjustment paths* that differ in the inflation-unemployment mix (Dornbusch and Fischer, 1994: 525).

Suppose that there is a macro-economic shock which causes the inflation rate to rise significantly, and a policy of disinflation has to be pursued (see, for example, Hall and Taylor, 1993: 251-4). There are economists who argue that a credible shift in policy regime can achieve the required adjustment of expectations without disinflation, but most macro-economists suppose that a reduction in the inflation rate can only be brought about at the cost of higher unemployment. To take the 'First Pass' model of Blanchard (1997: 367), a reduction in inflation from 8% to 4% can be achieved by 4 years of unemployment at 1 percentage point above the natural rate. This is based on the assumption that what is required is a total of 4 percentage point-years, so that an alternative would be 2 years of unemployment at 2 percentage points above the natural rate. Unemployment would be more intense, but for a shorter period and inflation would be reduced more rapidly.

Now we have to investigate the implications of these different adjustment paths for household poverty.

Unemployment, inflation and household poverty

If unemployment causes people to fall below the poverty line, then on an individual basis we would expect a 1:1 relationship between the poverty rate and the unemployment rate: i.e. close to the Blank-Blinder result for the United States. (In making this calculation, it is assumed that the poverty line is smoothed to avoid variations with macro-economic conditions.) This however assumes that all the unemployed become poor and that none of the employed are below the poverty line. Neither is the case. Unemployment does not fall uniformly. There are grounds for expecting the newly unemployed to be drawn from the lower part of the distribution of workers, already doing poorly-paid jobs, so that they were already exposed to the risk of poverty. Even if their poverty is intensified by the loss of the job, this reduces the impact of higher unemployment on the overall poverty rate. In the opposite direction, disinflation may increase the risk of poverty for workers who remain in their jobs. As has been argued by Pissarides (1991), there is likely to be more fluctuation of wages in the secondary sector of the economy, so that a recession particularly depresses the earnings of those already close to the poverty line, and may push them below it.

Whether unemployment itself causes poverty depends on the degree of replacement provided by social insurance and social assistance. Replacement rates, net of tax and working costs, are typically considerably less than 100%, and some people are not eligible or do not claim the benefit to which they are entitled. The unemployed can therefore expect a fall in their income. At the same time, the extent of the associated rise in poverty depends on the characteristics of social protection and hence varies across countries. A country with a lower replacement rate, and less extensive benefit coverage, can expect to see a larger rise in poverty per 1% increase in the unemployment rate. This points to particular problems within the European Union if countries pursue different strategies with regard to social protection. There may be a common macroeconomic policy, but it may have quite different implications for the financial status of households.

The same issue arises when we turn to the impact of inflation on individual incomes. The standard position is that inflation has distributional effects:

> real wages stay ahead, which hurts firms' profitability ... Those on fixed incomes and limited political clout, such as pensioners or dole recipients, generally lose out. ... wealth shifts from lenders to borrowers (Burda and Wyplosz, 1997: 417).

Those adversely affected include groups overrepresented at the bottom of the income distribution, so that there may be a positive relationship, as found in the United States by Blank and Blinder, between the rate of inflation and poverty. It does however depend on the intervening institutions. If company profits are reduced, then the impact depends on the beneficial holders of the shares in these companies. In a country such as the United Kingdom where a sizeable fraction of company shares are held by pension funds, the effect may be quite different from that in a country with a different structure of the capital market. The state itself is an important intervening institution, and the effect of inflation depends on the adjustments made to social security, notably the extent of automatic indexation.

The links between unemployment, inflation and poverty are further complicated when we recognise that many people are part of a wider living unit, and take the household as the unit of analysis. If all of the newly unemployed have partners who are in well-paid jobs, then the rise in unemployment may leave household poverty unaffected. The same may be true if the newly unemployed all have partners in receipt of income-tested benefits, if the lost earnings are fully replaced by additional social assistance. The impact of a rise in the unemployment rate is, therefore, less predictable, since it depends on the joint distribution of economic circumstances.

Changes in the household composition of unemployment can affect the relation between the unemployment and poverty rates. In the UK, there have been periods when the overall unemployment rate has not increased but there has been an increase in the proportion of households without work (Robinson, 1996). Unemployment has become more concentrated among households. Where the poverty rate of no-earner households exceeds that of 1-earner households by more than the latter exceeds that of 2-earner households, poverty can be expected to increase even though the overall unemployment rate is no different.

The need to go from individual income experience to household income is one reason why the link between unemployment and poverty is a complex one. When we allow for this, and for differences in national social protection systems, it is not surprising that a number of European countries have seen a large rise in unemployment from the late 1970s to the early 1990s without a commensurate rise in poverty (Atkinson, forthcoming). This does not however mean that unemployment ceases to be of concern. Unemployment has costs even if it does not give rise to financial poverty. For this reason, it is right to take account of both unemployment and poverty rates, in addition to the inflation criterion.

Conclusion

Bringing together the two strands of the article - quantitative study of the achievement of national goals and the interface between macro-economic policy and social objectives - I conclude that there is an urgent need for further thought about the links between macro-economic variables and poverty in Europe. If, as I have proposed, the European Union sets a poverty reduction target alongside its objectives for inflation and unemployment, then we have to know more about how these are related. How would these different criteria be weighted? What is the nature of the macro-economic trade-off? How would the figures in a Europe-wide *The Poor and the Poorest* be affected by different decisions about the response to macro-economic shocks? This is an ambitious research agenda, but answers will be needed by a twenty-first century Brian Abel-Smith advising the governors of Europe.

References

Abel-Smith, B. and Townsend, P. (1965) *The Poor and the Poorest*. London: Bell.
Atkinson, A. B. (1969) *Poverty in Britain and the Reform of Social Security*. Cambridge: Cambridge University Press.
Atkinson, A. B. (1996) 'Promise and performance: Why we need an official poverty report', in P. Barker, ed. *Living as Equals*. Oxford: Oxford University Press.
Atkinson, A. B. forthcoming. *Three Lectures on Poverty in Europe*. Oxford: Basil Blackwell.
Blanchard, O. (1997) *Macroeconomics*. Upper Saddle River: Prentice Hall.

Blank, R. M. (1993) 'Why were Poverty Rates so High in the 1980s?', in Papadimitriou, D. B. and Wolff, E. N., eds. *Poverty and Prosperity in the USA in the Late Twentieth Century*. Basingstoke: Macmillan.

Blank, R. M. and Blinder, A. S. (1986) 'Macroeconomics, Income Distribution, and Poverty', in Danziger, S. H. and Weinberg, D. H., eds. *Fighting Poverty*. Cambridge, Massachusetts: Harvard University Press.

Bradshaw, J. and Chen, J.-R. (1996) 'Poverty in the UK: A Comparison with Nineteen Other Countries'. *Luxembourg Income Study Working Paper* No. 147, CEPS/INSTEAD.

Burda, M. and Wyplosz, C. (1997) *Macroeconomics*. Second edition. Oxford: Oxford University Press.

Callan, T. and Nolan, B. (1991) 'Concepts of poverty and the poverty line: a critical survey of approaches to measuring poverty'. *Journal of Economic Surveys* 5: 243-262.

Dornbusch, R. and Fischer, S. (1994) *Macroeconomics*. Sixth edition. New York.

Hagenaars, A., de Vos, K. and Zaidi, A. (1994) *Poverty Statistics in the late 1980s*. Luxembourg: Eurostat.

Hall, R. E. and Taylor, J. B. (1993) *Macroeconomics*. Fourth edition. New York: W.W. Norton.

Mankiw, N. G. (1994) *Macroeconomics*. Second edition. New York: Worth Publishers.

National Anti-Poverty Strategy (1997) *Sharing in Progress*. Dublin: Stationery Office.

Nolan, B. and Whelan, C. T. (1996) *Resources, Deprivation, and Poverty*. Oxford: Clarendon Press.

OECD (1995) *Historical Statistics 1960-1993*. Paris: OECD.

OECD (1997) *Historical Statistics 1960-1995*. Paris: OECD.

Pissarides, C. (1991) 'Macroeconomic adjustment and poverty in selected developed countries'. *World Bank Economic Review* 5: 207-229.

Rogerson, R. (1997) 'Theory Ahead of Language in the Economics of Unemployment'. *Journal of Economic Perspectives* 11 (Winter): 73-92.

Robinson, P. (1996) *Labour Market Studies: United Kingdom*. Brussels: European Commission.

Van den Bosch, K. with Marx, I. (1996) 'Trends in Financial Poverty in OECD Countries'. *Luxembourg Income Study Working Paper* No. 148, CEPS/INSTEAD.

PART 1

PENSIONS AND RETIREMENT

1.1 The economic impact of widowhood in the United States in the 1990s: The role of social insurance and private pensions

Karen C. Holden and Cathleen D. Zick

Introduction

This study uses the 1990 and 1991 SIPP panels to examine the economic status of women prior to and after the death of their husbands. The economic experience of continuously married women, weighted for age comparability to eventual widows, provides a comparison. We find that, compared to continuously married women, eventual widows already have lower incomes many months prior to their husbands' deaths. Income does not decline as couples approach widowhood but widowhood itself is a major economic shock. Husbands' disabling conditions play a role in lower incomes of eventual widows, but are not the full explanation. While we cannot explain fully the long-standing differences in economic well-being prior to widowhood, we do find that income from pensions and earnings plays a pivotal role in minimizing the decline in economic status at the time of the husband's death and the subsequent risk of falling into poverty. Our findings suggest the continuing need to increase awareness of the risk of widowhood and perhaps to improve insurance against the economic consequences of pending death as well as of the widowhood event itself.

While the economic status of older Americans has improved over the past couple of decades, widowed women continue to be an economically vulnerable group. Research using panel survey data from the 1970s and early 1980s has documented the large negative impact of widowhood on the economic well-being of women widowed during those decades. Since then married women continue to report higher earnings and longer work histories, the private insurance industry has developed new insurance options against the loss of income in case of retirement and death, and federal pension legislation has been passed that seeks to increase the share of a couple's resources paid to a widow after her husband's death (e.g., the 1984 Retirement Equity Act). Singularly or in combination, these forces may have improved the economic position of women who have more recently been widowed.

This chapter presents a descriptive analysis of the changes in income that occur in the months immediately preceding and following the death of a husband, using data from the 1990 and 1991 panels of the Survey of Income and Program Participation (SIPP). The economic experiences of women who are widowed during the panel periods are compared to the economic experiences of similarly aged women who remain married throughout SIPP. In addition, event-history techniques are used to examine the factors that influence the risk of falling into poverty for initially nonpoor widows.

The literature

Longitudinal analyses using annual data from the Panel Study of Income Dynamics (PSID) (1968-1984) or biannual data from the Retirement History Study (RHS) (1969-1979) provide a background for the current investigation. Most of these studies focus on assessing the extent of decline in income at the time of the widowhood and in the years that immediately follow. The consensus of these studies is that at the time of the husband's death there is typically a substantial decline in economic resources and a commensurate rise in the risk of falling into poverty (Bound, et al., 1991; Holden, Burkhauser, and Feaster, 1988; Hurd and Wise, 1989). The immediate post-widowhood years are characterized by somewhat greater economic stability - albeit typically at a lower level of well- being. Fewer studies track changes in economic status during the period that precedes widowhood. Zick and Smith (1991a) use 1968 to 1984 data from the PSID to compare continuously married couples' and to-be-widowed couples' income adjusted for needs during the pre-widowhood years. They find that the to-be-widowed group has significantly lower average income-to-needs ratios than the continuously married group even five years prior to the death. This finding is consistent with that of Hurd and Wise (1989) and Burkhauser, Holden, and Myers (1986) who, using RHS data from the 1970s, observe long-standing wealth and income differences between couples whose widowhood is observed and couples who remain intact. It is also consistent with research that links lower economic well-being with a higher risk of mortality (Duleep, 1986; Hadley, 1982; Zick and Smith, 1991b).

Of course, not all newly widowed women experience an economic decline. Yet, the literature has not firmly established what factors substantially improve the economic security of women when their husbands die. Race, education, and age (either the husband's or the wife's) at the husband's death are included in most studies of widowhood as indirect measures of employer-provided insurance, savings, and age-related benefits that may be drawn on when husband's income ceases. Fewer studies include direct measures of the impact of changes in specific income sources such as social security and private pension plans.

Bound et al. (1991), Holden, Burkhauser, and Feaster (1988), and Zick and Smith (1991a) find that white widows fare better economically and, all else equal, also experience smaller declines in income than do nonwhite widows. While Hurd and Wise (1989) find no relationship between the chances of a widow becoming poor upon widowhood and the husband's age at his death, Burkhauser, Butler, and Holden (1989), Holden, Burkhauser, and Feaster (1988), and Smith and Zick (1986) find that the risk of poverty is modified for women who are 60 or older when widowed. This suggests that benefits payable to widows at age 60 by the U.S. Old Age and Survivors Insurance program (or Social Security) protect older widows from economic difficulties. Only two studies (Holden, Burkhauser and Feaster, 1988; Burkhauser, Butler, and Holden, 1991) examine the joint roles of Social Security and private pension coverage in cushioning the economic shock of widowhood among RHS widows. Not surprisingly, higher Social Security primary insurance amounts (PIA) and pension receipt by widows was found to both reduce the hazard of falling into poverty and modify the decline in income-to-needs upon widowhood.

The picture that emerges from these studies of widowhood during the 1970s and 1980s is one where couples in which the husband was about to die had lower pre-widowhood resources compared to similarly aged couples where the husband did not die. The former group of couples then experienced a further decline in income at the time of the husbands' deaths. And, in the years that followed his death, the average widow did not see gains in economic status that would put her back on par with either her married counterparts or her own pre-widowed status. Declines in income upon widowhood were modified by higher benefit amounts from Social Security and pensions, with some evidence that Social Security survivor benefits paid to widows were important in stabilizing their incomes. In many ways these findings are not surprising, but do indicate the importance of public and private insurance benefits for widows in these earlier decades. Why some couples did not have access to or choose to extend to widowhood that protection remained unexplained.

The current descriptive work builds on past studies in several ways. First, by using data from the 1990 and 1991 SIPP panels, we are able to examine patterns of income change among more recent cohorts of widows who, as we noted earlier, should be enjoying greater economic security than past cohorts. Changes in income-to-needs and the chances of entering poverty are used as indicators of income security. The second contribution of the current work is that by using SIPP we are able to examine *monthly* changes in economic well-being rather than annual or biannual changes. Finally, we expand the standard set of risk factors beyond age, education, and race to include measures of household composition, disability status of the husband before his death, and whether or not the widow receives income from various sources (i.e., earnings, pensions, social security, property/assets, and other income) immediately after her husband's death.

Methods

The analyses. Our goal is to provide a description of the changes in household income adjusted for needs that occur in the months immediately preceding and immediately following the death of a spouse. Some of these changes may be due to widowhood, but others may be due to external events that would have changed the economic status of these women even if their husbands had not died. As a measure of what income changes would have been observed over the same period for reasons other than widowhood, data are presented for a comparison group of married women whose husbands did not die during the panel.

We graphically compare the pattern of average monthly income/needs during the pre- and post-widowhood periods for the eventually widowed and continuously married couples. Two income regressions are estimated for the eventually widowed and continuously married couples. These regressions provide a more detailed picture of whether the pre-widowhood income/needs levels of eventually widowed couples are affected by sociodemographic and economic factors in a substantially different way than for couples who do not enter widowhood and of which sub-groups of widows (if any) are particularly disadvantaged as they experience widowhood.[1]

The sample. Each SIPP panel is a nationally representative sample of households whose members are interviewed at four-month intervals over approximately a 32-month period. At each interview, data are collected on household composition and the incomes of each household member over the four preceding months. Our sample of 382 eventual widow households and 2184 continuously married households comes from the 1990 and 1991 SIPP panels. We combine the two panels using the SIPP-recommended weights for aggregating these particular panels where the interview periods in fact overlap. The eventual widow sample includes all women age 40 or older at the first SIPP interview, with husband present at the first interview, whose husbands died at some point during the panel, and who are interviewed at least once as a widow. The continuously married comparison is a one-quarter sample of women also 40 and older at the first SIPP interview and who are married throughout the 32-month panel. In all of the estimations individuals in the sample are weighted by the appropriate SIPP sample weights. In addition, because married couples are younger than those who become widowed, a weight developed for the purposes of this study is applied to the continuously married women to make their age distribution equal to that of the (older) eventual widows. Thus differences in patterns of and contributors to income change between the two sets of couples are net of differences in age structure.

Because calendar month of widowhood is different for each eventually widowed woman yet we want to compare households by months prior to and after widowhood, we choose an approach first used by Zick and Smith (1991a) where one identifies all person-month observations generated by the eventual widow households and flags them according to their time since widowhood (e.g., if '0' is the month of death, then '-4' is four months prior to the death, '+6' is six months after the death). To compare incomes of eventual widows in these redefined months to the incomes of our comparison sample of continuously married couples, we assign a month of 'widowhood' to each continuously married couple in such a way that the distribution of 'deaths' by calendar month for the continuously married couples is identical to that of the actual deaths for eventually widowed couples. We flag all pre- and post-widowhood months accordingly around the month of actual death for eventual widows and assigned death for the continuously married.

Our approach has the advantage of illustrating the comparative economic trajectories for each group. For example, a married woman who is (actually or by assignment) widowed in month ten of the panel contributes nine months of data to the pre-widowhood period (i.e., months -9 to -1) and 22 months of data to the post-widowhood period (i.e., months +1 to +22). Another woman, widowed in month 28 of the panel contributes 27 pre-widowhood months and 3 post-widowhood months. While the continuously married couples are in fact never widowed, arraying their monthly incomes around an assigned widowhood month allows us to control for the effects of other shocks that may destabilize income for all couples - both married and those about to be widowed - during all months of 'pre- and post-widowhood'. In this way we can distinguish what widows could have expected to happen to them, for example, as they entered retirement from the event of widowhood itself. In the comparison we ignore the month in which the husband died since income reported for the wife will be a combination of income received as a wife and widow. The first month post-widowhood is the first full month spent as a widow.

The results. Descriptive statistics for the eventual widows and continuously married couples appear in Table 1.1.1. In the two months preceding the death the eventual widows average 0.6 lower income-to-needs (using the standard U.S. Census Bureau needs calculations) than their continuously married counterparts.[2] Their income-to-needs ratio drops by 0.73 on average immediately after the death, while the continuously married couples experience virtually no change in income over this period of 'widowhood'.[3]

Table 1.1.1 Descriptive statistics: eventual widows and continuously married couples

Variables	Pre-widowhood Eventual Widows		Post-widowhood Eventual Widows		Pre-widow Continuously Married		Post-widow Continuously Married	
2-Month Avg. Income Needs [a]	3.4	-2.05	2.67	-2.34	3.98	-2.73	3.91	-2.74
Wife's Education (1= gt 12 years; 0=otherwise)	0.24	-0.39	-	-	0.26	-0.4	-	-
Ethnicity (1=white, 0=otherwise)	0.89	-0.29	-	-	0.9	-0.28	-	-
Other Adults Present (1=yes, 0=no) [b]	0.16	-0.34	0.17	-0.34	0.17	-0.35	0.18	-0.35
Minor Children Present (1=yes, 0=no) [b]	0.03	-0.16	0.04	-0.17	0.06	-0.22	0.06	-0.22
Wife's Age < 60 (1=yes, 0=no)	0.19	-0.35	-	-	0.18	-0.35	-	-
Wife's Age 60-64 (1=yes, 0=no)	0.14	-0.31	-	-	0.16	-0.33	-	-
Husband Disabled and < 70 (1=husband < 70 and disabled, 0=else)	0.29	-0.42	-	-	0.12	-0.29	-	-
Husband Not Disabled and < 70 (1=husband <70 & not disabled, 0=else)	0.19	-0.35	-	-	0.39	-0.45	-	-
Wife Has Labor Income (1=yes, 0=no) [b]	0.17	-0.34	0.16	-0.33	0.17	-0.35	0.17	-0.27
Husband Has Labor Income (1=yes, 0=no) [b]	0.19	-0.36	-	-	0.27	-0.41	-	-
Wife Has Pension Income (1=yes, 0=no) [b]	0.17	-0.34	0.31	-0.42	0.17	-0.46	0.17	-0.46
Husband Has Pension Income (1=yes, 0=no) [b]	0.61	-0.44	-	-	0.49	-0.46	-	-
Wife Has Social Security Income (1=yes, 0=no) [b]	0.75	-0.39	0.81	-0.13	0.75	-0.4	0.75	-0.32
Property and Interest Income (1=yes, 0=no) [b]	0.77	-0.38	0.74	-0.4	0.86	-0.32	0.85	-0.32
Other Income (1=yes, 0=no) [b]	0.3	-0.41	0.15	-0.33	0.14	-0.32	0.12	-0.29

[a] Income-to-needs is averaged over months -2 and -1 for the pre-widowhood period and +1 and +2 for the post-widowhood period.

[b] In the case of the pre-widowhood measures, these variables take on a value of 1 if the condition is met in one or more of the three months prior to the husband's death (i.e., months -3, -2, and/or -1). Similarly, in the case of the post-widowhood measures, these variables take on a value of 1 if the condition is met in one or more of the three months that immediately follow the husband's death (i.e., +1, +2, and/or +3). In those instances where a widow did not provide at least three months of post-widowhood data (either because of attrition or because the SIPP panel ended), we take the information from the one or two months that are available for this descriptive table. (See footnote a in Table 1.1.3 also.)

When comparing the two age-adjusted samples on socio-demographic characteristics other than income, we find that the eventual widow households are similar to their married counterparts in terms of education, ethnicity, and household composition prior to widowhood.[4] What's more, the percentage of wives reporting receipt of income from earnings, pension, and Social Security is almost identical across the two groups. There are, however, marked differences between the two groups in the pre-widowhood months for the husbands' income sources. In particular, husbands who are about to die are more likely to be drawing on Social Security and pension income and less likely to have labor income than are their married counterparts. This is not surprising given the greater frequency of younger disabled husbands in the to-be-widowed sample and husbands' pending deaths.[5] Immediately after the husbands' deaths, there is no change in household composition or in the percentage of wives working. Not surprisingly, the percentage of women receiving a pension and Social Security rises above that of their married counterparts, although in contrast to the 61 percent of men who were receiving pensions prior to their deaths, only half that many widows receive a pension. The decline in 'other income' recipients among widows may also reflect the loss of husbands' income since this income category includes non-pension annuities.

Figure 1.1.1 tracks household monthly income adjusted for basic needs over the full pre- and post-widowhood periods for which we have data for these couples. The story told by this graph is strikingly similar to the findings of the studies that have made use of data from the 1970s and early 1980s. Eventual widow households have persistently lower levels of economic resources than their continuously married counterparts (i.e., about 0.6 lower income-to-needs) and for a substantial time prior to their husbands' deaths incomes are stable for both groups. The additional drop in economic resources that occurs at the time of the deaths worsens the widows' situations, and during the immediate post-widowhood months their monthly income-to-needs stabilizes at roughly 60 percent of that of the continuously married couples. There are no substantial changes observed in *average* income-to-needs over the months preceding or following widowhood, although it should be cautioned that we observe a relatively short pre- and post-widowhood period. Nevertheless, the lower economic status of widows compared to married couples appears to be composed of two somewhat equal parts: long-standing economic differences and a drop in economic status that occurs at the time of the death.[6]

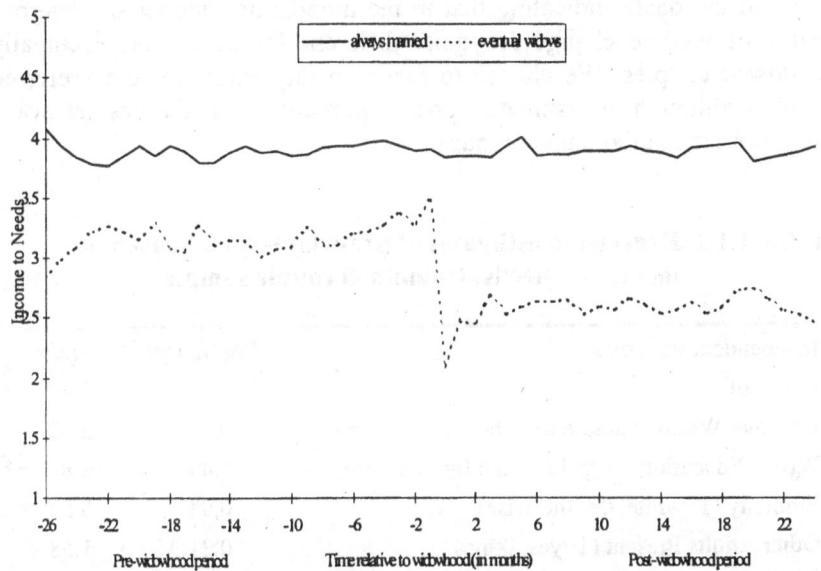

Figure 1.1.1   Always married couples and eventual widows: Full sample

We estimate regressions using dependent measures that capture the two major differences between our couples: (1) the income/needs level in the months immediately preceding the death and (2) the change in income/needs between the two-month average that immediately precedes the death and the two-month average that immediately follows the death. We run regressions where the eventual widow and continuously married samples are combined and a dummy variable reflecting group membership is included (model A). We also run regressions where sample membership is interacted with all of the other independent variables (model B) and where estimation is done separately for each sample (model C). While models B and C are statistically equivalent, model C offers a more straightforward presentation of the results than model B. We need model B, however, to conduct an F-test to identify whether models A or C should be preferred statistically. F-tests indicate that model A is preferred in the case of estimating income-to-needs in the month preceding, that is, interaction effects do not add to the explanatory power. Model B/C is preferred when estimating the change in income-to-needs at the time of the death indicating that in the months of widowhood determinants of income change are quite different for intact and eventually widowed couples. We choose to focus on the results for the preferred models although the estimates for the alternative formulations are available from the authors upon request.

Table 1.1.2 Regression estimates of pre-widowhood household income-to-needs: Combined couple sample

Independent variables	Coefficient	t-ratio	
Intercept	0.89	3	**
Eventual Widow Sample Member (1=yes, 0=no)	-0.33	-2.32	**
Wife's Education (1=gt 12 years; 0=otherwise)	1.49	12.8	**
Ethnicity (1=white, 0=otherwise)	0.93	5.54	**
Other Adults Present (1=yes, 0=no)	0.21	1.58	
Minor Children Present (1=yes, 0=no)	-1.34	-5.92	**
Wife's Age < 60 (1=yes, 0=no)	-0.08	-0.31	
Wife's Age 60-64 (1=yes, 0=no)	0.48	2.8	**
Husband Disabled and < 70	-0.6	-3.58	**
Husband Not Disabled and < 70	-0.2	-1.44	
Wife Has Labor Income (1=yes, 0=no)	0.79	5.04	**
Husband Has Labor Income (1=yes, 0=no)	2.11	14.31	*
Wife Has Pension Income (1=yes, 0=no)	0.31	2.27	**
Husband Has Pension Income (1=yes, 0=no)	0.79	7.28	**
Wife Has Social Security Income (1=yes, 0=no)	0.08	0.39	
Husband Has Social Security Income (1=yes, 0=no)	-0.27	-1.46	
Property and Interest Income (1=yes, 0=no)	1.12	7.89	**
Other Income (1=yes, 0=no)	0.19	1.37	
Panel Year (1=1991, 0=1990)	-0.02	-0.2	
Adjusted R-Squared	0.27		
F-Statistic	53.18	**	

*p < .10
**p < .05

Note: Dependent Variable: Household Income Averaged Over Months -2 and -1.

The parameter estimates for the descriptive regressions appear in Tables 1.1.2 and 1.1.3. Table 1.1.2 shows the predictors of pre-widowhood income-to-needs. Being in the to-be-widowed group has a negative and statistically significant effect on the pre-widowhood level of income-to-needs. Being white, being a wife with more than a high school education, and being a wife who is age 60-64 are all socio-demographic factors that are associated with higher levels of income-to-needs for both groups. In contrast, having minor children present and having a young husband who is disabled all contribute to lower income-to-needs for households. The receipt of property and interest income, husband's labor income, wife's labor income, husband's pension income, and wife's pension income are all associated with higher levels of income-to-needs. The insignificant effect of Social Security receipt does not mean that this program has no effect on these couples' well-being, but rather that receipt of benefits from this universal program does not place couples in higher or lower income-to- needs categories.[7]

Turning to the change regression (Table 1.1.3) we focus our discussion on the coefficients associated with the widowed sample. In this table, the coefficients obtained with the intact couple sample can be viewed as a benchmark for comparison: specifically, they allow us to assess how socio-demographic characteristics and the receipt of income from various sources enhance or inhibit changes in economic well-being more generally, when the death of the husband is not the catalyst for change. In both regressions, we include a control for income-to-needs at month '-1.' This takes account of the initial conditions from which both samples begin. We also include the dummy variable that identifies which panel the household came from, and a dummy variable that identifies whether the change in income-to-needs is calculated using the 'seam' months in SIPP (Dodge, 1995; McGarry, 1995).[8] Defining the dependent variable as post-widowhood income minus pre-widowhood income means that a positive coefficient implies a *smaller* drop (or larger increase) in income-to-needs upon widowhood. Conversely, a negative coefficient implies the variable increases the decline (or reduces the increase) in income-to-needs.

Table 1.1.3 Regression estimates of change in income/needs

Variables	Eventual Widows Sample (N=358) Coefficient [a]		Always Married Sample (N=2184) Coefficient [a]	
Intercept [b]	-1.48	**	0.16	
Income/Needs at Month '-1' [b]	-0.53	**	-0.24	**
Wife's Education (1=gt 12 years; 0=otherwise) [b]	1.27	**	0.06	
Ethnicity (1=white, 0=otherwise)	0.73		0.24	**
Other Adults Present (1=yes, 0=no)	0.39		0.25	**
Minor Children Present (1=yes, 0=no)	0.12		-0.01	
Husband Disabled < 70 [b]	0.06		0.29	**
Husband Not Disabled < 70 [b]	0.25		0.56	**
Wife Has Labor Income (1=yes, 0=no)	1.27	**	0.15	
Wife's Age <60 (1=yes, 0=no)	-0.01		-0.03	
Wife's Age 60-64 (1=yes, 0=no)	-0.55		0.22	*
Wife Has Pension Income (1=yes, 0=no) [b]	1.36	**	0.14	*
Wife Has Social Security Income (1=yes, 0=no)	0.35		0.11	
Property and Interest Income (1=yes, 0=no)	0.62	**	0.51	**
Other Income (1=yes, 0=no) [b]	0.88	**	-0.06	
Panel Year (1=1991, 0=1990)	0.1		-0.08	
Death Occurs in 'Seam' Month (1=yes, 0=no) [b]	0.32		-0.17	**
Adjusted R-Squared	0.34		0.15	
F-Statistic	11.62	**	27.19	**

*p   <.10
**p   <.05

Note: Post-Widowhood Minus Pre-Widowhood Two-Month Averages is the Dependent Variable.

[a] The sample size for this regression is slightly smaller because widows who had left SIPP before month +3 (either because of attrition or because the panel ended) are deleted from the regression.

[b] When the widowed and intact couples are grouped together and group membership is interacted with all of these independent variables, the estimated coefficients associated with the interactions for these variables are significant at the .05 level.

The estimated coefficients show that being white and having more than a high school education appear to protect widows from large economic declines when their husbands die. Consistent with previous studies is the finding that a higher pre-widowhood income leads to a larger decline in income upon widowhood. Higher-income wives have more to lose upon widowhood, and survivor benefits from Social Security and pension may replace a smaller share of pre-widowhood income. On the other hand, that higher-income households suffer a larger change indicates a failure of private markets to fully insure. In addition, beyond their roles in enhancing pre-widowhood income-to-needs, income from paid work, pensions, assets, and 'other' sources all provide protection against large income declines upon widowhood. The magnitude of the estimated coefficients suggests that the receipt of labor income and pension income is especially protective of wives as they are widowed. While asset income is also protective, it is no more so for widows than for married couples.

Interestingly, the only income source that appears not to lessen the severity of the economic decline that occurs at widowhood is Social Security income. This happens despite the fact that we observe an increase in the percentage of women in our widowed sample who report receiving some Social Security income between these two periods. Again, this is likely because of the broad-based receipt of benefits from this program by widows; receipt (in contrast to PIA amount) does not differentiate women who have greater or smaller income changes. Finally, the husband's disabling condition does not affect the widow's economic status beyond its effect on pre-widowhood income. In contrast income declines are greater for continuously married couples with younger husbands (both those disabled and nondisabled), probably because of their entering retirement over this period.

Discussion and conclusions

Even for women who became widows in the early 1990s, widowhood remains an economically risky event. Widows are disadvantaged because even before they entered widowhood period in which their incomes adjusted for household consumption needs were already significantly lower than for their continuously married peers. Nevertheless, widowhood itself was accompanied by a large decline in average income-to-needs. These results are unexpectedly similar to those of earlier studies that looked at widowhood during the 1970s and 1980s. Despite gains in income among the elderly, changes in pension legislation that aim to protect women against the loss of their husbands' earnings and pensions, and changes in labor force work and earnings among women, on average women continue to experience a major drop in economic well-being when husbands die.

Our understanding of the relative importance of sociodemographic and economic factors in explaining the relatively disadvantaged economic situation of widows prior to their husbands' deaths remains poor. Additional work needs to be done to identify the causal relationships that lead to the rather long-standing differences in economic well-being during the pre-widowhood period between the to-be-widowed households and otherwise similar continuously married couples. The similarity in demographic characteristics between the two groups of couples prior to widowhood and the striking absence of interaction effects between widowhood and the other independent variables in the pre-widowhood income-to-needs level equation (Table 1.1.2) shows that these two groups of couples are similarly affected by socio-economic conditions. What distinguishes them in the pre-widowhood period is the husbands' disabling conditions, but when and how these conditions affected income in the pre-widowhood period could not be observed in the SIPP panel data. Figures 1.1.2–4 demonstrate the puzzle that remains to be understood. Both groups of couples with husbands younger than 70 and disabled have comparable (and lower) pre-widowhood income but eventual widows still experience a sharp decline in income-to-needs (Figure 1.1.2) upon the husbands' deaths. Nevertheless, both non-disabled young eventual widows and older eventual widows report lower pre-widowhood incomes and sharp declines upon widowhood (Figures 1.1.3 and 1.1.4).

The current work does identify several income sources that appear to be critical in cushioning the economic shock of the widowhood event itself. In particular, we find that the post-widowhood receipt of labor income or pension income significantly lessens the income decline at the time of the husband's death. The importance of these income sources is all the more sobering when we recognize that a mere 16 percent of the newly widowed women in our sample had labor income and only 31 percent had pension income in the months immediately following the death. While receipt itself of Social Security does not distinguish among widows with larger or smaller income declines, it does provide a floor of protection to all widows.

Another consistent finding in this study is that race and education matter even after controlling for other factors. White widows fare better than nonwhite widows and widows who have more than a high school education fare better than those who do not. In large part, these variables may be capturing differences in the *amounts* of various types of income that are received by certain household types. For example, given the presence of earned income, widows with more than a high school education are likely to have higher amounts of earned income than widows with a high school education or less. Regardless of the underlying cause, our analysis does point out that the economic consequences of widowhood do not cross race and class lines in an even manner.

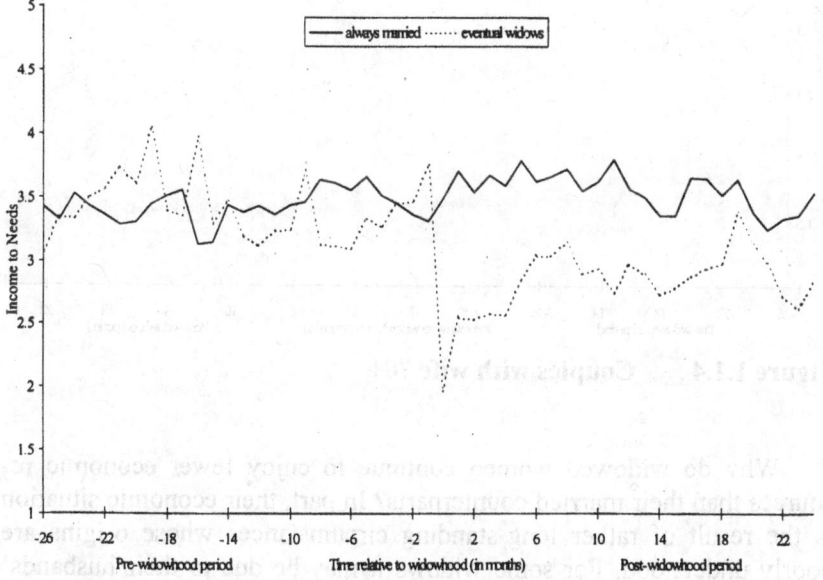

Figure 1.1.2   Couples with wife < 70 and husband disabled

From a public policy perspective, it is clear that the risk faced by widows needs to remain on the national policy agenda. Despite the potential for women's work and pension coverage to protect against the economic consequences of widowhood, this protection is still far from universal in the U.S. The almost universal coverage of Social Security probably contributes to the finding that receipt of Social Security, in and of itself, does not significantly enhance pre-widowhood economic well-being nor does it soften the economic shock that occurs at the time of the husband's death except at the very low end of the income spectrum.

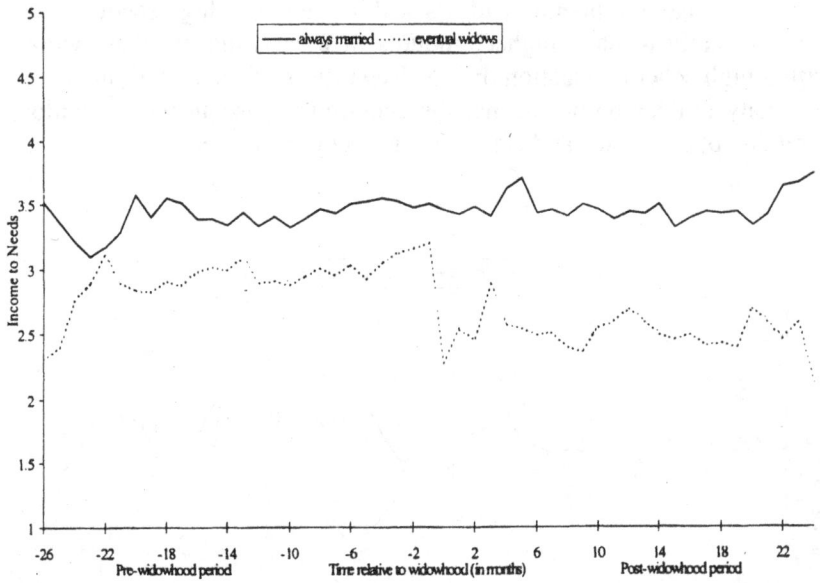

Figure 1.1.4 Couples with wife 70+

Why do widowed women continue to enjoy fewer economic resources than their married counterparts? In part, their economic situation is the result of rather long-standing circumstances whose origins are poorly understood. For some widows it may be due to their husbands' long-standing disabling conditions that reduce income prior to widowhood. This analysis did reveal that the receipt of income from certain sources could soften the substantial decline that occurs at the time of the death. It may be that women do not realize the change in their own economic status that could occur if their husbands were to die. If pension legislation, the expansion in Social Security coverage, and wives' own greater work roles have soothed couples into thinking that the wives are protected against the economic consequences of widowhood, it appears that education to the contrary may be in order.

Notes

1. Conversely, a widow who was just above the poverty threshold when married may enter poverty with only a small decline in income upon widowhood. Thus, because poverty hazards are measuring the influence of factors on ending up in a particular income category, the results may be quite different than for income changes.

2. Income-to-needs is the ratio of household income to the U.S. poverty threshold. A ratio of less than one indicates a poor household by the U.S. definition. The poverty threshold is specific to household size. Apart from measuring household income to the threshold, a decline (rise) in this ratio when a husband dies indicates that income falls by more (less) than the change in consumption needs of the now smaller household.

3. Compared to women widowed in the 1984 SIPP, these widows are better off both before and after widowhood. Women widowed in that SIPP panel had income-to-needs of 3.1 in the pre-widowhood period, declining to 2.0 for the two months after widowhood (Holden, 1990).

4. Age is also identical, but this is a result of weighting the continuously married sample to conform to the eventual widows' age distribution. In part because of this weighting, other demographic characteristics are also more alike than between the actual population groups. On the other hand, the similarity in characteristics indicates that the initially lower income of about-to-be widowed couples is not due to differences in income related to differences in wife's education, household structure, etc.

5. The disability variable comes from a core question on work-limiting disability that is updated at each interview. It is asked only of respondents under 70. Because the two samples are weighted to achieve age comparability, differences in disability categories reflect disability rate differences between the two samples

6. The '0' month is the month in which the husband dies. The dip in income-to-needs is an artifact most likely of the husband not being considered present in that month and, therefore, his income not accounted for even though he was there part of the month. This results in an inaccurate accounting of the income the widow could draw on during that month. See Holden (1989) for a discussion of the problems associated with the first accounting period of widowhood.

7. This does not contradict studies reviewed above which find that potential Social Security benefit (measured by the primary insurance amount) cushions women against the economic shock of widowhood. The SIPP public use file includes only actual Social Security benefit amounts.

8. The seam occurs when two consecutive months come from different interviewing waves in SIPP. McGarry (1995) has demonstrated that researchers should find larger shifts in income across these seam months than across consecutive months within an interviewing wave simply because they come from different interviews.

References

Bound, John, Duncan, Greg J., Laren, Deborah S. and Oleinick, Lewis (1991) 'Poverty Dynamics in Widowhood.' *Journal of Gerontology: Social Sciences* 46: S115-S124.

Burkhauser, Richard V., Butler, J. S. and Holden, Karen C. (1991) 'How the Death of a Spouse Affects Economic Well-Being After Retirement: A Hazard Model Approach.' *Social Science Quarterly* 72 (3): 504-519.

Burkhauser, Richard V., Holden, Karen C. and Feaster, Daniel (1988) 'Incidence, Timing, and Events Associated with Poverty: A Dynamic View of Poverty in Retirement.' *Journal of Gerontology* 43: 546-552.

Burkhauser, Richard V., Holden, Karen C. and Myers, Daniel (1986) 'The Dynamics of Poverty among the Elderly: Income Transitions at Older Stages of Life.' *Gerontologist*, 26: 292-297.

Dodge, Hiroko H. (1995) 'Movements Out of Poverty among Elderly Widows.' *Journal of Gerontology: Social Sciences* 50B: S240-S249.

Duleep, Harriet. O. (1986) 'Measuring the Effect of Income on Adult Mortality using Longitudinal Administrative Record Data.' *Journal of Human Resources* 21: 238-251.

Hadley, J. (1982) *More Medical Care, Better Health? An Economic Analysis of Mortality Rates*. Washington DC: The Urban Institute.

Holden, Karen C. (1989) 'The Transition from Wife to Widow: Data Issues in Measuring First-Period Income Effects in SIPP and the RHS.' In: *Individuals and Family in Transition: Understanding Change through Longitudinal Data*. Washington, D.C.: U.S. Bureau of the Census.

Holden, Karen C. (1990) 'Social Security Policy and the Income Shock of Widowhood.' The Robert M. La Follette Institute of Public Affairs Working Paper No. 3.

Holden, Karen C., Burkhauser, Richard B. and Feaster, Daniel J. (1988) 'The Timing of Falls into Poverty After Retirement and Widowhood.' *Demography* 25: 405-414.

Hurd, Michael and Wise, David (1989) 'The Wealth and Poverty of Widows: Assets Before and After the Husband's Death.' In Wise, David A. (ed.) *The Economics of Aging*. Chicago: University of Chicago Press.

McGarry, Kathleen (1995) 'Measurement Error and Poverty Rates of Widows.' *The Journal of Human Resources* 30: 113-134.

Smith, Ken R. and Zick, Cathleen D. (1986) 'The Incidence of Poverty Among the Recently Widowed: Mediating Factors in the Life Course.' *Journal of Marriage and the Family* 48: 619-630.

Zick, Cathleen D. and Smith, Ken R. (1991a) 'Patterns of Economic Change Surrounding the Death of a Spouse.' *Journal of Gerontology: Social Sciences* 46: S310-S320.

Zick, Cathleen D. and Smith, Ken R. (1991b) 'Marital Transitions, Poverty, and Gender Differences in Mortality.' *Journal of Marriage and the Family.* 53: 459-487.

1.2 Old-age provision for women: Bismarck or Beveridge?

Christopher Prinz

Pension systems in Europe

Pension systems in the countries of the European Union differ in many aspects, such as coverage, financing, qualifying conditions, extent of public involvement, level of old-age and survivor benefits, and type and level of minimum pensions (see, for example, U.S. Social Security Administration 1995, European Economy 1996, and Ploug & Kvist 1996). While there is little uniformity in those rules essentially three types of systems can be identified: (i) corporatist pension schemes which offer a contribution-related old-age benefit and survivor benefit to the employed; (ii) universal pension schemes which offer a (usually tax-financed) basic old-age benefit; and (iii) mixed systems which offer a basic benefit and a (smaller) supplementary contribution-related old-age benefit and survivor benefit. Corporatist systems focus on maintaining the standard of living (after retirement and after death of the insured spouse), universal systems on securing a basic income in old age, and mixed systems on a combination of both. Though not fully distinguishable on that kind of categorization, living standard maintenance is the main element of the Bismarck social security philosophy, while avoidance of poverty is the major goal of the Beveridge approach. Therefore, notwithstanding the slight incorrectness, throughout this paper Bismarck is equated with corporatism and Beveridge with universality.

Table 1.2.1 broadly characterises the systems in the fifteen EU countries. Nine pension schemes (in Austria, Belgium, France, Germany, Greece, Italy, Luxembourg, Portugal, and Spain) are clearly of the Bismarck-type, although Luxembourg also has a basic benefit which is related to the length of contribution to the system. Four schemes (in

Denmark, Finland, Sweden, and the United Kingdom) are built according to Beveridge-principles and supplemented by a contribution-related second pillar; so we can speak of mixed systems. However, in the UK it is optional to contract out of the earnings-related pension program. Two schemes (in Ireland and in the Netherlands), finally, have only a basic pension, although in the Netherlands this is supplemented for over 90% of the employed by industry or enterprise workers supplementary earnings related old age and survivor pension schemes. In the Netherlands this basic pension depends on the period of residence in the country, in Ireland on the period of contribution to the system (although low income earners are exempted from contributing). With one exception, all systems also offer a survivor benefit, although with widely differing entitlement criteria and levels. Only in Sweden survivor pensions were abolished in 1990 and replaced by a so-called adjustment pension which is paid for only one year. In mixed systems, a basic survivor pension usually replaces the basic pension while the survivor pension from the contribution-related second pillar is paid in addition; this is also the case in all corporatist schemes.

While different pension systems naturally result in different income distributions at old age, this is particularly true for women. Female life biographies - in contrast to men's - are often characterised by career interruptions due to periods of child care, problems in reconciling work and family life, and resulting disadvantages on the labour market (regarding salaries, opportunities for promotion, and the like). Disadvantages during adulthood are to a large extent reproduced and manifested in old age, depending on how the pension system is constructed. In a purely earnings-related scheme, for instance, with discontinuous work biographies, women are often unable to achieve (sufficient) pension claims in their own right. Systems which implicitly assume women's maintenance through their husbands can create financial dependency, paradoxical pension deficiencies and also unnecessary pension accumulation. The pension scheme has a decisive impact on the adequacy of female pension claims in relation to those of men's but also on the income distribution between different groups of women (according to marital status, number of children born, level of labour income, and the like).

Table 1.2.1 Pension schemes in the fifteen countries of the European Union

Country	Contribution-related old-age benefit	Contribution- or tax-financed basic benefit	(Contribution-free) survivor benefit
Austria	xx	-	xx
Belgium	xx	-	xx
Denmark	xx	xx	xx
Finland	xx	xx	xx
France	xx	-	xx
Germany	xx	-	xx
Greece	xx	-	xx
Ireland	-	xx	xx
Italy	xx	-	xx
Luxembourg	xx	x	xx
Netherlands	-	xx	x
Portugal	xx	-	xx
Spain	xx	-	xx
Sweden	xx	xx	(x)
United Kingdom	xx	xx	xx

Source: U.S. Social Security Administration 1995, Social Security Programs Throughout the World - 1995.
For explanation of appearance of one or two x's see text.

In order to study the impact of the pension system on pension levels and the distribution of retirement incomes of women and to answer the question whether, from the point of view of women in today's Europe, a pension system of the Bismarck- or of the Beveridge-type is to be preferred, one can choose between two different strategies. One possibility is comparing the distributions of women's pension across Europe. This procedure, however, has a number of drawbacks. First, various national pension systems have to be understood and compared in detail. Small details in some of the regulations can often have an important effect. Most systems are composed of a set of supplementing and counteracting rules which make the identification of the principles difficult. And second, countries differ in many socio-economic aspects such as the level of female economic activity, family and fertility behaviour, labour market segregation, income differentials, cultural and ideological background, or social protection and family policy apart from pension regulations. A reasonable comparison has to take all these factors and differences into account.

For this study, an alternative strategy is chosen. Instead of focussing on different schemes in different countries the focus is on a set of hypothetical pension schemes in just one country, namely Austria. This is done by model calculations on the basis of a set of assumptions concerning the pension scheme. This procedure avoids considering national differences and enables us to compare stylised 'ideal' pension schemes. In doing so, we can also answer the question which type of system - corporatist, universal, or mixed - would best account for the great variety of different female life (i.e. work and family) biographies. The only problem with this strategy is that potential effects of different policy settings on individual behaviour (for example concerning female labour force participation or family and fertility behaviour in general) are neglected.

All calculations are taken from 'Independent old-age pensions for women in Austria', a recently completed research project on behalf of the Austrian Federal Minister for Women's Affairs (see Prinz et al. 1996). The aim of this project was to propose pension reform solutions which would improve the situation of women in old age by guaranteeing a sufficient, individual pension claim in its own right for everybody. While recent reforms of the Austrian pension system were driven by pure financial considerations, increasingly it is acknowledged that the Austrian system is unfair, systematically discriminating against some groups (especially women) and privileging others (most particularly civil servants, but also widows in general). Although pension reforms in the future are likely to be equally driven by budgetary considerations, even more so when population ageing gains in significance, recent and expected future changes in the society in general (such as changing family behaviour and labour market conditions) and the gender aspect in particular give a more structural pension reform urgent. There is some hope that forthcoming reforms might consider both financial and structural arguments in order to find a fair and sustainable policy solution.

Alternative pension models

Five alternative pension models are compared in the analysis: (i) the current Austrian, corporatist pension scheme, (ii) the current system complemented by splitting pension claims between married or divorced spouses, (iii) a two-pillar system similar to the Scandinavian schemes (a universal basic pension supplemented by a contribution-related component), (iv) an individual mandatory insurance scheme for everybody (still Bismarck-type, but covering the total population), and finally (v) a system which combines elements of (i) and (iv). The model calculations are based on the assumption of 'expense neutrality' which means that both the individual contribution to the pension system (22.8 per cent of gross earnings) and the contribution by the government (currently around 20 per cent of total pension expenditures) is held constant.

The current system is used as a reference model. Its basic characteristics as of 1996 are the following: the legal retirement age is 60 years for women and 65 for men. Early retirement is possible at 55 and 60 years, respectively. The pension benefit amounts to 1.83 per cent of average earnings in the best 15 income years per annum over the first 30 insurance years, plus 1.675 per cent for each subsequent insurance year until the 45th, with a 2 per cent increase for each year beyond age 56 (for women) or 61 (for men); maximum: 80 per cent of average earnings. These benefits are payable if there are at least 15 contributory or 25 insurance years. There is an income-tested allowance for those with a pension claim, but no minimum pension. Four contribution-free years of insurance are credited for each child (less than four years with shorter birth intervals). The survivor pension amounts to 40-60 per cent of the pension of the insured spouse, depending on the income difference between the partners (on average, it is 58 per cent for women and 42 per cent for men; with equal income the percentage is 52). Divorced women and men are not entitled to a survivor pension. In conclusion, pension claims in this system are strictly related to contributions (= length of employment and level of earnings) or marital status (= level of contributions of the spouse).

The split pension variant complements the current system with splitting individual pension claims between married or divorced partners according to the number of years married before retirement (the exact period of marriage being irrelevant). All other regulations remain unchanged, except for the survivor benefits which are reduced by 17 per cent (to 33-50 per cent of the pension of the insured spouse) in order not to violate the expense neutrality. Under this system, the situation of divorced women, but also of married women in general, should be improved.

The two-pillar system offers two types of benefits: a basic benefit of ATS 6600 per month (approximately 550 US$) which only depends on the duration of residence in the country and which guarantees a minimum income in old age; and a contribution-related benefit equivalent to the current system but with a lower benefit rate (only 1.2 per cent for each year of insurance, with a maximum of 54 per cent). The survivor pension is abolished altogether except for an adjustment payment for widow(er)s below retirement age. Other regulations (retirement ages, credits for child care, etc.) remain unchanged. This system would essentially mean introducing a minimum income security in old age for all residents at the expense of reduced contribution-related claims and annulled derived claims, thus favouring low income groups in general.

The mandatory insurance system supplements the current contribution-related system by an individual mandatory insurance for all persons above age 20, who do not belong to the labour force. In doing so, it strengthens the insurance principle but at the same time introduces a minimum pension for everybody, irrespective of the work biography. The minimum contribution is ATS 2220 (or US$ 185) per month. This contribution has to be paid either by the state (during the first four years after the birth of a child; also for employed mothers), or by the respective insurance body (health insurance institutions in case of long-lasting illness, care insurance institutions during times of old-age care, unemployment insurance institutions in case of unemployment), or by the married spouse (with a certain subsidy for low income groups). Again, the survivor pension is abolished altogether. Due to the additional contributions, the benefit rate is slightly higher in this model (2 per cent for each year of insurance, but again with a maximum of 80 per cent).

The combined system is again a mandatory insurance scheme but keeps certain elements of the current system. The minimum contribution is only ATS 1500 (or US$ 125) per month, leading to a lower minimum pension which is - if necessary - increased by a certain allowance in order to surpass the individual poverty level (in this model, in contrast to the current system, this allowance is not means-tested). The contribution paid by the state after the birth of a child is both higher (twice the minimum during the first four years) and of longer duration (minimum contribution until the youngest child reaches age ten). The survivor pension is not abolished, but instead reduced to one-third (then amounting to 13-20 per cent of the pension of the insured spouse), thus keeping a certain maintenance of the standard of living after the death of the spouse. The benefit rate is reduced to 1.73 per cent for each year of insurance (resulting in 69.2 per cent after 40 years of insurance, the maximum still being 80 per cent of average earnings).

Selected life biographies

In order to analyse the effect of these five alternative pension schemes on the income distribution of women in old age, typical and critical female life biographies are constructed which differ by marital status, number of children born, length of career interruption, and income. The following four biographies are compared (see also Table 1.2.2):

1. A working married woman with one child who interrupts her career for three years (in the following labelled 'working spouse'); this woman benefits from the current system to the extent that she receives both an old-age and a derived pension (or a double-pension).

2. A non-working married woman with three children who gives up gainful employment after the birth of the first child (labelled 'non-working spouse'); in the current system this woman is entirely dependent on her husband, be it through his earnings or pension or through her derived pension claim.

3. A non-working woman with the same biography as the one above who experiences a divorce at age 50 and re-enters the labour market at that age (labelled 'divorced spouse'); in the current system this woman has to rely on her own, very small old-age pension entitlement, since she does not have a derived pension claim.

4. And finally a working single mother with one child who interrupts her career only during the two-year period of parental leave (labelled 'single mother'); her pension level essentially mirrors her earnings level.

Each of these four biographies are combined with two assumptions concerning the women's (and their husband's) income levels, resulting in eight different cases altogether. A first assumption is that both partners earn average gender-specific incomes (which is 33 per cent lower for women), the other that both earn only a low income corresponding to the average in the gender-specific lowest income quartiles (which is slightly above half of the overall gender-specific average).

Table 1.2.2 Selected typical and critical female life biographies: Basic assumptions

Parameter	Working spouse	Non-working spouse	Divorced spouse	Single mother
Marital status	married	married	divorced	single
Age at labour market entrance	18	18	18	18
Age at marriage	22	22	22	-
Age at first birth	24	24	24	24
Age at second birth	-	26	26	-
Age at third birth	-	28	28	-
Age at labour market re-entrance	27	-	50	26
Age at retirement*	55	(60)	60	55
Age at widowhood	74	74	-	-
Age at divorce	-	-	50	-
Life expectancy	82	82	82	82
Total contributory years	34	6	16	35
Total insurance years	37	14	24	37

* The age at retirement differs because only some women fulfil the early retirement requirements. The non-working spouse is not entitled to any pension in the current system; in other systems her retirement age is set to 60. In the mandatory insurance scheme, for comparative purposes the retirement age is set at 58 for all biographies.

Main model results

Table 1.2.3 (for women or couples with an average income) and Table 1.2.4 (for those with a low income) summarise the results, focussing on the following six indicators.

The lifetime old-age benefit gives the accumulated old-age pension payments from retirement - at age 55 or 60 - until death, in million Austrian Shillings (12 ATS is 1 US$). Pension duration is calculated on the basis of average female life expectancy at age 58, which is currently 82 years. This indicator is an overall measure of the old-age pension level of a particular woman. To calculate the lifetime total benefit one had to add to this figure the accumulated derived survivor pension payments, given that the husband dies when the wife turns 74. This indicator is the most relevant when comparing the overall effect of a pension scheme on the pension income of women, since it also shows how a higher old-age entitlement might possibly compensate for a lower derived entitlement.

We define the old-age income replacement ratio as the monthly old-age pension divided by the monthly average earnings of the best 15 income years (the earnings base on which the pension is calculated). This is a reasonable indicator of living standard maintenance at retirement. The survivor income replacement ratio, on the other hand, is defined as the ratio between the woman's total pension after the death of the spouse (monthly old-age plus survivor benefit) and the sum of both partners' individual monthly old-age pensions before the husband has died. This is a measure of living standard maintenance when becoming a widow. Both ratios are measured as a percentage.

The husband's lifetime benefit is the accumulated lifetime old-age benefit (from retirement at age 60 until death) for the corresponding partner, again measured in million ATS. The husband's survivor benefit is put equal to zero, because - for an average couple - the man will always die before the woman. With an equal monthly old-age pension entitlement, the husband's lifetime old-age benefit will invariably be lower than that of his wife, simply because his life expectancy at retirement (at age 60) is significantly lower. The wife/husband pension ratio, finally, gives the wife's monthly old-age pension claim, if any, divided by that of her husband, thus measuring gender differentials in pension income.

The current, earnings- and marriage-related Austrian pension system is particularly beneficial for the working spouse with one child, who - over her lifetime - receives 3.7 million ATS old-age benefit (which gives a 65 per cent old-age income replacement ratio) and an additional 1.2 million ATS survivor benefit (see Table 1.2.3, average income group). This gives her a very high (74 per cent) survivor income replacement ratio at the death of her husband, although her old-age pension is only 54 per cent of that of her husband. Would she die before him, his survivor income replacement ratio would even be as high as 80 per cent. The non-working spouse or full-time housewife, who has three children, receives the same amount of survivor benefit, but no individual old-age benefit because she fails to accumulate 15 contributory years. Her survivor income replacement ratio is 60 per cent. In absolute terms her pension income after the death of her husband is around half of that of the working spouse. The single mother with one child, on the other hand, obtains the same lifetime old-age benefit as the working spouse (slightly higher because she has worked one year longer), but no derived benefit. For that reason, with almost the same life biography (35 contributory years and one child), her lifetime total pension benefit is almost one-quarter lower than that of the working spouse. The divorced spouse with three children, who re-enters the labour market at age 50, is again in a peculiar position. With 16 contributory years, she is able to arrive at an old-age pension which is exactly half of that of the working spouse or the single mother. Since she also does not receive any survivor benefit (but a small allowance, see below for details), her lifetime total pension benefit is only 41 per cent and 53 per cent, respectively, in relative terms compared to the two other biographies. On average, the total lifetime pension income of the divorced spouse is 50 per cent higher than that of the non-working spouse, who - on the other hand - can still count on her husband's income or pension. Would the husband of the non-working spouse die already at age 60 (or immediately after retirement) her lifetime survivor pension benefit would be almost twice as high as the divorced spouse's lifetime old-age benefit - simply because 60 per cent of the old-age pension of the (deceased) husband is still twice as much as the old-age pension of the divorced spouse.

The main difference for the low income group is produced by the means-tested allowance (the so-called 'Ausgleichszulage') which raises the pension to 7900 ATS (or 660 US$) a month for an individual and 11500 ATS (or 960 US$) a month for a couple if a pension claim exists. The old-age pension of the divorced spouse and the single mother and the survivor benefit of the widowed non-working spouse are indeed lower than this level and increased accordingly - this is not true for the working spouse who receives a double pension which is higher than this level (which is often seen as the official poverty line in Austria). As a result, the relative position of the working spouse worsens (see Table 1.2.4). Her lifetime pension benefit is below that of the single mother, because her lifetime survivor pension claim is lower than the single mother's lifetime allowance. Indeed, due to this allowance, the old-age income replacement ratio of the single mother (and also of the divorced spouse) with low income reaches 94 per cent. Similarly, the survivor income replacement ratio of the non-working spouse goes up to 80 per cent. The income-tested allowance considerably improves the income position of low income groups in general, not only of women; just to give an example, the husband of the non-working spouse also receives such an allowance, which raises his pension claim by roughly 12 per cent (see Table 1.2.4).

While all the four alternative pension schemes aim at improving the income position of women in old age, one way or the other relieving the disadvantages resulting from career interruptions due to child care, the distributional mechanisms and effects are quite different.

The split pension variant increases old-age pension entitlements of women significantly if the woman is or was married and if the husband had a reasonable income himself. The lifetime total pension entitlement of the divorced spouse increases by 60 per cent with an average income, but only by 20 per cent with a low income. In the latter case, the increase in the old-age benefit of the divorced woman is largely compensated for by a reduced allowance payment. The non-working spouse benefits even more than the divorced spouse (plus 160 per cent with average, and plus 100 per cent with low income). However, her husband's pension is reduced accordingly. One consequence of this shift is that the survivor income replacement ratio of the non-working spouse becomes much higher - 74 per cent, exactly the same as for the working spouse. The old-age benefit of the working spouse is also one-third higher, her survivor benefit - which is calculated on the basis of her husband's old-age pension - one-fourth lower. In other words, pension splitting leads to a totally different income distribution between two partners. Irrespective of the work biography or the length of career interruption, a married woman's old-age benefit is around 90 per cent of that of her husband's. A real improvement results for divorced women (and a similar deterioration for divorced men): her pension income reaches three-quarters of his pension for the average income group, and even 100 per cent with low income. By definition, this variant has no effect on the pension income of single mothers.

The Beveridge-type two-pillar system - with a first, universal and a second, contribution-related component - results in a significant redistribution to the benefit of low income earners. Particularly for women with a continuous work biography and a low income, a situation which is often typical for lowly educated blue-collar workers, this scheme would be ideal.

Table 1.2.3 Selected results for four biographies under average income

Indicator	Working spouse	Non-working spouse	Divorced spouse	Single mother
Lifetime old-age benefit (mio. ATS)				
Current system	3.7	0.0	1.8	3.8
Split pension	4.9	2.7	3.2	3.8
Two-pillar system	4.5	2.1	2.9	4.5
Mandatory insurance	4.7	2.8	3.9	4.8
Combined system	4.3	2.3	3.6	4.4
Lifetime total benefit (mio. ATS)				
Current system	4.9	1.2	2.0	3.8
Split pension	5.8	3.2	3.2	3.8
Two-pillar system	4.5	2.2	2.9	4.5
Mandatory insurance	4.7	2.8	3.9	4.8
Combined system	4.7	2.7	3.6	4.4
Old-age income replacement (%)				
Current system	65	-	51	65
Split pension	87	-	88	65
Two-pillar system	79	-	81	78
Mandatory insurance	83	-	88	83
Combined system	75	-	83	75
Survivor income replacement (%)				
Current system	74	60	24	-
Split pension	74	74	42	-
Two-pillar system	41	34	35	-
Mandatory insurance	39	29	36	-
Combined system	5.2	43	38	-
Husband's lifetime benefit (mio. ATS)				
Current system	4.6	4.6	4.6	-
Split pension	3.8	2.4	3.5	-
Two-pillar system	4.4	4.4	4.4	-
Mandatory insurance	5.2	5.2	5.2	-
Combined system	4.5	4.5	4.5	-
Wife/husband pension ratio (%)				
Current system	54	0	32	-
Split pension	90	90	73	-
Two-pillar system	69	39	55	-
Mandatory insurance	65	42	57	-
Combined system	67	39	61	-

Source: Prinz et al., 1996.

Table 1.2.4 Selected results for four biographies under low income

Indicator	Working spouse	Non-working spouse	Divorced spouse	Single mother
Lifetime old-age benefit (mio. ATS)				
Current system	1.9	0.0	1.1	2.0
Split pension	2.7	1.4	1.8	2.0
Two-pillar system	3.3	2.1	2.5	3.3
Mandatory insurance	2.8	2.7	2.7	2.8
Combined system	2.4	1.9	2.2	2.4
Lifetime total benefit (mio. ATS)				
Current system	2.6	0.9	2.0	2.9
Split pension	3.1	1.8	2.4	2.9
Two-pillar system	3.3	2.2	2.5	3.3
Mandatory insurance	2.9	2.7	2.7	2.9
Combined system	2.6	2.1	2.6	2.9
Old-age income replacement (%)				
Current system	65	-	94	94
Split pension	88	-	112	94
Two-pillar system	109	-	113	107
Mandatory insurance	86	-	91	86
Combined system	80	-	94	94
Survivor income replacement (%)				
Current system	74	80	49	-
Split pension	74	80	59	-
Two-pillar system	43	44	41	-
Mandatory insurance	42	42	42	-
Combined system	52	51	48	-
Husband's lifetime benefit (mio. ATS)				
Current system	2.5	2.8	2.5	-
Split pension	2.0	1.7	2.0	-
Two-pillar system	3.0	3.0	3.0	-
Mandatory insurance	2.8	2.8	2.8	-
Combined system	2.4	2.4	2.4	-
Wife/husband pension ratio (%)				
Current system	53	0	67	-
Split pension	90	90	100	-
Two-pillar system	75	57	68	-
Mandatory insurance	69	73	73	-
Combined system	68	61	70	-

Source: Prinz et al., 1996.

With low income, the old-age pension of the working spouse and of the single mother increases by almost 70 per cent; with average income, the increase is roughly 20 per cent. The old-age income replacement ratios reach 78-79 per cent with average income and even 107-109 per cent with low income. For men with a low income the increase is also in the order of 20 per cent. For the divorced and for the non-working spouse the effect of the two-pillar system is very positive too, although for the average income group this system is less beneficial than the split pension variant. The huge improvements in old-age pension income under this scheme come at the expense of two groups of the population (see also Table 1.2.5): first, men with an average income lose around 5 per cent (the higher the income, the higher the loss); and second, survivor benefits are abolished altogether. For that reason, the lifetime total benefit of the working spouse with an average income is 8 per cent lower than under the current system. With low income, however, the surplus gained from the basic pension component by far exceeds the loss of the survivor pension in a lifetime perspective. Since there is no survivor benefit anymore, also in this case the survivor income replacement ratio falls below 50 per cent for all widows, irrespective of the income level, and in some cases even below 40 per cent.

The 'universal Bismarck-type' mandatory insurance system turns out to be optimal for those people, in particular women, with significant career interruptions. While there is no extra benefit for low income groups gaps in the working biography disappear by means of the mandatory insurance also covering all those who are not in the labour force (most particularly people taking care of a child or a dependent elderly). The consequence is that, in the low income group, the non-working spouse reaches practically the same old-age pension as the three other categories of women. The explanation is found in the fact that the benefit for this group in this system, is about the same as the contribution resulting from a low income job (this is no longer the case in the combined system, see below). Comparing average income earners the non-working spouse reaches an old-age pension which is approximately 60 per cent of that of the working spouse or the single mother, two biographies with, on the average, virtually no career interruption. On the other hand her pension claim is only 12 per cent lower than under the split pension variant - and that with no corresponding pension loss of her husband. In fact, also men benefit from this system because the additional old-age benefits for women do not result from a gender redistribution, but rather from additional contributions (which are, however, partly to be paid by the husbands) and from a shift from derived to individual benefits.

With average income the old-age benefit of the working spouse and of the single mother increases by more than one-quarter. The lifetime total benefit of the divorced spouse even doubles, reaching a level as high as for the single mother under the current system - again, with no corresponding loss of the divorced former husband. For all women with average income the old-age income replacement ratio is comparable to that under the two-pillar system (more than 80 per cent). In contrast to the Beveridge-type two-pillar system, however, this ratio is only little higher for the low income groups. Due to the abolition of derived pension claims the survivor income replacement ratio is again around 40 per cent for women (again even lower for the non-working spouse) and 60 per cent for men.

The combined system, which is again a universal Bismarck-type scheme, tries to overcome some of the major shortcomings of the two-pillar and the mandatory insurance systems. By keeping a reduced survivor pension entitlement, living standard maintenance at the death of the husband is re-introduced. And by lowering the minimum contribution the additional burden of traditional married couples with only one income is reduced. On the other hand, these measures lead to a parallel reduction of old-age benefits, in particular for women with career interruptions. Compared to the mandatory insurance scheme the lifetime old-age benefit of the non-working spouse is 18 per cent (with average income) and 30 per cent (with low income) lower. In a lifetime perspective, for a woman with a husband with average income, this reduction is fully compensated by the survivor benefit. With a low income husband only one-third of this difference is compensated. For those women without significant career gaps, such as the single mother, the old-age benefit is reduced by around 8 per cent. With a low income the reduction would theoretically be larger, but is fully compensated by the income-tested allowance. Overall, the main effect of the combined system, compared to the pure mandatory insurance variant, is a reduction of the old-age income replacement ratio to around 75 per cent (not for low income groups, who receive an allowance) and an increase in the survivor income replacement ratio to around 50 per cent. Because of the derived pension claims and the significantly lower additional contributions, the average pension of a man is also lower - just about the same as under the current system.

Assessment and conclusion

The answer to the basic questions, first, which of the systems is most attractive to women, and second, is a (corporatist) Bismarck- or a (universal) Beveridge-type scheme to be preferred, is quite complex. Depending on the group of women at interest, be it non-working housewives, divorced women, working spouses, single mothers, or low income groups, very different pension systems turn out to be optimal (see Tables 1.2.3 and 1.2.4, and Table 1.2.5 below). For working spouses, the current system is very attractive since they can expect to become 'double-pensioners'. For most of these women only the split pension variant could increase their benefit level but only through a proportional pension loss of their husbands. For non-working spouses any change in the system would be an enormous improvement. A mandatory insurance scheme is generally most appropriate for this group since this scheme 'fills' the career gaps. Pension splitting can be even more advantageous for these women if the husband had a reasonable income. However, splitting would of course not increase the combined pension income of the couple. The situation is similar for divorced spouses, although for them a mandatory insurance scheme leads always to higher benefits than the split pension variant. Also single mothers would benefit from a mandatory insurance scheme while they naturally could not profit from a splitting of pension entitlements. Finally, women with a lower income in general (and men with a low income as well), would mostly benefit from a Beveridge-type two-pillar system, in particular if they have a continuous work biography with very short or even no career gaps.

What is the essence of this contradictory summary? Apparently, the evaluation of these crucially different pension schemes very much becomes an ideological issue. Depending on what model of the family and the society one has in mind, one or the other scheme seems more appropriate. Consequently, different political parties and pressure groups will clearly promote different solutions. From a social-democratic point of view, a Beveridge-type two-pillar scheme should be advanced as this is the scheme with the most significant redistribution flows. However, a mandatory insurance system gives similar results, and that with a stronger focus on individual benefits and without hurting the insurance principle. From a more conservative point of view, the split pension variant might look appropriate since it supports the middle-class marriage model, just as the current system does, but at the same time solves the precarious situation of the divorced. Clearly, the current Austrian system is most contradictory in itself. On the one hand it supports the traditional marriage model, since it offers generous contribution-free survivor benefits, thus being particularly beneficial for the middle-class. On the other hand, it is exactly the non-working spouse which would, on average, benefit the most from a two-pillar or a mandatory insurance scheme; offering individual instead of derived entitlements. These schemes more or less redistribute the pension income of non-working spouses over the life-cycle. The critical point is that there is a very important income component. The higher the income of the husband, the more beneficial is the current system, implying a massive redistribution to the benefit of high income class widows.

Table 1.2.5 Winners and losers under alternative pension schemes

Pension scheme	Winners		Losers	
	in general	in particular	in general	in particular
Current system	most men and survivors	-	most women	discontinuous work biographies
Pension splitting variant	married and/or divorced women	divorced spouses	married and/or divorced men	ex-husbands of the divorced spouses
Two-pillar system	lower income groups	women/couples with low income	higher income groups	widow(er)s, men with avg. income
Mandatory insurance	discontinuous work biographies	non-working spouses	widows and widowers	-
Combined system	discontinuous work biographies	non-working spouses	-	-

Next to the pure income distribution effects, other outcomes of the proposed alternative pension schemes should also be analysed. The most important issue in this context is incentives and disincentives given by the different systems, in particular with regard to female labour market participation. For high income groups the current system has strong incentives for women to withdraw from the labour market, although an - always unforeseeable - divorce could or would have disastrous consequences. The pension splitting variant gives equally contradictory work incentives, since in this case men who would provide security for the possibility of a divorce should like to see there wives paying contributions to the pension scheme. From a woman's point of view, on the other hand, even the risk of divorce is cared for - in so far, this system would clearly support the traditional (non-)sharing of paid and unpaid work. For low income couples, there is a strong incentive for the woman to earn part of the living to secure daily survival - irrespective of the particulars of the respective pension scheme. The two-pillar and the mandatory insurance systems clearly encourage women's economic activity, as these schemes do not offer a derived pension entitlement and only a relatively low individual benefit for the non-employed. To what extent this would also favour an equal sharing of unpaid care work is a different issue, of course. The mandatory insurance system has an even greater incentive for women to re-enter into the labour market, because the husband would have to pay contributions in any case. However, since the state takes over these contributions during the first four years after the birth of a child (and given the paternal leave allowance, which is paid for 1½-2 years), there is quite a strong incentive to leave the labour market during a certain period, though not necessarily for the whole four years.

Given all these ideological elements, what strategy could and should be applied? Essentially, there are two steps involved. The prerequisite is an agreement on the aims of the pension reform. Since these aims are ideologically different as well, it will only be possible to agree on - hopefully not entirely contradictory - minimum aims. In the Austrian context, the following basic aims might be agreeable: first, securing an individual minimum pension above the poverty level for everybody; second, securing a certain living standard maintenance after retirement and after the death of the spouse; and third, strengthening the insurance principle ('contribution equivalence or fairness').

Given these aims, the next step is to propose systems which fulfil the aims by combining several elements, an example of which is given above. With the aim to bridge the different ideologies and to be fair and balanced, such a combined system seems to be the best, if not the only solution. In other words, a balanced combination of Bismarck- and Beveridge-type elements would serve the whole group of women the best. The resulting redistribution effects of the combined system indeed look very promising (see again Tables 1.2.3-1.2.5). For none of the selected biographies is this variant optimal; however, the most critical problems and discriminations are removed. Everybody reaches an individual pension above the poverty line; the situation of women with significant career gaps is considerably improved (both for divorced and for married spouses); living standard maintenance at retirement is clearly improved for women, with almost no change (or a 4 per cent reduction) for men; living standard maintenance at the death of the spouse is not abolished, though considerably reduced; and the insurance principle is very much strengthened. Moreover, any kind of still remaining redistribution is made explicit.

The future will tell whether such a combined system will indeed be the only solution, at least in the Austrian context.

References

European Economy (1996) *Ageing and Pension Expenditure Prospects in the Western World*. European Commission, Directorate-General V: Brussels/Luxembourg.

Ploug N. and Kvist, J. (1996) *Social Security in Europe. Development or Dismantlement?* Kluwer Law International: The Hague/London/Boston.

Prinz Ch., Rolf-Engel, G. and Thenner, M. (1996) 'Neue Wege der eigenständigen Alterssicherung von Frauen - Ausgangslage und Reformmodelle'. [Independent old-age pensions for women - reform models for Austria]. *Final Project Report*. European Centre for Social Welfare Policy and Research/Austrian Federal Ministry for Women's Affairs: Vienna.

U.S. Social Security Administration (1995) 'Social Security Programs Throughout the World - 1995'. *SSA Publication* No. 13 - 11805. U.S. Government Printing Office: Washington.

1.3 Employment and retirement: Conflicting aims within the welfare society

Martin Rein and Barry L. Friedman

The aging of the population is likely to drive up the costs of largely pay-as-you-go public pension systems in many countries. As policy makers have grappled with possible solutions, it has become clear that the pension system does not stand alone, but is linked to other systems. For example, there has been extensive interest in the mutual links between the pension system and capital markets, and the success of policies such as pre-funding depends on how these links are managed. There are also links between employment and pension systems. Of course, there are behavioural links. A person's work and retirement decisions and wage history help determine pension benefits, and parameters of the pension system may influence work decisions. But there are also links in terms of policy. It has often been asserted that encouraging retirement is a way to open employment opportunities for younger workers. Whether that is true is uncertain, but employment policy has at least sought to remove workers from the labour force, the young by keeping them in school longer and the old by enabling and encouraging retirement earlier. Countries have used not only the retirement system itself, but other programs such as unemployment insurance and disability insurance to get workers out of the labour force before the official retirement age. In terms of policy, the links have involved mainly using retirement and related programs as tools for achieving employment goals. However, this kind of linkage has financial consequences for the retirement system. When pension costs were still relatively small, possible financial burdens could be overlooked. Now, with pension costs likely to rise substantially in many countries, the issue is more serious. There is a new view that argues that retirement may not be a desirable tool for solving employment problems, a view that would shift the balance between the needs of employment policy and the financial burden of the pension system.

Typical of the new view is the argument of Steuerle and Bakija. They argue that there are many individuals who for a variety of reasons have labour market problems and may need help with those problems. However, such individuals may be found in all age groups. Using early retirement as a tool to solve employment problems makes available to all people in the age bracket a benefit that only some need. They say:

> If the needy, unemployed, or disabled are only a minority of any age group, then there is little justification for entitling all members of this group to benefits required by that minority. It is not a question of whether need exists, but, rather, which needs most demand society's resources (Steuerle and Bakija, 1994: 201).

They urge that needs be met through programs such as unemployment and disability insurance. They assume that such programs are targeted, just at those with the indicated risk, and are not available to the general population of older workers. They assume also that the benefit and hence the cost is less than in the pension system. In a similar vein, the World Bank report, *Averting the Old Age Crisis*, argues:

> Early retirement, though appealing in the short run, is a costly and shortsighted way to reduce unemployment and facilitate enterprise reform. It reduces the country's labour force (especially its experienced labour force), shrinks potential output, reduces political pressure to cut unemployment, and results in regressive redistributions. Pension benefits are often much higher than unemployment benefits, and these costs continue for many years (World Bank, 1994: 125).

The new view is a reaction to the fact that the function of the retirement system has been blurred, making it in effect into unemployment insurance for older workers who are still below the original retirement age. Basically, it argues that the pension system should be de-linked from employment policy, and that this would reduce one of the financial strains on the system. Instead of drawing pensions, those with real problems should be directed to the programs that deal with their specific risk such as unemployment and disability insurance. The view is that if, these programs are run appropriately, participation will be restricted to those with the stated risk, and benefits in these programs will be lower than in the pension system. Of course, this view is not really new. As the names of the programs suggest, they were designed to deal with specialized risks in the first place. However, it is difficult to resurrect their original functions. Not only has the mission of the retirement system been blurred to meet employment goals, but unemployment and disability insurance have been blurred to make them pathways into retirement in which role they also serve employment goals. Moral hazard has long been recognized as a problem in unemployment and disability programs. Workers may try to take advantage of these programs, and employers might seek to direct workers into them as a cheap way to reduce the work force. The important development has been, however, that the state has also assented to, or even encouraged, the expansion of coverage beyond those with the specified risk. Rather than meet specific risks, many programs have been blurred to make them serve multi-purpose needs. Although blurring is a fairly general phenomenon, the form it takes differs by country. In France, it was the retirement system itself that was used to absorb unemployment when the retirement age was dramatically lowered from 65 to 60. In Germany, unemployment and disability insurance were adapted into pathways to early retirement, and in addition the retirement age in the pension system was lowered so a person could make a smooth transition along the pathways into retirement. In the Netherlands, the old retirement system kept the retirement age at 65, but new early retirement programs were created.[1] If the redirection approach is to be used, it faces the challenge of undoing the blurring that has emerged over many years. In recent cases where countries have attempted to close pathways to those without the designated risk characteristics, it appears that new pathways have been created to substitute for the old. If pathway substitution becomes an important phenomenon, that will further complicate the redirection of people to the programs that match their risk characteristics.

Given the tendency to blur program missions and to create new pathways when old ones are blocked, there is reason to doubt that retirement policy can be successfully de-linked from employment policy simply by targeting - or re-targeting - programs. The tendency to use retirement and other programs to absorb older workers out of the labour force on a long-term basis is expensive. At a time when pension systems are being strained in any case, it is worth considering whether there are ways to ease this particular source of strain. However, re-targeting alone does not address the real issues if costs related to early retirement are to be controlled. There are several factors that affect program cost no matter which pathway is used in a country. Reducing the benefit level and the participation rate are ways to reduce program costs. It may also be possible to shift costs from the public sector to the private sector which can then make its own choice about whether it is willing to pay the cost. These are tools for controlling cost no matter which pathways are used. Re-targeting will make a difference only if it will change one of these cost control factors. At the same time, these tools may be used even without re-targeting.

Given that employment policy has in some ways redirected the mission of retirement and other programs and added to their cost, the main focus of this paper is on the possibility of easing this burden, containing costs while still being attentive to employment needs. We look first at how employment policy came to influence retirement policy. Then we look at three tools for cutting program costs. The first is adjustment in benefits. It turns out that most programs that allow early retirement actually subsidize in present value terms to those who retire early. We examine the magnitude of the subsidy and explore the possibility of setting benefit levels that would eliminate it. The second is restrictions on participation. Here we consider mainly incentives relating to participation and employment and look at data concerning these. While the first two measures reduce total cost, the third examines the possibility of shifting costs. To shift from one public program to another does not help the public budget. However, a shift to the private sector may ease public costs while allowing the private sector to decide whether the cost is really worthwhile.

Retirement as a tool of employment policy

Although employment policy has come to play an important role in retirement policy, there have been other factors such as mortality rates and family solidarity. When national public old age insurance schemes were first introduced in the late 19th century in Germany entitlement to benefits was set at age 70. Over the years retirement was gradually reduced to age 65 in most countries at the same time longevity was increasing. In Eastern Europe where longevity is lower, the retirement age is 60 for men. One principle shaping retirement policy was the importance of maintaining family solidarity by creating policies that avoid having a younger wife stay in employment after an older husband has retired. Most countries therefore set a retirement age for wives between 3 and 5 years lower. In more recent years it has become widely recognized that the principle of family solidarity seems to conflict with the principle of equal gender treatment. Thus countries have had to decide whether to lower the retirement age of men or raise the age for women. Most countries raised the retirement age of women.

Although these other factors have been important, unemployment problems have also come to influence the design of public retirement systems in most Western countries. Social security was first enacted in the US during the Great Depression. Some of the distinctive features of European retirement systems developed in times of high unemployment. However, unemployment could be viewed as a general problem of all age groups and not just the aged. To some extent, policies have sought to remove workers of various ages from the labour force, keeping the young in school longer, for example, as well as encouraging early retirement among older workers. Nevertheless, there has been a tendency in some countries to offer particularly strong inducements to early retirement. Considering arguments that justify targeting older workers, a perennial is that exit by older workers opens more opportunities for younger workers. While this is possible, it is also possible that exiting older workers simply reduce overall employment without opening new opportunities. Even if early retirement does not increase the number of jobs for others, it has been argued that older workers have special problems keeping their jobs. Perhaps employers seek to renege on long-term contracts as the wages of older workers rise above their marginal products. Perhaps the skills of older workers actually become obsolete. Or, perhaps economic restructuring has devalued the skills of older workers more than those of younger workers. These are all difficult propositions to prove, but as ideas, they can influence the design of policy. Because of arguments such as these, countries generally have been concerned about the situation of older workers. However, countries have differed in the ways they addressed this concern. Some countries have moved only to enable the early retirement of older workers. In contrast, others have actively sought to encourage it.

The active encouragement of early retirement has involved two kinds of policies. First, countries have eased eligibility standards, either within the pension system itself or in other programs such as unemployment and disability insurance which can serve as pathways to retirement.

This means in turn (1) easy tests to qualify initially for those above some minimum age, and (2) prolonged eligibility, generally until age 65. Second, not only must workers qualify, but they must choose the option of early retirement. A key element in inducing this choice is to offer a benefit sufficiently high. There are two dimensions to this: (1) a benefit that does not penalize early retirees by being set below the level for those who wait until normal retirement age; (2) a benefit that is high relative to the final wage. High benefits are not only an incentive, but also serve equity goals. If older workers really have poor employment opportunities, leaving them to the mercy of the labour market consigns them to low wages or no work at all. But after contributing to the economy for many years, it is considered fair to protect older workers from a significant decline in their standard of living. Moreover, it is argued that equal treatment for all at relatively high levels can promote solidarity. Thus, the idea of encouraging early retirement tends to begin with a belief in the asymmetric lack of opportunity for older workers, reinforced by value considerations. We illustrate the variety of approaches by comparing the US which enables early retirement with France and the Netherlands which have been among the countries most aggressively encouraging it.

In the US debate over social security, there was considerable support for a retirement age of 60 as a way to remove unemployed workers above this age from the labour force. This age was ultimately rejected because of reasons of cost. There was also support for a retirement age of 68 or 70, but the concern over high unemployment induced decision makers to keep the age at 65. There were provisions to discourage work by those over 65 including the loss of benefits for those whose earnings exceeded $15 per month, and not counting earnings after 65 in determining benefits (Graebner 1980: 184-89). One member of the committee which drafted the legislation was once asked if the attention to employment objectives did not make the program political. She replied that such concerns were not political, but rather economic and social.[2] Even in the US, there was intense concern over unemployment. Later, when early retirement was introduced, employment was again an important consideration. Even in the late 1940s, there were advocates of a lower retirement age for women to ease employment problems in textiles and other industries. When the age for women was lowered to 62 in 1956, employment effects were one consideration, although there were others such as a belief that husbands and wives should retire at the same time. Again, when the male retirement age was reduced to 62 in 1961, there was concern that job opportunities for older workers were limited (Graebner 1980: 221-23). US policy allowed early retirement for those who chose it, but did not make it a primary goal. In allowing early retirement, a penalty was imposed which could reduce the pension amount up to 20% below that of a person retiring at the normal age of 65. Even for those retiring at the normal retirement age, replacement rates were generally well below 50% except for those with the lowest earnings.

France, in contrast, promoted early retirement more actively. France after World War II had a retirement age of 65. It did allow early retirement at age 60, but with highly restricted eligibility and with a 50% penalty below the pension at normal retirement age. Eligibility conditions in the pension system were eased somewhat over time, but France turned initially to its unemployment insurance system to deal with the employment problems of older workers. Beginning in 1972, dismissed workers over 60 were eligible for a guaranteed income program not available to younger workers. The benefit would be guaranteed until the person could draw a pension at age 65. The benefit amounted to 80% of net final wages which was higher than the 60% available in the pension system. Upon retirement at age 65, the person would receive a full pension as if she had continued working. In 1977, this benefit was extended to those over 60 who resigned voluntarily. In accord with the new view, workers were directed to a program other than the retirement system, but unlike the new view, there were no eligibility restrictions (after 1977) related to risk, and the cost was actually higher than that of the pension system. In view of the rapidly mounting costs of this program, France in 1982 began redirecting those over 60 back to the pension system. The retirement age was reduced to 60 with no penalty for early retirement. There was some reduction in overall cost since the pension benefit was lower than the guaranteed income, but still relatively high compared to other countries. The predominant view was that older workers should be drawn out of employment. Over time, one program was substituted for another, but both offered high benefits without penalties for retiring early. Still concerned over unemployment, France also began targeting special unemployment insurance benefits to older workers who were below age 60 (Guillemard 1991).

The Netherlands also went far in removing older workers from the work force. The pension system itself is a flat benefit available only from age 65, and that retirement age has not changed. However, the disability and unemployment insurance systems expanded coverage for older workers under 65, becoming in effect pathways to early retirement. The disability program was initially targeted, but became less so over time. A person qualified if she was unable to earn her final wage in 'suitable work.' In the seventies, the eligibility determination came to focus more on the availability of work. Labour market conditions came to play a greater role than the inherent condition of the worker, making the disability program more like an unemployment program. The benefit was 80% of the final wage for those with the highest level of incapacity, but lack of an available job came to be considered full disability.

Moreover, the duration of the benefit was indefinite, and could last until age 65 when regular retirement could begin. The unemployment insurance system also broadened its coverage of older workers in the seventies, in particular, allowing prolonged benefits for workers over 57.5. Replacement rates in both programs were relatively high. In addition, negotiations between labour and employers produced supplementary benefits for both programs which brought the replacement rate to 100% for many recipients. There is one more option provided by the private sector, known as VUT, which has drawn many workers into early retirement. It was available initially to workers age 62.5, with the eligibility age eventually coming down to 59.9 years. It paid benefits replacing 75 to 85% of final wages. The idea arose in a time of high unemployment that workers should be entitled to a period of retirement before the pension age. With these generous benefits available, it is not surprising that labour force participation among those 60 to 64 fell from 74% in 1971 to 19% in 1994 (Blomsma and Jansweijer 1996).

Even in the more generous countries, cost has become an issue. However, there is also a belief in the appropriateness of encouraging early retirement and there is political support for it. In such an environment, cost-cutting can produce unexpected results. We turn to a discussion of the variables most likely to make a difference.

Benefit rates for early retirees

One way to cut the costs of a program is to cut benefit rates. Since we are concerned with early retirement, our interest is primarily in the rates paid to those who draw pensions before the normal retirement age. Since benefit levels are often specified in relation to the normal retirement age, changing it can also change benefits for early retirees. In a country like France, there is no penalty for early retirement. A retiree will get the same benefit whether she retires at age 60 or 65. Most countries, however, have some penalty. In the US, for example, younger retirees get a permanently lower benefit rate. If there is no penalty, early retirees over their lifetimes clearly draw more from the pension system than those retiring at the normal retirement age. In other words, there is a net subsidy to those who retire early. On the other hand, it is possible to set a penalty rate such that there is no extra cost to the pension system, no net subsidy. This section explores the magnitude of the early retirement subsidy and the early retirement penalty rate that would be needed to eliminate the subsidy.

The subsidy can be calculated in terms of present value. Compare the net present value of benefits from the pension system for two individuals at age 62, the earliest age to qualify for a pension in the US. One chooses to retire early at age 62, while the other continues working and contributing to the pension system until the normal retirement age of 65. The present value can be broken into three components:

1. the benefits received before age 65 (by the early retiree, but not the age 65 retiree);
2. the benefits received after age 65 by both, but smaller for the early retiree;
3. the contributions into the system out of wages (by the age 65 retiree, but not the early one).

Consider first just benefits alone. The difference between the individuals in item 2 measures the amount the pension system can recover through the early retirement penalty. If the penalty is large enough, this can exceed the early benefits in 1 and there is no net subsidy. Table 1.3.1, Part A, estimates these magnitudes for low-wage male earners in the US. Males are used because they have lower life expectancy and thus will get a higher subsidy (the case of females is considered below). It calculates first the subsidy in total benefits, taking account of items 1 and 2. Then it calculates the subsidy in net benefits taking account of item 3 as well. The early retiree gets $2,347 more in the present value of lifetime benefits than the retiree at the normal age of 65. This amounts to 3.6% of the present value of the age 65 retiree. This may understate the difference since the age 65 retiree continues working and hence contributing into the social security system. Considering the overall expected impact of the social security system as of age 62 on the age 65 retiree, the present value of his net benefit is lowered by the subtraction of the present value of contributions. No such adjustment is needed for the age 62 retiree since he does not contribute further to the system. Taking account of contributions, the early retiree gets a net present value $5,980 higher than that of the age 65 retiree, or 9.8% of the net present value of the latter.

Instead of looking at the subsidy resulting from the current benefit structure, an alternative is to ask what benefit reduction for early retirees would be just sufficient to eliminate the subsidy. Again, the zero subsidy rate can be calculated either taking account of the contributions of the age 65 retiree or not. Assuming real values, the current US benefit for an age 62 retiree is 80% of that for the age 65 retiree.[3] To eliminate the subsidy in the benefit alone, the benefit for the early retiree would have to be lowered only to 77.2%, the small difference reflecting the fact that the subsidy itself is not large. Taking account of the difference in contributions, the subsidy is a little larger, and an early retiree rate of 72.8% would be needed. At these rates, the early retirement of males would be of no concern to the pension system. There would be no difference in cost to the system no matter when the worker retired.

An individual account system automatically achieves the result that early retirement does not change the cost of the system. If a person retires early, benefits will be reduced to account fully for the fact that there will be no further contributions and benefits will be drawn for a longer period - there is no source of funds other than what the person has already put in. The person is free to retire at any time, but must absorb fully the financial risk from that decision. As our calculations show, it is possible to set a benefit rate that will achieve the same result in a defined benefit plan. However, there are some practical problems in doing so, because several assumptions are needed.

First, should the contributions of the age 65 retiree be included, and, if so, how should they be valued? From the point of view of the financial condition of the system, not only may extra benefits be paid to the early retiree, but three years of contributions are lost. The zero-subsidy benefit calculated this way is what is needed to neutralize fully the adverse effects from early retirement. On the other hand, it could be argued that employment may not be a realistic alternative for many of those who retire early. In this view, early retirees should not be punished for something they cannot control. The zero-subsidy benefit calculated without taking account of lost contributions avoids this penalty.

Table 1.3.1 Subsidies to early retirees

A. Case I

Retirement age	65 ($)	Difference 65-62 ($)	Subsidy ($)	Subsidy as % of age 65 total or net benefit
Annual benefit	6863			
1. Present value of benefits, age 62-64	-	-15236		
2. Present value of benefits from age 65	64446	12889		
Present value of Total Benefits	64446	-2347	2347	3.6
3. Present value of contributions	3633	3633		
Present value of Net Benefits	60813	-5980	5980	9.8

B. Benefit Rate Required for 0 Early Retirement Subsidy
(as % of PIA for retiree age 62)

for 0 subsidy in total benefits	72.2%
for 0 subsidy in net benefits	72.8%

(current rate is 80%)

C. Alternative Cases
Summary of total and net subsidies (present value)
Other cases differ from Case I in just the one variable indicated

	total subsidy		net subsidy	
	$	%	$	%
Case I	2347	3.6	5980	9.8
Earnings always at US Social Security maximum	4998	3.6	17620	14.1
Age 62 benefit is 100% of PIA (similar to France)	19045	29.6	22678	37.3

All present values calculated as of age 62.
Assumptions:
1. US retiree in 1994 who had always earned the minimum wage;
2. all values real (constant over time);
3. real interest rate of 4%;
4. life expectancy at age 62 of 17 years (male figure in 1992);
5. wage after age 62 continues at federal minimum;
6. age 62 benefit is 80% of PIA, age 65 benefit is 100% of PIA.

A counter-argument, however, is that all early retirees get the subsidy, but only some have no alternatives while others choose early retirement voluntarily. Not establishing a sufficient penalty gives an incentive for a kind of behaviour that the state does not need to subsidize. But again, some European countries have argued that the state does have an interest in inducing older workers out of the work force. Finally, with the coming aging problem, some countries will need major increases in contribution rates if they do not undertake other reforms. The state will be losing more from lost contributions, and so it will become increasingly important to take account of them in the zero-subsidy calculation. Whichever argument is preferred, two alternative calculations are presented. Incidentally, the lower present value for age 65 retirees does not necessarily mean that they are worse off. They do have earnings for an extra three years which probably increases their overall net worth relative to early retirees. The calculation concerns only the person's standing with respect to the social security system and the cost to it of the person's retirement choice.

Another assumption concerns life expectancy. While the above results are for a single male, those for single females are different because of differences in life expectancy. The state recovers some of the extra costs from early retirement by paying a lower benefit compared to the age 65 retiree. This recovery begins at age 65 when both draw pensions (item 2 above). The longer life expectancy, the longer the time to recover costs. Thus, the subsidy to early retirement will be smaller the longer life expectancy. Using the longer life expectancy for females, Part C of Table 1.3.1 shows that there is no subsidy for total benefits (negative numbers). There is still a subsidy in terms of net benefits (taking account of contributions), but it is about half that for males. If life expectancy continues to increase, the subsidy to early retirement will diminish on its own. But at a given point in time, decision makers would have to decide whose life expectancy to use.

The above calculations were for a person who had always earned the minimum wage. The table also shows the subsidy to a worker who always earned the social security maximum. Not surprisingly, the absolute early retirement subsidy is larger for the high-wage early retiree. Considering just the benefit side, the percentage subsidy is the same for all income groups. However, taking account of contributions, the subsidy rate is considerably higher for the higher-earning people. An increase in benefits alone changes present values in the same proportion. However, because of the progressivity in the US benefit formula, the increase in contributions is greater than the increase in benefits, resulting in a larger subsidy to high-income early retirees. This is another one of the inadvertent redistributions which arise in defined benefit pension systems.[4] The rationale for subsidizing early retirement at all is not clear. Even more so, the rationale for giving subsidies larger in absolute amount and (on one measure) larger relatively to high-earning early retirees is questionable, but it is one of the consequences of the US-defined benefit formula.

Finally, consider the case of no benefit reduction at all for early retirees as is the case in France. In this case, there is no possibility of recovering the cost of the extra benefits paid out early. The bottom line of Table 1.3.1 shows that the subsidy to early retirees in terms of benefits alone amounts to 30% of the whole present value for an age 65 retiree. Taking into account contributions, the subsidy is 37%. These are the subsidies for a person retiring at age 62 with the life expectancy of a US male. However, in France a person can retire on a full pension at age 60. The subsidy at this age is no doubt considerably larger. The US does subsidize early retirement, but at an amount that is small in comparison to a French-style system. The French are committed to the goal of getting older workers out of employment, and they pay a high subsidy to each early retiree in order to do that. In addition, the benefit reductions in the US system are close to the point where more early retirement would not drive up the cost of the system. In France, however, variations in the number of early retirees will have big impacts on the cost of the system.

Employment, participation, and program costs

Program participation in an early retirement program generally affects program cost, although it would not if a zero-subsidy benefit rate were set. But there are additional links between participation, benefits, and program cost. Participation is generally related to employment. Workers generally leave employment completely or at least partially in order to participate in early retirement programs or pathways. The workers also balance the gains from participation against the gains from work. Program benefits may be one of the factors influencing this balancing decision. In particular, the lower the benefits, the greater the incentive to stay employed. Thus, the effects on cost come together. Lower benefits reduce cost and diminish the adverse effects from participation. Lower participation, if it has an effect, will tend to reduce cost. And lower benefits will provide an incentive for lower participation.

While there is a chance that benefits are at the zero-subsidy level, a degree of subsidization is common in many countries, although that degree can differ substantially. Thus, it is worth knowing the extent of participation and employment, and, if possible, factors affecting them. One factor particularly relevant to this paper is the level of program benefits. If high benefits not only drive up costs directly, but also draw people out of employment and into the programs, this accentuates the cost effects. Evidence that employment is sensitive to benefit levels in early retirement programs would be useful and would suggest that unemployment is not wholly intractable, but this finding alone would not help resolve the policy dilemmas. There is often heterogeneity of response to a stimulus, and in this case it would be of particular concern to policy. There are individuals who have labour market problems which would likely keep them from work no matter what the program incentives. There are others who can be induced to retire early, given a suitable inducement. The new view would seek to separate people into these parts, targeting income support to those with problems and employment incentives to the others. Policy would require evidence on how to distinguish the groups. Another view, however, is that policy should promote solidarity and should treat all alike. Targeting is contrary to the basic values of this approach. Nevertheless, evidence would help. If it turned out that the group of potential workers is large and that they are responsive to the disincentive effects of high benefits, it would suggest that the cost of the solidarity approach is high and that employment policy could be managed better by cutting benefits rather than expanding or maintaining them. Unfortunately, we lack the evidence to resolve these issues. Instead, we simply look at a few pieces of data concerning employment, retirement, and pathway programs.

Table 1.3.2 presents some incentive measures related to program features and the labor market. These data come from the Luxembourg Income Study (LIS). Pathways are defined to include 5 variables, disability, military war benefits, accident insurance, sick pay, and unemployment insurance. Military benefits and accident insurance are pretty small in most countries. Social retirement is benefits in the regular retirement system, and in most countries is not available before age 60. The first measure indicates the penalty of drawing a benefit before age 65 from a pathway by taking the ratio of pathway income for each age group relative to the mean social retirement benefit at age 65.[5] The next two lines measure the opportunity cost of choosing either a pathway or social retirement relative to employment: they take the benefit relative to the contemporaneous wage. The last line is an indicator of the wage gain from staying employed longer and is measured as the ratio of the wage for an age group relative to the wages of those below 55. The data for the Netherlands show the high pathway income relative to the flat social retirement benefit. The only other country with such high pathway income relative to social retirement is Australia where the social retirement is means tested. The other measure of the attractiveness of pathways is its ratio to wages. Here the Netherlands again stands out as the highest, but not Australia. Indeed, most other countries in the table are similar in pathways relative to wages.

The earned income of family heads age 55-59 is higher in every country compared with the earnings of those under age 55. However the size of increase varies across countries. In Canada, Switzerland and the United States earnings are higher by 13-14% for the 55 to 59 group, whereas in Australia and the Netherlands it is only 6-8% higher. After the peaking of earning at age 55-59 it begins to decline. By age 65-69 the earnings declined by two-thirds to three-quarters compared to those under 55 years of age. One explanation of the observed decline in participation rates and the high age-wage profile is a selection bias of those who continue to work. Those with good jobs and high earnings are likely to continue to work and those with bad jobs and low earnings will drop out. Data for the US for 1991 support this argument. Focusing on the age group 60-64 the following story emerges. The earners in this age group account for only 6% of all workers in the American economy. On the other hand about 68% of all heads of households are working in the 60-64 age group. However when we divide the households into those at the bottom 40% and top 60% of the income distribution a quite different pattern emerges. Only 17% of those in the bottom of the distribution have income from earning as compared with over half of those at the top of the income distribution. In most countries the earnings of the wife follows a similar pattern. However in the Netherlands and in Switzerland wives' earnings seem to peak later in life after age 65. Thus the rising earnings of these wives appears to offset the declining earnings of their male counterparts. This is an interesting theme, but it clearly requires more careful analysis.

Table 1.3.2 Work incentive measures (per cent)

	Age group			
	<55	55-59	60-64	65-69
The Netherlands, 1987				
Pathway income relative to social retirement at age 65-69	129	170	194	149
Pathway income relative to wages	47	57	71	71
Social retirement relative to wages				48
Wages relative to age <55	100	109	100	77
Switzerland, 1982				
Pathway income relative to social retirement at age 65-69	56	62	68	59
Pathway income relative to wages	19	19	22	29
Social retirement relative to wages			23	50
Wages relative to age <55	100	113	105	69
Canada, 1991				
Pathway income relative to social retirement at age 65-69	52	48	60	61
Pathway income relative to wages	17	14	21	29
Social retirement relative to wages			19	47
Wages relative to age <55	100	114	94	71
Australia, 1989				
Pathway income relative to wages retirement at age 65-69	75	112	105	114
Pathway income relative to wages	17	24	27	33
Social retirement relative to wages			20	29
Wages relative to age <55	100	107	88	78
US, 1991 (CPS)				
Pathway income relative to social retirement at age 65-69	40	63	58	56
Pathway income relative to wages	12	16	18	27
Social retirement relative to wages			24	47
Wages relative to age <55	100	112	96	61

Source: Luxemburg Income Studies Database.

Table 1.3.3 shows the percent of people receiving wage and pathway income along with the percent self-employed and with earning spouses for the same countries and years. The Netherlands has the lowest percent having wage income in every age group, and the fall is particularly dramatic over 60. On the other hand, in a substantial minority of households, people continue to work after age 65 in every country except the Netherlands. Similarly, pathway participation is substantially higher in the Netherlands while the US is lowest. Although this is a limited sample of countries, it supports the idea that the generosity of benefits may influence both employment and participation in pathways. Additional information on employment rates comes from the Employment Outlook Report for July 1996 put out by OECD. Data are reported on the employment activity rate of men 55 to 64 between 1979 and 1995. The data tell a dramatic story. Nine countries show a decline in this period. Norway, the US and Sweden all declined, but in 1995 still had employment rates of over 64 percent. But the decline in the other countries produced rates of employment as low as 38.4% in France, 41.1% in the Netherlands, and 48.8% in Germany. In other words, less than half of men 55 to 64 were working in these three countries. By contrast, in 1979 none of these countries had had male rates in this age group below two-thirds. Actually, three groups of countries can be identified among those experiencing a decline. The low group has rates below 50%, including France, Germany, and the Netherlands. A medium group has rates hovering around 50% (54-56%) in Canada, Australia, and the UK. The high group has rates between 64-70% including the US, Sweden, and Norway. Although all these countries experienced declines, some others did not. For example, in Denmark and Japan there was no decline, rates being 63% and 80% respectively. There is also no trend data for Switzerland where rates are 79%. Unfortunately, we do not have good measures of program incentives for these countries to test whether the variations in employment are explained by program features.

Table 1.3.4 looks at the share of household income coming from selected sources. The sample is broken into those in the top 60% of the income distribution and the bottom 40%. Not surprisingly, the differences are substantial. Gross wages are considerably higher for the top 60% than for the bottom 40%. While wages diminish as a share of income as both groups age, it is particularly noteworthy that earnings of those over 65 among the bottom 40% are negligible in almost every country: the top 60% in this age group gets over 20% of its income from earnings in several countries. The bottom income group depends more heavily on social retirement, and to the extent they are available, on pathways. In other words, those at the bottom not only are less likely to work, but are relatively more dependent for income on the public sources.

Table 1.3.3 Percentage of heads and spouses receiving income, by source

	Age group			
	<55	55-59	60-64	65-69
The Netherlands, 1987				
Wages	734	58.7	26.9	6.3
Self-employment	80	11.5	7.8	3.1
Spouses' wages	257	9.1	6.5	2.0
Pathway	110	34	43.4	1.1
Switzerland, 1982				
Wages	962	88.0	72.4	38.0
Self-employment	111	16.6	13.3	-
Spouses' wages	211	22.1	14.7	8.3
Pathway	37	111	27.1	-
Canada, 1991				
Wages	870	772	58.9	28.9
Self-employment	134	17.0	140	73
Spouses' wages	456	39.6	237	120
Pathway	294	26.5	232	104
Australia, 1989				
Wages	828	66.4	50.0	199
Self-employment	147	15.5	12.9	4.5
Spouses' wages	454	30.7	17.5	6.0
Pathway	168	25.7	33.6	39.7
US, 1991 (CPS)				
Wages	875	76.9	60.4	36.4
Self-employment	98	11.3	11.4	7.4
Spouses' wages	446	38.4	27.0	13.7
Pathway	150	16.0	15.8	72

Source: Luxemburg Income Studies Database.

Table 1.3.4 Percent of household gross income from selected source

	Top 60%				Bottom 40%			
	<55	55-59	60-64	65-69	<55	55-59	60-64	65-69
Netherlands, 1987								
Gross wages	74.1	59.6	25.2	6.4	46.2	26.1	5.6	0.1
Self-employment	3.7	6.7	1.2	2.9	8	7.7	9.9	0
Spouses' earnings	13.1	4.2	2.7	1.1	3.4	0.4	0.2	0.1
Pathways	5.5	18	32	2	11.3	34.9	42.2	1.9
Social retirement			2	42.9			0.4	895
Switzerland, 1982								
Gross wages	82.8	68.2	59.1	22.9	82.9	53.4	28.8	8
Self-employment	7.1	9	7.3	0	2.6	2.4	2	0
Spouses' earnings	5.9	5.5	4	4.1	3.6	2.6	1.3	1.4
Pathways	0.4	1.6	4.7	0	2.4	10.1	21.7	0.1
Social retirement			2.4	31			24.1	65.7
Canada, 1991								
Gross wages	69.3	63.3	54	20	55.1	42.1	22.2	6.4
Self-employment	5.1	4.4	5.6	3.7	5.5	5.1	7.2	1.4
Spouses' earnings	18	13.4	9.5	5.7	8.4	6.9	3.5	1.7
Pathways	2	1.9	1.9	1.1	6.6	6.9	4.4	1.0
Social retirement	0.4	2.1	4.8	27.2	1.5	4.2	20.1	63
Australia, 1985								
Gross wages	69.8	65.4	52.1	29.6	42.5	17.5	4.8	1.9
Self-employment	7.3	8.5	6.5	5.4	11.7	11.2	4.6	1.1
Spouses' earnings	15.4	8.5	6.5	5.4	4.2	3	1.9	0.4
Pathways	1.6	2.7	4.1	6.2	17.1	29	21.2	6.8
Social retirement	0.3	1.1	2.1	7.1	4.2	18.9	30.1	51.2
US, 1986								
Gross wages	70.8	62.7	46.9	23.2	59.1	36.2	26.5	8.7
Self-employment	5.7	6	4.9	2.7	5.5	7.8	4.4	
Spouses' earnings	16.5	13.9	11.4	7.2	10.3	8.1	4.1	2.7
Pathways	0.9	1.1	2	1.5	2.2	3.4	6.2	2.4
Social retirement	0.7	2.2	8.8	25.9	3.1	14.4	31.6	65.2
Germany, 1984								
Gross wages	72.2	69.7	44.9	7.8	61.9	41.4	18.3	3.5
Self-employment	6.2	12.1	7.8	6.3	3.4	11.5	4.5	0.4
Spouses' earnings	14.2	8	6	2.2	7	3.2	1	2
Pathways	0.1	0.7	0.8	0.2	3.7	1	1.7	0.2
Social retirement	1.4	4.2	34.7	76.5	3.8	28.9	65	87.5
United Kingdom, 1991								
Gross wages	64.5	58.1	40.8	11.4	25.1	21.3	11.4	1.8
Self-employment	7.7	6.1	4.6	2.7	6	8.4	0.1	0.5
Spouses' earnings	13.5	9.8	7.5	3.6	6.1	2.1	2.5	0.4
Pathways	3.4	6.8	8.5	6.3	7.3	14.1	11.5	3.7
Social retirement	0.5	3	7	30.4	1.9	11.7	25.5	66.2

Source: Luxemburg Income Studies Database.

Several conclusions emerge from these data. There has been a rather dramatic decline in employment activity rates in all countries. But there are also sharp differences across countries, some having high exit from employment and others low. Despite the high exit from work, employment remains a significant source of household income for a sizable minority of households. The wages of those who do work from age 55-64 remain surprisingly high relative to the earnings of those below the age of 55.

Returning to the question of what induces the decline in employment among older workers and whether program features contribute to it, Japan suggests interesting possibilities, both because it did not have a decline and because of its unique system. In Japan, it was customary for workers to retire at age 55, receiving a combination of severance pay and a pension from their company. However, most workers did not withdraw from work at this point, but rather sought new employment, many from their old company. But the new jobs were generally at considerably lower wages and rank. Thus, the Japanese system could be viewed not so much as a retirement system, but as a way to induce older people to work at a lower wage. But what about the reservation wages of the workers? Why would they continue to work at lower pay? If they stopped work, they would get the company pension, but would not qualify for a public pension for several years. Thus, the alternatives to work were not attractive. At the same time, Japanese workers knew from the time they started work that their wages would go down at age 55. It was fully incorporated into their expectations. There were thus strong cultural factors influencing the reservation wage of Japanese workers. European countries lack the same cultural factors and have the inducement of high benefits in early retirement tending to keep their reservation wage high. There is, however, another side of the Japanese system. The wages of most workers were in effect reduced at age 65, but not all workers suffered a decline in productivity. If the goal is to keep workers employed, there is a need to reduce the reservation wage only of those whose productivity falls. However, the cultural mechanism probably would work on a selective basis. It is because all are affected alike that all think it is normal to accept a reduction in pay. Thus, European countries have avoided targeting in drawing workers out of employment, while Japan has avoided targeting in keeping workers employed through the mechanism of reduced wages.

Cost shifting and pathway substitution

One form of cost shifting is to find a new form of financing for an existing program. This could reduce the financial burden of the program without a need to cut participation or benefits. More commonly, however, cost shifting comes from shifting participants from one program to another. This is particularly common in the case of early retirement where several programs may accomplish the same thing. Costs are, indeed, shifted, but whether this results in a net cost reduction depends on whether the new program restricts participation or pays a lower benefit or is financed out of a different, less burdensome source. Most cases of cost shifting are related to shifting participants between programs. In such cases, the savings to one program are generally far greater than the net cost reduction to the programs combined. The patterns of shifting can be complex and produce unanticipated results. For example, there have been efforts to reform a single program by restricting eligibility. However, new pathways emerge to substitute for the old. We term this situation 'pathway substitution'. Such substitution may or may not result in a change. It is critical to focus on the factors influencing cost in examining such changes, benefit levels, program participation levels, and the degree of cost shifting. Several examples illustrate the issues.

Many countries have at times attempted to contain costs through some form of cost shifting. In the case of France discussed above, the reduction in the retirement age in 1982 was part of a process of shifting participants below age 65 from the unemployment insurance system to the pension system. Participation in the pre-retirement program had expanded rapidly. But the benefit offered under this program was more generous than that in the regular pension program. Not only were costs shifted from one program to another, but it was expected that the new costs should be smaller. On the other hand, the same reform that eliminated the expenditures of the unemployment program on 60- to 64-year-olds opened a new form of pre-retirement coverage for those age 55 to 59. The reform was not only a cost-cutting effort, but that part of it that shifted costs between programs may have achieved a modest economy.

In the Netherlands, the unemployment insurance program has reduced the level of benefit, and the disability program has restricted eligibility somewhat. However, there are supplementary benefits in these areas financed by contributions from employers and employees, such that the total benefit from both public and private sources has been near

100% of the final wage. Once the public sector cuts opened a gap below this level of support, there were efforts to 'repair' it by increasing benefits in the supplementary programs. To the extent that this has happened, the total benefit to a recipient has been maintained at the same level as before. The incentives to work are as small as before. But the costs of the program are being shifted increasingly to the private sector. If the public support level were reduced sufficiently, at some point the private organizations might opt not to close the benefit gap fully. Given the still high level of public benefits, the private organizations still are willing to top them up fully. This is a case of cost shifting where so far there has not been much change in the total benefit, but the cost to government has been reduced by shifting the financing. For those no longer covered under these programs, there were also the new VUT pensions paid to early retirees without a risk factor. These are paid by the private sector. Thus, one kind of coverage may be substituted for another, but again there is a shift in financing to the private sector.

Sweden provides a case of pathway substitution. Sweden introduced a number of reforms aimed at containing cost and slowing the rapid decline in the male employment rate by 14% between 1979 and 1995. Sweden has had a partial pension system since 1976, administered separately from the regular pension system, and available to workers between 60 and 65 who want to continue working, but at a reduced schedule. In 1994, the partial pension system was tightened in three ways: (1) the age of entitlement was increased from 60 to 61; (2) the replacement rate decreased from 65% to 55%; (3) the maximum amount of work time allowed to qualify for the partial payments was decreased from 23 hours per week to 10 hours. Combining part-time work and partial pensions therefore lost its attractiveness, and for all practical purposes it is as if the system was disbanded. People began to look for full-time retirement opportunities. A second area of reform was the disability insurance system. There had been a provision for disability for social reasons. If an older person could not get a job at age 58.3, he was regarded as socially disabled because employment was socially not available. But this provision was eliminated. Thus, there was a search for new pathways to retirement.

One new pathway was private: firms began buying pensions from insurance companies. Employers and employees valued early retirement enough that employers were willing to pay for it. The new pension costs were only 75% of gross wages, and there was a large saving on the social security tax. This new pathway substituted for the old one as a form of retirement, but allowed a shift in costs from the public program to the private sector. A second new pathway made use of the unemployment insurance system, and involved tacit, informal agreement between employers and the government. Unemployment insurance benefits last for 1 year and 9 months. Then the employer agrees to re-employ the worker for 5 months, and then lay her off again, qualifying her for another 1 year and 9 months. There is a burden for government associated with the new pathway, but it is now only intermittent. And there is an additional contribution by the employers who agree to take back workers for periodic 5 month stretches. For those who use these two substitute pathways, there is still effective retirement, perhaps less work than in the case of partial benefits, perhaps more work when the periodic unemployment benefits are used. But for both substitute pathways, at least a portion of the previous cost is shifted onto the private sector.

An example of a pathway shift that achieves a small cost reduction is that in Austria. Unemployment insurance lasts at most for two years, the time varying with age and years of prior employment. However, when these benefits end, the person can enter into the social assistance system for an indefinite period of time and receive a benefit equal to 92% of her unemployment insurance benefit. Austria is unusual in that the social assistance and social insurance benefits are so close. In this case, both are provided by government, so there is no cost shifting to the private sector. There is a cost saving, but it only amounts to 8%, and the second pathway is of indefinite duration. It turns out that Austria has one of the lowest rates of employment among men age 55 to 64: only 41% of them work, a level similar to that found in the Netherlands (Boeri and Edwards 1996).

It is very difficult to close pathways or to substantially cut benefits. Both employers and workers often share a common interest in encouraging the exit of older workers from employment. Indeed, social values and public policy sometimes share the same interest. Pathways arose in the first place out of the common desire to create retirement opportunities before the normal retirement age. When one pathway is closed, this same set of shared interests tends to create alternatives. Nevertheless, although something similar to the old benefits may be preserved, the new pathway is generally not identical with the old. There may be reductions in coverage as some individuals no longer qualify for the new benefit. The new pathways may pay smaller benefits, since one goal in closing pathways is to save money. One important outcome is that cases of pathway substitution often, but not always, shift some program costs to the private sector. In principle, the private sector can make its own evaluation of whether to maintain a benefit or itself cut costs. In practice, however, in many European countries private decisions concerning benefits are made in negotiations between groups of employers and labor unions. It is difficult in such a setting for individual companies to make their own adjustments. One of the biggest difficulties arises for analysts who have a hard time evaluating the magnitudes of cost savings, cost shifting, and changes in benefits and coverage that emerge from the complex process of pathway substitution.

Conclusion

Out of concern over employment problems, many countries blurred the mission of their pension systems. To get workers out of the work force, they came to be encouraged to retire early, before the normal retirement age. Countries differed from simply enabling early retirement to actively encouraging it. However, this activity came at a cost, and most countries in some degree subsidized early retirees in the sense that the present value of benefits to early retirees was greater than that for retirees at the normal age. Given current life expectancies, the subsidy in the US is small, but it can be one-third or more of the present value of benefits to a person retiring at the normal age in a country such as France. Not only was the mission of the pension system blurred, but also that of other programs such as unemployment and disability insurance when confronted with unemployment problems. Programs which originally had been targeted to meet specific risks came to serve a wider array of clients as their eligibility standards were eased. Depending on the country, large numbers of older workers could use these on a prolonged basis as pathways to early retirement. Or, in some countries they could move from one pathway to another with similar outcome. Thus, the effective retirement system became the array of these programs.

Now with pension systems facing increasing financial burdens, it is necessary to look at ways to control costs, and there are costs related to early retirement. Of course, controlling these costs would not solve the overall problem, but would be only one step among many. To explore the possibilities, however, this paper looked at three tools, reducing benefits, restricting participation, or shifting costs elsewhere. We estimated benefit levels that would reduce the early retirement subsidy to zero, in other words, neutralize the adverse consequences of more people retiring early, which in the US is only a little below the current rate. We looked at policies relating to the rate of employment and program participation. Not surprisingly, there has been a sharp drop in the rate of employment in many (but not all) countries in the last two decades. We did not prove that this was due to the features of programs, although some of the most generous countries also have among the lowest participation rates. Assuming that program features do play a role, however, it would mean that policy should be having multiple effects on cost. Higher benefits mean higher subsidies to those who retire early, but it is these countries that tend to have the most early retirees. Finally, we looked at the possibility of cost shifting. Of course, if costs are shifted from one public program to another, that will help the budget of the one program, but not government as a whole unless the new program has lower benefits or participation. On the other hand, when costs are shifted, eventually they may go to someone who makes a decision to control them. Perhaps shifting to the private sector could eventually achieve this outcome, although private decisions about benefits are highly constrained in many countries by group processes among companies and labor unions.

Working against the process to control costs are the strong belief that early retirement is a way to reduce unemployment and the political force of people who like the benefits they have. There have been cases where the attempt to close one pathway to retirement has simply led to the substitution of another. Because of this easy substitution of pathways, it is probably naive to expect that we could return to a situation of programs neatly targeted to specific risks. Instead, cost cutting will have to come from hard choices such as cutting benefits or restricting eligibility for early retirement. But as the costs of social security systems mount, countries might become more willing to consider measures aimed at reducing the encouragement to early retirement.

Notes

1. For an examination of the policies by country, see Kohli et al., 1991.

2. Asked of Barbara Armstrong, member of the Committee on Economic Security which drafted the old age and unemployment security provisions of social security, and reported in Graebner, p. 186.

3. A person's Primary Insurance Amount (PIA) is set at age 62. Subsequent earnings usually do not change the value of the pension. There is sometimes a recalculation of benefits when wages after age 62 are substantially higher than before, but we do not consider this possibility.

4. See Martin Feldstein and Andrew Samwick, 'Social Security Rules and Marginal Tax Rates,' *The National Tax Journal*, 45 (1), 1992, pp. 1-22 for a long list of distorting, although probably unanticipated incentives in the social security system.

5. The data are based on actual benefit amounts and wages. Thus, the benefit amounts are not pure measures of program characteristics since benefits generally depend on individual behavior. Also, the figures are based on mean amounts for those who received that income source. Thus, the numerator and denominator in a ratio do not necessarily relate to the same set of individuals. Finally, there is likely to be selection bias since those who do not draw the income source may differ systematically from those who do.

References

Blomsma, Martin and Roel Jansweijer, *The Netherlands: Growing Importance of Private Sector Arrangements*, 1996 (unpublished manuscript).

Boeri, Tit and Scott Edwards, *Long-Term Unemployment and Short-Term Unemployment Benefits*. Institute for Advanced Studies, Vienna, Nov. 1996.

Graebner, Wiliam, *A History of Retirement*. Yale University Press, New Haven, 1980.

Guillemard, Anne-Marie, 'France: Massive Exit through Unemployment Compensation'. In Martin Kohli, et al., *Time for Retirement*, Chapter 5.

Kohli, Martin, et al., *Time for Retirement*. Cambridge University Press, Cambridge, England, 1991.

Steuerle, Eugene C. and Jon M. Bakija, *Retooling Social Security for the 21st Century*. Urban Institute Press: Washington, DC, 1994.

The World Bank, *Averting the Old Age Crisis*. Oxford University Press: New York, 1994.

1.4 Cross-national patterns of labor force withdrawal

Timothy M. Smeeding and Joseph F. Quinn

I. Introduction

During the post-war period, life expectancies, age distributions and retirement patterns have changed significantly in the developed, industrialized nations. Between 1950 and 1990, for example, the life expectancies for men and women in the United States increased by 6.1 and 7.3 years. Similar at birth changes, and often larger ones, can be found in other OECD countries (U.S. Bureau of the Census 1993, Figure 3.1). At the same time, men (and less often women) have been leaving the labor force earlier and earlier in these same countries (OECD 1995a, Table 2.1; OECD 1996, Table A2). The result has been an increasing period of labor market inactivity at the end of the life cycle. As these nations age, the ratio of workers to retirees is falling, presenting potential fiscal difficulties for these governments and economies (Boivenberg and van der Linden 1997).

In the United States, several public policy initiatives have been undertaken to encourage more work and later retirement among older Americans. Labor force participation data over the past decade suggest that these policies may be working - the early retirement trend seems to have stopped. The purpose of this article is to analyze retirement patterns in the United States and six other OECD countries to compare their levels and to see if any changes in trends can be discerned over recent years.

In order to investigate this issue, we will focus on differences and similarities between labor force participation and several other concepts of retirement. Many people view labor force withdrawal and retirement as synonymous, but recent research has shown that retirement patterns are many and varied. The purpose of this article is to examine these issues with an eye toward answering several questions:

- How does one measure retirement across many nations?
- Has their been change in the age of retirement, however defined, over time?
- Does work stoppage mean receipt of retirement income, and vice versa?
- Does retirement mean full work stoppage or a more gradual withdrawal from the labor market.
- Finally, does retirement mean impoverishment?

This work builds on previous research by both authors (Smeeding 1992; Quinn 1997). We will argue that retirement and labor force withdrawal mean different things to workers and to family economic status depending on the nature of each nation's disability, unemployment and retirement system, and on their labor market institutions.

We begin by reviewing some of the potential uses and operational meanings of the term 'retirement' and the seismic demographic transition which prompts wide policy interest in this topic (Section II). We then describe our data and variables (Section III), results (Section IV) and conclusions (Section V). The bottom line is in one sense straightforward; labor force withdrawal is still continuing at early ages in most wealthy nations. Unless we find ways to induce older workers to remain in the labor market longer, the demographic tsunami of the baby boom will create severe fiscal problems for most of the nations examined here. In another sense, this article is more complicated. 'Retirement' is a very complex issue which may require different definitions depending on the policy issue at hand.

The results of this article are based on the Luxembourg Income Study (LIS) database. LIS offers a choice of 25 nations where labor force withdrawal can be examined. Here we chose seven: Australia, Canada, the United States, The Netherlands, Sweden, the United Kingdom, and Germany. We chose these seven for several reasons.

First, they are among the economically most important nations within LIS. Only Japan (where the data are not available) and France and Italy (where the data are old) are alternatives on these grounds.

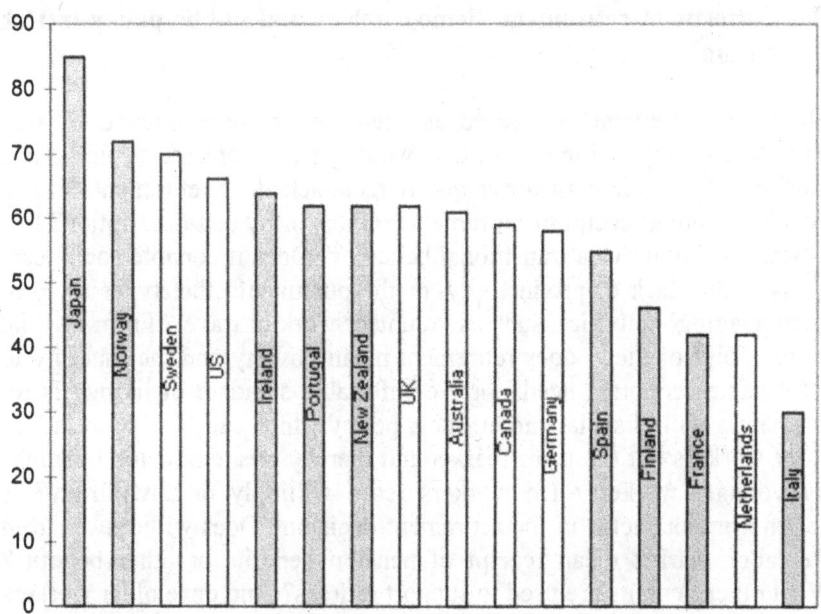

Figure 1.4.1 **Overall labor force participation rates for men aged 55-64 in 1995**
Source: OECD Labor force database.

Second, these nations represent a broad range of experiences with respect to the labor force participation of male workers nearing traditional retirement age. In 1995, only 42 percent of men aged 55 to 64 in The Netherlands were still in the labor force, compared to about 60 percent in Australia, Canada, West Germany and the United Kingdom, 66 percent the United States and 70 percent in Sweden. These fairly well span the range of national experiences found in OECD nations (Figure 1.4.1). Only Italy (30 percent) has a lower participation rate at these ages than does The Netherlands, while Norway and Sweden have the highest participation rates except for Japan.

Third, these seven nations were first visited on this issue by Smeeding (1991a, 1992) and we now return to them for an update. Finally, we are Americans presenting this article in both Sweden and the United Kingdom where there is interest in these issues.

II. Patterns of retirement, demographics and public policy in rich nations

The term 'retirement' or 'retired' is often used in social science research on public policy and the aged. One would be hard pressed to find a less murky term or one with fewer questions attached. Is retirement defined by labor supply, receipt of retirement income, or by self-description? Is it a 'state' behavior or a transitional behavior? Does it connote social uselessness and lack of productivity, or the pursuit of other types of 'productive aging' activities, such as volunteer work or travel? From a social policy point of view, does retirement mean poverty and the inability to meet basic economic needs, or a comfortable standard of living? Is retirement a tool of social and business policy which can be used to induce older workers out the labor market and thereby create new job openings for younger workers? Do workers retire willingly or unwillingly? Is health a major factor in the retirement decision? Does withdrawal from the labor market mean receipt of pension benefits or other benefits? What other benefits are used to support retirees? And once older workers leave their lifetime jobs do they continue to work? If so, where, doing what, and for how long? Does receipt of retirement benefits mean total stoppage of work or movement to a less time intensive 'bridge job' to ease the transition? In short, how one defines retirement has a lot to do with the uses to which one would want to make of the term. And our use is to highlight public policy issues, particularly those that affect the social cost of retirement.

Demographic change: experiences of nations

The age distributions of the populations of the OECD nations are changing dramatically. As life expectancies increase and the post-war baby boom cohorts age, the proportions of the populations that are of traditional retirement age are increasing and will continue to do so. In 1960, only 9.4 percent of the OECD population was aged 65 or over. Today, the OECD average is between 13 and 14 percent and well over 14 percent in the European countries. By 2030, when the last of the baby boomers will have turned age 65, 22.5 percent of the OECD population is projected to be aged 65 or older (and 10.4 percent will be aged 75 or older). Between now and 2030, percentage aged 65 or older in the United States will have increased by 75 percent, from 12.5 to 21.9 percent.

Several nations, including Germany, Italy, Japan, and The Netherlands, will have over 25 percent of their populations aged 65 or older (OECD 1996, Table A2).

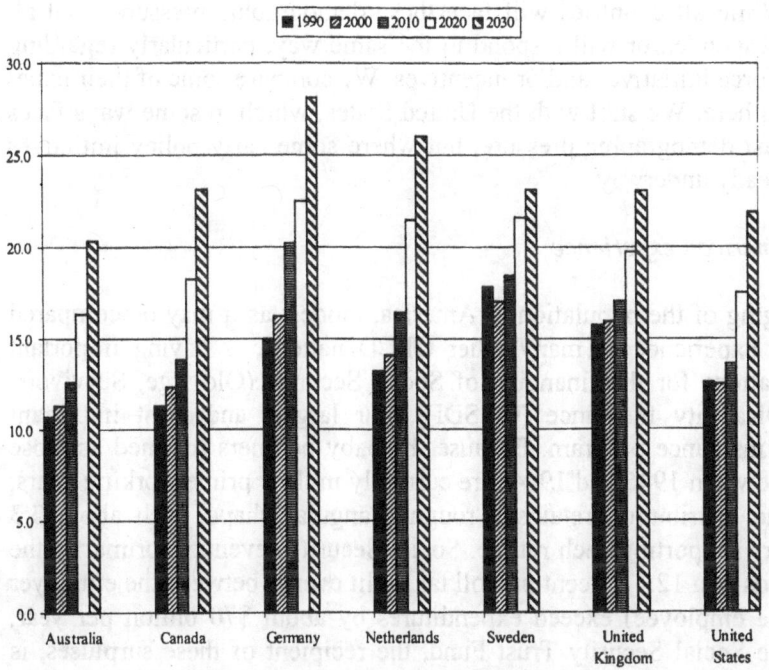

Figure 1.4.2   Percentage of the population aged 65 or over in selected OECD countries 1990 - 2030

Source: OECD, 'Ageing in OECD countries', *Social Policy Studies* no. 20, Paris: OECD, 1996, Table A2.

Figure 1.4.2 shows the percentage of the populations aged 65 or older at ten year intervals between 1990 and 2030 for the seven OECD countries whose retirement trends are discussed in this article. Among these seven countries, the experience of the United States was at the low end in 1990; it had a larger percentage aged 65 or older than did Australia or Canada, about the same fraction as The Netherlands, but a substantially lower percentage than Germany, Sweden, or the United Kingdom. By 2030, however, only Australia is projected to have a lower percentage than the United States. In fact, several Western European countries are more than two decades ahead of the United States on the aging curve. Germany, Sweden, and the United Kingdom all had substantially higher proportions of people aged 65 or older in 1990 than the United States is projected to have in 2010.

While all countries will face these demographic pressures, not all have responded or will respond in the same way, particularly regarding labor force initiatives and/or incentives. We compare some of their experiences here. We start with the United States, which in some ways faces the least demographic pressure, but where some early policy initiatives are already underway.

The American experience

The aging of the population in America, modest as it may be compared to the experience of many other OECD nations, is having important implications for the financing of Social Security (Old Age, Survivors, and Disability Insurance (OASDI)), our largest and most important social insurance program. Because the baby boomers (defined as those born between 1946 and 1964) are currently in their prime working years, the age distribution retains a rough triangular shape, with about 3.3 workers supporting each retiree. Social Security revenues (primarily the proceeds of a 12.4 percent payroll tax, split evenly between the employer and the employee) exceed expenditures by about $70 billion per year, and the Social Security Trust Fund, the recipient of these surpluses, is increasing rapidly. Beginning about 2020, however, under current tax and benefit rules, expenditures will exceed revenues, and the Trust Fund reserves will have to be used to make up the difference. Were no changes to be made, the OASDI Trust Funds would be depleted, and Social Security technically bankrupt, by 2029, about three decades from now.

America, as most other industrialized nations, has witnessed a significant increase in early labor force withdrawal during the post-war period. Whereas about one out of every two American males aged 65 or older was working in 1950, only one in six are employed today. This decline in work effort and the simultaneous increase in early receipt of Social Security benefits will accentuate the impacts of population aging on Social Security finances. Because of the impending bankruptcy of our primary social insurance system, some important changes in Social Security rules and in retirement behavior are inevitable. Some combination of revenue increases and benefit decreases or delays are necessary to bring Social Security back into long-range actuarial balance. The longer we wait to make such changes, the greater are the changes that must be made.

In the United States, several important public policy initiatives have already been enacted to encourage later retirement by older Americans. Mandatory retirement, which once covered about half of the work force, was first delayed from aged 65 to 70 (in 1978) and then outlawed altogether (in 1986). The amount of money that Social Security recipients could earn each year without losing benefits was increased, and is now indexed to wage growth. (For those aged 65 to 69, this 'exempt amount' is scheduled to increase by much more than wage inflation, from $13,500 in 1997 to $30,000 in 2002.) The age of eligibility for 'normal benefits', which has been age 65 since the beginning of the program in the late 1930s, is scheduled to rise to age 66 early next century and then, after a 12 year hiatus, to age 67. This will not only lower the benefits of those who continue to retire at age 65, but will also send an important societal message about retirement timing. Finally, the financial reward for delaying receipt of benefits beyond the 'normal age' is being increased, from 3 percent to 8 percent per year of delay, thereby encouraging additional work by older Americans.

On the private sector front, there has been a steady decline in the relative importance of defined-benefit (DB) employer pension plans (in which pension rules determine the dollar benefit that the worker will receive, usually as a function of years of service and terminal salary), and a simultaneous increase in defined contribution (DC) plans (in which the employer guarantees only a contribution to the worker's retirement account, the size of which determines the annual benefit at retirement) (EBRI 1995). Considerable research has shown that DB plans often incorporate strong retirement incentives (or work disincentives) beyond some age, usually the earliest age of eligibility (Kotlikoff and Wise 1989; Quinn, Burkhauser, and Myers 1991). Many DB plans penalize those who stay on the job past some optimal point, by reducing the present discounted value of the expected benefit stream with each additional year on the job. Econometric evidence indicates that people respond to these incentives. DC plans, in contrast, are age-neutral, and have no such work disincentives. Although DB plans remain important in America, the rise in the extent of DC plans is slowly reducing the importance of these age-specific retirement incentives.

There is some evidence that these public and private policy changes are working. Casual empiricism suggests a break in retirement patterns in the mid-1980s. Labor force participation rates (one definition of 'retirement') of older American men declined steadily form 1950 until about 1985, but have been flat since then, and there is even a suggestion of a slight increase over the past few years.

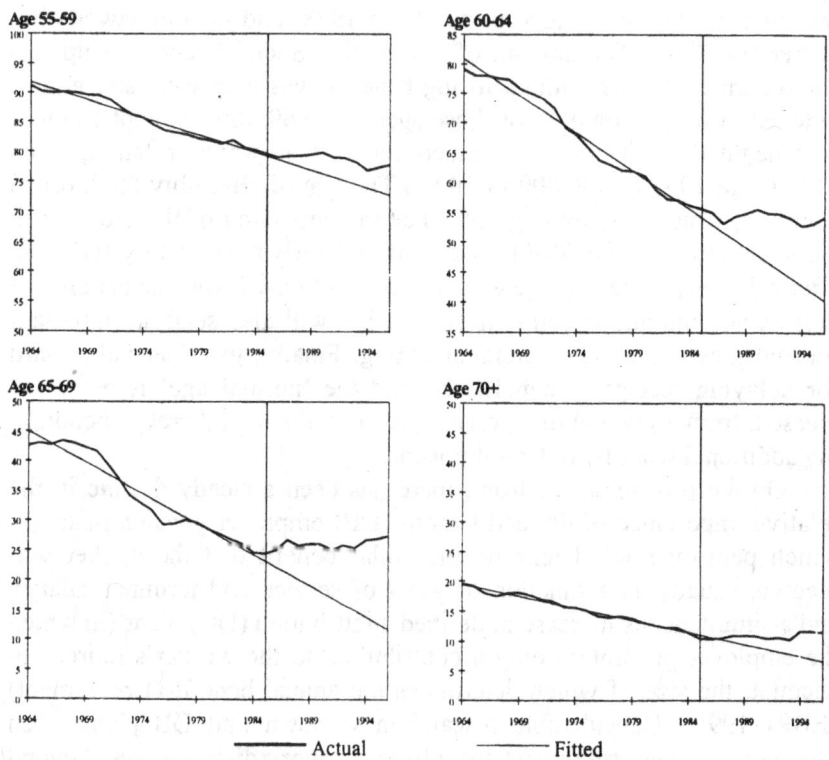

Figure 1.4.3 Labor force participation rates, United States males, by age group

Source: Author's calculations based on LIS data (see below).

Figure 1.4.3 provides clear evidence of a break in the prior trends in the United States. It shows, for men aged 55 to 59 through aged 70 and over, both the actual labor force participation rates and predicted rates based on a simple extension (from a time series regression) of the 1964 to 1985 age-specific time trends. The differences between the actual and predicted values from 1986 on illustrate the new regime. Participation rates since 1986 have been higher (and often substantially higher) than the prior trend would have predicted. There is even a suggestion of a slight increase over the past few years.

The changes in the long-term trends are consistent with the policy changes described above, indicating that changing retirement incentives by means of changing policy parameters may have an important impact on behavior. However, determining the actual causes of these changes in trend is difficult, and has been muddied by the very strong economic performance of the United States economy over the past five years, during which the overall unemployment rate dropped from 7.5 percent in 1992 to 4.8 percent today. This macroeconomic strength may have increased the desire and the ability of older Americans to stay on the job longer than they would have in the past, and may therefore have contributed to the change in trend noted above. However, the break in behavior for men in all age groups began in the mid-1980s and has persisted since then despite a recession (1990-1991). Thus, secular forces as well as cyclical forces are at work here.

The American concept of retirement

In America, 'staying on the job' can mean many things. For some, it means delaying departure from a career position. But for others - a substantial minority - it means leaving the career job (often when employer pension incentives dictate), but staying in the labor force in a new position, often part-time and sometimes as a self-employed worker. Many Americans, although still not most, retire gradually, in stages, utilizing 'bridge jobs' between full-time career employment and complete labor force withdrawal (Quinn 1997). This makes the concept of 'retirement' difficult to define.

American retirement definitions span the range outlined above. For some researchers, retirement means complete labor force withdrawal - the absence of earnings. For others, it is defined by the receipt of retirement income, either Social Security or benefits from an employee pension plan, regardless of whether the individual is still working or not. Others look for a significant decline in hours or earnings, or a job switch late in life. Still other analysts utilize a subjective definition - how respondents in a survey described themselves. These different definitions can lead to different conclusions about the proportion of a population that is 'retired' at any given age or point in time.

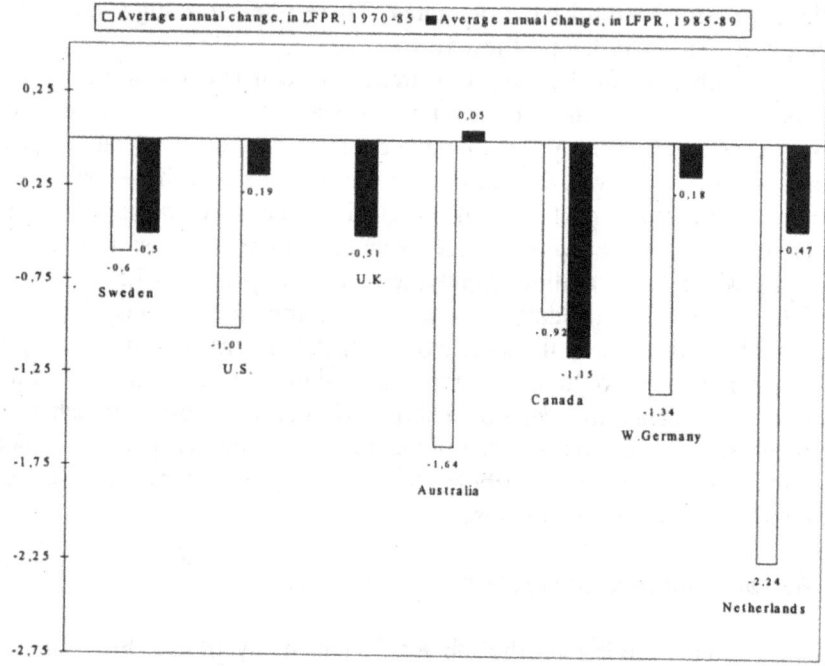

Figure 1.4.4 Average annual change in overall labor force participation rates for men aged 55-64 in 1995: 1970-85 and 1985-95

Source: OECD labor force database.
UK has data for 1985-95 only.

Experiences of other nations

The United States experience is interesting because of the dramatic change in the post-war retirement tend, coincident with several public policy initiatives that were expected to encourage more work late in life. In this section, we compare the United States retirement trends with those in several other OECD nations, and find a variety of situations - some similar to that in the United States, and others in which the post-war trend has continued unabated.

Figure 1.4.4 illustrates how trends in labor force participation among men aged 55 to 64 have changed in the nations studied here. In Figure 1.4.1 we saw that participation rates are currently lowest in The

Netherlands (42 percent) and highest in Sweden (70 percent). While these different participation rates can be corroborated from other sources,[1] the trends may be more important than the level. In fact, participation rates for these men dropped significantly in all seven countries during the 1970 to 1985 period, by an average of about 0.6 points per year in Sweden, by about 1.0 point per year in the United States and Canada, and even more in West Germany (-1.34 points/year), Australia (-1.64 points/year) and The Netherlands (-2.24 points/year). During the past decade, however, participation rates for men aged 55 to 64 were almost unchanged in Australia, West Germany, and the United States. They continued to decline, although more slowly than prior to 1985, in The Netherlands. In Sweden and the United Kingdom, the rate of decline continues at about -0.5 points per year, close to the Dutch trend since 1985. Only in Canada, which currently has the highest rate of labor force exit, do we find an increasing trend toward early retirement.

Table 1.4.1 Standard age of entitlement and public expenditures on social retirement: 1995 and 2030

	Standard Age of Retirement for Men in 1992	Social Retirement Pensions as a Percent of GNP *			Difference as %
		1995	2030	Difference	1995
United States	65	4.1	6.6	2.5	61.0
Germany	65	11.1	16.5	5.4	48.6
United Kingdom	65	4.5	5.5	1	22.2
Canada	65	5.2	9.0	3.8	73.1
Australia	65	2.6	2.9	0.3	11.5
Netherlands	65	6.0	11.2	5.2	87.0
Sweden	65	11.8	15.0	3.2	27.1

* Assumes continuation of current trends.
Source: OECD (1996), table 2.1 and table 2.3.

Labor force withdrawal is only one issue involved in the fiscal cost of retirement, outlays for public social retirement and related programs are also important. For instance, Table 1.4.1 provides some cross-national evidence for public pension costs and standard age of entitlement to public pensions courtesy of the OECD (1996). The first contrast of obvious interest is the limited usefulness of the standard age of retirement as a predictor of retirement behavior. While standard age of benefit receipt does have some effect on retirement as noted by 'spikes' in labor force leaving behavior, considerable labor force withdrawal has already occurred by them.

While all seven of our nations have the exact same age of normal retirement for men (of these only the United Kingdom has a lower age for women), the costs of public pensions as a fraction of GDP very enormously across these nations. Australia has no social insurance system but rather an income-tested pension in old age which guarantees most workers about 60 percent of the median overall level of disposable income. Thus, benefits are very targeted at the bottom of the distribution and cost only about 2.6 percent of GDP in 1995. This allows the Australians to control their outlays and they predict only an 11.5 percent change by 2030 when the number of aged are expected to peak. The United States and the United Kingdom faced the next lowest levels of program costs in 1995. The United Kingdom forecasts a relatively modest 22 percent rise in pension claims by 2030. The British achieve much of their savings by offering private accumulation pension plans (SERPS) in addition to a modest first tier social retirement benefit plan. The Americans anticipate a steep 61 percent increase in their social retirement costs. While many Americans regard as cataclysmic the rise in public pension outlays expected over the next century (e.g., Peterson (1996)), America will only spend 6.6 percent of GDP for this purpose by 2030, third lowest and still far below 1995 levels of outlay in Germany and Sweden. The Canadians and Dutch face the largest increases in outlays. While the Canadians will still be below 10 percent of GDP in outlays in 2030, they face a 73 percent (3.8 point) rise in total outlays over the next 35 years. The Dutch will see their outlays nearly double from 6.0 to 11.2 percent of GDP. Financially, the Germans and the Swedes begin with 1995 pension to GDP rates of over 11 percent, far above the other nations examined here.[2] They are expected to further expand another 3.2 (Sweden) to 5.4 (Germany) percentage points *beyond* these already high levels. The bottom line is that with the exception of Australia, each of these nations is facing a large increase in the fiscal burden of pension outlays over the next 35 years if current policies are not changed.

Because policies will likely be changed, these forecasts are not likely to occur. In fact, even the 1995 figures are in some ways just 'estimates'. For instance, *none* of the figures in Table 1.4.1 include the cost of 'early retirement' benefits that fall under 'disability,' 'extended unemployment' or 'unemployment retirement' schemes. Given low rates of male labor force participation *prior* to age 65, the standard age of retirement in all of these nations, something else must be supporting early labor force departures. These issues can be faced as they were in the United States where there is evidence of labor force turnaround. But cost forces are pushing up the retirement burden in two directions: from below (early retirement) and from above (life expectancy). As we mentioned earlier, overall lifespan and life expectancy at age 65 has been growing in all nations. According to Preston (1996), the United States social retirement actuaries are liable to be seriously underestimating expected gains in life expectancy at older ages over the next 30 to 40 years. If he is correct more generally, *all* nations will be facing even larger burdens in 2030 than those forecast by OECD because of underestimates of life expectancy. From 1935 to 1985, added years of life expectancy at age 65 all by themselves produced a 28 percent increase in social pension outlays (Smeeding 1991b). Finally, increases in public health care costs due to an aging society have not been figured into these estimates. Rough estimates from the OECD (1996, Table 3.3) indicate that population aging could add another 1.5 to 2.5 percentage points of GDP to the cost of providing health care for these elders. What is now painfully clear to each of these nations is that the fiscal costs of an aging society are growing rapidly (OECD 1996).

Social policy and retirement

Labor force withdrawal at older ages depends on both demand and supply factors. On the demand side, the productivity of older workers and pay practices (age-earnings profiles) are important, as is the macroeconomic strength of the economy. Government policies to protect against age discrimination, firing rules, and laws against mandatory retirement all limit the ability of employers to affect retirement decisions.

Government social insurance programs can have significant impact on labor supply decisions, and may help explain why actual retirement ages are often so much lower than official standard ages. In fact, many European workers claim retirement at much earlier ages. When asked their status on the 1992 European Labor Force Survey, 65 percent of Germans, 56 percent of Dutch, and 89 percent of British aged 60 to 64 list themselves as 'retired.' The figures for men aged 55 to 59 were 39 percent in Germany, 29 percent in The Netherlands, and only 17 percent in the United Kingdom (Theeuwes 1997).

On the income support side, three different types of policies are used to bridge the income gap between job departure and full old age social retirement benefits. In Germany, The Netherlands, the United Kingdom, Sweden, and Australia, the unemployment insurance system has special provisions for extending unemployment compensation until the official age of retirement. In Germany, The Netherlands and Sweden, this is even called an 'unemployment pension.' However, 'unemployment retirement' is not always separately identified from 'unemployment insurance.' Because much of unemployment insurance may be cyclical as well, receipt of unemployment insurance may or may not be used as a bridge to retirement.

A second well-traveled route to social retirement is disability benefits. All nations reviewed here, especially Sweden, Germany, The Netherlands, the United Kingdom, and Australia, face important challenges in both eligibility for disability pensions and benefit generosity. When unemployment is high and workers are near retirement, the idea of relaxing the criteria for disability is attractive to public officials.

A third way that public social benefit policy can directly affect early retirement is by means of early retirement benefit receipt. Most nations have arrangements under which qualified workers can elect early receipt at a reduced benefit level. In Germany, early retirement with full benefits is allowed in specific cases. While this third way is the easiest to affect via public policy, no country, except Germany, has recently changed these rules. As suggested by Theeuwes (1997), to study the retirement decision in old age, at least two (disability and early retirement) and perhaps all three (including unemployment) types of benefits need to be simultaneously evaluated.

A separate retirement determinant behavior mentioned earlier is the occupational pension. Here employers (in the private and public sector) can exert considerable influence over job departure, especially when the pension is of the defined benefit (DB) type. In Canada, the United Kingdom, The Netherlands, and the United States, employer pensions often affect departure from the firm. However, while employer pensions are 'work-conditioned' from the firm's point of view, there is no penalty for work in alternative employment. Workers accepting pensions from specific employers often take new jobs, and combine earnings and retirement benefits.

With respect to public retirement benefits, most nations administer a 'retirement test' to determine beneficiary status. These range from Germany, where there is a substantial penalty for work, to the United Kingdom, where there is no work penalty. In Sweden, partial public pensions can be mixed with part-time work, and in the United States where there is a substantial earnings disregard (about $8,600 per year for those aged 62 to 64, and $13,500 for those aged 65 to 69). In our empirical work below, we will see that work and retirement are frequently combined in some of these countries.

Conclusion

Among the seven nations we are studying here, there is both considerable similarity and substantial difference across nations. Every nation is facing a severe demographic challenge, some more than others. Yet every nation has one or more avenues for early retirement at the same time that life expectancy at older ages and overall economic well-being among the aged are increasing. One solution to the fiscal crisis of old age is to try to keep potential beneficiaries employed and to limit these avenues of labor force retreat.

The first step in formulating these policies is to see how workers and their families mix earnings and other sources of income around retirement ages. In the sections below, we demonstrate the complexity of defining retirement within any one country and across countries. We will follow the lead of Smeeding (1992), and use several definitions of 'retirement' to examine retirement patterns across nations. We will see to what extent beneficiaries mix employment and social pensions and will investigate the impact of retirement on one aspect of economic well-being - poverty.

III. Data and definitions

The data used in this article come from the Luxembourg Income Study (LIS), a social science database that now covers 25 nations and 75 databases.[3] The LIS countries and data years used in the article are Australia (1985-1986 and 1989-90), Canada (1991, 1994), The Netherlands (1987, 1991), Sweden (1987, 1992), the United Kingdom (1986, 1991), the United States (1986, 1994), and West Germany (1984, 1989).

These data allow us to identify separately earning and retirement income receipt for family heads, spouses, and other adults.[4] However, one should remember that these data provide only time-specific cross-sectional 'snapshots' views of several measures of 'retirement' at particular points in time, or short trends in these snapshots. To fully analyze the dynamic process of retirement from a cross-national perspective, comparable panel data such as that used by Burkhauser et al. (1997) is necessary. Unfortunately, these panel data are currently available for only three of the seven nations studied here, and even these are limited in scope to three to ten years of recent retirement behavior.

The major variables used to define retirement here and elsewhere are lack of earnings (labor force departure) and/or receipt of retirement income. Earnings include cash compensation from all types of employment (wages and salaries, self-employment, and farming). Retirement income includes all forms of social pensions, occupational pensions (from private or public employers), and government employee pensions. Retirement income is also defined here to include long-term disability pensions and other types of special 'younger age' pensions offered to workers by enterprises and/or governments. While long-term disability benefits could be excluded, they serve as an early retirement device in many nations. In fact, the inclusion or exclusion of long-term disability income can create large differences across nations. For instance, the inclusion of long-term disability benefits and unemployment insurance as retirement income, raises the fraction of Australian heads aged 55 to 59 having retirement income from 29 to 39 percent. In The Netherlands, the proportion of heads in this same age range with retirement income rises from 47 to 65 percent once disability is included. The widespread use of disability benefits as a bridge to retirement income in most of the nations studied here is widely acknowledged (Haveman, Halberstadt, and Burkhauser 1984; Burkhauser et al. 1997; Aarts and DeJong 1992). It is important to note that our retirement income definition does not include short-term worker disability benefits, nor does it include means-tested 'welfare' or 'special assistance' benefits (except in Australia where all 'old age pensions' are income tested). These income components are, however, included when determining poverty status.

We could also include unemployment insurance as a type of retirement income. However, because unemployment insurance is received by many older workers who will indeed return to work, we are hesitant to label it as retirement benefit and have not done so here.[5]

All of our analyses define the retirement status of households (or families) based on the earnings, income, and characteristics of the 'head' of the household (which is the male in two adult units) or based on the incomes of the entire household. Households are generally defined to include all persons related by blood, marriage, or adoption plus single persons living alone or with or without other unrelated persons (Coder 1990).

While retirement may be an individual phenomenon, social policy analysts are generally concerned about the way that retirement effects household economic status. Since lack of earnings or receipt of retirement income by an individual head may nor may not coincide with low family income, we concentrate on persons in families as the main unit of analysis in all comparisons of family economic status. To measure poverty or low income, we adopt a relative measure based on equivalence adjusted disposable cash income for the entire nation. Disposable cash income includes all forms of money income received by the family including retirement income, earnings, and all forms of transfers and property income net of direct income and payroll taxes. All family disposable incomes are normalized to the income of a three-person family using an equivalence scale with family size adjustments, where equivalent disposable income ($EDPI$) is agreed to unadjusted disposable income (DPI) divided by household size (S) raised to the exponent, ε:

$$EDPI = DPI/S^{\varepsilon}$$

While values of ε may range from 0 (full economies of scale) to 1 (zero economies as measured by per capita income), we follow recent practice and set $\varepsilon = .5$ (Atkinson, Rainwater, and Smeeding 1995). Poverty is therefore defined as all persons living in families with adjusted incomes less than half of the national median adjusted income, the most common relative poverty definition used by OECD, the United Nations and other bodies (e.g., Rainwater and Rein 1992; Foerster 1993; Smeeding 1997).

Table 1.4.2 Patterns of earnings and retirement income[a] defined by characteristics of family heads (percentage persons living in families with heads having given characteristics)

		Age			
		55-59	60-64	65-74	75+
Part I: All heads with zero earnings[b]					
Australia	1989	39.8	58.3	89.9	98.2
Canada	1994	32.7	57.7	90.6	99.1
Netherlands	1991	65.1	88.5	99.2	100.0
Sweden	1992	17.7	30.6	74.6	95.0
United Kingdom	1991	48.5	66.8	94.4	98.4
United States	1994	26.7	46.6	78.2	94.3
West Germany	1989	34.6	56.1	96.1	99.7
Part II: All heads with retirement income[c]					
Australia	1989	21.2	33.6	59.1	82.9
Canada	1994	19.9	49.9	99.1	99.1
Netherlands	1991	46.4	78.7	99.1	98.8
Sweden	1992	28.3	67.3	99.5	99.7
United Kingdom	1991	24.0	39.9	98.7	99.7
United States	1994	23.9	53.1	91.8	96.6
West Germany	1989	19.7	47.7	91.7	94.1
Part III: All heads with both zero earnings and retirement income[d]					
Australia	1989	16.9	30.0	55.4	82.3
Canada	1994	12.8	38.6	89.9	98.3
Netherlands	1991	37.7	73.3	98.2	98.8
Sweden	1992	11.6	27.4	74.2	94.7
United Kingdom	1991	17.6	34.4	93.2	98.2
United States	1994	12.0	35.0	74.0	91.2
West Germany	1989	14.2	38.9	88.7	93.8

a. Retirement income includes disability payments.
b. Percentage of persons living in families with a head who has zero earnings during the survey period.
c. Percentage of persons living in families with a head who receives retirement income.
d. Percentage of persons living in families with a head who has zero earnings and who receives retirement income.

IV. Results: differences in retirement patterns by retirement definition, work after retirement, and poverty

Here we take a look at retirement from a family income perspective. We first look at the effect of various retirement definitions on the level and trend in retirement. Next we ask if zero earnings means receipt of retirement income and conversely the ways that retirement income and work stoppage are mixed. Then we take a closer look at the relationship between work and retirement in general, and self-employment in particular. We close by examining the relationship between retirement and poverty.

Retirement definitions

We begin by investigating families ranked by age of head and head's earnings and retirement income patterns in seven countries using the latest data we have available for each country (Table 1.4.2). Three potential definitions of retirement are presented: families with heads having zero earnings (Part I), families with heads receiving retirement income (Part II); and families with heads having both zero earnings and receiving retirement income (Part III). We then create the same table with income and earnings characteristics based on all members of the household (Table 1.4.3). These two sets of figures together tell us the differences between basing the definition of retirement on heads' earnings and income characteristics versus household characteristics. The former is more akin to the usual treatment of retirement as a personal phenomenon while both provide a way to examine the welfare (or well-being) consequences of retirement and its impact on families.

The first definition of 'retirement' is lack of earnings (Table 1.4.2, Part I). Because not all LIS datasets measure head's self-declared labor force status, it is not possible to discern whether the family with a nonearning head is unemployed, retired or other. The older the head, the more likely the head is to be retired, but the correlation of not working and receipt of retirement income by the head or by any other household member is far from perfect.

The second definition of retirement is based on receipt of retirement income (Table 1.4.2, Part II). The head may or may not have a job while receiving retirement income. Similarly, in the household format, a head may be still working while someone else receives retirement income (Table 1.4.3, Part II). For those interested in the budgetary cost of retirement to society (in the case of retirement outlays), this definition of retirement may be preferred.

Table 1.4.3 Patterns of earnings and retirement income[a] defined by characteristics of family heads (percentage persons living in families with heads having given characteristics)

		Age			
		55-59	60-64	65-74	75+
Part I: All households with zero earnings[b]					
Australia	1989	22.8	38.0	76.2	86.9
Canada	1994	12.2	29.5	65.3	84.1
Sweden	1992	10.8	19.3	62.6	93.5
United Kingdom	1991	24.0	42.1	77.1	87.5
United States	1994	12.2	24.7	54.9	79.5
West Germany	1989	28.1	45.1	80.0	93.0
Part II: All households with retirement income[c]					
Australia	1989	25.4	39.8	62.1	84.7
Canada	1994	28.9	57.2	99.2	99.4
Sweden	1992	36.2	74.5	99.6	99.7
United Kingdom	1991	43.9	77.2	99.6	99.9
United States	1994	31.6	60.5	93.0	97.1
West Germany	1989	28.5	58.3	91.7	93.9
Part III: All households with both zero earnings and retirement income[d]					
Australia	1989	9.5	20.4	43.6	70.0
Canada	1994	7.0	24.5	65.3	84.1
Sweden	1992	7.9	18.1	62.2	93.2
United Kingdom	1991	15.3	37.0	76.8	87.4
United States	1994	6.1	19.9	52.5	77.3
West Germany	1989	12.8	30.8	72.5	86.9

a. Retirement income includes disability payments.
b. Percentage of persons living in families that have zero earnings during the survey period.
c. Percentage of persons living in families that receive retirement income.
d. Percentage of persons living in families that have zero earnings and that receive retirement income.

If one wants to be more certain that a head is fully retired, one could count only families whose heads have zero earners and receive retirement income (Table 1.4.2, Part III), or at households in which no one is working but at least one person is receiving retirement income (Table 1.4.3, Part III). This definition produces many fewer retired families, especially in the younger age ranges, as one might expect. Of course, we cannot tell if the head will ever return to work. Analyses of panel data in the United States indicate that less than 10 percent of those out of the labor force for at least two years will return to work (Quinn, Burkhauser, and Myers 1990). Comparable German panel data indicate a much lower fraction of Germans, about 5 percent, will return to work (Merz 1990). For analyses of economic well-being, e.g., poverty status and the adequacy of retirement income, this definition may be the preferable one.

Retirement levels The entries in Table 1.4.2 display considerable heterogeneity across countries. One straightforward conclusion here is that retirement, however defined, increases with age. Retirement is most likely in The Netherlands, particularly in the aged 55 to 59 and aged 60 to 64 categories, even when we impose dual criteria (Part III). Even with The Netherlands excluded, the intercountry variation is large, particularly in the aged 55 to 59 and aged 60 to 64 brackets. Excluding The Netherlands, between 20 percent (Canada and Germany) and 28 percent (Sweden) of all heads aged 55 to 59 received retirement income (Part II). In the same group, however, less than 18 percent of the aged in the United Kingdom, and even fewer in all other nations (except The Netherlands), have both stopped work and are receiving retirement income. Excluding Australia, at least 40 percent of all heads aged 60 to 64 in every country receive retirement income (Part II). But the fraction who also have zero earnings in this older bracket varies between 27 percent (Sweden) and 39 percent (Canada and Germany), except for The Netherlands, where a full 73 percent of household heads aged 60 to 64 have no earnings and receive retirement income.

Focussing on the most strict definition of retirement (Part III of Table 1.4.3), Sweden and Australia appear to have 'later' retirement patterns than do the other nations. The United States retires later at older ages (e.g., aged 65 to 74) but average or above at younger ages (aged 60 to 64).[6] The Germans start with low retirement in the youngest age group, but then quickly move to above average rates. The Dutch are, within all age groups, most likely to be fully retired, with the British second at the lowest (aged 55 to 59) and older (aged 65 and older) retirement ages.

If we shift focus to include the incomes of all household members, the situation is a bit different (Table 1.4.3).[7] The fractions with zero earnings are lower because we count other members' earned income (Part I), and the fractions with retirement incomes are higher because we count the retirement incomes of others as well (Part II). The net result (Part III) is a lower fraction of fully (doubly) retired households at all ages. In the critical age period of 60 to 64, only between 18 percent (Sweden) and 37 percent (the United Kingdom) of households have no earners and receive retirement income compared to numbers generally about 50 percent higher in Table 1.4.2. Taking the household resource definition, the most interesting pattern in Table 1.4.3 is found among those aged 65 to 74, and therefore beyond the age of normal retirement in all these countries. Here we find that over 70 percent of households are retired by both definitions in Germany and the United Kingdom, between 60 and 70 percent in Canada and Sweden, but only 52 percent in the United States and 44 percent in Australia. Yet in all but Australia, over 90 percent of these households have someone who is receiving retirement income (Part II of Table 1.4.3). This means that even if individuals do not do well mixing retirement income with work at older ages, households tend to do much better. We return to this issue below.

Trends Next we turn to changes in these measures between a beginning year (mid-1980s) and an ending year (1990s except for Germany (1989)) for each nation (Table 1.4.4). We concentrate on the trends facing heads here because the trend in households change is very similar.[8] The trend is presented as the absolute change in the variable of interest from the most recent to the earliest year. A value of -0.3 for Australian heads aged 55 to 59 with zero earnings indicate that in 1985 40.1 percent of Australian heads had zero earnings (Smeeding 1992, Table 4.1), compared to 39.8 percent in 1989. Hence 0.3 percent fewer heads had zero earnings in 1989. It follows that positive values mean more of the given characteristic while negative values mean less.

Patterns of labor force change for heads (Table 1.4.4, Part I) indicate retreats from work at all ages for Canadians and the Dutch especially at ages 60 to 64 in Canada and ages 55 to 59 in The Netherlands. In Australia, the reverse was true at all ages. The other countries show mixed results.[9]

Table 1.4.4 Absolute change in patterns of earnings and retirement income[a] defined by characteristics of family heads (percentage persons living in families with heads having given characteristics)

		Age		
		55-59	60-64	65-74
Part I: All heads with zero earnings[b]				
Australia	1985-1989	-0.3	-4.1	-2.8
Canada	1991-1994	4.5	11.4	2.9
Netherlands	1987-1991	15.2	6.4	0.4
Sweden	1987-1992	3.6	-2.9	-7.2
United Kingdom	1986-1991	5.0	3.6	-0.4
United States	1986-1994	-1.8	-1.0	0.1
West Germany	1984-1989	2.3	1.1.	1.3
Part II: All heads with retirement income[c]				
Australia	1985-1989	0.7	-15.2	-27.8
Canada	1991-1994	1.7	11.9	3.9
Netherlands	1987-1991	13.8	29.2	-0.4
Sweden	1987-1992	4.6	5.7	-0.4
United Kingdom	1986-1991	-9.7	-16.5	0.0
United States	1986-1994	0.3	3.5	0.9
West Germany	1984-1989	8.4	-4.6	-4.9
Part III: All heads with both zero earnings and retirement income[d]				
Australia	1985-1989	1.1	-12.6	-27.7
Canada	1991-1994	4.4	14.5	6.9
Netherlands	1987-1991	10.0	26.0	0.1
Sweden	1987-1992	2.7	-0.6	-7.6
United Kingdom	1986-1991	-6.4	-11.4	-0.3
United States	1986-1994	0.1	-0.5	-0.6
West Germany	1984-1989	7.7	0.4	-2.3

a. Retirement income includes disability payments.
b. Percentage of persons living in families with a head who has zero earnings during the survey period.
c. Percentage of persons living in families with a head who receives retirement income.
d. Percentage of persons living in families with a head who has zero earnings and who receives retirement income.

More disturbing from a policy perspective, receipt of retirement income (Part II) is rising in some age brackets everywhere but in the United Kingdom. Together these translate into a higher fraction of heads with zero earnings and retirement income (Part III) at critical younger ages in Canada, The Netherlands, and Germany. There were only modest increases in the United States and in Sweden over this period.

Table 1.4.5 Zero earnings and retirement income

Panel A: Do heads with zero earning always get retirement income?[a]
(percentage of heads with zero earnings who also have retirement income)

		Age			
		55-59	60-64	65-74	75+
All Heads					
Canada	1994	39.1	66.9	99.2	99.2
Netherlands	1991	57.9	82.8	99.0	98.8
Sweden	1992	65.5	89.5	99.5	99.7
United Kingdom	1991	36.3	51.5	98.7	99.8
United States	1994	44.9	75.1	94.6	96.7
West Germany	1989	41.0	69.3	92.3	94.1

Panel B: Do households with zero earnings always get retirement income?[a]
(percentage of households with zero earnings who also have retirement income)

		Age			
		55-59	60-64	65-74	75+
All Households					
Canada	1994	57.4	83.1	100.0	100.0
Sweden	1992	73.1	93.8	99.4	99.7
United Kingdom	1991	63.8	87.9	99.6	99.9
United States	1994	50.0	80.6	95.6	97.2
West Germany	1989	45.6	68.3	90.6	93.4

a. Retirement income includes disability payments.

Relationship between earnings and receipt of retirement income The next two tables (Tables 1.4.5 and 1.4.6) are designed to show that zero earnings among older heads does not always infer receipt of retirement income (Table 1.4.5), and vice versa (Table 1.4.6).[10] We perform these analyses for heads (Panel A) and for households (Panel B) in each table. In each of these cases, the variance is large across all countries. Hence, absence or presence of one characteristic should not be used to infer another, particularly for those heads between aged 55 and 64.

Table 1.4.6 Retirement income and work stoppage

Panel A: Does retirement mean total work stoppage?
(percentage of heads receiving retirement income[a] who also have zero earnings)

		Age			
		55-59	60-64	65-74	75+
All Heads					
Australia	1989	79.7	89.3	93.7	99.3
Canada	1994	64.3	77.4	90.7	99.2
Netherlands	1991	91.3	93.1	99.1	100.0
Sweden	1992	41.0	40.7	74.6	95.0
United Kingdom	1991	73.3	86.2	94.4	98.5
United States	1994	50.2	65.9	80.6	94.4
West Germany	1989	72.1	81.6	96.7	99.7

Panel B: Does retirement mean total work stoppage?
(percentage of families that receive retirement income[a] that also have zero earnings)

		Age			
		55-59	60-64	65-74	75+
All Households					
Australia	1989	37.4	51.3	70.2	82.6
Canada	1994	24.2	42.8	65.8	84.6
Sweden	1992	21.8	24.3	62.4	93.5
United Kingdom	1991	34.9	47.9	77.1	87.5
United States	1994	19.3	32.9	56.5	79.6
West Germany	1989	44.9	52.8	79.1	92.5

a. Retirement income includes disability payments.

Except in The Netherlands (58 percent) and Sweden (65 percent), the majority of heads aged 55 to 59 with no earnings are *not* receiving retirement (including disability) income. The correlation improves with age, and by age 65, nearly all household heads without earnings are receiving retirement benefits (Table 1.4.5, Panel A). In Panel B, we find that if there is no earned income in the entire household, retirement income is more prevalent than if we focus on the head alone. Beyond age 60, 80 percent or more of households with zero earnings also have retirement income everywhere but in Germany.

The fraction of heads for whom receipt of retirement income means total work stoppage is quite varied, with Sweden and the United States with the lowest numbers (Table 1.4.6). In Sweden, the majority of heads aged 55 to 65 with retirement income still work; in the United States, between one-third and one-half do. In the other nations, the vast majority of those receiving retirement income no longer work.

Once the earnings of other household members are taken into account (Panel B), the pattern changes, with the fraction of households without earners falling in all nations. For instance, at aged 60 to 64, only in Australia and in Germany do we find retirement income receipt means no earned income for half or more of the families.

Table 1.4.7 **Do household heads combine work and retirement? (percentage of persons living in families with heads receiving retirement income[a] where the head also has some earnings)[b]**

		Age of Head		
		55-59	60-64	65-74
Australia	1989	20.3	10.7	6.3
Canada	1994	35.7	22.6	9.3
Netherlands	1991	8.7	6.9	0.9
Sweden	1992	59.0	59.3	25.4
United Kingdom	1991	26.7	13.8	5.6
United States	1994	49.8	34.1	19.4
West Germany	1989	27.9	18.4	3.3

a. Retirement income includes disability payments.
b. 100 minus the ratio of '*All heads with both zero earnings and retirement income*' to '*All heads with retirement income*': (Panel A of Table 1.4.6).

This means that a large fraction of retirees, especially younger ones, continue to work. This pattern is most clearly seen in Table 1.4.7 which is derived directly from Panel A of Table 1.4.6. Work and retirement income are most often combined in Sweden and the United States where part-time retirement (Sweden) and a large earnings disregard (United States) encourage mixing work and retirement. In Germany, the United Kingdom, and The Netherlands, there is less mixing of work and retirement among household heads. The message from this final table is an important one. Nations such as Germany and The Netherlands where still larger pension outlays loom in the near future could perhaps help reduce these outlays by encouraging work among otherwise retired heads. Given recent changes in life expectancy and the changing nature of work from manufacturing to service sector jobs in all of these nations, there is room for policy to further increase work at older ages.

Does retirement mean impoverishment?

Perhaps the most important question asked about 'retirement' in a family/household context is its effect economic well-being and on poverty status. Regardless of whether they are pushed or pulled out of the labor market, are retirees significantly more (or less?) likely to be among the low income population? To examine this question, we prepared a final table that shows the rate of low income or poverty among persons living in older families (Table 1.4.8). As mentioned earlier, poverty is defined as living in a family with adjusted income less than half the median adjusted income for all families. Estimates are made for three groups of persons: all persons in the age group (Part I); all persons living with heads having retirement income (Part II); all persons living with heads with both retirement income and zero earnings (Part III). Finally, we have added a column for those aged 19 to 54 so that we can compare poverty status of the old to other adults.

Table 1.4.8 Does retirement mean impoverishment? (percentage of persons living in families with head having various characteristics defined as poor[a])

		Age				
		19-54	55-59	60-64	65-74	75+
Part I: Whole population[b]						
Australia	1989	11.7	12.0	13.3	17.0	24.9
Canada	1994	12.4	10.3	15.8	5.2	5.1
Netherlands	1991	18.4	12.4	7.8	2.8	3.8
Sweden	1992	6.0	2.6	3.1	3.9	9.0
United Kingdom	1991	13.1	12.4	11.9	17.7	27.9
United States	1994	19.5	12.2	16.2	16.7	23.2
West Germany	1989	4.0	4.7	5.3	5.7	8.5
Part II: Head receives retirement income[c]						
Australia	1989		25.4	23.0	19.8	26.6
Canada	1994		11.2	15.2	4.8	4.7
Netherlands	1991		12.1	5.1	1.9	2.3
Sweden	1992		1.7	2.6	3.8	8.7
United Kingdom	1991		8.4	13.7	17.5	27.8
United States	1994		11.6	15.2	15.1	21.4
West Germany	1989		13.2	2.6	5.4	8.5
Part III: Head with both zero earnings and retirement income[d]						
Australia	1989		29.3	25.6	21.0	26.7
Canada	1994		16.7	17.7	5.2	4.7
Netherlands	1991		14.9	5.5	1.9	2.6
Sweden	1992		2.7	6.1	4.9	9.2
United Kingdom	1991		11.4	15.4	18.4	28.3
United States	1994		21.7	20.6	18.1	22.4
West Germany	1989		14.0	3.2	5.6	8.4

a. Poor are persons in families with adjusted disposable incomes below half of median adjusted disposable income (DPI) for individuals. Incomes are adjusted by E=0.5 where adjusted DPI = actual DPI divided by household size (s) to the power E: Adjusted DPI = DPI/sE.
b. All persons in all families.
c. Persons in families whose head receives retirement income.
d. Persons in families whose head has zero earnings and receives retirement income.

The first result to note is that poverty varies more across countries than across age groups within countries (Table 1.4.8, Part I). For instance, the differences between the United States (or the United Kingdom) overall poverty rates and the German (or Swedish) rates are greater than the differences between the working age and older age poverty rates in each of these countries. Only in Australia (with a means-tested retirement program) and among Germans aged 55 to 59 are persons in families with retirement income (Table 1.4.8, Part II) more likely to be poor than is the entire population. In most age/country cells, poverty rates are actually lower for those with retirement income than are those for the population at large. This is less true among the group with retirement income and zero earnings, suggesting that combining work and retirement benefits may be a useful strategy to avoid poverty. In some nations, pockets of high poverty exist among those without earnings and with retirement income at younger ages (which is probably disability income in many cases). but poverty rates plummet around normal (age 65) retirement age. Canada, Germany, and The Netherlands have this pattern. This suggests that besides work, other social programs (e.g., disability, early retirement, and unemployment) also provide a 'bridge' to full retirement. In other high poverty nations, Australia, the United Kingdom, and the United States, poverty is high among workers and nonworkers alike at older ages. We conclude that poverty in old age depends on country of residence as well as work status.

V. Conclusion and policy implications

Several points emerge from this overview of retirement patterns in these seven countries:
– Retirement has many meanings, and the number of retired workers in a country depends critically on the definition chosen. Stereotypical retirement, a one time movement from full-time work to complete labor force withdrawal, is only part of the story in these developed nations. Many individuals nearing traditional retirement age supplement their retirement income with labor market earnings, and even more households combine the two (see also Palme 1990; Clark and Ogawa 1992). The most notable exceptions are Germany (at older ages) and The Netherlands (at all ages), where mixing the two sources of income is less common. These behavioral differences are related to institutional differences in the impact that earnings have on the size of retirement benefits. Sweden, the United States and

Canada appear to have the less restrictive earnings tests, and older workers respond accordingly.
- Brief trends in retirement patterns between the mid-1980s and the early 1990s (with slightly different beginning and ending dates in the different countries) display no common pattern. Canada and The Netherlands show the most movement toward continued early retirement, under either the 'earnings' or the 'retirement income' criterion. Australia is the only country to show delayed retirement over time at all ages, using the 'no earnings' definition, but a more ambiguous pattern appears when receipt of retirement income is used. The United States shows very little change since 1986, consistent with the labor force participation rate data in Figure 1.4.3. The other countries tend to show different patterns at different ages.
- Social programs can be very effective in preventing poverty among the retired. In the United States, the poverty rate among the elderly was cut in half in only seven years (from about 30 percent and twice the national average in 1967 to 15 percent in 1974) following large increases in real Social Security benefits in the interim. Sweden (at all ages), Germany and The Netherlands (at aged 60 and over) and Canada (at aged 65 and over) have been successful in nearly eliminating poverty among the retired. In the other countries, although the absolute levels of poverty are higher, retirement of the head is not necessarily associated with an increase in the probability of poverty. Our analyses, however, say nothing about the likelihood of being 'near-poor.' In the United States, the United Kingdom, and Australia, the elderly are more likely than the rest of the population to hover just above the poverty thresholds (Smeeding 1997).
- Finally, encouragement of gradual or partial retirement - the combination of retirement income and earnings - may be a good idea for several reasons. It may be better for the personal well-being of many retirees than an abrupt change. Although we did not explore this issue in this article, there is evidence, in the United States at least, that many older retirees who are out of the labor force would like to be working (often only part-time), and that many workers would like to work longer than they think they will (McNaught and Barth 1993; Quinn and Burkhauser 1994). In addition, combining the two is good for the household's financial well-being. Poverty rates are highest where retirement income was combined with zero earnings. In the United States, poverty rates are substantially higher

among those elderly without labor market income. Finally, delayed retirement may relieve the fiscal pressures on governments and economies, by reducing the benefits during the intermediate periods of those who successfully blend work and retirement.

Notes

1. A recent paper (Burkhauser et al. 1997, Table 3), indicates that in 1993 only 59 percent of Dutch men age 55, 44 percent of those age 59, and 16.8 percent of those age 61, were still working in 1993. In the United States, in contrast, the figures were 77 percent at age 56, 69 percent at age 59, and 66 percent at age 61.

2. The outlays for some nations, e.g., The Netherlands, may be understated because disability, early retirement, and extended unemployment schemes are not taken into account here.

3. A description of LIS and the specific surveys used in this article can be found in de Tombeur (1997) or at http://lissy.ceps.lu/index.htm.

4. The terms 'household' and 'family' are used interchangeably. With the exception of Sweden, all persons living together are a family or household in this article. The Swedish family definition is more narrow, treating all unmarried units aged 65 and over as separate persons. For an analysis of the older segment of the population, these nuances might take a marginal, though not significant difference.

5. Survey respondents may classify benefits as either unemployment or social retirement and thus, we are unable to determine 'unemployment retirement' from standard 'unemployment compensation' on most surveys.

6. The earnings rules for Social Security benefits are more lenient in the United States for recipients aged 65 to 69 then they are far those aged 62 to 64 (a higher disregard, and then a smaller benefit loss (0.33 vs. 0.50) for each dollar earned above the disregard). At age 70, one can earn any amount without any reduction in Social Security benefits.

7. Here we have excluded The Netherlands due to incomplete information on other household member incomes.

8. The trends in households are available from the authors.

9. It should be noted that both levels and trends in zero earnings in Tables 1.4.2 onward may differ from labor force participation rates and trends in Figures 1.4.1 and 1.4.4 because of differences in definitions, samples, and questions. For instance, most labor force surveys ask about current labor force status while income surveys measure

earnings over the entire year.

10. We omit Australia in Table 1.4.5 because asking the questions we pose here do not make sense given the means-tested nature of their retirement income system. We omit The Netherlands in Panel B of both Tables 1.4.5 and 1.4.6 due to incomplete information on other household members' incomes.

References

Aarts, Leo J.M. and De Jong, Philip R. (1992) 'Early Retirement of Older Male Workers Under the Dutch Social Security System.' In Atkinson, A.B. and Rein, M. (eds.), *Age Work, and Social Security*. New York: MacMillan.

Atkinson, A.B., Rainwater, Lee and Smeeding, Timothy M. (1995) *Income Distribution in OECD Countries: The Evidence from LIS*. Paris: Office for Economic and Cooperative Development.

Boivenberg, L. and van der Linden, A. (1997) 'Pension Policies and the Aging Society,' *OECD Observer*, 205: 10-14.

Burkhauser, Richard V., Dwyer, Debra, Lindeboom, Maartin, Theeuwes, Jules and Woittiez, Isabel (1997) 'Health, Work, and Economic Well-Being of Older Workers Aged 51 to 61: A Cross-National Comparison Using the United States HRS and the Dutch CERRA.' Working Paper, Center for Policy Research, The Maxwell School. Syracuse, NY: Syracuse University, mimeo.

Clark, Robert and Ogawa, Naohiro (1992) 'The Effect of Mandatory Retirement on Earnings Profiles in Japan,' *Industrial and Labor Relations Review*, 45(2): 258-266.

Coder, John (1990) 'Technical Issues,' *Luxembourg Income Study Newsletter*, II(1) (April): 5-7.

deTombeur, C. (1997) 'LIS/LES Information Guide,' LIS Working Paper #7. Luxembourg: Luxembourg Income Study, February.

Employee Benefit Research Institute (1995) *EBRI Data Book*, 3rd edition. Washington, DC: EBRI.

Foerster, M. (1993) 'Comparing Poverty in 13 OECD Countries: Traditional and Synthetic Approaches,' LIS Working Paper #100. Luxembourg: Luxembourg Income Study, October.

Haveman, Robert H., Halberstadt, Victor and Burkhauser, Richard V. (1984) *Public Policy Toward Disabled Workers: A Cross-National Analysis of Economic Impacts*. Ithaca, New York: Cornell University Press.

Kotlikoff, Laurence J. and Wise, David A. (1989) *The Wage Carrot and the Pension Stick*. Kalamazoo, MI: The W.E. Upjohn Institute for Employment Research.

McNaught, William and Barth, Michael (1993) *The Untapped Resource*. Final Report on The Americans over 55 at Work Program. New York: Commonwealth Fund, November.

Merz, Joachim (1990) Tabular data provided to the author.

Office for Economic and Cooperative Development (1996) *Aging in OECD Countries: A Critical Policy Challenge*, Social Policy Studies No. 20. Paris: OECD.

Office for Economic and Cooperative Development (1995a) *The Transition from Work to Retirement*, Social Policy Studies No. 16. Paris: OECD.

Office for Economic and Cooperative Development (1995b) *The Labour Market and Older Workers*, Social Policy Studies No. 17. Paris: OECD.

Palme, Joachim (1990) 'Pension Regimes and Retirement: Age and Income in a Cross-National Perspective,' LIS Working Paper #51. Luxembourg: Luxembourg Income Study, June.

Peterson, Peter G. (1996) *Will America Grow Up Before It Grows Old?* New York: Random House.

Preston, Samuel (1996) 'American Longevity: Past, Present, and Future,' Center for Policy Research Policy Brief No. 7, The Maxwell School. Syracuse, NY: Syracuse University.

Quinn, Joseph F. (1997) 'The Role of Bridge Jobs in the Retirement Patterns of Older Americans.' In Philip deJong and Theodore Marmor (eds.), *Social Policy and the Labour Market*. Aldershot: Avebury Publishers.

Quinn, Joseph F. and Burkhauser, Richard V. (1994) 'Public Policy and the Plans and Preferences of Older Americans,' *Journal of Aging and Social Policy*, 6(3) (Fall): 5-20.

Quinn, Joseph F., Burkhauser, Richard V. and Myers, Daniel A. (1990) *Passing the Torch: The Influence of Economic Incentives on Work and Retirement*. Kalamazoo, MI: W.E. Upjohn Institute for Employment Research.

Rainwater, Lee and Rein, Martin (1992) 'Economic Well-Being among Men 55-64 Without Earnings - A Six Country Comparison.' In A.B. Atkinson and M. Rein (eds.), *Age, Work, and Social Security*. New York: MacMillan.

Schmähl, Winfried (1991) 'Changing the Retirement Age in Germany.' Paper presented at the European Society for Population Economics Annual Conference, Pisa, Italy, June 6.

Smeeding. Timothy M. (1991a) 'The Meaning of Retirement: Cross-National Patterns and Trends.' In L. Rainwater, M. Rein, and F. Naschold (eds.), *The Interplay between Social Policy and Labor markets*. Armonk, NY: M.E. Sharpe, Inc.

Smeeding, Timothy M. (1991b) 'Mountains or Molehills: Just What's So Bad About Aging Societies Anyway?' In J. Hubek (ed.), *Consequences of Aging Societies for Individuals*. Newbury Park, CA: Sage, pp. 208-220.

Smeeding, Timothy M. (1992) 'Cross-National Patterns of Retirement among Men and Women in the Mid-1980s: Full Stop or Gradual Withdrawal?' In Atkinson, A.B. and Rein, M. (eds.), *Age, Work, and Social Security*. New York: MacMillan, pp. 91-114.

Smeeding, Timothy M. (1997) 'Financial Poverty in Developed Nations: The Evidence from LIS.' Fiscal report for the UNDP. LIS Working Paper #155. Luxembourg: Luxembourg Income Study, April.

Theeuwes, Jules (1997) 'Work and Well-Being: The Experience of the Elderly in Europe.' Paper presented to the Conference on Emerging Policy Issues on Aging in Asia and the Research Response, Taipei, Taiwan, January 13-15. Mimeo. The Netherlands: University of Leiden.

U.S. Bureau of the Census (1993) *An Aging World II*, International Population Reports P95/92-3. Washington, DC: U.S. Government Printing Office.

PART 2

EMPLOYMENT AND SOCIAL SECURITY

2.1 The welfare state and full employment

Robert H. Haveman

The purpose of this article is to prompt discussion about the structure of income protection policies in the OECD countries, and the adverse employment side-effects that they may generate. In my discussion, I first sketch the nature of the income protection programs in OECD countries, emphasizing the substantial differences among them in terms of the generosity and accessibility of support available. For purposes of discussion, I contrast the European Community countries with those of North America, neglecting important distinctions among the European countries.[1] In the second section, I characterize both the pros and the cons of having a generous and accessible income support system, emphasizing the negative labor supply effects of such an arrangement. I also point out that the negative side effects of generous systems are even greater if the systems are loosely administered or open-ended in the duration for which individuals can receive benefits. Section III. summarizes the trends in employment, inequality, and the generosity and accessibility of social protection within the OECD countries. I note that those countries with the most accessible and generous systems also tend to have the slowest growth in employment, and the most serious poverty/joblessness traps.

In Section IV, I ask: 'Is there not an alternative approach that can both protect against poverty and encourage work and self-sufficiency?' I conclude that there is, and set forth a simple and stylized approach for policy reform. It rests on the judicious combining of a variety of proposals for reform, all of which address but a single aspect of the problem. While this multi-pronged strategy has an attractive set of characteristics, in Section V, I address this issue and suggest an approach that might lessen resistance to large-scale change.

I. The income protection systems among OECD countries

Among the larger and more industrialized OECD countries, a large and financially costly system of income protection is in place. While the levels of coverage, generosity and accessibility of these systems differ substantially over the countries, the following characteristics tend to be common to all or nearly all of them:[2]

An *unemployment benefit program* seeks to replace earnings losses due to the involuntary separation of a worker from a job. These programs tend to replace a substantial proportion of the earnings losses - from 30 to 80 percent - among the OECD countries. Moreover, in many countries unemployment benefits can be received for a long period of time, often a year or more. In some of the countries, the expiration of unemployment benefit eligibility triggers eligibility for an alternative benefit program, such as disability benefits.

A *disability benefits program* provides earnings replacement to workers who become handicapped during their working years, either on or off the job. These programs tend to replace a substantial proportion of the lost earnings, but again the replacement rates vary substantially across the countries. Receipt of benefits is typically of long duration.

Provision for early retirement from the work force is available in most of the countries, which provision is often a transition from the receipt of unemployment or disability benefits to the receipt of retirement pensions. The replacement of earnings in early retirement schemes is typically less than if retirement is delayed until the normal retirement age, but in several countries the replacement rate extends up to 70 percent after age 60.

All of the countries have in place a *safety-net welfare system* that provides coverage to working-age individuals and families headed by such individuals. Benefit levels in these programs range widely across the countries, and in some cases vary significantly across various regions within a country. Many OECD countries have welfare program benefit levels that assure recipients of an income level around one-third to one-half of the median income level in the country.

Many of the countries have a legal *minimum wage policy* that requires employers to pay a minimum wage rate (or a minimum weekly wage for full-time workers) to employees irrespective of their education, skill, training, or productivity. This policy typically applies to all workers, including school leavers without work experience and recipients of unemployment and disability benefits should they decide to return to work. Other countries achieve an effective minimum wage arrangement through more or less comprehensive collective bargaining agreements. In a few countries, some groups of workers are not covered by minimum wage laws; in others (e.g., the Netherlands) wages below the minimum are permitted for some groups of workers (e.g., young workers).

Many of the countries have *employment regulations* that constrain the ability of employers to alter the size of their work force in response to changes in the demand for their output; hence, an employment contract becomes a fixed cost to the employer, generating caution in the addition of permanent workers to the enterprise. Such regulations also lead to disguised unemployment in periods or places of slack demand, as employers are constrained from releasing workers, even if there is insufficient demand to retain them.

II. The pros and cons of a generous and accessible social protection system

The constellation of policies yielding a full coverage, generous and accessible safety net of social protection has both positive and negative economics impacts. Both positive and negative consequences are positively related to the comprehensiveness, generosity and accessibility of the system;, however, only negative effects stem from administering the system in a loose or open-ended manner.

As a result of a comprehensive and generous social safety net, income poverty is reduced and the disparity between high- and low-income families that results from the unfettered operation of labor markets is moderated. In the process, workers are protected from severe income losses due to illness, disability, unemployment, and retirement, and homemakers experiencing divorce or child bearing out of marriage have their incomes and those of their children supported. The security against adverse events that these policies afford is of value to both to those who are directly protected by them, and to others on whom burdens would fall were it not for this protection. Moreover, many of these programs provide employment protection which fosters long-term employer-employee relationships and the training-productivity benefits that are inherent in such relationships. Similarly, the provision of income support during periods of short-term unemployment may foster job search and efficient employment matches.

However, these policies can also have distinctly negative effects on economic performance to the extent that they:
- reduce the demand for labor (especially low-wage, low-skilled labor), and encourage the substitution of temporary employees for permanent workers. The latter effect reduces the level of job training offered by firms to employees, and erodes the benefits from establishing long-term employer-employee relationships;
- reduce the willingness to work, and the incentive to engage in job search, for those who are recipients of income support benefits which may be available for a long duration, e.g., unemployment and disability benefits. Such working-people, living at relatively low levels of assistance are described as being in a 'poverty trap' or a 'joblessness trap';
- increase the costs of enterprises that are required to pay taxes to cover the costs of the benefits or higher-than-market wages; for the open economies that characterize many of the OECD countries, these costs reduce the demand from foreign markets for the goods and services produced;
- create rigidities in the labor market, keeping wage rates from equilibrating and labor demand from expanding to its true potential;
- erode the incentive for diligence and effort for current job holders, as the possibility of job loss is reduced by employment regulations, and the alternative of available income support from public transfer programs provides income protection in the face of job loss.

These negative economic effects are viewed by many as prejudicing the rate of productivity growth, inhibiting employment and economic growth, increasing joblessness of low-wage, low-experience, and low-skilled workers, and creating a low-income or joblessness trap for many individuals and families who receive income support benefits. It is into this context that analysts, advocates, and policymakers propose reforms of welfare state policies, typically with the objective of reducing these adverse economic effects of social protection.[3]

These adverse effects of generous and accessible income protection policies are even more serious if the income protection policies are loosely structured, poorly integrated or ill-managed. Numerous examples

of such program inefficiencies in either design or administration have been documented in the social welfare literature. These include:[4]
- failure to verify if job search activities are being pursued in unemployment benefit programs;
- failure to detect voluntary job-leaving as a basis for benefit claims, or concealed employment among beneficiaries of unemployment programs;
- benefit reduction (marginal tax) rates equal to or approaching 100 percent in some assistance programs;
- lax administration of income support programs attributable to central-government, rather than local, financing;
- acquiescence in infinite duration unemployment benefit programs through either legislation or the allowance of cycling between benefit recipiency and active labor market program participation;
- arrangements such that movement from unemployment benefits to disability benefits to early retirement programs is encouraged.

If the incidence of such problems is as widespread as anecdotal evidence suggests, the availability of income protection benefits can increase program costs, increase measured unemployment rates beyond true rates of unemployment, promote the demand for benefits and the resulting joblessness, and undermine the effectiveness of active labor market policies. Such program structures or administrative practices exaggerate the adverse effects that stem directly from the provision of income support in the absence of employment.

III. Trends in employment, inequality, and social protection within the OECD countries: a summary

The first page of a recent volume on *Reducing Unemployment* summarized the global unemployment problem as follows:[5]

> While unemployment will ebb somewhat as countries recover from the recent global recession, millions are likely to remain jobless for a variety of structural reasons. Moreover, there is a disturbing trend in many industrialized countries toward long-term unemployment, especially among low-skilled workers. This trend has had less effect on measured unemployment in the United States than in Europe in part because U. S. workers have greater incentives to accept low-wage jobs. Nonetheless, virtually all in-

dustrial countries face a jobs problem that impairs living standards and threatens a breakdown in social cohesion.

This description contains two key points. The first is the emphasis on structural barriers to the reduction of unemployment (or non-employment) in OECD countries - namely, high minimum wages, generous and accessible income protection programs, and stringent labor market regulations. The second is the contrast in unemployment, joblessness, and inequality among OECD countries, especially between North America and Europe.

While the relative demand for low-skilled workers has fallen in all higher income, industrialized economies, countries in these two regions tended to respond in quite different ways. The differences in policy and employment experiences between the U.S. and Europe suggest a trade-off between a North American package consisting of:
- low minimum wages;
- a relatively modest social protection system, with relatively low levels of income support;
- few institutional barriers to hiring, firing, and geographic mobility.

These policies have been accompanied by:
- rapid employment growth, especially for low-wage workers;
- high and rising wage inequality;
- slow wage control.

This contrasts with a European-style package of:
- generous and accessible social benefit programs;
- high minimum wage levels;
- relatively stringent labor market regulations and constraints.

This policy stance has been accompanied by:
- high unemployment and joblessness;
- slow employment growth;
- low and steady wage inequality;
- relatively high wage growth.

Whether or not the trade-off between social policy and economic performance is as explicit as this characterization, high levels of available income support to working-age people through unemployment, disability, sickness, and early retirement programs - in combination with relatively high and rigid minimum wages - do appear to contribute to a 'poverty-trap' or 'jobless trap' for low-skilled workers. When confronted with the choice between continued employment at relatively modest wage rates and a life without a job supported by public benefits equal to a relatively high proportion of potential net earnings, many choose the nonwork/recipiency option. Similarly, facing high minimum wages, employers tend to find the hiring of low-skilled workers an unprofitable option. Conversely, low minimum wages and the availability of relatively low social protection benefits encourage high levels of employment and job growth, but with the side effect of high and growing wage inequality and poverty.

A few statistics will make the comparison between the North American and European experiences clear.

Employment growth

Relative to other industrialized regions, North America has been a 'job creation machine'.[6] From 1960 to the present, employment in North America has doubled, while the number of jobs in European Community has increased by less than 20 percent. Over the decade of the 1980s, the number of new jobs created in North America and Australia was well above 20 percent of the level of 1979 employment. That for the remainder of the OECD country groupings ranges from essentially zero to about 10 percent.[7]

Unemployment levels and changes

This differential pattern of job growth is also reflected in the unemployment experience among countries. In North America, the standardized unemployment rate in the 1990s (1990–1993) was 6.9 percent, which is about 110 percent of its level over the period from 1960–1990. By contrast, the 1990s unemployment rate in the European Community (9.2 percent) was equal to its value in the 1980s, but more than 300 percent of its level during the 1960s and 1970s.[8]

Joblessness levels and changes

Much the same pattern is seen if one focusses on joblessness, rather than unemployment. Among males aged 25–54, a group that excludes those who have chosen early retirement or continued schooling in the face of poor labor market prospects, the male jobless rate in the United States has gone from about 9 percent in the 1970s to about 12 percent in the 1990s, an increase of about one-third. For the European Community, however, the male jobless rate for workers in this age range has doubled from about 7 percent in the 1970s to 14 percent in the 1990s.[9]

Generosity and accessibility of unemployment benefit programs

These differential changes in unemployment and jobless patterns between North America and Europe appear to be related to changes in the generosity and accessibility of public income support programs. For example, among the 12 European Community countries, 6 increased the maximum period for which unemployment benefits are available over the 1961 to 1991 period; there was no increase in this benefit accessibility indicator in North America.[10]

A composite indicator of overall unemployment benefit generosity provides an even clearer comparison of this differential pattern. A simple average of this generosity indicator across the European Community countries (excluding Luxembourg) stood at 17.4 in 1961. By 1991, the index had increased to 31.5, representing an increase of more than 80 percent. For the EFTA countries, the increase was from 8.3 to 34.5, or an increase of more than four times-fold. By contrast, the simple average indicator for North America stood at 19.5 in both 1961 and 1991.[11]

Generosity and accessibility of other income protection programs

Besides unemployment benefits, other income support programs also enable working-age individuals to opt for nonwork/recipiency status. Early retirement and disability benefit programs are two such alternatives. A calculation of the simple average of replacement rates of the disability benefit programs among the European Community countries shows a slight increase from the mid-40s to the upper 40s from 1974 to 1993. For North America, the replacement rate increased from a level of about one-half of that in the European Community in 1974 to about 30 percent in 1993. While the absolute amount of the increase is about the same in the two regions, the difference in the average level of the replacement rates is notable.[12]

Minimum wage levels

While the European Community countries tend to support the income of non-working people at a substantially higher level than in North America, where legislated minimum wages exist, these too are higher in Europe than in North America.[13] For example, in the early 1990s the minimum wage in the Netherlands and France stood at over 50 percent of the average wage, while in the North American countries the minimum wage was about 35 percent of the average wage.

The trend in average earnings

Consistent with the patterns of income support, unemployment and joblessness, one would expect the pressures for productivity improvements to be greater in those countries with the highest social protection and minimum wage levels, relative to those with more flexible and less constrained labor markets. As a result, wage growth in the latter countries (e.g., North America) would be expected to lie below that of the former (e.g., the European Community).

In a quite distinct break from the early post-war period in the United States, when the real wage of the average worker grew about 2.0 percent per year, the real hourly earnings of the average worker haves been virtually constant since the early 1970s. The basic cause of the sharp decline in average earnings growth is the fall in the rate of productivity growth, to which gains in average compensation are ultimately tied. From 1948 to 1973, output per worker in the U.S. business sector increased nearly 2.9 percent per year; since 1973, the average gain has been about 1 percent per year. While this pattern explains why average earnings growth has been so anaemic, it leaves the question of why the rate of productivity growth has stagnated since the early 1970s. Since 1970, the 10 percent real wage growth of the United States contrasts with real wage growth of nearly 60 percent in the European Community; conversely, over the same period the nearly 60 percent employment increase in the United States compares with a small 10-15 percent increase in the European Community.

The level and trend in earnings and income inequality

In most OECD countries, there has been a widening of wage rate and earnings differentials since the late 1970s, although the patterns among countries vary widely. In North America, Australia, Japan, and the United Kingdom, the relative wage of low-skilled workers has fallen by from 10 to 25 percent during the 1980s. On the other hand, the relative wage of low-skilled workers in most continental European countries was about the same at the beginning of the 1990s as it was in 1980.[14] This pattern likely reflects the higher relative minimum wage established either through legislation or bargaining in Europe relative to North America and the United Kingdom.

The high and accessible level of income protection benefits and high minimum wages in Europe have successfully maintained a relatively low level of income inequality, even in the face of rising unemployment and joblessness. Figures for the late 1980s indicate that the simple average Gini coefficient for North America (Canada and the United States) equalled 31.5, while that for the European Community countries (excluding Denmark, Spain, Portugal, and Greece) was 27.9, and that for the primary EFTA nations stood at 22.0.[15]

The level and trend in poverty

Poverty rates among OECD countries vary widely. North America and Australia all have poverty rates well above the average, while the continental European countries of Austria, Belgium, Germany, Luxembourg and the Netherlands have the lowest rates. France, Ireland, Italy, Sweden and the United Kingdom have rates close to the average, with France and Sweden falling at the low end of this group.[16]

Evidence on changes in poverty rates is not available for most of these countries. For the United States, however, the level of official income poverty has risen substantially since the early 1970s, from an already high level. At the beginning of the 1970s, the rate of poverty defined by the United States government stood at about 11 percent; by 1992, over 14.5 percent of the nation's population lived in poverty. Between 1973 and 1992, the number of people officially classified as poor increased from 23 million to 37 million persons. This pattern is consistent with the growing earnings inequality that has occurred during the past two decades, and again reflects the implications of the lack of generosity and accessibility of income protection programs, and the relatively low minimum wage.

In Europe, then, wage rates at the bottom end have been maintained by a variety of measures, including policies and collective bargaining arrangements that result in a high effective minimum wage (as a percent of the average wage). Moreover, income protection policies (viz., unemployment benefits, disability benefits, early retirement policies, and welfare benefits) are more accessible and generous in Europe than in North America. As a result, the declining relative European demand for new labor market entrants and other lower-skilled workers has been revealed in high unemployment and joblessness rates, and in the increasing prevalence of long-term unemployment. Given the pattern of labor demand growth, the structure of income protection programs in the European countries has tended to create a 'poverty trap' or a 'joblessness trap' for workers with low potential earnings.

In North America, on the other hand, a lower minimum wage, less generous and accessible social benefits, and fewer other barriers to employment creation haves encouraged job growth for low-skilled workers. The overall unemployment rate has not shown an upward trend - unlike that in Europe. As a result, a high percentage of all workers occupy minimum-wage, low-earnings jobs in North America. Wage rates and earnings have fallen substantially for low-skilled, low-education, young, and minority workers, and as a result wage-rate and earnings inequality has grown substantially. While the growth in earnings inequality has been effectively checked in Europe by a comprehensive set of social protection programs, this is not the case in North America. This, among other factors, has led to a rapid increase in the poverty rate in the United States of over 30 percent, and an increase in the number of the poor people by more than 60 percent.

However, in nearly all OECD nations, unemployment and joblessness haves become increasingly concentrated among youths and other low-skilled workers. While the incidence of joblessness and part-time work (especially for younger and minority male workers) has increased substantially in North America since 1973, both of these indicators have increased more in the European Community.

IV. Is there not an alternative approach?

The patterns described in Section III. prompt the question of whether there are alternative approaches to social policy that could simultaneously address the problems of both:
- high aggregate unemployment, growing joblessness and poverty traps in the (primarily European) countries with generous, accessible, and in some cases ill-managed income protection programs; and
- stagnant wages, high rates of non-employment among low-skilled workers, and increasing inequality and poverty that characterize the (primarily North American and Australian) countries with relatively modest income protection programs.

I would suggest that for both of these quite different sets of labor market problems, a common prescription could attain the following objectives:
- provide a minimum income floor under all individuals and families, equal to, say, one-third of per capita median income;
- eliminate the serious work disincentives implicit in existing social policies, and create positive incentives for increases in the labor supply of low-skilled workers; and
- stimulate the demand of private and public employers for the services of low-skilled workers.[17]

A wide variety of *individual measures* have been put forth as contributing to these objectives. They range from simple retrenchment of the eligibility conditions and benefit generosity of existing programs, to substitution of a costly universal, high level Basic Income Guarantee (BIG) program for the existing constellation of often ill-integrated measures. Other proposals also cited as improvements for categorical and difficult-to-administer systems include the Negative Income Tax (NIT) and Credit Income Tax (CIT) programs (as substitutes for existing categorical measures), earnings supplementation plans (e.g., earned income tax credits), and wage rate and employment subsidies operating on both the demand and supply sides of the low-wage labor market.[18]

Taken alone, each of these individual measures could make a contribution to the effectiveness of social policy, especially in the high-benefit welfare states. However, a review and assessment of them leads to one clear conclusion:

No single approach is capable of both assuring adequate income support to those without sufficient earnings (i.e., poverty reduction) and attaining the employment objectives cited above. The 'iron law' of income support dictates that an income guarantee assuring all citizens an 'adequate' level of living requires a structure of marginal tax rates on both benefit recipients and taxpayers that may imply substantial work disincentives. And, the higher the minimum income guarantee, the more severe are the work disincentives.

This conclusion suggests that a *combination of measures* is necessary to accomplish the goals set out above. For example, a CIT or an NIT could be effective instruments for 1) providing a minimum income floor below which no individual or family would fall, and 2) reducing the serious disincentives to work that are implicit in some existing social policies (e.g., unemployment, disability, and welfare income support policies with relatively high benefit levels and few restraints on duration). However, these policies would be unlikely to induce a sizeable increase in the supply of or the demand for the services of low-skilled workers, and overall employment levels.

Conversely, the work-conditioned policies - earnings supplements, wage rate subsidies, and employer-based marginal employment subsidies - are capable of 1) increasing the returns to labor supply and work, 2) increasing the effective demand for the services of low-skilled workers, and 3) contributing to the reduction of poverty through increasing the rewards from working. Such measures, however, are not effective in providing a minimum income floor beneath all individuals and families.

These conclusions suggest that a judicious combination of a moderate minimum income guarantee, supply- and demand-side labor market programs, and measures to tighten program monitoring and administration could be implemented simultaneously to accomplish these employment and income support goals. The stimuli to the demand for and the supply of low-skilled labor are designed to increase the employment and earnings of this high-joblessness/high-unemployment group. The minimum income guarantee would eliminate economic destitution, but not be so high as to seriously diminish the attractiveness of earnings from work. The increased stringency of program administration would seek to ensure that those able to work would not fail to seek labor market options.

In the following section, I provide a rough sketch of one possible combination of income support and labor market reform policies. Such a draconian package of changes should be viewed as illustrative of a general strategy designed both to reduce poverty and promote self-sufficiency. Hence, its objective is to stimulate discussion leading to policy changes with this goal, and not to argue the superiority of this prototypical approach relative to alternatives with a similar purpose.

Employment-centered social policy: a stylized reform strategy [19]

This suggested strategy is designed to be relevant to *both* those OECD countries with generous and accessible income protection systems (e.g. many of the European Community and EFTA countries) *and* those with less generous and accessible arrangements (such as those in North America and Australia). While the former countries tend to have more severe unemployment and poverty trap problems caused by generous and easily accessible public benefits than do countries with less generous benefit arrangements, the latter countries have problems of increasing wage inequality and poverty. The proposed reform is designed to mitigate both sets of problems.

The core policy changes that could comprise this 'blueprint' include:

1. *Adoption of a two-pronged employment subsidy program for low-skilled workers.*[20] The proposal offered here is two-pronged, and is aimed both at disadvantaged workers and those who hire them. Its effect would be to alter the terms on which workers could be hired - in effect, to make hiring low-skilled workers a more profitable and attractive proposition than it is now. Both prongs of the policy are designed to offset constraints on labor demand from market rigidities, to increase the employment of less-skilled workers, and to increase the returns to them from the work that they do. In the process, business costs would tend to fall, while output would tend to increase.[21]

   a. *An employer-based marginal employment subsidy.* This prong of the program would provide financial incentives to employers who hire low-skilled workers over and above the amounts that they would otherwise hire. One possible form of marginal employment subsidy targeted on enterprises might work as follows: the government would provide a tax credit (or other financial subsidy) to any enterprise equal to (say) 50 percent of the first (say) $10,000 of wages paid to the (say) 50 workers hired in a firm above (say) 102 percent of the firm's previous year's employment. Hence, the subsidy would be marginal in nature, affecting the decisions of firms regarding both the level of inputs to hire and their composition. While this arrangement does not distinguish among workers by their unemployment or poverty status, the subsidy (and hence the incentive to hire workers) is a higher percentage of the wages of low-skilled than it is for more skilled workers. By attempting to directly expand the demand for the services of low-wage workers, this form of employment subsidy seeks to reduce poverty and unemployment by directly changing the structure of the labor market.[22]

b. *A wage rate subsidy.* The second prong of this program focuses on the low-skilled workers themselves. An employee-based wage rate subsidy program would be instituted for disadvantaged workers and those with long-term and persistent unemployment problems. Some portion of the wage rate of low-wage workers would be subsidized by the government, giving the worker a labor market advantage, and hence an incentive to seek work. Workers would have incentive to exercise job-seeking initiative on their own behalf.

Such a wage rate subsidy program would require the establishment of a target wage rate which is socially determined. For any worker earning a wage rate below the target amount, a per hour subsidy is paid equal to some percentage (the subsidy rate) of the difference between the target wage rate and the actual wage rate. For example, if the target wage rate were set at $8.00 per hour while the subsidy rate was .5, a worker earning $5.00 per hour would receive a subsidy of $1.50 per hour worked ($1.50 is .5 of the difference between the target wage rate of $8.00 per hour and the actual $5.00 per hour wage). The 'take-home' wage rate of that person would then be $6.50 per hour.

A wage rate subsidy is but one example of what have become known as 'in-work benefits', all of which are characterized by the provision of support only when accompanied by market work. Other examples include the Family Credit in the United Kingdom, the subsidization of work in markets which are intensive in employing low-skilled labor (e.g., home cleaning and lawn and garden work), as is currently being pursued in

Denmark and the Netherlands, and an earnings subsidy of which one variant is the Earned Income Tax Credit of the United States.

The U.S. earned income tax credit provides a supplement to earnings below $8,000 per year of 26.3 percent for families with one child and 30.0 percent for families with more than one child). Beyond $8,000, the supplement of $2,038 (for one child; $2,528 for two children) remains constant until earnings of $11,000, and then is phased out at a rate of about 16 to 17 percent. The credit is totally phased out at an earnings level of about $24,000. Clearly, the EITC has strong work incentives for lower-income families - especially those experiencing the 'negative' marginal tax rate. However, the EITC causes reduced work incentives for families (with two children) who are earning more than $11,000, and it is in this region of the earnings distribution that the density of the population becomes heavy. Offsetting this disincentive effect is the positive work effect of the incentive to move from joblessness to employment.[23]

The new labor market environment generated by a two-pronged supply-side and demand-side policy proposal will improve the employment prospects of disadvantaged workers by generating ongoing job creation pressures at reasonable cost. By targeting the additional employment on segments of the labor market with the most severe unemployment problems and the greatest susceptibility to 'poverty trap' problems created by existing tax and transfer programs, employment and output could be increased without significant inflationary pressure. This two-pronged labor market program will fundamentally alter the wage structure in private labor markets, raising the take-home pay of low-skilled workers relative to those with more secure positions in the labor market. It would reduce inequality in employment and earnings in a way that encourages independence, work, and initiative.

2. *Establishment of a Credit Income Tax program.* In this program, a family's income would be defined comprehensively, and a tax credit would be awarded to each living unit (or taxpaying unit) according to how large it is and who lives in it (for example, the adult/child composition of the unit). This credit would guarantee to taxpaying

units a minimum income that would be set at a modest level, perhaps two-thirds of the explicit or implicit poverty line in the country. Units with no other means of support would receive the full amount of the credit as a grant; those with some other income would receive smaller net payments; better-off families would receive no net payment, and would pay positive taxes. This program would be integrated with the positive income tax, so as to yield a smooth marginal tax rate pattern.

As a result of this low-guarantee plan, 'hard-core' poverty would be eliminated, as the bottom tail of the nation's income distribution would be cut off. However, the minimum income which is ensured by this base income support plan is low (as a percentage of median income) relative to accepted benefit levels for unemployment, disability, and retirement pension programs (and safety-net welfare programs) in those OECD countries with large and generous transfer systems.[24]

A central gain from this component of the proposal arrangement is the substantial increase in work incentives relative to those inherent in the existing high benefit-reduction rates of the income support programs of most of the larger OECD nations. A universal CIT would also strip away the complexity of the melange of current programs, and eliminate much of the stigma associated with welfare programs; however, the moral hazard problem associated with such support would still exist. With a CIT integrated with the standard income tax structure, incomes would be taxed and support provided in a simple, open, universal, and just manner.[25]

3. *Elimination of existing programs for disability income transfers, unemployment compensation benefits, and welfare benefits (or scaling back the benefit levels in these programs, and establishing them as supplements to the Credit Income Tax described in 2. above).* The elimination or scaling-back of these programs would free up budgetary resources to support the new programs, and would eliminate or moderate the effects of those aspects of these programs in many OECD countries that contribute to high work disincentives and the poverty/joblessness trap.

V. Obstacles to an employment-centered social policy reform

The objective of this proposed new direction is to simultaneously provide income support to the poor families of a nation and, at the same time, to encourage work effort and individual initiative, consistent with the objectives stated above. As in any proposed change that represents a major policy adjustment, this new direction also confronts several obstacles.

One concern with this approach is that the income guarantee level that lies at the base of the 'blueprint' lies well below the implicit income minimum provided by existing programs in those OECD countries with the most generous and accessible benefits. Clearly, a minimum income guarantee of this level could not be sustained were universal income support measures (e.g., a CIT or NIT) to be substituted for a set of individual of categorical benefit programs. Were a general CIT or NIT to provide an income guarantee level as high as even 50 percent of per capita median income in these countries, the marginal tax rate imposed on *all* earnings would be intolerably high if the policy reform were to be budget neutral.[26] While the poverty/-unemployment trap would be reduced for current benefit recipients, severe work disincentives would be imposed on the remainder of the population. Such a policy substitution seems economically unworkable.

Two options seem possible. First, those OECD countries desiring elimination of the poverty trap and an increase in work incentives and employment for low-skilled workers must face the fact that the replacement rates and eligibility standards now in force in some of their programs need to be scaled back if incentives to retain or to seek work are to exist for lower-skilled workers. While this is a bitter political pill to swallow, the 'iron law' of income support policy described above indicates that high guaranteed incomes and strong work incentives are incompatible objectives.[27]

There is also a second option. Governments could set the level of the income guarantee in a CIT or NIT at a rather low level (say, one-third of per capita median income), and this guarantee would cover citizens. However, people included in restricted categories (e.g., the disabled or the unemployed) could be eligible for supplemental benefits in categorical programs designed for them.

With such a two-tiered arrangement, a comprehensive and universal income support system as supplemented by such categorical programs could be financially feasible and workable. A modest income floor would be established below all working-age families, and work incentives would be maintained. However, in this case it must be admitted that workers receiving benefits from programs in the special categories will not face the desirable work incentives that confront the remainder of the population; for them, something of a poverty trap will persist. If this strategy is followed, it would be essential that eligibility restrictions on benefits from these programs be tightly enforced, that recipients judged able to work be monitored for unreported work and job search activities, and that program administration be geared to returning beneficiaries to the work force. Moreover, it could be desirable to erode over time the seriousness of the trap by incrementally reducing the replacement rates incorporated into these programs, and simultaneously restricting the eligibility criteria applied in granting access to benefits.

Discussion of this obstacle to an employment-centered social policy raises the question: 'if such an employment-centered reform strategy is so attractive, why have countries not adopted such large-scale changes?' One answer to this question highlights yet another obstacle to a sizable employment-centered social policy reform - namely, the losses that would be experienced by those individuals now receiving benefits in the unemployment, disability and early retirement programs of countries with high replacement rates and easily accessible benefits (and people who would expect to be beneficiaries in the future) would be adversely affected by the change. There is no easy way to assess the strength of this potential political obstacle, though efforts to retrench social benefit programs by reducing replacement rates or tightening eligibility standards inevitably generate heated opposition from those who reflect the interests of beneficiaries, or who otherwise support the status quo.

Another obstacle to an employment-centered strategy rests on the argument that generous and accessible systems (especially if tightly administered) do provide the security that the future incomes of all citizens will not be subject to a large downside risk. A corollary of this argument is the observation that systems that do provide transfer support to otherwise well-off classes tend to have strong systems of social protection that insure low levels of poverty and inequality. While such arrangements may, indeed, reduce both poverty and inequality, they do come at the cost of reduced overall work effort and lower measured national income. Perhaps the only way to blunt the force of such arguments for generous and accessible systems is to make as clear as possible the large efficiency toll that the incentives in such systems impose on the society as a whole. Such arguments, unfortunately, tend not to be persuasive in the face of those private interests that benefit from the generous systems in place. Here, then, may lie the ultimate dilemma.

Notes

1. These distinctions are emphasized in the paper by Fritz Scharpf, presented at the OECD Beyond 2000 conference, November 12-13, 1996.

2. The following description focuses on the programmes providing support to the working-age population, and hence does not discuss the work incentives implicit in the Social Security retirement programmes. Descriptions of the nature of welfare and labor market policies among member countries are available in several OECD publications. A basic description of the eligibility and coverage provisions of several of the programmes is U.S. Social Security Administration (1995). The effects of benefit programmes, employment protection, and minimum wage programmes on employment, joblessness, wage adjustment, and economic growth are discussed in OECD (1994), Chapters 5, 6, 8, and 9.

3. Edmund Phelps has analyzed the effect of these distortions in the framework of 'natural unemployment rate' theory, concluding that their impact is to drive up the natural rate. See Edmund S. Phelps (1994). The theoretical underpinnings of Phelps' natural rate model have been challenged by a number of reviewers; these challenges are alluded to in Phelps (1995). See also Richard Layard, Stephen Nickell, and Richard Jackman (1991), and Assar Lindbeck (1996). A helpful discussion of the implications of alternative theoretical frameworks in analyzing the effects of the welfare state on economic welfare is found in Anthony Atkinson (1995). This analysis makes clear that the direction of the impacts suggested above persists irrespective of the labor market assumptions made, though the anticipated magnitude of the effects may vary.

4. These examples, and numerous others, are discussed in OECD (1994), Chapter 8. The study concludes as follows: '...If unemployment is to be kept low, it is vital to limit entitlements to benefit and refuse benefit to people who are not available for work' (p. 213).

5. Higgins (1994).

6. A good summary of recent trends in the United States labor market is found in Peter Auer (1995).

7. See OECD (1994).

8. Calculations from data in John P. Martin (1994).

9. If the jobless rate for males aged 20 to 64 had been shown, the difference between North America and Europe would have been even larger; youth joblessness and early retirement has grown in both regions, but more in Europe than America.

10. Three of the four EFTA countries increased the maximum benefit period over this time period, and Sweden adopted a procedure that enabled a virtual permanent extension of unemployment benefit eligibility.

11. For the United States alone, the indicator fell from 17 to 11. These calculations are from data in OECD (1994).

12. For the EFTA countries the replacement rate of disability benefits was a very high 66 percent in 1981; by 1993, it had fallen slightly to 61 percent. A regression fit over the OECD countries relating the percent of those aged over 55 receiving disability benefits and the generosity of disability benefits as measured by the replacement rate has a regression coefficient of 0.48, a standard error of 0.2, and an R-squared of 0.3. Data in this paragraph are from Blondal and Pearson (1995).

13. Among the larger OECD countries, statutory minimum wages exist in the United States, Canada, Japan, France, the Netherlands, Spain and Portugal. Several other countries have established de facto wage minima through tri-partite and other collective arrangements, but not through legislation. Data are available only on statutory wage minima. In a number of countries, primarily in Europe, an effective wage floor is established by benefit levels in social protection programs. These wage floors tend to be a higher proportion of the average wage than is the minimum wage in the North American countries. (For Germany and Australia, however, evidence suggests that the minimum wage is effective for adults but not for youths.)

14. See OECD (1994).

15. Calculations from OECD (1994). Evidence necessary to indicate differential trends in income inequality between North America and Europe is not available.

16. The data on comparative poverty rates are from Michael Forster (1994). The criterion for measuring poverty is the percentage of people living in households with disposable income adjusted for family size (using an equivalence scale with an elasticity of .55) which is less than 50 percent of the median household income in the country.

17. A more full-bodied statement of these objectives might read as follows: 1) insure that public programs that guarantee income support do not inhibit the willingness of people to work at prevailing market wages, and constrain the duration of support for which workers qualify, 2) increase employment opportunities for low-skilled labor and stimulate the willingness of workers to accept work at prevailing wages in a manner that encourages investments in education and training, and 3) increase the monitoring of recipients in terms of unreported work and job search efforts, and improve aspects of program integration and administration.

18. Elsewhere, I have discussed these various approaches as potential reforms for existing, high-benefit welfare state systems, and assessed their advantages and disadvantages. See Haveman (1996).

19. A recent Australian comprehensive reform package contains many of the elements emphasized in the prototypical plan presented here. They include: subsidies to youth, the long-term unemployed, and those at risk of long-term unemployment for job search, employment and training; employer subsidies for hiring/training people in these categories; reform of income support (unemployment benefit) programs so as to provide incentive for job search and work; intensive case management and a 'compact' between workers and the public sector indicating mutual obligations. See Commonwealth of Australia (1994).

20. This component of the blueprint rests on the view that most OECD countries face a situation where minorities, youths, older workers, disabled workers, and single mothers - all characterized by low levels of skill and education - face relatively bleak labor market opportunities. Given prevailing wage standards, union wage contracts, and the fringe benefits and payroll taxes that businesses are required to pay for every standard worker, hiring low-skilled workers simply does not generate much additional output and profit for employers. These constraints on labor market flexibility, hence, contribute to the labor market disadvantage of the low-skilled.

21. The case for such a labor market strategy is made in Robert Haveman (1994), Appendix to Chapter 7. See also the paper by David Betson and John Bishop in Haveman and Palmer (1982). Edmund Phelps estimates that wage incomes of $7,000 or less could be raised to about $11,000 with an employment subsidy program that would cost about $100 billion per year for the United States. The empirical basis for this assertion is unclear. See also Edmund S. Phelps (1994a).

22. A possible structure for this program is the New Jobs Tax Credit that was in place in the United States during the late 1970s. Evaluations of the New Jobs Tax Credit program concluded that it was a potent and cost-effective measure to increase employment of low-skilled workers. A wide variety of modifications could be made to its structure to increase its employment generating potential. For evidence on the effect of the New Jobs Tax Credit on employment levels, see Haveman and Bishop (1979); and Perloff and Wachter (1979).

23. The design and effects of the Earned Income Tax Credit in the United States have been analyzed in Scholz (1994). An earnings supplementation plan can easily be integrated with a credit income tax. Haveman (1996) discusses this option and its advantages and disadvantages.

24. As a result, if these programs were to be replaced with only the universal CIT, poverty rates would be increased, even though 'hard core' poverty would be eliminated. As an alternative, income losses by recipients of existing generous programs could be offset either by increased earnings associated with improved incentives for labor supply and the employment subsidies which are also part of this proposal, or the

adoption of supplemental categorical unemployment, disability, and retirement programs.

25. Reform proposals with a negative income tax or a credit income tax at their heart have been recently debated in the United Kingdom. Nobel Laureate James Meade (1995) suggests such an arrangement in his recent volume. Similarly, Roger Douglas (1995), former Finance Minister of New Zealand, has also proposed a Guaranteed Minimum Family Income at the base of his reform suggestions. In a commentary on these proposals, Samuel Brittan (1995) states that: 'Meade has always insisted that if people are to be priced into work, whether through free market forces or direct intervention, there must be an adequate safety net for those whose earnings in the market place do not provide a reasonable standard of living.' This sentiment motivates the employment-centered social policy reform that the 'blueprint' represents. A basic income guarantee for the non-elderly population, conditional on 'participation' (defined to include work, sick though employed, unemployed though seeking work, in education or training, and caring for young, elderly and disabled), has also been proposed by Anthony Atkinson (1996).

26. See OECD (1994).

27. Viewed this way, the policy strategy suggested above would seem more feasible for those OECD countries with benefit levels and replacement rates set at lower percentages of median income (such as the United States) than for countries with higher percentage rates (such as some of the Northern European countries).

References

Atkinson, Anthony (1995) 'The Welfare State and Economic Performance'. *National Tax Journal*, Vol. XLVIII, No. 2: 171-198.
Atkinson, Anthony (1996) 'The Distribution of Income: Evidence, Theories, and Policy'. *The Economist*, Vol. 144, No. 1: 1-21.
Auer, Peter (1995) 'The American Employment Miracle.' *inforMISEP*. Employment Observatory Policies, Employment in Europe. European Commission, Directorate-General for Employment, Industrial Relations, and Social Affairs. No. 49 (Spring): 18–27.
Blondal, Sveinbjorn, and Pearson, Mark (1995) 'Unemployment and other Non-Employment Benefits.,' *Oxford Review of Economic Policy*, Vol. 11, No. 1.
Brittan, Samuel (1995) 'No, not the next budget.,' *Financial Times*, November 9.
Commonwealth of Australia (1994) *Working Nation: Policies and Programs*, Australian Government Publishing Service Canberra.
Douglas, Roger (1995) *Unfinished Business*. Wellington: New Zealand Random House.
Forster, Michael (1994) 'Measurement of Low Incomes and Poverty in a Perspective of International Comparisons'. OECD Labor Market and Social Policy Occasional Paper No. 14.
Haveman, Robert (1996) 'Reducing Poverty while Increasing Employment: A Primer on Alternative Strategies, and a Blueprint'. *OECD Economic Studies*.

Haveman, Robert and Bishop, John (1979) 'Selective Employment Subsidies: Can Okun's Law Be Repealed?' *American Economic Review* 69 (May): 124–130.

Haveman, Robert and Palmer, John (eds.) (1982) *Jobs for Disadvantaged Workers: The Economics of Employment Subsidies*. Washington, D.C.: Brookings Institution.

Higgins, Bryon (1994) 'Symposium Summary.' In *in Reducing Unemployment: Current Issues and Policy Options*. A symposium sponsored by the Federal Reserve Bank of Kansas City.

Layard, Richard, Nickell, Stephen and Jackman, Richard (1991) *Unemployment: Macroeconomic Performance and the Labor Market*. Oxford: Oxford University Press.

Lindbeck, Assar (1996) 'The West European Employment Problem.' Seminar paper no. 616; Institute for International Economic Studies, August, 1996.

Martin, John P. (1994) 'The Extent of High Unemployment in OECD Countries.' In *Reducing Unemployment: Macroeconomic Performance and the Labor Market*. Oxford University Press.

Meade, James (1995) *Full Employment Regained*. Cambridge: Cambridge University Press.

OECD (1994) *The OECD Jobs Study: Evidence and Explanations*. Paris: OECD.

Perloff, Jeffrey M. and Wachter, Michael (1979) 'The New Jobs Tax Credit: An Evaluation of the 1977–78 Wage Subsidy Program.' *American Economic Review* 69 (May): 173–179.

Phelps, Edmund S. (1994a) 'Low-Wage Employment Subsidies versus the Welfare State.' *American Economic Review* 84 (May): 54–58.

Phelps, Edmund S. (1994b) *Structural Slumps: The Modern Equilibrium Theory of Unemployment, Interest, and Assets*. Cambridge, Mass.: Harvard University Press.

Phelps, Edmund S. (1995) 'The Structuralist Theory of Employment.' *American Economic Review* 85 (May): 226–231.

Scholz, John Karl. (1994) 'The Earned Income Tax Credit: Participation, Compliance, and Antipoverty Effectiveness.' *National Tax Journal* 47 (March): 59–81

U.S. Social Security Administration (1995) Office of Research and Statistics, 'Social Security Programs Throughout the World–1995' Social Security Administration Publication no. 13-11805, Research Report no. 64, Washington, D.C., July.

# 2.2 Government mandates, health insurance, and the deterioration of the low-wage labor market: Are they connected?

Barbara L. Wolfe, Amy Wolaver and Timothy McBride

Introduction

In the current attempt to improve upon the rather poor economic performance of many industrialized countries in Europe and to learn from the far better performance of the U.S. economy, attention is turning to the role of non-wage labor costs - the costs of social assistance and social protection, including health insurance coverage. Certain trends seem clear: increased global competition has brought pressure to reduce costs of production, to achieve labor market flexibility, and to privatize such benefits as health insurance. At the same time, declines in jobs and labor force participation have brought calls for a strategy to increase employment opportunities. With these trends comes a certain amount of pressure to 'reduce the commitment to equity'.[1]

This article addresses the question of the link between employer-provided health insurance and the level of employment, especially among low-wage or low-skilled workers. More precisely, it explores the question of whether the U.S. employer-based health insurance system, combined with its high cost and with regulation requiring that all full-time workers must be offered coverage, may be related both to a decline in coverage and to deterioration of the low-skilled labor market. Implications of the link for other industrialized nations are discussed.

The vast majority of persons in the United States are covered through private health insurance coverage, most of it employer-based. In

1994 this included 70.1 percent of the non-elderly population, representing a decrease from the 1980s, when nearly 79 percent of this population was insured. (See Table 2.2.1.) Full-time workers are far more likely to be offered coverage than part-time workers, and the probability of coverage also varies by industry, size of firm, and occupation. In general, those in higher-prestige occupations are more likely to be offered coverage. Table 2.2.2 compares these patterns in 1993 to those in 1988.

Health insurance tends to be employer-based rather than individual- (or family-) based for two main reasons: coverage through a firm may bring tax advantages, and firm-based coverage tends to reduce loading charges, because administrative costs are lower and insurers can reduce uncertainty by offering policies to a large group (spreading the risk).[2]

Table 2.2.1 Private health insurance coverage, United States: 1980-1994, for persons under age 65

Characteristic	1980	1984	1989	1994
	(Percentage of population covered)			
Total, age adjusted	78.8	76.9	76.6	70.1
Age under 15 years	74.7	71.9	71.7	63.0
15 - 44 years	79.3	77.0	76.6	69.9
45 - 64	83.6	83.6	80.7	80.5
Race				
White	81.9	80.0	79.7	73.6
Black	60.1	58.9	59.2	52.0
Family Income [a]				
Low	38.6	34.1	34.6	24.7
Low-middle	61.1	71.3	71.4	54.0
Middle	79.0	88.3	87.9	78.4
Middle-high	90.2	93.1	92.4	88.5
High	93.7	95.2	95.7	92.7

Source: *Health United States*, 1992 and 1995.
a Categories in order, are < $7,000, $7,000-$9,999, $10,000-$14,999, $15,000 - $24,999 and $25,000 or more in 1980; <$10,000; $10,000-$18,999; $19,000-$29,999, $30,000-$39,999 and $40,000 or more in 1984; <$14,000, $14,000-$24,999; $25,000-$34,999, $35,000-$49,999 and $50,000 or more in 1989 and 1994.

Table 2.2.2 Employer-based health insurance in the United States: 1988 and 1993

	1988			1993		
Characteristic	Offered %	Covered %	Not Offered %	Offered %	Covered %	Not Offered %
Total of work force	77.6	67.9	5.7	75.6	65.1	6.3
Full-time workers	84.3	76.3	3.2	83.4	74.0	3.0
Part-time workers	40.4	20.9	19.9	36.6	20.6	22.5
Firm size						
< 25	45.8	36.3	3.1	40.9	31.8	2.9
25 - 99	77.5	65.7	5.9	74.8	61.2	6.0
100 - 249	85.3	73.1	6.5	82.8	70.8	6.9
250 - 999	88.9	79.1	5.7	87.4	75.4	6.9
1000+	90.3	82.4	6.0	88.6	79.0	6.9

Source: Employee Benefit Supplements to the 1988 and 1993 Current Population Surveys, conducted by the U.S. Bureau of the Census.

Tax advantages take the following form: premiums paid by the employer for an employee are not counted as income to the employee in calculating income or payroll taxes (or state or local taxes); the premiums are considered a cost of business to the firm, just as cash wages are considered. Thus, for an employee facing a high marginal tax rate, premiums paid by the employer are heavily subsidized relative to a privately purchased plan. Workers at lower marginal tax rates receive less subsidy, but all gain from the lower overhead and the spreading of risk.

To be eligible for favorable tax treatment, private firms since 1978 have been obliged by nondiscrimination laws to offer fringe benefits to all full-time workers, rather than only to high-wage employees. Fringe benefits include pensions, health insurance, and a variety of other benefits.

The nondiscrimination laws may have negative consequences for the population they are designed to help: namely, low-wage employees. The reason is that the cost of health insurance is a fixed cost, not related to earnings, raising the relative cost of hiring low-wage as opposed to higher-wage employees. The costs to employers of premiums (or fringe benefits in general) are largely passed back to employees by a reduction in total cash compensation, and as the cost of fringe benefits grows, this effect becomes larger. But minimum wage laws set a floor beneath which cash wages cannot fall. For workers at or near the minimum wage, it is not possible to reduce wages sufficiently to cover the cost of insurance. Thus high or increasing costs of coverage, together with minimum wage laws, are likely to decrease employment of low-wage workers. The decrease may take the form of fewer hires, or a shift to part-time employment, when fringe benefits are not offered to part-time workers; or firms may hire vendors (i.e., outsource) to perform tasks normally performed by low-wage workers.

In this article we explore the extent to which U.S. nondiscrimination laws, together with the increasing costs of providing health insurance, have led to a change in the composition of labor demands by skill and education level. We do so by using, from work described in an earlier article (Wolaver, McBride, and Wolfe, 1997), a three-stage simultaneous model including wages, the offer of a job by a firm offering benefits, and working full- versus part-time. The special Employee Benefits Supplements to the U.S. Census Bureau's Current Population Surveys for 1988 and 1993 are used to provide empirical evidence on this issue. These surveys are unique in that they include, with their usual labor force questions, an extensive set of questions on health insurance coverage of employees.

Background and significance

The sluggish growth in family incomes and the long-term trend toward increased income inequality in the United States has captured the attention of many analysts and policy makers in recent years. Between the peaks of the business cycle in 1979 and 1989, real median family income grew only 4 percent.[3] Family incomes declined in the first four years of the next business cycle, from 1989 to 1993, and, despite an increase in incomes in 1994 and 1995, still have not returned to their 1989 level. The shares of income received by the highest income quintile increased from less than 44 percent to nearly 49 percent from 1967 to 1995, while the shares received by the lowest income quintile have decreased from 4.0 to 3.7 percent in the same period (Weinberg, 1996).

Wage inequality has been increasing for more than twenty years, and the lowest-wage workers have fared particularly poorly. Since the 1980s there has been some additional shift in trends: most workers have seen declines in real wages, with the exception of only the highest-wage workers (Mishel, Bernstein, and Schmitt, 1996). The wages of the average male without a college education fell 10.1 percent from 1979 to 1989 and another 7.2 percent between 1989 and 1995. The wages of a young male high school graduate dropped 21.8 percent in the 1980s and another 6.9 percent in the 1989–95 period. Over the 1989–95 period, real wages declined for the bottom 80 percent of men and the bottom 60 percent of women.

A number of theories have been offered as explanations for the increase in wage inequality (e.g., Solow, 1994). An explanation favored by many economists is that technological change, especially the increased use of computers, has favored high-skilled workers (Krueger, 1993; Burtless, 1994). Other explanations include the shift in jobs from manufacturing to services, the drop in unionization, sluggish growth in worker productivity, increasing returns to education, especially university education, and the impact of international trade on wages and employment.[4]

What role for fringe benefits?

In addition to the explanations offered above, another source of the sluggish growth in wages could be the cost of fringe benefits. Total compensation for employees consists of wages plus fringe benefits, and the cost of fringe benefits has been increasing for many years. There are several indicators of this trend. First, wages have become a smaller share of compensation: the ratio of wages to total compensation declined by roughly 14 percent from 1955 to 1994 and by 5.5 percent from 1975 to 1994 (Social Security Administration, 1996). Second, the current aggregate cost of fringe benefits, as measured by the amount of 'tax expenditures' lost by excluding from federal personal income taxes the employer's contribution to fringe benefits, is high: the exclusion for medical insurance was $65 billion in 1996.[5]

A third indicator of the growth of fringe benefits comes from the Employment Cost Index (ECI), maintained by the Bureau of Labor Statistics (BLS), a broad measure of trends in total compensation, wages, and fringe benefits. From the second quarter of 1982 to the fourth quarter of 1996, the ECI shows an increase of more than 108 percent in the benefits paid to workers, far above the 73 percent increase in wages and salaries.[6]

What is the impact of rising fringe benefits on workers, especially low-wage workers? Slower growth in wages, and/or changes in employment (hours worked) are both possible. Slower growth would be due to the increased share of one component of compensation, fringe benefits, crowding out another form, cash wages. Much if not all of the cost of fringe benefits is passed through to employees. As outlined by Gruber and Krueger (1991), the amount of pass-through will depend on the elasticities of demand and supply for labor, as well as a term they describe as the 'value' of the insurance to the employee. A worker will accept lower wages to the extent that she values the benefits. If she values the benefits at less than a dollar-for-dollar basis, employers will be faced with paying higher cash salaries and hence will hire fewer workers (assuming labor supply is not perfectly inelastic).[7] Thus, the provision of employer-provided benefits comes with concomitant effects on employment and wages, and these are both considered here. Empirical evidence suggests that employers pass most of the costs (perhaps 80 percent) of employer-sponsored coverage onto employees, but that the remaining costs may result in employment effects.[8]

The nondiscrimination law governing fringe benefits

Beginning in 1978, private firms have been obliged under nondiscrimination laws (including 401 (a) (4) of the Internal Revenue Act) to offer fringe benefits to all full-time workers (not just highly compensated employees) in order for fringe benefits provided by the firm to receive favorable tax treatment. As of 1978 this requirement was extended to include health insurance. (Appendix 1 presents an excerpt from the revenue code.) The nondiscrimination law can be viewed as a mandate: if a firm decides to offer fringe benefits to its high-wage workers, the government mandates that it must offer benefits across the board to all full-time employees.

For several reasons, the nondiscrimination laws may have negative consequences on the population it is meant to help: low-wage workers. Nondiscrimination laws may lead to a lowering in the demand for such workers because their cost (wages plus fringe benefits) increases relative to other, higher-paid workers. These problems are exacerbated for the lowest-wage workers because firms may not be willing or able to pass the costs of fringe benefits back to their lowest-wage employees. Minimum wage laws limit the ability of firms to pass the costs back to their low-wage workers because the wage cannot be lowered below the minimum wage. Employers will then find it attractive to substitute capital for such labor (limited by cost and technology); and to hire services from vendors (to outsource) rather than hire low-wage service workers themselves. Hence the demand for numerous services that were performed by low-wage workers in generally high-wage firms will be reduced through substitution using capital and/or outside service firms.

It is possible for employers to get around the effects of nondiscrimination laws on total compensation through employment changes. In particular, employers can increasingly hire low-wage workers on a part-time basis, thus making them not qualified for the nondiscrimination rules, or they can 'outsource' tasks normally assigned to low-wage workers. Alternatively, employers who decide to offer benefits to all workers, including low-wage workers, may respond by hiring some low-wage workers to work for longer hours, in order to spread the fixed-cost fringe benefits across more hours. The first of these possible responses is explored empirically in this article.

Publicly mandated coverage for all employees: other industrialized countries

Are the negative employment consequences discussed above likely to be the case in other countries with employer-based health insurance that faces government mandates of various forms? The most common form of employer-based coverage[9] requires that low- and middle-wage workers must be covered at their place of employment with a 50–50 split in cost (or an alternative split), while high-wage workers are covered separately, through their own private purchase of health insurance. This means that the employer faces a higher relative cost of hiring a low- or middle-wage worker, compared to a high-wage worker, unless the full cost of the coverage is borne by the employees through reduced cash compensation. (In cases such as Germany, which has an earnings ceiling on the payroll tax, the effect is likely to be even greater, since the relative cost difference between low- and higher-wage workers will be greater than without a ceiling.) The result of the mandate requiring firms to provide coverage should be similar to that in the United States, in which demand for low-wage workers is reduced relative to that for high-wage workers. However, unlike the United States, where the premium is a fixed amount, the financing in these countries tends to be through a payroll tax or percentage of the payroll. Hence the impact should be considerably less than in the United States under the nondiscrimination law, because the relative costs of low- and high-wage workers are changed far less.[10] Furthermore, all firms must offer coverage so that outsourcing to a lower-cost alternative should offer less cost savings. However, the 'substitute' for outsourcing is likely to be a movement of production offshore or to other countries where the cost of labor is lower, or possibly hiring services 'off the books,' through use of the underground or unreported economy. Thus, the model developed here can be extended to be a model that relates higher costs of labor owing to the health insurance mandate (and payroll tax) to a decline in the demand for low-wage workers in countries with this form of employer-based health insurance. In these countries the results may be (1) a demand for fewer low-wage workers, (2) fewer hours of work when there is no earnings ceilings on the payroll tax, (3) an increase in overtime work when there is an earnings ceiling, (4) an increase in work outside of the countries' borders, (5) a growth in the 'underground' or unreported economy.[11]

We have some evidence on such patterns. In Belgium an experiment, Operation Maribel, implemented in 1981, suggests that employment may be sensitive to the rate of payroll tax on employers. Employer payroll taxes were reduced by slightly more than 6 percent at that time, from a high of 30 percent. Other taxes were used to make up the deficit. The plan, implemented only in part, reduced labor costs and stimulated the economy. Any effect on employment, however, was weak. In Italy in the 1970s and 1980s, average payroll taxes were nearly 15 percent for health and maternity, and an additional 30 percent for other benefits. These taxes were paid up to a ceiling. In response to this tax scheme, firms tried to substitute away from labor - to employ workers overtime and to hire workers clandestinely, so that they did not pay payroll taxes for them (see Glazer, 1991, Chapter 6). Official unemployment rates were extremely high during this period. In Spain, the rapid surge in wages and in social insurance payroll costs in the late 1970s has been credited with increasing a deep recession, high 'official' unemployment, and the rapid development of an underground economy.[12]

How high are these payroll tax rates currently? Table 2.2.3 gives examples of rates for medical insurance as of 1995, not including the full rate for pensions or other benefits tied to this tax. In the European Union as a whole, these non-wage costs or rates tend to be significantly higher than in the United States. According to the European Commission (1995), 'Employers' statutory social security contributions...tend to be much higher than in the competitor economies.' This report highlights the far bigger difference for those with low pay than for the higher-paid, because non-statutory health insurance contributions in the United States tend to be high and to be paid more often for higher-wage workers. This tends to reduce the difference in the non-labor costs for higher-paid workers in the European Union as compared with the United States. As to whether these costs play a role in the high unemployment rates, there clearly is not a one-to-one relationship, since the exchange rate, the interest rate, and other factors influence opportunities, competitive pressures, and the behavior of firms. Nevertheless it seems unlikely that these high rates would not lead to a substitution of capital for low-wage labor and to motivation to produce certain items abroad or through alternative routes to avoid these high taxes. The larger underground economy in most of these countries as compared with the United States is also consistent with an attempt to avoid high non-wage costs.

Evidence on the impact of fringe benefits on wages in the United States

As noted above, higher fringe benefit costs may be passed through to workers, the amount of pass-through depending on the elasticities of demand and supply for labor, as well as a term described as the 'value' of the insurance to the employee (Gruber and Krueger, 1991). Empirical studies suggest that employers pass most of the costs of employer-sponsored coverage onto employees, but that the remaining costs may result in employment effects (Aaron and Bosworth, 1994; Gruber and Krueger, 1991; Loprest et al., 1994; Summers, 1989). In a survey of these studies, using widely accepted estimates of the appropriate elasticities, Loprest et al. (1994) concluded that about 80 percent of health insurance premiums were borne by the worker in the form of lower wages.

Empirical findings suggest that while the increase in total compensation may be expected to reflect increases in the marginal productivity of workers, the rising cost of fringe benefits may 'crowd out' increases in wages, as employers are forced to use most increases in total compensation to pay for fringe benefits. Trends in these data tend to support this hypothesis (Figure 2.2.1). From the second quarter of 1982 to the fourth quarter of 1996, the average annual growth in real total compensation was 0.59 percent, but real wages increased by only 0.24 percent annually. In contrast, benefits increased by 1.57 percent annually during this period, suggesting that the growth in benefits contributed to the slower growth of wages, relative to total compensation, during this period. In fact, in almost every quarter since the Employment Cost Index has been collected, the growth in fringe benefits has exceeded the growth in total compensation, resulting in growth in wages lower than the growth in total compensation. A notable exception are the eight quarters ending in the fourth quarter of 1996, in which the growth in wages has exceeded the growth in fringe benefits (Figure 2.2.1).

Little (1995) also found evidence that payments for employer-sponsored health insurance and social security benefits have exacerbated between-group and within-group wage inequality. Little found that in recent years changes in health insurance provision have tended to favor high-wage workers, increasing inequality in total compensation. Blank (1990) explores the quality of part-time jobs by exploring the impact of part-time status on wages. She finds that occupation wage differentials between part-time and full-time workers are not as pronounced as would be expected. Female part-time service workers appear to earn higher average wages, while male part-time workers earn less except in the professional category. Others, including Lettau (1995), have been unable to replicate this finding and provide evidence that part-time employment pays less and offers much lower benefits per hour, even if the job is 'the same' as a full-time one at the same firm.

The limited literature in this area suggest that employers have responded to the increase in the cost of health insurance benefits in general, and the imposition of the nondiscrimination law in particular, through slowing the rate of increases in wages and increasing hours worked among low-wage workers who are employed full-time. However, the evidence of a relationship between the nondiscrimination law and changes in the employment patterns and wages of part-time workers is quite limited. Below we explore further evidence which might support the hypothesis that the nondiscrimination law has contributed to the deteriorating employment and income picture for low-wage workers in the United States.

Table 2.2.3 Payroll tax rates for medical insurance, 1995

Country	Employer Share	Employee Share	Extent of Coverage
France	12.8% of total payroll	6.8% of total earnings.	72% of workers
Germany	4.0 to 8 % of payroll[a]	4.0 to 8 % of covered earnings	All wage earners, apprentices, unemployment beneficiaries, salaried employees and some categories of self-employed persons earning up to DM 70.200 a year (E-DM 57.600).
Belgium	6.00[b]	4.7	Employed persons and apprentices (must enroll with mutual benefit society or public auxiliary fund).
Netherlands	8.20%[c]	10.95% of earnings	Compulsory coverage for wage earners and salaried employees earning less than 58.950 guilders a year of payroll.
Spain	6.2% of payroll[d]		1.6% covered earnings
Sweden	zero[e]	zero	
Japan	4.1% of basic wage	4.1% of basic wage	Employees of firms in industry and commerce (government-managed programs, unless member of health insurance society). Voluntary coverage for other employees.[f] Maximum basic wage for contribution and benefit purposes: 980.000 yen a month; minimum, 92.000 yen a month.

Source: Social Security Programs throughout the World, 1995.

a   Employer: pays (up to earnings ceiling) according to fund (8.0 percent to 16 percent for employees earning less than DM 610 a month). Insured person: pays according to fund (no contribution if earnings less than DM 610 a month).

b   Employer: Medical benefits, 3.8 percent of payroll. Cash benefits, 2.2 percent of payroll plus 0.15 percent to finance maternity benefits. Insured person: Medical benefits, 3.55 percent of earnings. Cash benefits, 1.15 percent of earnings.

c   Employers share includes 7.25 percent for medical benefits, 0.95 percent for cash benefits. Insured person pays 1.10 percent for medical benefits, 1.00 percent for cash benefits, and 8.85 percent for exceptional medical expense insurance.

d   Maximum earnings for contribution and benefit purposes: 269,940 to 362,190 pesetas a month (separate ceilings for each occupational class).

e   No contribution for medical care but contribution required for cash benefit from both employer and employee. For Employer: Cash benefits 6.23 percent of payroll. Employee, 2.95 percent of wages.

f   This is a dual social insurance systems. National Health Insurance provides medical benefits, Employees Health Insurance provides cash and medical benefits.

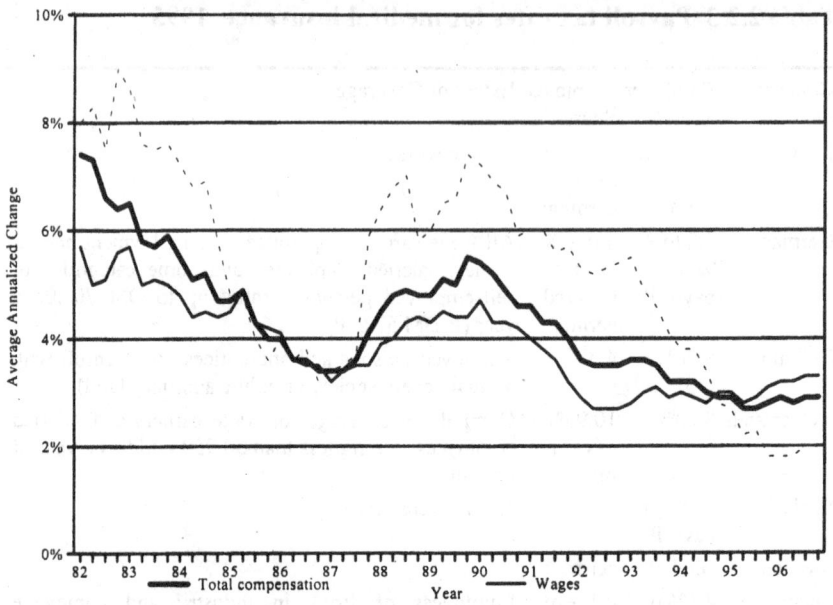

Figure 2.2.1　Change in employment cost index
Source:　US Bureau of Labor Statistics, Employment Cost Index, seasonally adjusted annual average change.

Other evidence related to the impact of fringe benefits on employment

There is empirical evidence suggesting that the use of part-time workers has increased. Between 1968 and 1993, the percentage of workers employed part-time increased from 14.9 percent to 18.8 percent. The peak year for part-time employment was 1982, when 20.2 percent worked part-time. Since 1980 (the year immediately after the imposition of the nondiscrimination law), the proportion of the workforce working part-time has never dipped below 18 percent.[13]

There is also some evidence that firms have raised their levels of outside contracting. Abraham and Taylor (1996) use U.S. Bureau of Labor Statistics data to provide evidence that firms have increasingly resorted to outsourcing some services. Over the period from 1972 to 1993, evidence suggests that building services establishments grew 288 percent, compared to total nonagricultural employment's growth of 50 percent. Similarly high rates of growth occurred in engineering and architectural services (124 percent), and accounting, auditing and bookkeeping employment (151 percent). In addition, using an establishment level sample from the Industry Wage Surveys from 1979 to 1986, they also find that the proportion of firms contracting out these services grew over the period, especially janitorial services and computer services, accounting for significant portions of the growth in employment in these industries (ranging from 20 to 40 percent).

The relationship between wages and employment of workers has been the focus of empirical literature over the years. A small subset of this literature has specifically focussed on the effect of employee benefits on the employment of workers (especially low-wage workers) and the hours worked by these workers. Cutler and Madrian (1996) examine the implications of quasi-fixed labor costs on hours demanded per worker. Although their theoretical construct does not distinguish between offering health insurance benefits to some or all workers, specifically the possibility of excluding part-time workers from eligibility, their findings suggest that rising health insurance costs have increased hours worked by 3 percent, controlling for changes in the demand for skilled workers and predicted wages (since benefits are likely to be correlated with wages).

Theoretical approach

Firms make several decisions in the employment process, deciding whether it pays to offer health insurance to their employees, whether to hire workers full-time or part-time, and what wages to pay to workers. (Or, in the prototype European case, they decide whether to hire a worker, whether to hire him or her full- or part-time, and the wages to offer.) In response, workers choose from an array of employment opportunities that may differ across several characteristics, including insurance coverage, hours, and wages. How do health insurance costs, and specifically the nondiscrimination clause, affect these decisions? This is the issue of importance here, because we are exploring the possibility that health insurance costs and the nondiscrimination clause are affecting the employment prospects and wages of low-wage workers relative to high-wage workers.

The hiring decision process can be simplified to these steps: (1) the firm decides whether to offer health insurance to any employees, (2) the firm then makes hiring decisions, including which workers to hire for full- and part-time work, and (3) the individual chooses to work as a full-time/part-time worker at a firm that offers/does not offer health insurance benefits at a given wage. (The first step is eliminated and the third simplified in a case such as Germany, where all firms are required to offer coverage. If, however, firms can make choices among alternative providers of insurance, or Sickness Funds, then this choice must be added to the process and there will also be three steps in this simple hiring model.)

Insurance offer decision

Employers offer insurance if the benefits of offering insurance to employees exceed the costs associated with this decision, i.e., if the firm increases profit by offering insurance benefits to employees. On the face of it, the costs of insurance to the employer are equal to the premiums paid on behalf of employees. However, the decision is much more complicated than that. Since employers pass most of the costs of employer-sponsored coverage onto employees (Gruber and Krueger, 1991), then it might seem that neither employers nor employees would face incentives to obtain insurance coverage through the workplace. This point ignores some important factors that encourage employers to offer insurance to their employees.

First, employees could prefer to obtain their health insurance through their employer (rather than from some other source) and employers, in order to maximize their production, would seek to accommodate these employees by acting as their 'agent' in the health insurance process. Employees might prefer employer-sponsored health insurance because employees can obtain insurance at a cheaper price when it is obtained through the employer, primarily because insurance purchased through employers is excluded from income taxation (Pauly, 1986; Feldstein, 1973) and because employees are often able to obtain insurance at a lower premium than would be offered to individuals because of lower loading fees in the employer group (Congressional Budget Office, 1991). Second, employers could reap some direct and indirect benefits from offering insurance if the productivity of workers increases when the employer offers insurance. This could occur if offering insurance allows the firm to attract higher-quality employees for some occupations, discourages employee turnover, and/or increases workers' health status through increased access to medical care.

To the firm, the cost of providing insurance includes two components: (1) the direct costs of administering the insurance through the firm, and (2) the net costs of the insurance to the employer after some share of these costs has been passed on to the employee. As noted above, this share may be significantly less than 100 percent of the employer-paid health insurance premium (Loprest et al., 1994).

Up to this point, it has been assumed that employers offer insurance either to all their employees or to none, and no distinction has been made between total employment and total hours worked. When employers have the flexibility to hire some workers full-time, some part-time, and outsource some employment, then they can selectively provide insurance to only certain of these employees; in such cases, the impact of insurance on employment and earnings becomes more complex. This also adds the potential for differential impact on high-wage and low-wage workers. Unless the full costs of benefits are borne by all employees, increasing benefit levels will lead to demand curves shifting further downwards for firms that offer benefits; to the extent that high-wage workers bear the full cost or nearly the full cost but low-wage workers bear a smaller share, employment effects will be more likely and larger for low-wage workers. As noted above, two federal regulations - the minimum wage and nondiscrimination laws - will exacerbate these problems, as employers will have an incentive to demand fewer workers than are willing to work at the minimum-wage level or to increasingly substitute part-time/temporary workers for full-time workers. At the same time, since health insurance is a fixed per-worker cost, firms that still offer the benefits will demand more hours from insured workers.

Firms working in countries with payroll-tax-based health coverage will face a somewhat different set of incentives. In those with such a tax and a minimum wage, the cost of low-wage workers will be increased, and fewer may be hired (demand will be reduced.) Workers in other countries without these mandates or constraints may be more fully employed, 'off the book' employees may be used, or capital may replace these low-wage workers. In countries with a ceiling or cap on the level of wages subject to the payroll tax, low-wage workers who are employed may be expected to work overtime. Such a ceiling or cap may also lead to some substitution of higher-wage workers for low-wage workers.

Our model suggests that rising health insurance premiums will shift the labor demand curves of those firms offering benefits downward, making employment effects more likely. Firms may then find it profitable to offer the benefits to only some workers, particularly if high-wage workers value the provision of fringe benefits more than low-wage workers. For low-wage workers, it is increasingly likely that the nondiscrimination and minimum wage laws will lead the firms to demand fewer workers than are willing to work at that wage/benefit level, leading firms increasingly to substitute part-time/temporary workers. At the same time, since health insurance is a fixed per-worker cost, firms that still offer the benefits will demand more hours from insured workers.

This gives rise to two key hypotheses for empirical testing in this article:

1. Firms that offer health insurance will be less likely to hire low-wage workers.
2. Firms that offer health insurance are more likely to hire low-wage workers to work part-time.

In fact, since we use individuals as the unit of observation rather than firms, we actually test the following two hypotheses:

1. Low-wage workers will be less likely to work for firms that offer health insurance.
2. Low-wage workers will be more likely to work part-time for firms that offer health insurance and be denied an individual offer of benefits.

Econometric methods

We are interested here in two important related decisions of employers and employees, both affected by the size of health insurance premiums: (a) whether the employee is offered insurance coverage by their employer, and (b) whether the employee works part-time or full-time. These probabilities can be expressed as: $P(I=1|X_{oi})$ for the probability that the worker is offered insurance and $P(PT=1|X_{pi})$ for the probability that the worker works part-time, where $I=1$ if worker i is offered insurance, $PT_i=1$ if the worker works part-time. The decisions are assumed to be a function of characteristics affecting the offer decision (denoted as X_{oi}), as well as characteristics affecting the acceptance decision (X_{pi}).

Here, this decision process can be modeled using two equations: (a) an equation that explains the relationship between individual characteristics and the probability of getting an insurance offer, and (b) an equation that explains the relationship between individual characteristics and the probability of working part-time. Following standard analysis of decision models in the economics literature (Greene, 1993), these probabilities can be modeled in the following way:

$$Offer^*_i = X_{oi}{}^* b_o + \_o \quad (1)$$
$$Parttime^*_i = X_p{}^* b_p + \_p$$
$$Offer_i, Parttime_i = 1 \text{ if } Offer^*_i, Parttime^*_i > 0, \text{ else} = 0$$
$$\_o, \_p \sim h(0,0,1,r)$$

Offer and Part-time are not observed directly, but observed if for individual i their value exceeds zero.

Given the correlation between these two decisions, a bivariate probit model is the appropriate method for estimation of these equations (Greene, 1993). In this model, the error terms are assumed to have a bivariate standard normal distribution with correlation r. Modeling these probabilities as a bivariate probit allows estimation of the correlation between the unobserved factors that affect both the probability of being offered insurance and the probability of working only part-time. It is important to estimate these equations with the possibility that the errors are correlated, because assuming r=0 could introduce bias into the measured coefficients. A positive correlation would indicate that workers with offers of health insurance would be more likely to work part-time and a negative correlation would indicate the opposite. A priori we expect the sign to be negative.

It is likely that firms will make three decisions simultaneously: whether it pays to offer health insurance to its employees, whether to hire workers full-time or part-time and what wages to pay to workers. Thus, examining the relationship between insurance offers and benefits, hours, and wages should ideally be done within the context of a simultaneous equations model. In this article, we simplify and estimate the *Wages* model first and then employ this equation to create a predicted value of wages which is included in our bivariate model of part-time and offered health insurance (our measure of benefits.)

We estimate equation (2), and substitute the resulting predicted wages from equation (5) into the bivariate probit model, represented by equations (3) and (4).

$$Wages = \alpha_0 + \alpha_1 *Offer + \alpha_2 *Parttime + \alpha_3 * Winst + A*X + \_{}_i \quad (2)$$
$$Parttime = \beta_0 + \beta_1 *Offer + \beta_2 *Parttime + \beta_3 * Hinst + B*X + \_{}_p \quad (3)$$
$$Offer = \gamma_0 + \gamma_1 * Premium + \gamma_2 *wages + \gamma_3 OInst + \Gamma *X + \_{}_{o'} \quad (4)$$
$$Wages = \_{}_0 + \_{}_3 * Winst + \_ *X \quad (5)$$

where X are worker/job characteristics, $\_{}_i$ are the estimated coefficients from equation (2), and *WInst, HInst,* and *OInst* are instrumental variables for wages, part-time status, and offer.[14] The coefficients of equation (2) will be biased with the inclusion of endogenous variables on the right hand side, but including this prediction does not bias the coefficient estimates in equations (3) and (4) because only the exogenous variables are used to form the prediction, and the result is a wage based on working full-time with the overall or mean probability of being offered fringe benefits.

Data

Ideally, in order to test this model, we would utilize data on employees collected within firms so that we would have matched firm and employee data. Unfortunately, such data are not available. Instead we use data on employees which are unique in the level of detail on benefits provided by the firms for whom they work. Data from the Survey of Employee Benefits supplement to the May 1988 and April 1993 Current Population Surveys (CPS) are used to answer the questions posed here.[15] These supplemental surveys are very rich in detailed information on employment and on health insurance coverage. Although the supplements include only employed persons over age 14, information about the socioeconomic, demographic, and health insurance status of all households common to the two months is available on the file containing the Survey of Employee Benefits supplement. The Census Bureau has merged the files so that data from each of the three months are available for each individual in each houschold.

In both the 1988 and 1993 surveys, employed workers (age 14 and older) were asked whether they were covered by employer-provided health insurance, and if not, why not. Some people worked for firms that offered coverage to the workers in the firm, some did not. Some workers in firms offering coverage were not offered employer insurance for various reasons, while others rejected coverage even when it was offered. Thus, it is possible to know (1) if the individual works for a firm that offers coverage; (2) whether they were offered coverage and (3) if the individual accepted. This is unusual in that most surveys with health insurance coverage simply obtain data on whether they are currently covered and if so by what type of insurance, and if they have been covered all year.[16]

For the data used here, the characteristics of each adult respondent (worker) are linked to everyone else in their family, including spouses and children. This is important because the spouse characteristics may help to determine how the decisions of employees are impacted by the characteristics and decisions of the spouse. This is especially important under two circumstances: first, the insurance coverage of a worker's spouse could be an important determinant of a worker's decision to accept jobs with and without insurance offers. Second, the characteristics of a spouse, especially the availability of insurance coverage from a spouse, are likely to impact a worker's decision to work full-time or part-time. For example, since part-time jobs are less likely to offer insurance coverage, a worker will be less likely to accept a part-time job if the other worker is not covered by health insurance.

We omit from our sample workers with missing information on their probability of offer, those who have no wage information, or those whose imputed hourly wage is less than $1 or greater than $250. We also omit self-employed workers, since their decision to buy insurance is very different from a firm's decision to provide insurance for its workforce. Respondents older than age 65 are excluded as well, since they are covered by Medicare.[17]

Table 2.2.4 Variable definitions, means and standard deviations

Variable	Definition	Full sample		Weighted Mean, Full Sample s		LOWWAGE Workers (Wage> LOWCUT)		HIGHWAGE Workers (Wage> LOWCUT)	
		Mean	(S.E.)						
FOFFER	= 1 if firm offers health insurance, else 0	.834	(.372)	.830	(.782)	.550	(.498)	.885	(.319)
IOFFER	= 1 if firm offers to worker, else 0	.773	(.419)	.767	(.880)	.383	(.486)	.843	(.364)
ACCEPT	= 1 if covered by employer, else 0	.665	(.472)	.663	(.984)	.223	(.417)	.745	(.436)
RHICOST[a]	Employer premium imputation	1972	(773)	1998	(1611)	2167	(591)	1937	(796)
PARTTIME	= 1 if PARTTIME	.164	(.370)	.162	(.766)	.453	(.498)	.111	(.314)
WAGE!	Hourly wage, if known, else usual weekly earnings/ usual hours	9.94	(7.62)	10.00	(16.33)	3.72	(.760)	11.06	(7.76)
LOWCUT	Real minimum wage + RHICOST/1750	4.52	(.448)	4.54	(.933)	4.64	(.361)	4.50	(.459)
LOW WAGE	=1 if real hourly wage<LOWCUT	.153	(.360)	.157	(.756)	—		—	
AGE	Age/100	.376	(.118)	.372	(.247)	.336	(.140)	.383	(.112)
MALE	= 1 if male	.506	(.500)	.520	(1.04)	.331	(.471)	.538	(.499)
MIDWEST	= 1 if Census region midwest	.261	(.439)	.251	(.903)	.293	(.455)	.255	(.436)
NEAST	= 1 if Census region northeast	.225	(.418)	.198	(.829)	.170	(.376)	.235	(.424)
WEST[b]	= 1 if Census region west	.200	(.400)	.204	(.840)	.187	(.390)	.202	(.401)
FRM1000	Firm size>1000	.412	(.492)	.421	(1.03)	.262	(.440)	.439	(.496)
FIRMMED[c]	100<Firm size≤1000	.185	(.389)	.180	(.800)	.124	(.330)	.196	(.397)
INDMAN	Manufacturing industry	.196	(.397)	.201	(.834)	.114	(.318)	.211	(.408)
INDFIN	Finance industry	.0663	(.249)	.0691	(.528)	.0285	(.167)	.0732	(.260)
INDTRADE	Trade industry	.191	(.393)	.195	(.826)	.406	(.491)	.152	(.359)
INDTRANS[d]	Transportation industry	.0767	(.266)	.0772	(.556)	.0254	(.157)	.0860	(.280)
AHRSWK	Usual Hours	37.31	(13.76)	37.06	(28.80)	32.39	(16.61)	38.19	(12.99)
OCCOPER	Operator occupations	.227	(.419)	.228	(.874)	.186	(.389)	.234	(.424)
OCCPROF	Professional services occupations	.254	(.435)	.246	(.897)	.0814	(.273)	.284	(.451)
OCCSERV[e]	Service occupations	.121	(.326)	.121	(.679)	.302	(.459)	.0877	(.283)
SINC2030	20,000<Spouse Income≤30,000	.122	(.327)	.118	(.672)	.0911	(.288)	.128	(.334)
SINC3040	30,000< Spouse Income≤40,000	.0645	(.246)	.0618	(.501)	.0432	(.203)	.0684	(.252)
SINC40P[f]	Spouse Income>40,000	.0553	(.229)	.0546	(.473)	.0356	(.185)	.0588	(.235)
Y1992	% in 1992 data	.479	(.500)	.499	(1.04)	.574	(.495)	.461	(.499)
CLASGOV	Gov. class of worker	.194	(.396)	.182	(.803)	.0970	(.296)	.212	(.409)
HHSIZE	Household size	3.12	(1.46)	3.11	(3.08)	3.35	(1.67)	3.08	(1.42)
KIDLT6	Child < 6 in household	.237	(.425)	.230	(.877)	.194	(.395)	.245	(.430)
FKIDLT6	Female w/child < 6 in household	.109	(.311)	.102	(.630)	.143	(.350)	.102	(.304)
EDUCHS	Highest education level, high school	.477	(.499)	.477	(1.04)	.619	(.486)	.451	(.498)
EDUCCOLL	Highest education level, some college	.488	(.500)	.486	(1.04)	.309	(.462)	.520	(.500)
URBAN	= 1 if urban	.724	(.447)	.795	(.841)	.620	(.485)	.743	(.437)

Table 2.2.4 (continued)

NONWHITE	= 1 if nonwhite	.121	(.326)	.143	(.729)	.151	(.358)	.115	(.319)
TENLT1YR	Job tenure < 1yr	.169	(.375)	.174	(.789)	.373	(.484)	.132	(.338)
TEN1T4	1–4 years job tenure	.355	(.479)	.363	(1.00)	.435	(.496)	.340	(.474)
TEN5T9[h]	5–9 years job tenure	.192	(.394)	.188	(.814)	.107	(.309)	.207	(.405)
UNION	= 1 if covered by collective bargaining contract/union	.203	(.402)	.205	(.841)	.0468	(.211)	.231	(.422)
FOFFPEN	Firm offers pension	.649	(.477)	.646	(.996)	.398	(.487)	.696	(.460)
MARRIED	= 1 if married	.640	(.480)	.619	(1.01)	.468	(.499)	.671	(.470)
FMARR	(1-MALE)*MARRIED	.300	(.458)	.282	(.936)	.358	(.480)	.291	(.454)
SPINS	Spouse has health insurance	.523	(.499)	.499	(1.04)	.311	(.463)	.562	(.496)
N		35,382		35,382		5,431		29,951	

Source: 1988 and 1993 CPS, Employee Benefits Supplement, excluding self-employed.
Notes: All variables in 1988 real dollars.
a   Source: Nelson imputation from NMCES and CPS.
b   Omitted category, south.
c   Omitted category, firm size less than 100 workers.
d   Omitted category, service industries.
e   Omitted category, technical occupations.
f   Omitted category, spouse income less than $20,000.
g   Omitted category, highest level of education, primary.
h   Omitted category, ten or more years of tenure.

Descriptive results

Table 2.2.4 presents the definitions of variables used here, with descriptive statistics for each variable in the entire sample. In the table, the first three variables describe the nature of the health benefits offered by the firm. These are followed by our estimate of the direct cost to the firm of providing health insurance; which is based on a procedure developed for imputation to the CPS by Charles Nelson of the Census Bureau.[18] Individual and firm characteristics follow. Four sets of descriptive statistics are presented: the full, merged sample from 1988 and 1993, this sample weighted and two subsamples (low-wage workers and higher-wage workers). We separate out low-wage workers as they are the group for whom a firm will be less able to pass on the full cost of the health insurance premium even if they were to work full-time. This group is the central focus of this study. The cost of the health insurance premium and the minimum wage are both employed in defining the low-wage and non-low-wage groups. Roughly 15 percent of the sample falls into this category.[19]

Turning to the insurance coverage variables, as expected according to the definitions of the three variables on insurance coverage, the highest proportion of workers are employed by a firm that offers coverage (83 percent) but a smaller proportion are themselves offered coverage (77 percent). Only two-thirds of all workers actually accept an offer.[20] However, the interesting feature to note from this table is that the probability of firm offer, individual offer, and part-time status vary between the groups of workers in ways that are consistent with the hypotheses identified above. High-wage workers are far less likely to work part-time, are far more likely to work for firms that offer health insurance benefits, and are much more likely to have an individual offer. High-wage workers are more than twice as likely as low-wage workers to have an insurance offer. Perhaps unexpectedly, the reported average premium cost for the employer share of health insurance is nearly $200 (or nearly 12 percent) higher for their firms as reported by low-wage workers compared to the value reported by high-wage workers. Most likely this reflects the likelihood that low-wage workers have lower overall health, tend to work for firms in which the employees face greater risks, or work for smaller firms which face higher risk premiums and/or administrative charges. For example, low-wage workers are more likely to work for smaller firms. Unfortunately, from the perspective of wishing to achieve greater health insurance coverage, the very last variable in the table shows that not only are the low-wage workers less likely to be offered coverage in their own employment, but they are also less likely to have a spouse who has health insurance coverage.

Low-wage workers are *far* more likely - more than four times as likely - to be employed part-time than are high-wage workers; nearly 50 percent of the low-wage workers in our sample work part-time. This compares to the overall weighted proportion of about 16 percent. Low-wage workers differ in other ways from the average or the high-wage worker in our sample. They are somewhat younger than the high-wage workers in our sample (33.6 compared to 38.3 years on average), more likely to be female (nearly two-thirds compared to just under half); less likely to work for the largest-size firms, much more likely to be employed in a trade or in the service industry, less likely to work for the government sector, and less likely to have any education above high school. They are somewhat more likely to live in the industrial Midwest than in the Northeast or West. Perhaps surprisingly, they are not more likely to have young children than higher-wage workers.

Table 2.2.5 Weighted probabilities of characteristics, conditional on FOFFER

Pr(X | FOFFER)	No Firm Offer	Firm Offer
PARTTIME, LOWWAGE	2149	404
PARTTIME, HIGHWAGE	1546	786
FULLTIME, LOWWAGE	2081	617
FULLTIME, HIGHWAGE	4224	8194
PARTTIME, Wage<$6	28.34	660
PARTTIME, Wage≥$6	861	529
FULLTIME, Wage<$6	3309	1624
FULLTIME, Wage≥$6	2995	7186
Tenure <1 Year	3153	1427
1–4 Years of Tenure	4426	3414
5–9 Years of Tenure	1357	1963
10+ Years of Tenure	1065	3196
Less Than High School	865	273
High School	5845	4547
Some College	3289	5180
INDALLOT	5363	4411
INDFIN	387	753
INDMAN	865	2245
INDTRANS	335	862
INDTRADE	3050	1729
OCCTECH	4346	3986
OCCOPER	2228	2291
OCCPROF	1210	2720
OCCSERV	2216	1004

Source: Authors' calculations from 1988 and 1993 CPS, Employee Benefits Supplement.

The variable means and standard deviations for the two sample years separately are presented in Appendix 2 (Appendix Table 2.2.1). The probability of firm offer, individual offer, and coverage has declined over time, and the imputed premium cost to the employer has grown in real terms over this period. In addition, these results show an increasing trend toward more part-time work over this six-year period. They also show the increasing share of workers who are in the low-wage sample rather than the high-wage sample (12.5 to 18.3). This is consistent with the hypothesis that the increasing cost of health insurance has led to a decline in full-time options for low-skilled workers.

Table 2.2.5 provides a more detailed exploration of the tie between worker characteristics and whether or not the firm for which they work offers coverage. We interpret it here as the demand side of the labor market.[21] The results show a very different pattern of distribution of part-time and low-wage by the two types of firms; firms that offer coverage and those that do not. Those who work for firms that offer coverage are more than twice as likely to be full-time, high-wage workers than those who work for firms that do not offer coverage (compare 82 to 42 percent). On the other hand, less than 5 percent of workers in firms that offer insurance are low-wage part-time workers compared to more than 21 percent in firms which do not offer coverage. Firms that offer coverage also have a far smaller proportion (6 versus 21 percent) of workers who work full-time but are low-wage workers. Combining the low-wage groups we find that more than 40 percent of the workforce of firms that do not offer coverage is made up of low-wage workers, as compared to only slightly more than 10 percent of the workforce of firms that offer insurance. Again, this is likely to reflect the inability of firms to pass the cost of the health insurance premium fully to these workers. The remaining cells are also consistent with expectations. They suggest that firms which offer coverage may well 'discriminate against' low-wage workers; they hire a limited number, and of these, hire few to work full-time, which would make them eligible for the health insurance benefit.[22]

Table 2.2.6 Probability of offer, conditional on part-time/wage status

Offer	PARTTIME LOWWAGE	PARTTIME HIGHWAGE	FULLTIME LOWWAGE	FULLTIME HIGHWAGE
FOFFER	49.15	71.62	59.92	90.66
IOFFER	24.62	51.93	49.71	88.37
ACCEPT	8.16	30.83	34.14	79.92
% of sample	6.96	9.42	8.39	75.23
Workers with firm offer, job tenure over one year only				
IOFFER	54.32	76.14	92.04	98.81
% of subsample	2.87	7.75	4.65	84.73

Table 2.2.6 explores the tie between health insurance coverage and work characteristics. Perhaps most striking is the difference in probability of offer and coverage by low- and high-wage and part-time/full-time status, shown in the top section of Table 2.2.6. Less than half of low-wage/part-time workers work for a firm that offers health insurance benefits to anyone in the firm, compared to 91 percent of high-wage/full-time workers. The difference in the probability of individual offer is even more striking, since only a quarter of part-time/low-wage workers have an offer of health insurance benefits through their employer, compared to 88 percent of full-time/high-wage workers, and roughly half of full-time/low-wage workers and part-time/high-wage workers. While these results show that firms are much less likely to offer benefits to part-time workers, it might also reflect the short job tenures of low-wage and part-time workers, since workers with short job tenures are often denied coverage until a specified period (rarely exceeding one year). To isolate these effects, the bottom panel of Table 2.2.6 presents these values for workers who are (1) employed by a firm that offers coverage to at least some of its employees and (2) have a job tenure of more than one year. The results indicate that even part-time workers with tenures exceeding one year are less likely to be offered insurance, with only slightly more than half of the part-time low-wage workers offered coverage compared to more than three-quarters of the part-time high-wage workers. However, nearly all of the low-wage full-time workers are offered coverage, as would be required by the nondiscrimination laws. One other factor is of note however; only 7.5 percent of the workforce of these firms is made up of low-wage workers - less than half of the overall proportion of low-wage workers.

These sample descriptive statistics clearly suggest that firms are acting to minimize their cost of health insurance coverage. The outcome of this is that low-skilled workers face very limited opportunities to work for firms that offer health insurance benefits. This could also be viewed as firms taking advantage of the loopholes in the nondiscrimination law. However, simple descriptive statistics do not provide evidence of causality. For example, it might be that all of these worker characteristics are correlated with skill level and firm characteristics which affect both the probability of part-time work and the probability of health insurance offer. To address these possibilities, a more complete multivariate analysis designed to provide a better test of our model follows.

Econometric results

Table 2.2.7 presents the core bivariate probit regression results for the model with two dependent variables: part-time and working for a firm that offers health insurance. The estimates are presented for the entire sample and separately for low-wage and high-wage workers. The separation is based on our calculation of whether or not the firm can pass on the cost of health insurance to the workers if they were to work full-time. For each subsample, the models are estimated with and without a variable measuring the predicted wage; the results change in minor ways between the two models, and, as one would expect, become slightly less precise with the addition of the predicted wage.

The primary purpose of these estimates is to measure the limit on opportunities due to the cost of insurance and the requirement of nondiscrimination rules. Thus the estimation models need to (and do) control for a wide variety of other factors that might lead workers to chose to work part-time (presence of young children), or to work for a firm that does not offer coverage (spouse has coverage). The control variables used here include background sociodemographic characteristics, several variables measuring the income of one's spouse for those with a spouse, and a variety of measures describing the worker's job. Also included in the FOFFER equation is the expected cost to the firm of offering coverage and whether or not one's spouse has health coverage through his or her own place of employment. The model is identified by the inclusion of presence of young children and the interaction with sex, household size, and spouse income, which are only included in the part-time equation and by the inclusion of the cost of health insurance to the firm and of whether or not one's spouse has employer-based coverage in the offer equation. The resulting coefficients on these control variables are consistent with expected relationships based on existing literature.

The results seem to support the central hypotheses identified above. In particular, workers who are more likely to work in firms that offer health insurance coverage are less likely to work part-time in these firms. This result is found by noting that the signs are reversed on several of the variables in the two equations, especially those reflecting job characteristics: firm size, industry, occupation, union coverage, job tenure, and educational status. To cite a specific example, the signs on the coefficients indicate that a worker working for a large firm is more likely to work in a firm that offers insurance coverage, but less likely to work part-time for that firm. This finding is consistent with the central hypotheses explored here, because it indicates that jobs that offer insurance coverage are also less likely to be part-time jobs. Another result which supports our central hypotheses is the estimated correlation, or r, between the two equations, which is negative and significant in all circumstances. This result provides evidence that unmeasured worker characteristics that are associated with firm offers of insurance are also associated with lower probabilities of part-time work, again suggesting that firms that offer insurance coverage are less likely to hire workers part-time (unless they are low-wage workers).

Table 2.2.7 Bivariate probit estimation results, dependent variable = PARTTIME, FOFFER

Variable	Full Sample				HIGHWAGE Sample				LOWWAGE Sample			
	Model 1		Model 2		Model 1		Model 2		Model 1		Model 2	
PARTTIME Equation												
Constant	0.44	(.12)*	.32	(.13)*	-.14	-0.15	-.20	-0.16	.51	(.22)*	0.37	(.29)*
CLASGOV	0.01	-0.028	0.03	-0.029	-0.1	(.032)*	-0.1	(.033)*	.44	(.071)*	.46	(.073)*
AGE	-13.3	(.51)*	-14.11	(.65)*	-10.91	(.64)*	-11.56	(.81)*	-12.6	(1.00)*	-13.4	(1.40)*
AGE2	17.2	(.65)*	18.09	(.77)*	14.39	(.79)*	15.09	(.95)*	17.00	(1.29)*	17.79	(1.67)*
FIRMMED	-0.2	(.027)*	-.20	(.027)*	-.16	(.032)*	-.17	(.032)*	-.21	(.061)*	-.21	(.061)*
FIRM1000	-0.15	(.023)*	-.17	(.024)*	-.14	(.027)*	-0.16	(.029)*	-.039	-0.046	-.055	(.051)*
INDFIN	0.15	(.050)*	.14	(.050)*	.11	(.056)*	.10	-0.056	.57	(.12)*	.56	(.13)*
INDALLOT	.57	(.034)*	.57	(.034)*	.54	(.040)*	.54	(.040)*	.69	(.074)*	.69	(.074)*
INDTRADE	0.69	(.036)*	.72	(.040)*	0.5	(.044)*	0.52	(.048)*	.79	(.074)*	.82	(.085)*
INDTRANS	0.48	(.049)*	0.45	(.051)*	.47	(.054)*	.45	(.056)*	.56	(.14)*	.53	(.14)*
MALE	-0.2	(.031)*	-.27	(.043)*	-.15	(.039)*	-.21	(.056)*	-.12	(.054)*	-.18	(.092)*
OCCPER	0.09	(.030)*	.11	(.031)*	.048	(.036)*	.063	(.038)*	.13	(.059)*	.14	(.062)*
OCCPROF	-0.23	(.027)*	-.31	(.044)*	-.19	(.031)*	-.24	(.051)*	-.22	(.075)*	-.28	(.11)*
OCCSERV	0.35	(.027)*	.38	(.032)*	.33	(.037)*	.36	(.043)*	0.1	(.045)*	.13	(.063)*
EDUCHS	-0.16	(.050)*	-.21	(.053)*	-0.13	(.068)*	-.16	(.073)*	-.017	-0.079	-.051	-0.092
EDUCCOLL	-0.1	-0.052	-.18	(.066)*	-.057	-0.07	-.12	-0.088	0.24	(.085)*	.17	-0.13
NONWHITE	-0.11	(.028)*	-.083	(.031)*	-.15	(.035)*	-0.13	(.038)*	-.14	(.053)*	-0.13	(.059)*
UNION	-0.18	(.029)*	-.21	(.033)*	-.10	(.031)*	-.13	(.036)*	-.014	-0.096	-.038	-0.1
MARRIED	-0.54	(.037)*	-.57	(.039)*	-.47	(.044)*	-0.49	(.047)*	-.53	(.086)*	-.55	(.090)*
FMARR	0.67	(.045)*	.68	(.045)*	.67	(.054)*	.68	(.054)*	.55	(.097)*	0.56	(.098)*
TENLT1YR	0.65	(.033)*	.72	(.048)*	0.52	(.039)*	.58	(.058)*	.55	(.084)*	.62	(.12)*
TEN1T4	0.42	(.030)*	.48	(.040)*	.35	(.033)*	0.39	(.046)*	.44	(.082)*	.49	(.11)*
TEN5T9	0.19	(.033)*	.22	(.037)*	.18	(.036)*	.20	(.040)*	.22	(.094)*	.25	(.10)*
URBAN	-0.13	(.021)*	-.17	(.028)*	-.074	(.026)*	-.11	(.036)*	0	-0.039	-.053	-0.06

Table 2.2.7 (continued)

Variable	Full Sample Model 1		Full Sample Model 2		HIGHWAGE Sample Model 1		HIGHWAGE Sample Model 2		LOWWAGE Sample Model 1		LOWWAGE Sample Model 2	
Y1993	0.13	(.019)*	.14	(.019)*	.11	(.023)*	.12	(.023)*	-.044	-0.039	-.038	(.040)*
PWAGE	—		.042	-0.019	—		.029	-0.022	—		.040	-0.055
SINC2030	0.15	(.033)*	.15	(.033)*	.096	(.038)*	.095	(.038)*	.30	(.071)*	.30	(.071)*
SINC3040	0.33	(.040)*	.33	(.040)*	.31	(.045)*	.30	(.045)*	.37	(.097)*	.36	(.097)*
SINC40P	0.53	(.040)*	0.52	(.040)*	.50	(.045)*	.49	(.045)*	.51	(.11)*	.50	(.11)*
HHSIZE	0.11	(.0067)*	0.11	(.0067)*	.11	(.0085)*	.11	(.0086)*	.083	(.012)*	.083	(.012)*
KIDLT6	-0.18	(.046)*	-.18	(.046)*	-.17	(.053)*	-.16	(.053)*	-.17	-0.11	-.16	-0.11
FKIDLT6	0.35	(.053)*	.35	(.053)*	.40	(.061)*	.40	(.061)*	.22	-0.12	0.22	-0.12
INDALLOT	-0.7	(.033)*	-.70	(.033)*	-.69	(.038)*	-.69	(.038)*	-.75	(.076)*	-.75	(.076)*
INDTRADE	-0.68	(.036)*	-.67	(.040)*	-.53	(.043)*	-.50	(.049)*	-.75	(.074)*	-.75	(.084)*
INDTRANS	-0.31	(.051)*	-.32	(.053)*	-.32	(.056)*	-.34	(.058)*	-.34	(.15)*	-.33	(.15)*
MALE	0	-0.031	-.045	(.045)*	-.10	(.040)*	-.16	(.058)*	-.095	(.054)*	-.081	(.096)*
OCCOPER	-.092	(.028)*	-.087	(.030)*	-.098	(.033)*	-.081	(.035)*	-.070	-0.06	-.073	-0.063
OCCPROF	0.19	(.029)*	.17	(.047)*	.17	(.033)*	.11	(.054)*	.080	-0.077	.097	-0.12
OCCSERV	-0.24	(.029)*	-.23	(.035)*	-.17	(.040)*	-.14	(.046)*	-.056	-0.047	-.065	-0.067
EDUCHS	0.42	(.049)*	.41	(.053)*	.31	(.062)*	.28	(.068)*	.42	(.086)*	.43	(.098)*
EDUCCOLL	0.63	(.051)*	.61	(.068)*	.50	(.064)*	.42	(.086)*	.52	(.091)*	.54	(.14)*
NONWHITE	-0.15	(.029)*	-.15	(.031)*	-.15	(.036)*	-.13	(.038)*	-.043	-0.053	-.048	-0.059
UNION	0.4	(.035)*	.39	(.038)*	.31	(.038)*	.29	(.042)*	.63	(.11)*	.64	(.11)*
MARRIED	-0.12	(.038)*	-.13	(.040)*	-.16	(.045)*	-.17	(.047)*	-.060	-0.082	-.055	-0.086
FMARR	0.19	(.040)*	.19	(.041)*	-.20	(.049)*	-.19	(.050)*	-.13	-0.087	-.13	-0.088
TENLT1YR	-0.68	(.035)*	-.66	(.052)*	-.65	(.040)*	-.59	(.061)*	-.34	(.087)*	-.36	(.12)*
TEN1T4	-0.48	(.032)*	-.46	(.043)*	-.45	(.036)*	-.40	(.050)*	-.32	(.085)*	-.33	(.11)*
TEN5T9	-0.22	(.036)*	-.21	(.039)*	-.23	(.040)*	-.21	(.043)*	-.13	(.099)*	-.14	-0.11
URBAN	0.22	(.022)*	.21	(.029)*	0.18	(.026)*	.15	(.037)*	.089	(.042)*	.098	-0.063
Y1993	0	-0.021	-.0075	-0.021	0.01	(.024)	.020	-0.025	.040	-0.045	0.04	-0.047
PWAGE	—		.011	-0.021	—		.033	-0.024	—		-.011	-0.059
SPINS	0.29	(.030)*	.29	(.031)*	.23	(.036)*	.23	(.036)*	.33	(.063)*	.33	(.063)*
RHICOST	-2.09	(.15)*	-2.11	(.15)*	-2.09	(.17)*	-2.13	(.17)*	-.77	(.38)*	-.76	(.38)*
r	-0.32	(.013)*	-.32	(.013)*	-.32	(.017)*	-.32	(.017)*	-.20	(.025)*	-.20	(.025)*
Log-likelihood	21794		21791		15132		15130		5932		5932	
N	33541		33541		287476		287476		5065		5065	

* Statistically significant at the 5% level.
Source: Authors' calculations from 1988 and 1993 CPS, Employee Benefits Supplements.

Also consistent with our hypotheses is the finding that employees who work for firms that face higher costs in providing health insurance are less likely to work for a firm that offers coverage (as reflected in the negative and significant coefficient on the variable RHICOST).[23]

In a related set of estimates, we run the same model but substitute individual offer (IOFFER) for FOFFER as one of the two dependent variables. There are three notable differences in the estimates: (1) larger coefficients and greater significance on the cost of health insurance to the firm (in all six cases the sign remains negative); (2) the predicted wage becomes positive in the low wage sample estimate although it remains not statistically significant; and (3) the r increases in size and statistical significance.[24]

In terms of the control variables, the most significant finding is that persons with very low levels of education (less than high school) are both more likely to work part-time with the exception of the estimates on EDUCCOLL in the part-time portion of the bivariate probit in the low-wage sample and less likely to work for a firm that offers coverage. We interpret this to mean that those with less education (generally low-skilled workers) face limited opportunities for full-time jobs which offer coverage. In the high-wage sample, persons with higher predicted wages are more likely to work for firms which offer coverage. These are the same employees for whom the tax advantage of employer-based coverage is greatest. Low-wage workers who work for the government are able to combine working part-time and working for an employer who offers health insurance.

Finally, we also ran bivariate estimates over the subsample of workers who work for firms which offer coverage to at least some of their employees and who have worked for them for at least one year.[25] A comparison of these results provides a method for exploring the *direct* effects of the nondiscrimination clause on the employment patterns of workers (especially low-wage workers). This is because in these estimates we limit the sample to those workers who would be affected by the nondiscrimination clause, i.e., workers who work for firms that offer coverage and workers that have long enough job tenures to qualify for coverage. The first thing worthy of note is that only 35 percent (N=1,772) of the low-wage workers are included in this sample, compared to nearly 80 percent of the high-wage workers. Thus nearly two-thirds of low-wage workers are either working for firms that do not offer coverage or have worked less than one year for a firm that offers coverage. Additional evidence that firms are using the loophole to exclude part-time workers from coverage comes in the form of a more negative r[26] than estimated in the FOFFER/PARTTIME probit. To illustrate this, think of an extreme example where all firms hire part-time workers, regardless of whether they offer health insurance to some or all workers, but none offer part-time workers individual coverage. In the FOFFER bivariate probit, the r would be equal to zero, but in the IOFFER bivariate probit, the r would be equal to -1. In reality, not all firms hire part-time workers, and not all firms exclude part-timers from their health insurance coverage, so the estimates of the correlations between error terms in the two cases will not be as exact. However, we do find estimates consistent with this story, since the estimates are r=-.32 in the firm offer bivariate probit and r=-.69 in the individual offer bivariate probit.

In further comparisons of the results on these two samples (and of the subsample compared to the full sample) some central findings indicate that:
- large firms are less likely to offer coverage to low-wage employees in this sample, in which only firms that offer coverage are included;
- the higher the cost of health insurance to the firm, the less likely the firm is to offer individual insurance coverage, especially to low-wage workers.

This finding is found by comparing the size and statistical significance of the coefficient on the RHICOST variable in the IOFFER equation to the FOFFER equation. In the case of low-wage subsample estimates, the estimates for the smaller subsample are -1.9 to -2.0, both of which are statistically significant at the 1 percent level. In contrast, as reported in Table 2.2.7, the coefficients are -.77 and -.76, significant at the 5 percent level. This again suggests that firms attempt to reduce their employment cost by avoiding coverage to low-wage workers.

The bivariate probit results allow us to examine the association of one specific variable with the probability of offer or part-time status while controlling for other factors. However, the nonlinearity of the model makes it difficult to gauge the magnitude of the effects measured because the coefficient estimates are not the marginal effects of each variable on the associated probabilities. Some variables affect both the probability of firm offer and part-time, and it is difficult to assess which effect will dominate from looking at the coefficient estimates. To assess the magnitude of measured effects, we compute the predicted joint probabilities of working part-time and working in a firm with an insurance offer using the model results.[27] Predicted probabilities are computed for each respondent in the sample. We start by assigning each respondent the actual values of their observed independent variables. Thus for this 'baseline case,' we simply present the joint predicted probabilities of part-time work and firm offers, compared to the actual sample statistics. The results of this exercise using the FOFFER/PARTTIME regression are reported in Table 2.2.8.A, with similar results employing the IOFFER/PARTTIME regression reported in Table 2.2.8.B.

The strength of this simulation method lies in the ability to estimate directly the marginal effect of a change in worker characteristics on the associated probabilities. This can be accomplished by changing worker characteristics one at a time, while holding all others constant at their observed values, and recomputing the predicted probabilities. For example, the tables isolate the effects of health insurance premiums of various amounts. We highlight these results, as they are closely tied to our hypotheses, and the variation in premiums partially helps us identify our model, since we do not have data from both before and after the nondiscrimination clause.

As developed above, when health insurance premiums are high, or increase significantly, we predict this will have two possible effects on low-wage workers. First, fewer firms will offer insurance, and second, firms that do offer insurance will seek to deny low wage workers coverage, either through hiring low-wage workers part-time or through outsourcing and hence denial of coverage (and employment) to low-wage workers.

Our results tend to confirm these predictions.[28] Table 2.2.8.A shows that as health insurance premiums increase from the sample minimum premium to the sample maximum premium, the probability that a low-wage worker would work for a firm offering insurance declines from 58.0 to 35.6 percent, providing evidence in support of the first hypothesis. (The results for high-wage workers are also consistent with the hypothesis that firms will drop coverage if the cost of the benefit increases substantially, but in both simulations, a larger fraction of high-wage workers are predicted to work for a firm that offers insurance.)

We also have some support for the second hypothesis. Panels A and B of Table 2.2.8 both show that low-wage workers are much less likely to be working part-time for a firm that offers coverage at all (FOFFER = 1) or get an individual offer (IOFFER= 1) as health insurance premiums increase. For example, as health insurance premiums increase from the sample minimum amount to the sample maximum amount, the proportion of low-wage workers working part-time with a firm that offers insurance declines from 24.3 to 13.5 percent, all else equal.[29] But (from panel B), as the size of the health insurance premium increases from the sample minimum to the sample maximum, the proportion of low-wage workers working part-time *and with an individual offer of insurance* declines from 37.6 to 2.8 percent (given that the worker has a job tenure in excess of one year and works for a firm that offers insurance). Both of these findings support the proposition that firms with higher health insurance premiums seek to substitute away from low-wage workers working part-time and with insurance offers.[30]

Table 2.2.8.a **Predicted proportions of workers working part-time and with firm offers of insurance***

	Low wage workers				High wage workers			
	% with firm offer			%	% with firm offer			%
	Total	Part-Time	Full-Time	Part-Time	Total	Part-Time	Full-Time	Part-Time
Actual	55.2	22.3	33	45.4	88.7	8.0	80.8	11.1
Baseline	50.6	20.4	30.3	44	96.8	1.3	95.5	1.7
Real health insurance premium								
Sample minimum	58	24.3	33.7	45.5	99.5	2.4	97.1	2.5
Mean-one S.D.	52.1	21.1	31.1	44.6	98.6	1.8	96.8	2.1
Mean	50.8	20.3	30.5	44.1	97.2	1.4	95.9	1.8
Mean+one S.D.	49.3	19.5	29.7	43.5	94.9	1	93.9	1.6
Sample maximum	35.6	13.5	22.1	39.6	65.3	0.1	65.2	0.8
Education								
Less than high school	35.9	11.1	24.8	34.7	90.8	0.9	89.9	1.8
High school	50.9	16.3	34.6	37.2	96.1	0.9	95.2	1.4
College	55.2	28.0	27.2	57.1	98.2	1.6	96.6	2
Firm size								
< 100	28.4	8.5	19.9	43.1	97.4	1.1	96.3	1.7
Medium (100–999)	96.4	32.9	63.5	34.9	99.9	2.0	98	2
> 1,000	97.9	47.6	50.3	49.1	100.0	2.5	97.5	2.5

* Expected values based on PARTTIME/FOFFER bivariate probit regression.
Source: Authors' calculations based on bivariate probit results reported in Table 2.2.7 (see text for methods).

These findings are also consistent with the expectation that higher premiums will have a greater impact on the probability of offers to low-wage workers than on the probability of offers to high-wage workers. For high-wage workers, the probability of a firm offer does not fall steeply until premiums exceed the mean premium plus one standard deviation. The likelihood of insurance offers declines more rapidly for low-wage workers.

In the analysis of the results from Table 2.2.8.B, recall that only a small subset of low-wage workers works for such firms and hence are included in this table. Nevertheless, it is important to note that as the insurance premium increases, far fewer part-time workers are expected to be offered coverage, but the impact is mostly on low-wage workers. Specifically, as the health insurance premium increases, the proportion of low-wage, part-time workers with an insurance offer decreases from 37.6 percent to 2.8 percent (from the sample minimum to the sample maximum imputed premium). In contrast, the proportion of high-wage, part-time workers with an individual insurance offer decreases only from 3.2 percent to 0.1 percent as the premium increases by the same amount.

The remaining findings presented in Table 2.2.8.A and B present the marginal effect of other key variables that are predictive of part-time work and insurance statuses. They show the following: workers with more education are more likely to work for a firm that offers insurance, regardless of whether they are low- or high-wage earners. Shifting workers to large firms would be expected to increase the probability that they work for a firm that offers insurance, again regardless of income level. Curiously, the proportion of part-time workers is projected to increase as education increases. This finding may reflect an anomalous result for a small group of highly educated low-wage workers. There is a U-shaped effect of firm size associated with the probability of working part-time being lowest in medium-sized firms for low-wage workers, but an increasing fraction of high-wage part-time workers with increasing firm size. In panel B, however, there is a different pattern over firm size for low-wage workers. It appears, given that a firm offers insurance to anyone, that the probability of a low-wage worker having an individual offer of insurance actually *decreases* with firm size, driven by part-time workers being excluded from coverage.

Table 2.2.8.b Predicted proportions of workers working part-time and with firm offers of insurance only for workers with firm offers (FOFFER=1) and job tenure of one year or more*

	Low wage workers				High wage workers			
	% with firm offer			%	% with firm offer			%
	Total	Part-Time	Full-Time	Part-Time	Total	Part-Time	Full-Time	Part-Time
Actual	776	205	571	380	970	64	906	83
Baseline	843	236	607	355	995	25	970	26
Real health insurance premium								
Sample minimum	961	37.6	58.5	41.0	100.0	3.2	96.8	3.2
Mean-1 S.D.	872	27.6	59.6	37.5	99.9	2.9	97.0	3.0
Mean	846	24.1	60.5	35.8	99.6	2.6	97.0	2.7
Mean+1 S.D.	814	20.7	60.7	34.2	98.8	2.1	96.7	2.4
Sample maximum	490	2.8	46.2	22.2	87.4	0.1	87.3	0.4
Education								
< High school	954	43.0	52.4	46.9	100.0	3.3	96.7	3.3
High school	892	34.5	54.7	43.3	99.5	2.4	97.1	2.5
College	829	31.4	51.5	45.8	99.5	2.6	96.9	2.7
Firm size								
< 100	817	20.8	60.9	37.4	99.3	2.1	97.3	2.7
Medium (100–999)	810	16.1	64.8	32.7	99.4	2.0	97.3	2.6
> 1,000	771	15.7	61.4	34.7	99.3	2.1	97.2	2.7

* Expected values based on PARTTIME/IOFFER bivariate probit regression.
Source: Authors' calculations based on bivariate probit results reported in Table 2.2.8 (see text for methods).

Conclusions

This article has considered whether the growth in the standard fringe benefit package has played a significant role in the deterioration of the U.S. low-skilled labor market in the last two decades. Over this time period, most workers have seen declines in real wages, the lowest-wage workers being particularly hard hit (Mishel et al., 1996).

This article has concentrated on two major hypotheses:

1. low-wage workers will be less likely to work for firms that offer health insurance; and
2. low-wage workers will be more likely to work part-time for firms that offer health insurance and be denied an individual offer of insurance themselves.

Empirical support is found for both of these hypotheses - in the descriptive findings as well as in the results of multivariate analyses. In particular, low-wage workers are much less likely to work for firms that offer health insurance and much more likely to work part-time than high-wage workers. Evidence is found to support the hypothesis that firms offering insurance to any of their workers substitute away from low-wage workers. Moreover, as a firm's health insurance premiums increase, is less likely to offer coverage at all; but, contingent on continuing to offer coverage, the probability that a firm will deny benefits to their part-time workers increases. In the multivariate model, we find that there is a negative correlation between the probability of a firm offer and part-time employment, and an even larger negative correlation between individual offer and part-time work, which is consistent with firms' excluding low-wage/part-time workers from coverage.

These findings suggest that the U.S. nondiscrimination law, which was written to benefit low-wage workers, may actually be contributing to some of their employment and income problems. For example, we found that when health insurance premiums rise, fewer workers are employed by firms that offer coverage, but those that do tend to deny low-wage workers coverage either through hiring such workers part-time or through hiring fewer low-wage workers (and presumably outsourcing). The combination of increasing costs of providing coverage and regulation of the nondiscrimination law may have decreased opportunities, especially for low-wage workers, both in fewer full-time opportunities and more part-time work without offer of benefits.

A complete test of this model would require a fully simultaneous model, firm-based data, and a longer time horizon. Nevertheless, we believe the evidence presented here is rather compelling in arguing that the nondiscrimination law may be partly responsible for the significant deterioration in the employment opportunities facing low-wage (low-skilled) workers in the last two decades.

What might this evidence suggest for other industrialized countries? The member states of the European Union saw a 4 percent decline in the numbers of workers employed, or a loss of about 6 million jobs, in the three-year period 1991–94. Unemployment hit a record 11 percent in 1994. It has subsequently declined in several member states but increased in others. The rates are highest for the young and, among youth, those with limited education. All citizens have health insurance coverage, and although nonwage costs, including employer and employee taxes, vary, in most of these countries the 'combined tax and contribution system is far from being progressive' (European Commission, 1995, p. 25) and are highest either at the bottom end or in the middle.[31] The rather poor employment performance and these high costs suggest that current tax and social insurance policies may be partly at fault in limiting employment opportunities.

Notes

1. For example, in the case of health insurance, copayments and competition may be introduced to reduce the cost of coverage, but copayments raise barriers to care, and competition among either insurers or medical care providers may lead to discrimination among patients in a search for profit. If the cost of insurance is experience-based and/or the cost is paid through employers, there is the additional potential of hiring discrimination against those with higher-than-average expected medical care costs or against low-wage workers, whose cost of insurance coverage is a far higher component of total compensation. Policies to reduce the cost of hiring low-wage workers may include reduced social security contributions or other nonwage costs.

2. This is also related to a reduction of adverse selection for the insurer.

3. U.S. Bureau of the Census (1996); Mishel, Bernstein, Schmitt (1996). We should note here, however, that current debate and some studies in the United States suggest that inflation has been overstated and hence that real growth in family income may have been understated; see for example Boskin (1996) and Moulton (1996).

4. See, for example, Bluestone and Harrison (1986); Blackburn, Bloom and Freeman (1990); Murphy and Welch (1992); Acs and Danziger (1993); Porterfield and Sizer (1996); Burtless (1995); Krugman and Lawrence (1994); Freeman (1994); Bhagwati and Dehejia (1994); Lawrence and Slaughter (1993).

5. The exclusion of pension contributions in employer plans was somewhat smaller, or about $55 billion.

6. Total compensation increased by about 82 percent over this same period. In real dollars using the CPI-U, the increases are more than 24 percent for benefits compared to nearly 9 percent for total compensation and about 3.5 percent for wages and salaries. Source: U.S. Bureau of Labor Statistics, Employment Cost Index (ECI).

7. In addition, as already noted, the minimum wage limits the ability of an employer to 'pass through' the cost of fringe benefits to low-wage employees.

8. See for example, Aaron and Bosworth (1994); Gruber and Krueger (1991); Loprest, Winterbottom, and Zedlewski (1994); Summers (1989).

9. This discussion is based primarily on the German and Dutch systems.

10. The difference is that in the United States, the cost to an employer of providing health insurance is like a head tax - a fixed amount per employee - while in most other industrialized countries health insurance is financed by a payroll tax that is a percentage of earnings.

11. A recent headline in the International Herald Tribune reads 'New German Export: Jobs Head to Border,' April 8, 1997. The article goes on to say that the transfer of manufacturing to other countries has 'gained speed in the past 18 months, largely because German labor leaders refuse to accept cuts in wages or entitlements' (p. 4).

12. See Rica and Lemieux (1994) for an analysis of the link between public payroll-based health insurance and the growth of the underground economy in Spain.

13. The source for these figures is the U.S. Bureau of Labor Statistics.

14. To estimate this model, it is necessary to choose these instrumental variables. Following Blank (1990), several possible instrumental variables are considered here, for wages we rely on measures of region which are a proxy for state unemployment rate and other macroeconomic conditions that differ by region. For part-time status, we use family characteristics, such as presence of child under the age of 6, household size, female interacted with child under 6 years, and spouse income. For Offer, we use spouse offered insurance. These parameters are exactly identified if there is only one instrument each for hours and wages, and over-identified if there are multiple instruments.

15. The CPS is a monthly survey administered by the U.S. Census Bureau (see U.S. Bureau of the Census, 1978) to a representative sample of about 57,000 households, including more than 150,000 persons. In the March survey, respondents are asked about their health insurance coverage during the calendar year preceding the survey and are counted as insured if they had health insurance at any time during that period.

Respondents are organized into eight 'rotation' groups. Respondents in each group are interviewed for eight months over the course of a year and a half with each group interviewed during their first four months in the sample, not interviewed for the next eight months, and then interviewed again in months 13 through 16. Thus, each respondent in a rotation group is interviewed for the same four months in two consecutive years, then drops out of the sample. New rotation groups are added each month. All household members over the age of 14 are interviewed. One parent or guardian answers the questionnaire for all children (under age 14) in the household for whom they are responsible. In 1988 and again in 1993, the March survey was matched with the sample of employed workers interviewed in depth in the Survey of Employee Benefits about pension, leave, and health benefits received from their employers. This supplemental sample consisted initially of all of the respondents in rotation groups common to the March and May 1988 surveys and common to the March and April 1993 surveys. The sample was further reduced by omitting children under 14 and respondents over age 14 who were not employed. Thus, only employed persons are included in the supplemental surveys.

16. Different health insurance information is available on the two files. In 1988, data from the Supplement to the CPS are linked with data from the March Annual Demographic Surveys. However, questions concerning health insurance cover two different time periods - March and May. In the May supplement, survey respondents are asked about their employer-sponsored health insurance status, while in the March survey they are asked whether they were covered by health insurance at any time during the previous calendar year (i.e., 1987 in the case of the 1988 file). These answers may be inconsistent. For example, an individual may respond that they were offered employer-sponsored insurance and accepted it in May, though in March they reported themselves as uninsured. Thus, in 1988 it is impossible to determine whether workers not covered by their employer have insurance elsewhere. The 1993 file also is linked to the March survey. However, a few additional questions were added in the 1993 file, including a question asking directly about current health insurance coverage.

17. We omit 3705 observations for missing wage information, 285 with wages less than $1 or greater than $250, 2212 over age 65, and 3890 self-employed.

18. The procedure uses data from the National Medical Care Expenditure Survey (NMES) data for 1977. See Appendix B, Current Population Report, P-60, No. 182, August 1992, for more detail. The authors obtained a copy of the computer code for imputing the premium values from Charles Nelson and are grateful for his advice on implementing this procedure.

19. The cutoff point, LOWCUT, is defined as the real minimum wage plus the average cost of health insurance to the firm divided by 1750 (working 50 weeks a year for 35 hours per week). Any worker whose hourly wage is below that point is designated as a low-wage worker. We also tried a cut-off point of $6 per hour; results were robust to this change in definition.

20. While this might raise a question on the value that employees place on health insurance, it is important to keep in mind that many workers who do not accept coverage may still have coverage from another source, so very few are actually choosing to remain uninsured. In 1993, roughly 10 percent of workers were offered coverage by their employer but did not accept the offer. However, 6.6 percent of these workers had other coverage, most likely through their spouse. Only 1.9 percent of workers reported that they turned down coverage because they 'did not need' it or because it 'costs too much.' The remaining workers reported that the coverage was too limited or that there were 'other reasons' why they did not accept the employer's coverage. Also, it is important to note that the financial gain in having private employer-based coverage is greater for higher-income persons, since the subsidy level depends on the family's marginal tax bracket.

21. We discuss this table as though the data were collected by firms, which makes the implicit or underlying assumption that the sample of workers is also representative of workers within all firms.

22. Our evidence is not at all based on firm intent; rather we observe that they simply act in a way consistent with discrimination.

23. This is also evidence that firms with a higher cost of coverage are less likely to offer coverage.

24. These estimates are available from the authors upon request.

25. In these estimates which are available upon request, we exclude workers with tenure of less than a year from this estimation, because if they do not have an individual offer at the sample period, they may have one in the future, after a probationary work period.

26. In the estimates on the subsample of workers who are employed by firms who make offers the r are respectively -.69(.015)*, -.69(.015)*, -.68(.019)*, -.68(.018)*, -.62(.034)* and -.62(.034)* while in the larger sample results presented in Table 2.2.5, these values are -.32(.013)*, -.32(.013)*, -.32(.017)*, -.32(.017)*, -.20(.025)* and -.20(.025)*.

27. We follow Greene (1995, p. 458), in calculating the expected values of the variables Part-time* and Offer*. Note that the equations we use account for the correlation between these two decisions. In each case, if the expected value is positive, the individual is predicted to be part-time (or have a firm offer).

28. Recall as well that the estimated r in the FOFFER/PARTTIME and IOFFER/PARTTIME bivariate probits provides evidence consistent with firms taking advantage of the loophole in the nondiscrimination laws.

29. The basis of this result is that in our econometric specifications, premiums affect directly the probability of insurance offer, and through the probability of part-time conditional on offer. Higher premiums decrease the likelihood of a firm offer of insurance, and because r is negative, decrease the incentive for firms to hire lower-paid/low-skilled workers part-time. Hence, we derive our result that firms are using part-time workers and excluding them from coverage from our estimates of r.

30. Note also that over a smaller range (minimum cost observed to plus one standard deviation above the mean) the proportion of low-wage workers with individual offers of health insurance who are hired full-time actually increases from 58.5 to 60.7 percent (Table 2.2.8.B). This may be consistent with our hypotheses, since it suggests that firms will increase hours worked for low wage workers who have offers of coverage as premiums increase, at least within some range.

31. An exception is the United Kingdom, where the rate of social contributions paid by employers is considerably lower for low-wage workers than other workers.

References

Aaron, Henry J., and Bosworth, Barry (1994) 'Economic Issues in Reform of Health Care Financing.' *Brookings Papers on Economic Activity: Microeconomics*: 249–286.

Abraham, Katherine G., and Taylor, Susan K. (1996) 'Firms' Use of Outside Contractors: Theory and Evidence.' *Journal of Labor Economics* 14(3): 394–424.

Acs, Gregory, and Danziger, Sheldon (1993) 'Educational Attainment, Industrial Structure, and Male Earnings through the 1980s.' *Journal of Human Resources* 28: 618–648.

Bhagwati, Jagdish, and Dehejia, V. H. (1994) 'Freer Trade and Wages of the Unskilled - Is Marx Striking Again?' In Bhagwati, Jagdish and Kosters, Marvin H. (eds.), *Trade and Wages: Leveling Wages Down?* Washington, D.C.: AEI Press.

Blackburn, M. L., Bloom, D. E. and Freeman, R. B. (1990) 'The Declining Economic Position of Less-Skilled American Men.' In *A Future of Lousy Jobs? The Changing Structure of U.S. Wages*, edited by Burtless. Gary, Washington, D.C.: Brookings Institution.

Blank, Rebecca (1990) 'Are Part-Time Jobs Bad Jobs?' In *A Future of Lousy Jobs? The Changing Structure of U.S. Wages,* Burtless, Gary (ed.), Washington, D.C.: Brookings Institution.

Bluestone, B., and Harrison, B. (1986) 'The Great American Job Machine: The Proliferation of Low-Wage Employment in the U.S. Economy.' Study prepared for the Joint Economic Committee of the U.S. Congress.

Boskin, Michael (1996) Final Report to the Senate Finance Committee from the Advisory Commission to Study the CPI. Washington, D.C. Senate Finance Committee.

Burtless, Gary (1994) 'Rising Wage Inequality and the Future of Work in America.' In *Widening Earnings Inequality: Why and Why Now?*, Norwood, Janet L. (ed.) Washington, D.C.: Urban Institute Press.

Burtless, Gary (1995) 'International Trade and the Rise in Earnings Inequality.' *Journal of Economic Literature* 33(2): 800–816.

Congressional Budget Office (1991) 'Rising Health Care Costs: Causes, Implications and Strategies.' Washington, D.C.: CBO.

Cutler, David, and Madrian, Brigitte (February 1996) 'Labor Market Responses to Rising Health Insurance Costs: Evidence on Hours Worked.' NBER Working Paper no 5525, Cambridge, Mass.

European Commission (1995) *Employment in Europe 1995.* Luxembourg: Office for Official Publications of the European Communities.

Feldstein, Martin S. (1973) 'The Welfare Loss of Excess Health Insurance.' *Journal of Political Economy* 80 (2, Part I): 251–80.

Freeman, Richard (1994) 'Is Globalization Impoverishing Low-Skilled Workers?' In *Widening Earnings Inequality: Why and Why Now?* Norwood, Janet L. (ed.) Washington, D.C.: Urban Institute Press.

Glazer, William A. (1991) *Health Insurance in Practice. International Variations in Financing, Benefits, and Problems.* San Francisco: Jossey-Bass.

Greene, William H. (1993) Econometric Analysis. New York: Macmillan.

Greene, William H. (1995) LIMDEP Version 7.0 User's Manual. Bellport, NY: Econometric Software.

Gruber, Jonathan, and Krueger, Alan (1991) 'The Incidence of Mandated Employer-Provided Insurance: Lessons from Workers' Compensation Insurance.' In *Tax Policy and the Economy* Vol. 5, Bradford, David (ed.) Cambridge, Mass.: NBER and MIT Press.

Krueger, Alan (1993) 'How Computers Have Changed the Wage Structure: Evidence from Microdata, 1984–89.' *Quarterly Journal of Economics* 108(1): 33–60.

Krugman, P. R., and Lawrence, R. Z. (1994) 'Trade, Jobs, and Wages.' *Scientific American* (April): 44–49.

Lawrence, R. Z., and Slaughter, M. J. (1993) 'Trade and U.S. Wages: Giant Sucking Sound or Small Hiccup?' *Brookings Papers on Economic Activity: Microeconomics* 2: 161–210.

Lettau, Michael (1995) 'Compensation in Part-Time Jobs versus Full-time Jobs: What If the Job is the Same?' *Bureau of Labor Statistics Research Paper*, January.

Little, J. S. (1995) 'The Impact of Employer Payments for Health Insurance and Social Security on the Premium for Education and Earnings Inequality.' *New England Economic Review* (May/June): 25–40.

Loprest, Pamela, Winterbottom, Colin and Zedlewski, Sheila (1994) 'Estimating the Employment and Wage Effects of the Clinton Health Plan.' Urban Institute Working Paper. April.

Mishel, Lawrence, Bernstein, Jared and Schmitt, John (1996) *The State of Working America 1996–97.* Washington, D.C. Economic Policy Institute, December.

Moulton, Brent (1996) 'Bias in the Consumer Price Index: What is the Evidence?' *Journal of Economic Perspectives* 10(4): 159–177.

Murphy, Kevin M., and Welch, Finis (1991) 'The Role of International Trade in Wage Differentials.' In *Workers and Their Wages*, Kosters, Marvin (ed.) Washington, D.C.: American Enterprise Institute Press.

Murphy, Kevin M., and Welch, Finis (1992) 'The Structure of Wages.' *Quarterly Journal of Economics* 107(1): 285–326.

Office of Research and Statistics, Social Security Administration (1996) Social Security Programs Throughout the World - 1995. Washington, D.C. U.S. GPO.

Pauly, Mark V. (1986) 'Taxation, Health Insurance, and Market Failure in the Medical Economy.' *Journal of Economic Literature* 24(2): 629–675.

Porterfield, S. L., and Sizer, M. (1996) 'The North American Free Trade Agreement: Impacts on Manufacturing Wages.' Working paper. October.

Rica, Sara de la, and Lemieux, Thomas (1994) 'Does Public Health Insurance Reduce Labor Market Flexibility or Encourage the Underground Economy? Evidence from Spain and the United States.' In *Social Protection Versus Economic Flexibility*, Blank, Rebecca (ed.) Chicago: University of Chicago Press.

Social Security Administration (1996) Annual Report of the Board of Board of Trustees of the Old-Age, Survivors and Disability Insurance (OASDI) Trust Funds. Washington, D.C.: U.S. GPO.

Solow, Robert (1994) 'Introduction.' In *Widening Earnings Inequality: Why and Why Now?*, Norwood, Janet L. (ed.) Washington, D.C.: Urban Institute Press.

Summers, Lawrence (1989) 'Some Simple Economics of Mandated Benefits.' *American Economic Review* 79(May): 177–183.

U.S. Bureau of the Census (1978) 'The Current Population Survey: Design and Methodology.' Department of Commerce, Technical Paper 40. Washington, D.C.: U.S. GPO.

U.S. Bureau of the Census (1996) 'A Brief Look at Postwar U.S. Income Inequality.' *Current Population Reports,* Household Economic Studies, No. P60-191.

Weinberg, Daniel H. (1996) '1995 Income, Poverty and Health Insurance Estimates.' Press briefing, U.S. Bureau of the Census, September 29, 1996.

Wolaver, Amy, McBride, Timothy and Wolfe, Barbara (1997) 'Decreasing Opportunities for Low-Wage Workers: The Role of the Nondiscrimination Law for Employer-Provided Health Insurance.' Institute for Research on Poverty, University of Wisconsin–Madison, Discussion Paper no. 1124-97.

Appendix 1

Nondiscrimination Clause

The following is the relevant passage from the 1978 legislation requiring that employers offer insurance to all employees. Section 105 pertains to amounts received under accident and health plans. (Reprinted from U.S. Tax Code, Title 26, Subtitle A, Chapter 1, Subchapter B, Part III, Section 105: (h); http://www.fourmilab.ch/ustax/www/t26-A-1-B-III-105.html)

(h) Amount paid to highly compensated individuals under a discriminatory self-insured medical expense reimbursement plan

(1) In general

In the case of amounts paid to a highly compensated individual under a self-insured medical reimbursement plan which does not satisfy the requirements of paragraph (2) for a plan year, subsection (b) shall not apply to such amounts to the extent they constitute an excess reimbursement of such highly compensated individual.

(2) Prohibition of discrimination

A self-insured medical reimbursement plan satisfies the requirements of this paragraph only if

(A) the plan does not discriminate in favor of highly compensated individuals as to eligibility to participate; and

(B) the benefits provided under the plan do not discriminate in favor of participants who are highly compensated individuals.

(3) Nondiscriminatory eligibility classifications

(A) In general

A self-insured medical reimbursement plan does not satisfy the requirements of subparagraph (A) of paragraph (2) unless such plan benefits

(i) 70 percent or more of all employees, or 80 percent or more of all the employees who are eligible to benefit under the plan if 70 percent or more of all employees are eligible to benefit under the plan; or

(ii) such employees as qualify under a classification set up by the employer and found by the Secretary not to be discriminatory in favor of highly compensated individuals.

(B) Exclusion of certain employees

For purposes of subparagraph (A), there may be excluded from consideration

(i) employees who have not completed 3 years of service;

(ii) employees who have not attained age 25;

(iii) part-time or seasonal employees;

(iv) employees not included in the plan who are included in a unit of employees covered by an agreement between employee representatives and one or more employers which the Secretary finds to be a collective bargaining agreement, if accident and health benefits were the subject of good faith bargaining between such employee representatives and such employer or employers; and

(v) employees who are nonresident aliens and who receive no earned income (within the meaning of section 911(d)(2)) from the employer which constitutes income from sources within the United States (within the meaning of section 861(a)(3)).

(4) Nondiscriminatory benefits

A self-insured medical reimbursement plan does not meet the requirements of subparagraph (B) of paragraph (2) unless all benefits provided for participants who are highly compensated individuals are provided for all other participants.

(5) Highly compensated individual defined

For purposes of this subsection, the term 'highly compensated individual' means an individual who is

(A) one of the 5 highest paid officers,
(B) a shareholder who owns (with the application of section 318) more than 10 percent in value of the stock of the employer, or

(C) among the highest paid 25 percent of all employees (other than employees described in paragraph (3)(B) who are not participants).

(6) Self-insured medical reimbursement plan

The term 'self-insured medical reimbursement plan' means a plan of an employer to reimburse employees for expenses referred to in subsection (b) for which reimbursement is not provided under a policy of accident and health insurance.

PART 3

FAMILY POLICY AND ECONOMIC WELLBEING

3.1 Policy responses to household vulnerability: The Norwegian case in an international context

Einar Overbye

This chapter traces changes in social policies in the Norwegian setting, with a special emphasis on family policies. By limiting the study to one country, it is possible to provide a study rich in institutional detail across a wide range of policy areas. I argue that a series of incremental changes over the past 10-20 years add up to a possible reorientation of the Norwegian welfare state, a reorientation that can be regarded as a policy response to changes in household structure and gender roles. The Norwegian case is then placed in an international context, and the article briefly investigates similarities and differences in policy responses among countries experiencing similar societal transformations.

Increased differentiation of the household structure

During the last two decades in particular, the household structure in industrialized societies has gone through important changes. Between 1981 and 1991, the percentage of one-adult households increased in all countries belonging to the European Economic Area (EEA), although there is a North-South divide as to how far the process has moved. The Scandinavian countries are in the lead, with the Southern European countries and Ireland lagging (Hatland and Skevik 1996). The rise in single women with children displays a similar pattern, as does the number of births outside marriage (as a percentage of all births) (Hatland and Skevik, op. cit.).

The rise in one-adult households implies that the risk-dispersing potential of the household unit is diminished. As long as there are several adults in a household, the mere presence of others serves as mutual insurance against some social risks. For example, nursing risk during short or long spells of illness is cushioned if other household members may step in (temporarily or permanently) to care for the sick or disabled member. This risk-dispersing effect may be of particular importance in households with children. Single parents employed in the regular work force are particularly vulnerable if children become sick or disabled.

Increased differentiation of the household structure is correlated to a change in gender roles, including the percentage of women entering the labour force. The trend is everywhere on the increase, but Scandinavia heads the development (OECD 1992: 39). Two-income families are also vulnerable to the risk of sickness or disability within the household. In these families, there is no one to stay behind and nurse children who - for shorter or longer periods - are unable to attend school or kindergarten. Obviously, a similar problem arises with regard to the supervision of healthy children, to the extent that child care and after-school care are not available.

The risk of an income loss in conjunction with maternity also increases in line with increased female labour force participation.[1] The income loss is both direct, in the form of earnings foregone, and indirect, by missing pension points/accrued pension rights in the public pension system.

The gradual increase in the percentage of elderly, including frail elderly, puts additional burdens on the caring capabilities of the economically-active population. Neither single-parent nor two-income families have much time available to step in if relatives outside the household need temporary or permanent care.

The purpose of this article is to trace changes in social security legislation with special reference to the above-mentioned caring responsibilities, to see if and how social changes have been accompanied by changes in social policies. In order to present an in-depth account of changes, including incremental changes of various kinds, the analysis is limited primarily to one country (Norway). As pointed out by Hatland and Skevik, the rise in one-adult households, as well as the influx of women into the labour force, have been particularly marked in Norway, as in Scandinavia more generally. For these reasons, a study of the Norwegian response to various types of household vulnerability may be of some general social policy interest.

Policy responses: the Norwegian case

A substantial number of new policy initiatives have been implemented during the last decades, in order to deal with the above-mentioned types of household vulnerability. However, few brand-new welfare schemes have been introduced. Rather, we are witnessing a never-ending tinkering at the edges of existing welfare arrangements, which gradually - when looked at with the benefit of hindsight - add up to substantial reorientations. Existing social security schemes are 'stretched' to achieve new social policy objectives. In this process, the content of certain schemes has been transformed into something distinctly different (Koren 1997).

The transformation of sickness insurance

Since 1909, Norwegian employees have received partial compensation in case of absence due to sickness (Bjørnson 1994: 65). State employees got their own sickness scheme in 1918, and this served as a role model for similar schemes in the municipal sector and among salaried staff (Hippe and Pedersen 1992: 87). Compulsory sickness insurance for employees was introduced in 1953 and extended to cover the self-employed in 1956 (Hippe and Pedersen 1992: 89). The present system stems from 1978. It incorporates all employees (workers as well as salaried staff) in the same scheme, on equal terms (Pedersen 1996: 8-9). The 1978 reform provided 100 percent of previous earnings with no waiting days.[2] Although the primary aim of the reform was to insure employees, the legislators included a paragraph stating that sick pay could also be granted if a child in the employee's household got sick. Sick pay was granted for up to 10 days a year in case of children's illness. For single parents, this rule was extended to 20 days. In this fashion, Parliament enlarged the sick-pay scheme to cater also for the risk of income loss due to children's illness.

Since 1978, several piecemeal amendments have been made, which have enlarged this aspect of the sick-pay scheme (Koren 1997). In 1986, sick pay was extended to 365 days if a child has a serious or fatal illness, or if s/he must be admitted to a hospital or nursed at home in a 'serious phase' of the illness. In 1987, parents with chronically ill or disabled children were granted up to 20 sick days a year, bringing them on par with single parents. At the same time, the age limit with regard to chronically ill or disabled children was raised to 16 years, and the age limit was abolished altogether for mentally retarded children with life threatening or serious illnesses. Sick pay was introduced for up to 4 weeks to care for terminally ill 'close relatives' in 1990. Three years later, sick pay if a child has serious or life threatening illness was extended from one to two years, but then at 65 percent of earnings. In 1995, sick pay was granted also if the person who supervises the child is sick, but within the same quota (10 days a year) as the child itself. The same year, sick pay was extended to 15 days a year for parents with more than two children.

It is tempting to see these extensions of the sick-pay scheme to include children, near relatives, au pairs and the like (plus the more generous rule for single parents) as responses to increased female labour force participation, plus the rise in single-parent families. There are simply no grown-ups left in most Norwegian households during the daytime who may step in and assume caring responsibilities if dependent household members become sick, disabled or chronically ill.

While the sick-pay scheme has been extended to allow for a smoother functioning of the everyday life of working parents, the scheme has simultaneously been tightened as regards its initial (or core) function: to insure the employee in case of his/her own sickness. In 1983 an earnings limit was introduced, stating that incomes above 8 times the so-called 'base amount' (a core concept in the Norwegian social security system) would not give rights to sick pay. The income ceiling was brought down to 6 times the base amount in 1985 (Pedersen 1996: 9). This amounted to NOK 155400 in 1985, or 124 percent of the average male full-time wage in industry (Trygdestatistisk Årbok 1996: 22, 26). Since its introduction in 1967, the annual regulation of the base amount has trailed behind average wage growth, implying that an ever-larger segment of the working population reaches this income ceiling. Thus in 1995, 6 times the base amount only comprised 115 percent of an average production worker's wage (op. cit.).

To sum up: in the case of sickness benefits there has been a *retrenchment* of the initial purpose of the scheme: to insure employees (breadwinners) in case of sickness. But at the same time, there has been an *extension* of the scheme to cover the wider array of risk situations facing a modern-type household (i.e. a double-income or single-parent household). The development of sick pay in Norway is thus simultaneously characterized by expansion (in some areas) and contraction (in others). Funds have been made available to cover new (emerging) risk situations, but in order to make room for this expansion, compensation levels have been reduced, in particular for higher-income groups. This change of emphasis within the scheme implies a redirection of funds away from protecting the core (male) industrial working class against sickness, towards protecting two-income families and single-adult households against the consequences of sickness among dependent family members. The shift may possibly be interpreted as an effect of the somewhat weakened societal position of (male) industrial workers. Between 1981 and 1995, employment in industry, mining and construction work declined from 25 percent to 19 percent of total employment (Statistisk Årbok 1996: 163). At the same time, the ranks of part-time and full-time service professions grew rapidly, largely comprised of women (op. cit.).

The transformation of maternity benefits

The Factory Supervision Act of 1892 prohibited women from work until 6 weeks after birth, but without any wage compensation. As part of the Sickness Insurance Act of 1909, insured women were granted sick pay during these weeks (Haavet 1994: 131). In practice, these laws only encompassed women employed in industry. In 1936 women were also protected from being laid off due to absence resulting from pregnancy.

Gradually, protection was extended from women employed in industry to women working in other occupations. This extension of eligibility culminated in 1971, when public sickness insurance encompassed the whole working population. Employed women then got the right to maternity benefits up to 12 weeks, of which 6 weeks had to be postponed until after birth. In 1978, sick pay (including maternity benefit) was raised to 100 per cent of earnings and extended to 18 weeks. The same year, the father was allowed to take up to 12 of these weeks provided that the mother returned to work.

During the 1980s and 1990s, there has been a flurry of new legislative initiatives transforming the benefit from being primarily a protection of the female against immediate income loss (and/or layoffs) due to childbirth, into a system for easing the child-rearing period for working parents more generally. The benefit period was extended to 20 weeks in 1987, 22 weeks in 1988 and 24 weeks in 1989. In 1989 the time period could eventually be extended to 30 weeks, but then only at 80 percent of earnings. In 1990 this period was extended yet again to 28 weeks, or 80 percent over 35 weeks. The same year, fathers who were granted custody of their children after a divorce got an independent right to benefits, implying that it had now been fully transformed from a maternity benefit to a parental benefit. In 1991, the period was extended to 30 weeks (or 80 percent over 38 weeks), and in 1992 to 33 weeks (or 80 percent over 42 weeks).[3] The time period was raised again to 42 weeks in 1993, or 80 percent over 52 weeks. Of these, four weeks *must* be taken by the father, and three weeks by the mother *before* birth (replacing an additional two-week maternity benefit introduced in 1991, which had to be taken before birth). Finally, since 1994, the parental benefit can be combined with part-time work for a period up to 104 weeks. This arrangement has been named 'parental time account' (see Koren 1997: 15 for an elaboration of these reforms).

These incremental changes are clearly responses to mounting political demands from the growing number of working parents (single-parent families as well as two-income families) who find it difficult to pursue working careers and raise children at the same time. The transformation of maternity benefit to a parental time-account system makes it possible for parents to stay at home up to 104 weeks without serious income loss, or without fear of being laid off during this period.

Family allowances (child benefits)

Family allowances were introduced in 1946, granting the same flat amount to all parents with children less than 16 years of age. Initially, benefits were granted only from the second child onwards, but single parents received benefits also for the first child. Benefits per child were the same irrespective of the number of children in the household. In 1963 benefits were differentiated according to the number of children, granting higher benefits to families with many children (NOU 1996: 130). The reasoning behind the new benefit was to ease the living conditions of families with children, rather than to redistribute between high- and low income families; thus the benefit was not income-tested.

From 1970, benefits were granted to all families also for the first child. At the same time, Parliament decided to grant single parents benefits for one more child than they actually had, to enhance the economic situation of this particular group. In 1991, a special small-child supplement was introduced, providing larger benefits for children less than 3 years old.

Care and nursing services

Parallel to the rise in welfare transfers, publicly provided or sponsored services in the fields of child care and care for the frail elderly have been expanded, thus relieving working-age household members from addressing these needs.

The origin of kindergartens in Norway can be traced back to 1837, when the first 'children's asylum' was introduced in the city of Trondheim to ease the plight of parents employed in the new manufacturing industries (NOU 1996: 150). The asylum was inspired by similar British institutions established in the first decades of the 19th century. The asylums provided full-time care for children aged two up to school age. During the 1920s and 1930s, and even more after the war, a differentiation emerged between short- and long-term day care. In 1975, a law was passed regulating child-care facilities, to ensure a sufficiently high quality of this type of services. Between 1980 and 1994 the rate of coverage in publicly provided or sponsored child care rose from 22 to 44 percent of all children 0-6 years (NOU 1996: 152). In 1997/8 compulsory elementary school was extended from the 7-year-olds to include the 6-year-olds. This reform will naturally limit the demand for child care (which tends to increase with the child's age).

Parallel to this development, after-school care has been established to provide children in elementary school with additional hours away from home. After-school care has the same historical origins as children's asylums, but until the late 1970s only a few large municipalities (cities) had established such institutions. In 1991 the parliament introduced a special grant to encourage municipalities to expand after-school care. Between 1991 and 1995, the number of places available increased from 28,000 to 56,000. At that stage, 31 percent of all children 7-9 years old were served by these institutions, and the number of places is still on the increase (NOU 1996:152). Most are run by municipalities, although some are operated by private entrepreneurs. As with child care, they are financed on a tripartite basis by the state, municipality and parent(s).

At the other end of the age distribution, there has been an expansion of nursing homes and home-based care for the frail elderly, relieving other family members of nursing responsibilities. Although expanding, the growth in nursing homes has not wholly kept pace with the increased number of elderly. While in 1980 there were 33.5 places in nursing homes per 100 elderly above the age of 80, the rate of coverage dropped to 27.2 in 1993 (St.meld. 35 1994-95: 145). However, in this period there was a shift in emphasis toward home-based care, which has been allowed to expand much more rapidly. In 1970 there were 32 elderly (above age 66) per man-labour year which - one way or the other - was financed by tax revenues to care for the elderly. In 1990, there were only 10 elderly per man-labour year spent on various care activities (Sosialt Utsyn 1993: 396).[4]

Single parents

Single-parent families are obviously the most vulnerable of the new family types emerging. Consequently, these families are targets of a multitude of special benefits and care options to compensate for their exposed position.

As already mentioned, employed single parents are allowed ten extra days of absence to care for sick children, and they receive child benefits for one more child than they actually have, for children below the age of 16 (so-called extended child benefit).[5] In addition, single parents receive a special maternity grant alongside the general grant (NOU 1996: 181). Further, single parents are taxed in 'tax bracket II' in the tax code regardless of their income level, which amounts to a lower personal income tax than other wage earners. They also have access to certain tax deductions not open to other types of households (op. cit.). As regards services, single parents have privileged access to child-care facilities run by Local Councils. Seventy-one percent of employed single parents and 61 percent of at-home single parents with children 0-6 years of age used kindergartens in 1995 (NOU 1996: 13). Low-income parents pay less than high-income parents, implying that single parents usually pay less for this service.[6]

The so-called transitional allowance is the most important benefit reserved for single parents in particular. This social security benefit was introduced in 1964. Initially, only widows and unwed mothers were eligible. Widowers were included in 1967, and divorced and separated mothers in 1972 (NOU 1996: 179). Unwed, separated or divorced men in custody of children were made eligible for the transitional allowance in 1981 (op. cit.). The transitional allowance is tested against income from earnings, but with a sliding scale to preserve some economic incentive to work. As a general rule, the transitional allowance is paid until the youngest child is 10 years old, or 18 years old with regard to sick or handicapped children.⁷ Maximum benefit equals the minimum pension level. Transitional allowance is granted single parents even if they cohabitate, as long as the cohabitant is not the parent of the child, and no new child is born as a result of the new relationship. This rather generous eligibility rule is meant to encourage single parents to seek new partners, by allowing the new couple a trial period without having to fear a loss of benefits during this period.⁸ Perhaps as a consequence, remarriage (or birth of a new child within a common-law marriage) is a major reason for the termination of the transitional allowance. Terum (1993: 75) reported that 24 percent of single parents on transition allowance discontinued their benefit as a consequence of marrying a new partner, or giving birth to a child with a new cohabitant.⁹

Single parents may receive a 3-year grant to acquire higher education in addition to transitional allowance. If they attend school or work they may also receive a babysitter grant.¹⁰ Finally, the collection of child maintenance is organized through a special institution, the Maintenance Contribution Collection Agency (established in 1992). As a main rule, maintenance in Norway is determined as a percentage of the non-custodial parent's gross income: 11 percent for one child, 18 percent for two children and 24 percent for three children (Skevik 1997: 12). The introduction of the Collection Agency as a centralized institution to administer child maintenance was a response to the problem of getting the increasing number of non-custodial parents to pay up. Using the Agency is mandatory only if the single parent receives transitional allowance. However, approximately 90 percent of all maintenance cases are administered by this institution. The single parent may ask the Agency for advance maintenance, which is then reclaimed from the absent parent (Skevik, op. cit.). In this way, single parents are secured against the risk that absent parents do not contribute.

To sum up, single parents are secured through a wide array of cash benefits, taxation rules and collecting agencies, as well as privileged access to various types of services. Nonetheless, these institutional devices do not wholly suffice to secure single parents against the risk of poverty. Traditional, means-tested social assistance remains an important benefit of last resort utilized by a significant minority of single parents. In 1991 35 percent of all single parents on transitional allowance received social assistance as a supplement (Osmunddalen and Kalve 1993: 19).

Households comprising students or young unemployed

It is rather obvious that a rise in single parents increases household vulnerability. The increased vulnerability created by a rising number of student households is less obvious. Due to structural shifts in the demand for labour (toward skilled workers), the percentage of young people pursuing higher education has increased markedly over the last decades. The percentage of 17- to 19-year-olds reporting paid work as their major vocation decreased from 31 to 8 percent between 1975 and 1990 (NOU 1993: 17, 152). The percentage pursuing long educations is also rapidly increasing.

How is this related to vulnerability? Mainly because eligibility requirements to receive various social security benefits (in particular earnings-related benefits) are tied to previous employment records. As an increasing percentage of the population postpones entry into the labour market, they face a longer period where they are cut off from various social security benefits should they be sick, disabled, or in a position where they have to care for other family members (be they young or old). Policy measures to secure also this group take many forms. For instance, in 1981 youth below the age of 21 who became disabled were granted a disability pension *as if* they had been working and received an 'average wage' at the time of the incident. In this fashion, they were granted larger benefits than the minimum disability pension (awarded those older than 21 with no previous work record). Since 1981, this disability benefit has been increased several times, and eligibility extended to include youth up to the age of 24. Youth becoming disabled before the age of 24 may also receive enlarged amounts of certain income-tested benefits (St.meld. 35 1994-95,100-1).

Rising unemployment adds to the increased risk exposure of youth in general, since youth are a particularly vulnerable group in periods marked by high unemployment. Youth are often cut off from claiming unemployment benefits, as the receipt of such benefits requires some previous labour market experience. To counter the risk of unemployment among youth without previous labour market experience, the government introduced a so-called 'youth guarantee' in 1994, granting youth either work or educational opportunities until they reach the age of 20. This arrangement serves as a substitute for unemployment insurance proper for age cohorts too young to have gained a foothold in the labour market.

Retrenchment in other areas: toward a transformation of the overall welfare structure?

On numerous occasions during the last decade, politicians of most parties have emphasized the need to avoid tax increases, and stressed that additional expansions of public transfers and services must be countered by retrenchment in other areas. This indicates the emergence of increased priority conflicts *within* the public sector. For example, in St.meld. (Green Paper) no. 4, 1992-93, 1: 32-33, the government (then as now led by the Social Democratic party) made the following remark:

> Public expenditures must...not be allowed to grow...faster than GDP growth in mainland Norway [excluding offshore oil and gas production, large contributors to overall GDP growth]...Government proposals for new reforms must for the greater part be financed through increased efficiency, or corresponding reductions, in other budget areas (translation by author).

Escalating priority conflicts have certainly been witnessed within the Norwegian welfare sector. The expansion of transfers and services to accommodate new types of household vulnerability has to some extent been matched by cutbacks with regard to traditional social security. Of these, earnings-related benefits have borne the brunt of cutbacks.

The reduction in sick pay for middle and high income earners due to stricter income ceilings, plus less-than-adequate indexation of ceilings, has already been mentioned. Also, the formula for earnings-related old age and disability pensions was cut back in 1992, in particular for higher-income groups. Eligibility rules for disability have been tightened during the 1990s, and Norway anyway only grants a disability pension for disability leading to at least a 50 percent loss in work capacity.

The reduction of the income ceiling granting an earnings-related pension was combined with an extension as regards which types of work 'earn' superannuation benefits. In 1991, Parliament decided to grant women who stay home to rear preschool children, or look after frail relatives, pension points in the superannuation system *as if* they were earning an average wage (St.meld. 35, 1994-5: 188). In this fashion, the government reduced the indirect income loss (in the form of accrued pension rights foregone) for those who alternate between formal and informal work.[11] Notice the similarities with the transformation of the sick pay scheme: benefit levels are brought down, in particular for higher-income groups; but at the same time eligibility criteria are broadened to encompass other groups than the traditional working class.

It is also worth mentioning that Norway, together with Iceland and Denmark, has the highest formal retirement ages in the world: 67 years. Also, Norwegian governments have not introduced any public early-retirement plan. This must be seen in the light of low unemployment figures in Norway during the 1970s and 1980s, which dampened popular demand for early-retirement schemes (OECD 1992: 43). However, in the late 1980s and early 1990s Norway experienced rising unemployment, and a corresponding demand (from unions in particular) for early-retirement options. In the absence of a public scheme, the social partners agreed in 1988 to introduce a negotiated early-retirement scheme. The state carries some of the costs of this scheme for those above 64. The social partners extended the early-retirement option also to the 63- and 62-year-olds in 1997. The government agreed to introduce some tax concessions also for these age cohorts, but only under the threat of massive strikes. The reluctant response of the Social Democratic government to union demands for early-retirement options, despite this being *the* top priority item in the Confederation, further indicates growing priority conflicts within the Norwegian welfare sector.

The nature of policy responses

In the preambles to the 1948 UN Declaration of Human Rights, 'social security' is defined as policy measures aimed at 'protecting an individual in social situations and conditions in which his or her livelihood may be at risk' (Andreassen 1992: 336). There are many ways to provide social security (thus defined), but - at least in a European context - a major avenue has been to set up contribution-based social insurance schemes. A social insurance scheme is ideally a reciprocal system which is contractual in character. An individual is entitled to benefits only if in some sense s/he has earned it through previous work or contribution payments (Loedemel and Schulte 1992: 16). However, the new household-related risks are very difficult to deal with by way of contributory schemes. Being unable to encompass these risks within a contributory context, one might surmise that politicians would respond by expanding the social *assistance* system. Assistance benefits are financed from general revenues: they are granted regardless of previous employment or former contribution records.

As the above exposition has shown, the Norwegian response to the rise of new risks has *not* been to expand the social assistance system. Rather, the main line of response has been to encompass new types of vulnerability within the existing social insurance schemes, by watering down or simply forgetting the contribution requirement. This has been possible since the Norwegian social insurance system ('folketrygden') does not specify contributions according to scheme. Two sets of contributions (one for citizens, another for companies) finance the whole package of social insurance benefits, without differentiating between (say) transitional allowance and unemployment benefits or pensions, or between minimum and earnings-related benefits.[12] In this fashion, social assistance proper has been maintained as a residual safety net of last resort, catering only for those social risks that are so diffuse or multifaceted that they cannot be singled out for separate treatment within one of the social insurance schemes, or serving as a top-up on benefits granted through the social insurance system. The strategy of encompassing new types of vulnerability by redesigning existing social insurance schemes rather than expanding social assistance is a long-standing tradition of Norwegian social policy. It is also a major reason why the Norwegian social assistance system has been maintained as one of the most residual and least rights-based assistance systems in Europe - although with quite generous average benefit levels (Loedemel and Schulte op. cit.)

The dichotomy between social insurance and social assistance does not wholly exhaust the Norwegian response to increased household vulnerability. An additional strategy has been to mandate responsibility on behalf of employers. Thus in the sickness insurance system (including cases where children are sick), the employer is compelled to pay the first 14 days of sickness; the state only maintains financial responsibility for sickness periods beyond 14 days. This represents an indirect strategy, or *regulation strategy*, for providing citizens with social security. The so-called 'youth guarantee' further demonstrates the creativity of policy makers to deal with new vulnerability without having to expand social assistance in a traditional sense. Yet another organizational device is to use fiscal policy. Tax credits to parents who can document child-care expenses are of particular importance, alongside special tax rules for single parents. However, taking things as a whole, the major strategy in Norway to encompass new social risks has been to rig the formally contributions-based social insurance system rather than to expand social assistance, regulation policies or tax measures.

The pressure behind policy reforms

Political elites can be portrayed either as active entrepreneurs planning for social change, or passively responding to changes taking place. Some regard the designs of Scandinavian welfare policies as the result of some pre-designed, overarching strategy on behalf of the Social Democratic parties in particular. Gustafsson's (1995) delineating of a comprehensive Swedish welfare model, where all elements seem to add up to a unified grand design, may lend credibility to this assumption. However, Nordic politicians have also been portrayed as passively responding to social changes taking place around them. The former Danish Minister of Social Affairs, Bent Rold-Andersen (from the Social Democratic party), summed up his experience as follows:

> Twenty years ago there was probably no-one in Denmark who would even dream of an expansion of the welfare system [of the magnitude that has taken place]. This enormous expansion...has in fact taken place without having been planned by anybody [and] without having been decided by any responsible government organ... By this I do not say that no decisions have been made. In fact...thousands of politically elected citizens from all parties have been involved in the millions of single decisions which accumulated to shape the development... But nobody worked out a blueprint of the total development... Each political decision was an answer to challenges which were created outside the political sphere, by social changes, reflecting the changing behaviour of the citizens... The political authorities reacted passively and mechanically to the social revolution which took place around them. By doing so, maybe they unconsciously accelerated the changes, but not because they wanted to do so. Most Nordic politicians do not see themselves as masters of a social development, they prefer the much more modest role as providers of public services, the aim of which is to satisfy acute demands (Rold Andersen 1984: 39-40).

In Norway, changes took place under shifting governments and/or under widespread Parliamentary consensus (Kuhnle 1983, Pettersen 1987: 178). In the postwar years, the Social Democrats ruled as a majority party only between 1945 and 1961. Since then, the situation has been characterized either by coalition governments, or by a minority party (or a coalition of minority parties) seeking parliamentary support on a day-to-day basis (Narud 1996: 150). In 1965-71, 1972-73, 1981-86 and 1989-90 Norway was ruled by non-Socialist coalition governments, and since 1969 the Social Democrats have been able to rule only by relying on support from non-Socialist parties, usually from the liberal or agrarian centre parties, who control the strategic crossover vote. This, as well as the incremental character of the changes, suggests that they were not the outcome of any pre-planned grand design.

That, however, is not the same as arguing that there was no long-term strategic thinking whatsoever behind the changes. The relationship between social changes and policy making should probably be analyzed as an interrelated cause-and-effect relationship, rather than a one-way street in one direction or the other. Changing behavioural patterns within the population (of modest proportions to begin with) may provide outlets for political entrepreneurs to pick up new demands, and thus demonstrate initiative and ability to act. Social changes may also lead to the emergence of groups with new collective identities, groups that form the recruitment base for new political elites, who (by formulating demands on behalf of the group) may stimulate further changes, as well as foster group loyalties.

Who have been the main benefactors of the expansion of publicly provided/mandated/subsidized care and nursing benefits? If one can assume that care responsibilities, if left a wholly private responsibility, tend to fall disproportionately on women, there should be a gender dimension with regard to these policies. This hunch is substantiated by noticing that the emergence of Norwegian policy responses to changing household structures is correlated to the rise of women's factions within all major parties. The percentage of female MPs in Parliament rose from 9 to 36 between 1969 and 1989, while the percentage in Local Councils rose from 10 to 31 percent from 1967 to 1987 (Skjeie 1992: 91). At the leadership level the peak so far was reached in 1991-92, when not only the Prime Minister (Ms Bruntland from the Social Democrats), but also the leaders of the Conservative and Agrarian party (the two main opposition parties) were women (Skjeie 1992: 72). In assessing the impact of changed gender composition in Parliament on social policy initiatives, Skjeie concludes:

Parallel to women's integration into party politics new political agendas have been established. Women's inclusion is perceived as having caused changes in party attitudes on a wide range of political issues. Issues of care politics clearly dominate the Agenda of Change reported by Norwegian parliamentarians; in all parties the inclusion of care and care work concerns is thus pictured as the most influential contribution of women politicians at this point in time [although] an analysis of changes in party profiles over the past two decades shows how old political cleavage structures might be maintained even as parties come to embrace new political agendas (op. cit.: 178).

A general picture seems to emerge: not of retrenchment as such, but rather a reorientation of the Norwegian welfare state. There might be tensions not only between defenders and critics of social security as such, but also between proponents of different types of security, in a situation characterized by increased fiscal strain and mounting priority conflicts. New social and occupational groups, with different risk characteristics, are gradually making their security interests felt. At the same time, declining groups face mounting problems in defending, or expanding, those schemes that are of particular interest to them.

Scandinavian idiosyncrasies or worldwide trend?

As shown in Figure 3.1.1, the proportion of women in national legislatures is correlated to the proportion of women in the labour force ($r=.739$). The United Kingdom and the Netherlands are the only clear deviations from this trend, although it should be mentioned that the Nordic countries form a cluster of their own.[13]

If the surge in social policy initiatives to compensate for increased household vulnerability and lack of slack to cope with child-related risks is something more than a peculiarity of Scandinavian developments, we should be witnessing similar changes in social policy elsewhere. Gauthier (1996) observed converging as well as diverging trends in her examination of family policies in industrialized countries. Family allowances were expanded in all countries until the mid-1970s. In the 1980s and 1990s, the situation has been characterized by a mixed response of expansion and reduction. Expansionist measures include increased coverage and rates, as well as the introduction of special supplements. However, Gauthier also observed that family allowances had been subjected to means-testing in Australia (1988), Canada (1992), Germany (1983), Greece (1989), Italy (1988) and Spain (1991).[14] Incidentally, the question of means-testing has also been on the agenda in Norway, both in Parliament and within the ruling Social Democratic party, but so far the universality of the scheme has been kept. (In some sense, the change is in the same direction as with sick pay and public pensions: eligibility is broadened and new groups are brought in, but the scheme is made less attractive to higher-income groups.)

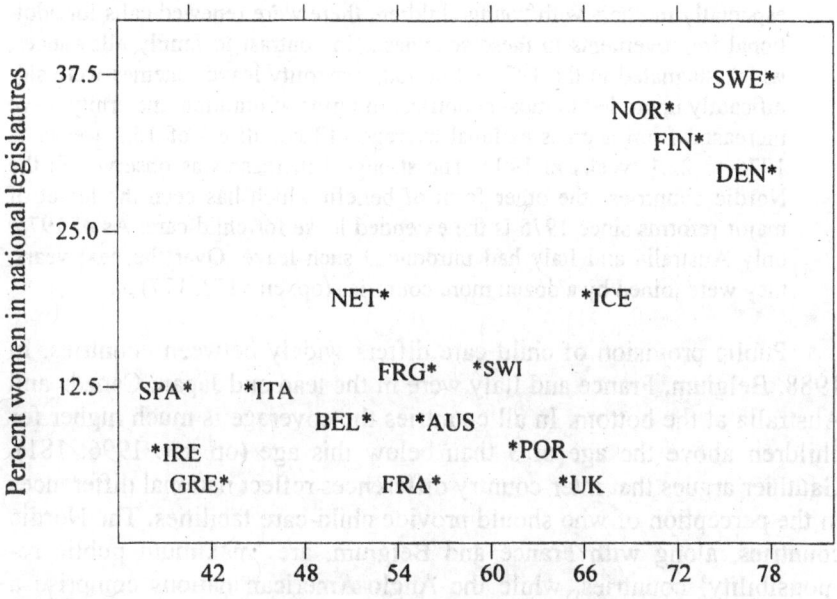

Figure 3.1.1 Correlation between female labour force participation* and percentage of women in national legislatures, 1990

* as a percentage of total female population aged 15 to 64.
Source: OECD, 1992: 39 and Skjeie, 1992: 87.

With regard to single parents, advance maintenance payment schemes (similar to the Norwegian 1992 legislation) were in place in Sweden and Denmark already from the 1960s. More recently, Belgium and Luxembourg have introduced similar legislation (op. cit.: 171). In contrast, the UK, US, Australia and Ireland still restrict the government's role in this area to the legal enforcement of maintenance allowance payments by the liable parent (ibid.). Gauthier further points out that Luxembourg and France introduced minimum guaranteed income schemes in 1986 and 1988, which might be of particular importance to low-income single parents.

The 1960s and 1970s saw major improvements in maternity leave and parental leave across the board. Gauthier writes:

> With further increases in women's participation in the labour force, and especially mothers with young children, there were renewed calls for additional improvements to these schemes... In contrast to family allowances, which stagnated in the 1975-90 period, maternity leave schemes were significantly upgraded in most countries. In terms of duration, maternity leave increased from a cross-national average (18 countries) of 15.5 weeks in 1975 to 22.1 weeks in 1990. The strongest increase was observed in the Nordic countries...the other form of benefit which has been the target of major reforms since 1975 is the extended leave for child-care. As of 1975, only Australia and Italy had introduced such leave. Over the next years, they were joined by a dozen more countries (op. cit.: 173, 177) .

Public provision of child care differs widely between countries. In 1988, Belgium, France and Italy were in the lead and Japan, Canada and Australia at the bottom. In all countries the coverage is much higher for children above the age of 3 than below this age (op. cit. 1996: 181). Gauthier argues that inter-country differences reflect national differences in the perception of who should provide child-care facilities. The Nordic countries, along with France and Belgium, are 'maximum public responsibility' countries, while the Anglo-American nations comprise a 'maximum private responsibility' group of countries (op. cit. 185). However, this picture might possibly be modified if taking into account subsidies to private care. For example, tax allowances and tax credits to families with dependent children appear more widespread in Anglo-America, in particular in the US and Canada, than in the Nordic countries (op. cit. 169). Differences between countries may to some extent at least represent differences in the *means* ruling elites employ to ease the burden of working parents with preschool children, rather than differences in policy responses per se. Some countries may rely primarily on tax-and-spend policies, others on a mix of tax subsidies and regulatory policies.

In a 1993 study comprising not only OECD countries but also newly industrialized (NIC) and developing countries, Cochran observed an increased emphasis on child-care policies and programs across the board, although the institutional designs of these policies displayed large variations. Cochran (1993: 638-41) differentiated policies along the following dimensions: 1) *Child versus parent/community as targets.* Some countries focus on the child as the receiver/benefactor of money and services, others on the parents (in particular the mother). 2) *Quality-quantity.* Some countries, in particular early entrants to the field, primarily emphasize coverage; others put a large emphasis also on quality. This is related to the 3) *regulated-unregulated* dimension. Regulations that serve to improve the quality of non-parental child care also increase the cost of the care. 4) *Younger/older children.* There is a tendency to focus on parental leave schemes, or family day-care homes, for the under-threes, and group care and early education experiences for the over-threes. 5) *Public-private financing.* Public revenues have been the major source of financing in China and former Communist Europe, where a large part of the national economy has been planned and/or run by the state. The Nordic countries employ large public sector investments and have discouraged the use of profit as an incentive to create more facilities, but expect parents to contribute on a sliding scale. In even more market-oriented countries the direct fee burden on parents is greater (but, as argued above, this may possibly be partly compensated by more liberal tax allowances). In the Anglo-American countries the profit motive is permitted, and at least in the US this has led to fully private companies that operate large networks of day care centres on a franchise basis. Spedding (1993: 542) also points out that virtually all US states offer kindergarten programs for five-year-olds, usually through the public schools.

Concluding remarks

In a historical perspective, the 20th century is marked by a common surge in social security devices across countries (Flora and Heidenheimer 1981; US Department of Health and Human Services 1992: xxxi). An influential hypothesis in trying to explain this common surge has been to focus on how the process of industrialization and urbanization ('modernization') exposes the population to new and old social risks, while at the same time weakening or destroying the old security/insurance institutions prevailing in an agrarian society, such as the guild, the village community, the extended family and the tribe. In a situation where old-style insurance institutions begin to crack, citizens will redirect their demands for security to new, 'modern' institutions, dominant among which is the *state*. Political elites of various colours may respond to these demands in order to conquer and/or maintain power. Through their competition for office, different types of welfare/social security devices emerge across all industrializing countries.

The social structure of industrialized societies did not turn static after the completion of the so-called industrial revolution. Rather, new societal transformations have long been under way, inducing further changes in our social structures. These changes may loosely be summed up under the labels 'post-modernization' or 'post-Fordism'. Increased differentiation of the household structure is one of the changes associated with this development.

In his comparative analysis of the history of social security, Baldwin (1990) stresses differences in risk characteristics in the population to explain controversies over social policies.[15] Baldwin points out that risk categories are correlated to social categories, and relates the demands for social protection on behalf of the industrial working class in particular to the high risk incidence of these occupational groups. Now it might be that risk categories are also correlated to gender differences, in particular with regard to care and family policies. If so, the risk perspective may contribute to an explanation as to why social policies seem to encompass a gender as well as (or in combination with) a class dimension (see also Nelson 1984).

This article has traced policy changes related to changes in household vulnerability. By limiting the analysis primarily to one country, I have aimed at an analysis rich in institutional detail across a wide range of social policy areas. Whether or not we are witnessing a cross-national trend will first and foremost depend on whether the redefinition of female roles, and the accompanying changes in household structures, are world-wide phenomena, or tied to specific national/cultural contexts. Cochran, although emphasizing the differential nature of policy responses, claims that one may nonetheless identify a common, underlying trend:

> The processes of industrialization and urbanization were major factors contributing to loss of traditional family roles and structures... The prevalence of the one-parent family...extends the more general shift from extended to nuclear family one step further in reduction of the child care resources available inside the family... It is easy to leave the impression that the public child care programs in a given society are a static resolution of...value tensions, when in fact historical analysis shows shifts over time in the way these pressures are addressed. Analysis of these historical changes across societies reveals what appear to be patterns that...transcend individual countries... The most powerful crosscutting trend...involves a shift in the direction of greater equality for women, both inside the family and in broader community affairs (Cochran 1993: 630, 631, 655).

However, it is not possible to distinguish between an assumption that all countries are marked by the same underlying transformation (the modernization/diffusion scenario), or if they belong on fundamentally different paths. We need longer time series before we can make more than educated guesses in this respect. Also, it is hardly likely that the *organizational designs* of policy responses should mimic the Scandinavian preference for tax-and-spend measures. The Scandinavian countries, including Norway, are unitary states with a tradition of centralized tax-and-spend policies. Countries with a lower tax take, and thus a limited scope for broad-based tax-and-spend measures, may possibly rely more heavily on indirect policy measures to satisfy new security demands (Castles and McKinlay 1979: 174, 177; Overbye 1997). One option might be to rely more heavily on tax relief, both to families and to businesses who set up and run child-care facilities. Another option might be to set up a more extensive regulatory framework, for example by mandating employer-sponsored periods of maternity and parental leave. Demands might also be levied on unions to pursue social protection measures through collective bargaining. Also, one should not forget that the extended family may still be operative, although the household unit has become steadily more individualized. Families may care from a distance, in particular if mobility is limited (children do not set up separate households too far away from their parents), and grandparents are not too involved in the formal economy, implying that they have time available for caring.[16] Finally, if all else fails the working-age population might also limit vulnerability simply by limiting the number of children per household.[17]

Be this as it may, the reorientation of the Norwegian welfare state may in any case illustrate a more general phenomenon: social changes change risk structures. And changed risk structures stimulate demands for new security devices, be they tax-and-spend policies, regulatory policies, tax credits, demands for trade union initiatives or other measures to reduce risk exposure to acceptable levels. In this sense, there is continuity in the development of social security institutions. During the late 19th and early 20th century the rise of industrialism and the breakdown of the traditional insurance institutions of an agrarian society spurred innovations and growth in a wide range of social policies. Today, the post-modernization and deindustrialization of our societies yet again change risk structures, which create new security demands, and provide new opportunities for politicians of various colours to suggest ways to cope with these issues, in their never-ending struggle to conquer office and realize their particular vision of the good society.

Notes

1. This is coupled with the risk of a depreciation of their human capital, to the extent that the birth of a child is followed by a prolonged period of absence from the labour market; implying that acquired skills may become obsolete, or not kept up to the mark (due to lack of continuous on-the-job training).

2. Sick pay is taxable income in Norway.

3. At the same time, a mother was granted 6 weeks of paid leave due to death of an infant.

4. 'Man-labour years' is the standard translation of the Norwegian concept 'årsverk'. However, with regard to those who are actually employed in these service professions, a much more accurate expression would be 'woman-labour years'.

5. However, a single parent who lives together with the father of the child, or cohabitates with another person more than 12 out of the last 18 months, loses the extended benefit (NOU 1996: 82).

6. Parents with handicapped children, parents from cultural minorities and refugees also have privileged access to kindergartens (op. cit.).

7. Transition allowance is in the process of being restructured. According to the government's proposal, benefit levels are to be raised but the duration of the benefit shortened, so that the allowance will 'normally' expire when a child reaches school

age. Also, the benefit is 'usually' to be limited to a time span of only three years. However, if the single parent starts a 'necessary' education, the benefit may be granted for up to 5 years (St.meld. 35, 1994-95: 126).

8. We are here witnessing yet another version of the old redistribution versus incentives dilemma: limiting the benefit only to those who are 'genuinely' single would target limited public funds more effectively at the weakest and most destitute single parents. However, it would also discourage single parents from trying to establish a stable relationship with a new partner.

9. Of these, 16 percent had a child with a new partner, and 8 percent married a new partner. Other reasons for the termination of the allowance were a) youngest child reached the age of 10 (28 percent), b) renewed cohabitation or marriage with initial partner (23 percent), c) rise in labour income (10 percent), lost custody of the child (3 percent), was eligible for other social security benefits (3 percent) and 'other reasons' (5 percent). The respondents were a random sample of Norwegian single parents who discontinued the transitional allowance between July 1989 and June 1990. N=579 (Terum 1993: 69).

10. The grant depends on the age of the child (higher grants for children less than 18 months of age) and the health of the child (higher grants for sick and disabled children).

11. The reform also somewhat reduced women's incentive to enter the formal labour force in the first place.

12. In addition, the state pays a substantial - and increasing - percentage of total costs through general revenues. The Norwegian system thus mimics Bismarckian-style tripartite financing.

13. The UK deviation may possibly be explained by the UK tradition of single-member constituencies. In single-member constituencies, the internal nomination process within each party is likely to be particularly intense, and the willingness of parties to award anybody but the safest of cards first place similarly limited.

14. Gauthier also mentions that means testing was introduced in Denmark (1976) and Japan (1978), but then abolished again in 1981 and 1985.

15. Interestingly, Barr (1992) also uses a risk perspective in explaining the surge in publicly provided social security devices. Barr points out that various market failures in insurance markets limit the ability of private markets to satisfy a popular demand for security, implying that this demand is redirected to the political agenda. Thus historians (Baldwin) and economists (Barr) intersect in moving the concept of risk to centre stage in the study of social policy.

16. Preretirement schemes should increase time available for grandparents to care for grandchildren while their working-age children are employed elsewhere. If so, generous preretirement options may possibly, to some extent at least, serve as a substitute to publicly provided child-care facilities. Also notice that increases in pensions and other wealth among the elderly, in conjunction with declining fertility (implying that there are fewer grandchildren per grandparent) may increase the scope for transfers between generations, to ease the life-cycle squeeze of parents with small children.

17. Interestingly, Hatland and Skevik (1996) notice that fertility rates as of 1993 are higher in Scandinavia than further south in Europe. Also, fertility has been on the increase in Scandinavia from 1983 till 1993, while it has declined further south.

References

Andreassen, B. (1992) Article 22, in Eide, A. et al. (eds.) *The Universal Declaration of Human Rights: a commentary*. Oslo/Oxford: Scandinavia University Press.
Baldwin, P. (1990) *The politics of social solidarity*. Cambridge: Cambridge University Press.
Barr, N. (1992) *Economic theory and the welfare state: a survey and interpretation*. Journal of Economic Literature, vol. XXX: 741-803.
Bjørnson, Ø. (1994) 'Sykeforsikringsloven - mellom tysk forbilde og norsk virkelighet' in Bjørnson, Ø. and Haavet, I.E. (eds) *Langsomt ble landet et velferdssamfunn*. Oslo: Ad Notam.
Castles, F. and McKinlay, R. (1979) 'Does politics matter? An analysis of the public welfare commitment in advanced democracies', *European Journal of Political Research* 7: 169-86.
Cochran, M. (1993) 'Public child care, culture, and society: crosscutting themes', in Cochran, M. (ed.) *International handbook of child care policies and programs*. London: Greenwood Press.
Flora, P. and Heidenheimer, A. (1981) *The development of welfare states in Europe and America*, London: Transition Books.
Gauthier, A. (1996) *The state and the family*, Oxford: Clarendon Press.
Gustafsson, B. (1995) 'Foundations of the Swedish model' *Nordic Journal of Political Economy*, vol. 22: 27-40.
Haavet, I. (1994) 'Befolkningspolitikk og familiepolitikk', in Bjørnson, Ø. and Haavet, I. (eds) *Langsomt ble landet et velferdssamfunn*, Oslo: Ad Notam.
Hatland, A. and Skevik, A. (1996) *Changes in the family*, paper presented at The European Institute of Social Security International Colloquium, 'The New Social Risks'. University of Nantes, October 3-5.
Hippe J. and Pedersen, A. (1992) *Når jobben betaler* Report no. 136, Oslo: Fagbevegelsens senter for forskning, utredning og dokumentasjon.
Koren, C. (1997) *Trygd og omsorgsarbeid*, report, Oslo: Norwegian Social Research.
Kuhnle, S. (1983) *Velferdsstatens utvikling*, Oslo: Universitetsforlaget.
Loedemel, I. and Schulte,.B. (1992) *Social assistance: a part of social security or the poor law in new disguise?* Paper presented at the SPRU conference, 'Social Security 50 Years after Beveridge'. York: September 27-30.

Narud, H. (1996) *Voters, parties and governments*, report no. 7. Oslo: Institute of Social Research.
Nelson, B. (1984) 'Women's poverty and women's citizenship: some political consequences of economic marginality', in Gelpi, B. et al. (eds.) *Women and poverty*, Chicago: The University of Chicago Press.
NOU (1993) *Levekår i Norge*, Green Paper no. 13, Oslo: Government Printing Office.
NOU (1996) *Offentlige overføringer til barnefamilier*, Green Paper no. 13, Oslo: Government Printing Office.
OECD (1992) *Historical statistics 1960-1990*, OECD: Paris.
Osmunddalen, Å. and Kalve, T. (1993) *Er pensjonene for lave?* Samfunnsspeilet vol. 7: 19-23.
Overbye, E. (1997) 'Convergence theory reconsidered: the politics of pensions in Scandinavia and Australia', *Australian Journal of Political Science* (forthcoming).
Pedersen, A. (1996) *Sykefraværet og arbeidslinja*, Working Paper no. 4. Oslo: Fagbevegelsens senter for forskning, utredning og dokumentasjon.
Pettersen, P. (1987) *Pensjoner, penger, politikk*, Oslo: Universitetsforlaget.
Rold Andersen, B. (1984) *Rationality and irrationality of the Nordic welfare state*, Daedalus, winter 1983/84: 8-52.
Skevik, A. (1997) *The state-parent-child relationship after family break-ups: child maintenance in Norway and Britain*, paper presented at FISS 4th International Research Seminar, 'Issues in Social Security'. Sigtuna, Sweden 14-17 June.
Skjeie, H. (1992) *Den politiske betydningen av kjønn*, report no. 11, Oslo: Institute of Social Research.
Sosialt Utsyn (1993) Oslo: Central Bureau of Statistics.
Spedding, P. (1993) 'United States of America', in Cochran, M. (ed.) *International handbook of child care policies and programs*. London: Greenwood Press.
Statistisk Årbok (1996) Oslo: Central Bureau of Statistics.
St.meld. 4, (1992-93) *Langtidsprogrammet 1994-97*, Oslo: Government Printing Office.
St.meld. 35, (1994-95) *Velferdsmeldingen*, Oslo: Government Printing Office.
Terum, L. (1993) *Stønad, samliv og sjølvforsørging* Report no. 1. Oslo: Institute of Applied Social Research.
Trygdestatistisk Årbok (1986) Oslo: Rikstrygdeverket.
US Department of Health and Human Services (1992) *Social security programs throughout the world - 1991*. Washington: Social Security Administration.

3.2 The state-parent-child relationship after family break-ups: Child maintenance in Norway and Britain

Anne Skevik

Introduction

A growing number of children is living in households with only one of their parents, and this parent is usually the mother.[1] This is not because their mothers are widowed, as has sometimes been the case in earlier periods, but because their parents have decided they do not want to live together: the growing numbers of lone-parent families are caused by increasing divorce rates and more women having children without being formally married. This is the case in the Anglo-American as well as in the Nordic countries, and also in most of the continental nations (Bradshaw et al. 1996). The 'reverse side' of this pattern is that a growing number of men have children they are not currently living with. This new family pattern has given rise to a number of questions, including how to determine fatherhood, how the rights of legal parenthood should be shared among non-married parents, the children's right to know both their parents, and the financial provision for children after relationship break-up.

Only the last of these issues will be addressed in this article: who provides for the children of divorced and never-married parents? The purpose is to investigate how the state intervenes in the mother-father-child relationship in situations of family break-ups. This will be done by conducting an in-depth study of two countries which have both introduced special types of legislation to deal with this particular issue: Norway and Britain. By conducting a detailed analysis of the institution of child maintenance in the two countries, it is possible to narrow in on differences in policy approaches as regards the relationship between the private and public sphere more generally. Moreover, these questions are likely to trouble the minds of legislators in an increasing number of countries, as most countries - like Norway and Britain - are now experiencing a similar breakdown of the 'standard nuclear family'. Consequently, politicians in a number of countries have to search for ways to deal with the increasing variety of household structures emerging across countries. The question of child maintenance arrangements therefore have relevance far beyond the countries studied.

Two aims of child maintenance

The fundamental idea of all child maintenance arrangements is that the responsibilities of parenthood go beyond the relationship with the other parent: bringing a child into the world is the work of two people, and those two people are jointly responsible for the child's well-being. That all children, including the children of lone parents, should have a certain minimum living standard is hardly a controversial statement. More controversial is the question of who is primarily - and secondarily, and tertiarily - responsible for providing the resources necessary for maintaining this minimum. Provision for children in lone-parent families is usually a matter of combining different sources of income, where the availability of each varies between countries (Millar 1994). Often, the mother will have an income from her own work outside the home - in some cases she will be fully self-supported. The countries differ to the extent their policies aim at enabling lone mothers to take up paid employment (Bradshaw et al. 1996), and to the extent they are willing to provide the lone parent with state benefits. Also, the availability of support from private sources will vary. Defining the right balance in the triangle wages-maintenance-benefits is therefore a matter of considerable political debate, where solutions vary between countries. Which politics should be adapted to protect the children of lone parents against poverty? This question, focusing on protecting children, provides one starting point for the debates on child maintenance.

Another political concern arising from the growing number of lone-mother families, particularly in the Anglo-American countries, is the question of the long-term effects these families may have on a number of issues, including the relationship between the sexes. On the one hand, there is the concern that men are marginalised within the family, that men will become 'superfluous' altogether. The existence of lone-mother families, not to mention the increasing prevalence of this family form, has been described as 'insulting' to the fathers who do stay married and provide for their families (Murray 1990). In addition, some observers worry about the consequences of children being deprived of their male role models (Dennis and Erdos 1992). These arguments are controversial in this form, with their inherent attacks on lone mothers. These ideas gain more widespread support when the searchlight is turned around - off the lone mother, and towards her ex-partner: bringing children into the world is the responsibility of two people, the argument goes - men should not be let 'off the hook' too easily when the relationship breaks down. Fathers should not be allowed to leave their families and place the entire burden of provision and caring for the children on the mother.

Child maintenance arrangements can thus have two different starting points, which I will call 'the child's right' and 'the father's duty'. Every child has a right to be adequately provided for: the right to food and shelter, clothes, and to live a life according to the prevailing living standards in his or her community. That the money to ensure this is available to the family, is more important than where the money comes from. Maintenance, whether it be from the mother's income, the father's payment or state transfers, is the right of the child. The other starting point is 'the father's duty'. According to this logic, the duty to maintain one's own children is absolute and unconditional, and cannot be 'transferred' to the other parent, the state or anybody else. This logic focuses on the father and the duties of parenthood rather than the right of the child, and implies that the state will only intervene where the family fails.

In real life, there is no absolute division between these two theoretical principles. They exist as analytical starting points, not as empirical examples. Furthermore, there is obviously a duality of the two principles: the parent's duty is the children's right, and vice versa. Still, the differing focus may be useful to keep in mind, as we move on to describe the different systems of Norway and the UK.

Norway and Britain

The most important reason for comparing Norway and Britain is that these are two of the relatively few countries which have moved the maintenance decisions away from the courts. Also, both countries have introduced a set of standardised rules for maintenance assessments. This contrasts with the traditional solution, which prevails in a number of European countries, where maintenance determination is largely dealt with in court on a case-by-case basis. Further, the institutional changes in the two countries happened at roughly the same time, and against the same demographic background of rising numbers of lone-parent families. Both these factors, the institutional and demographic similarity and the congruence in time, speak for selecting those two countries for a 'most similar case' approach. However, the political context in which the changes happened were rather different, as shown below.

In Esping-Andersen's by-now famous scheme, Norway is described as close to the prototypical Sweden in the social-democratic cluster, while Britain is in the liberal cluster and 'moving closer' to the USA (Esping-Andersen 1990). One of the dimensions Esping-Andersen uses to group the countries is the public/private, or the state/market dimension. This is one of the points where his theory has been attacked from a feminist point of view: conceptualising the interplay of public and private as the sharing of labour between state and market means downplaying the role of the family as a source of economic provision and care, and thereby making women's unpaid work invisible (Orloff 1993, O'Connor 1993, Sainsbury 1994). Starting from this point of view, Jane Lewis (1992) has argued that 'Esping-Andersen's identification of a Scandinavian welfare regime breaks down as soon as gender is given serious consideration. The Norwegian system, which has continued to treat women mainly as wives and mothers, is closer in many respects to that of Britain than it is to Sweden'. She conceptualises welfare states according to the degree they promote the 'male breadwinner model', and describes Britain and Ireland as strong male breadwinner states, France as a modified male breadwinner state, and - not surprisingly - Sweden as a weak male breadwinner state. As the traditional importance of the father's exclusive and unconditional duty to provide for his family is likely to influence the design of the child maintenance scheme, this debate is a further argument for a comparison between Norway and Britain.

The institution of child maintenance is controversial in both countries. Absent parents have criticised both systems and sometimes campaigned against them, yet the level of controversy is far higher in Britain, where the implementation of the Child Support Act has evoked 'a degree of unanimity previously only generated by the poll tax' (Glendinning, Clarke and Craig 1996: 287). The maintenance rules in Britain are also criticised by the lone parents, the recipients of maintenance (op. cit.; Abbott 1996). This has not been the case in Norway. This may imply that it is not the principle of child maintenance as such that provokes resistance, but that the degree of resistance is highly dependent on the actual design of the schemes. Comparing Norway and Britain may help to shed some light on which features are relevant in this respect.

Some knowledge of the different situations of Norwegian and British lone parents may be useful in this context. First, lone mother's labour market participation in Norway is higher than in the UK. 61% of Norwegian lone mothers are in paid employment, 72% of those full-time, compared to 41% in the UK, and only 41% of those full-time (Bradshaw et al. 1996, tab 1.3). In both countries, lone mothers with young children are entitled to benefits that replace wages - the transitional allowance in Norway, Income Support in Britain. The work requirement is relatively liberal in both countries: recipients of these benefits are not required to work until the youngest child is 10 (Norway) or 16 (Britain) years old. Forty-three per cent of those eligible are in receipt of full transitional allowance (1994) (RTV 1995), which equals 29% of all lone parents with children under 16.[2] In Britain, on the other hand, 70% of all lone parents with children under 16 are in receipt of Income Support (1994). However, the length of time in receipt of state support tends to be relatively short in both countries. Terum (1993) found that of all the recipients of transitional allowance, 51% are off benefit within two years, and two-thirds within three years. The mean period on benefit is three years. This is broadly the same picture as Bradshaw and Millar (1991) gave for the UK for recipients of income support.

The main rules

Britain

The establishment of a separate system for child maintenance in Britain began with the White Paper *Children Come First* in 1990. In this paper, two trends are explored: first, the government was concerned with the increasing number of lone-parent families. Second, and perhaps even more important, it wanted to do something about the increasing number of lone-parent families on Income Support - the fact that most lone-parent families were supported by state benefits. Before 1990, maintenance assessment was largely a matter for the courts, but this system was seen as ineffective. The estimated 'going rate' for maintenance assessments was low, a high percentage[3] of lone parents did not receive maintenance at all, and the procedure for reviewing awards was slow and difficult. This imposed high costs on the state budget - on the taxpayers, in the government's language. Thus the aim of the new system was to reduce public spending and to establish a more predictable and consistent system that made sure fathers 'honoured their responsibilities to their children', and that both parents' work incentives were maintained (Government White Paper 1990b). The Child Support Act, which was passed by Parliament in 1991, was presumed to encompass all these aims.

All non-custodial parents in the UK are liable to pay maintenance to their children. Following from the Child Support Act, the enforcement of this duty has been organised by the Child Support Agency (CSA) since April 1993. This duty is independent of the previous relationship between the parents, implying that a casual sexual partner has the same obligations as a divorced father (Fox Harding 1996). However, where none of the parties receive state benefits,[4] using the Agency is voluntary. Only parents in receipt of these benefits are required to co-operate. The child support legislation has been heavily criticised, and has been under constant review since it was set up. Some of the criticisms were met in the modifications made in February 1994 and January 1995, which at the time of writing were the last rounds of substantial changes to the CSA rules.

The formula for estimating the amount of maintenance is complex, taking into account the costs of raising children, the number of children and the income of the absent parent. Rates for the costs of children are based on Income Support rates, and represent the day-to-day living expenses of maintaining children. This amount also includes an allowance for the parent: a percentage of the adult person's allowance depending on the age of the children. On the side of the absent parent, an exempt income - the adult person's allowance, reasonable housing costs and costs of children with a new partner where this applies - is deducted from the absent parent's income, and 'left out' of the maintenance calculation. Since the 1995 changes, housing costs of a new parent and step-children are also allowed for in the exempt income. As a general rule, 50% of net income above the exempt income will be payable in maintenance. If this sum is lower than or equal to the maintenance requirement, this rule applies. If it is higher than the maintenance requirement, additional maintenance will be due: from 15% for one child and up to 25% for three or more children. If the absent parent's ability to pay is very low, there is a minimum maintenance of £4.80 a week (1996). The last step in calculating maintenance is to estimate the protected level of income, where the needs of the absent parent and everybody living in his household are included. This will be higher than the exempt income mostly where the absent parent has established a new family. The protected level of income should make sure that the absent parent and his new family are significantly better off than they would be on Income Support. If the family falls below the protected level of income, maintenance is reduced. In 1995 a further ceiling was introduced, limiting maintenance payments to a maximum of 30% of the absent parent's net income.

Exemptions to the main rules apply in a few cases. In cases where the custodial parent has a high income of her own, she is expected to contribute equally to the support of the child. In these cases, the child support assessment is divided in proportion to the size of parents' respective assessable incomes (Wasoff and Morris 1996). Because of the low labour market participation of British lone mothers, and the high prevalence of part-time work, this applies only to a minority. Special rules also apply in cases where care is shared, where the 'absent' parent cares for the child at least 104 nights a year (an average of two nights per week). The allowance made in the absent parent's net income for basic expenditure (exempt income) will then include amounts for the child, based on time spent with the parent. Since the 1995 changes, 'an allowance is made in exempt income for absent parents...who made a property and/or capital settlement to the other parent of at least £5,000 in consequence of a court order or written maintenance agreement made before 5 April 1993' (CSA 1996a: 34). This is a recognition of what is usually referred to as 'clean break settlements' and represents an easing of the rules and a limited opening for discretion in some cases.

As mentioned above, parents with care who are in receipt of state benefits are required to co-operate with the Child Support Agency. This co-operation means providing all information necessary to help trace the absent parent and to assess and collect maintenance due. Only if the custodial parent can argue that co-operation is likely to expose her, or the children living with her, to 'harm or undue distress' can parents be exempt from this requirement. How real this risk is - how seriously it should be taken and what proof should be provided - is one of the few elements of the British child support system that is left to the discretion of the CSA worker. However, mothers on Income Support have little incentive to co-operate with the CSA, as they are very unlikely to see any of the maintenance payments. Maintenance received is deducted from the IS payments with no disregard. To modify this situation, a 'back-to-work bonus' was introduced in 1995. There is still no maintenance disregard for recipients of state benefits, but part of the maintenance payment will be 'saved' and paid as a lump sum when (or if) the parent finds paid employment.

The lack of gain to themselves obviously makes many custodial parents unwilling to let the CSA into their lives. They do, however, have very little choice: a custodial parent who refuses to co-operate fully without proving 'good cause' may face reductions in her benefit payment. These are implemented after a 'cooling-off' period of six weeks, during which the lone parent has time to provide evidence of 'good cause' or to change her mind about co-operation. The benefit reduction is equal to 40%[5] of the parent's IS allowance, which amounts to £19.16 a week (1996/97 rates).

The requirement to co-operate is no less strict on the part of the 'absent' parent. Non-custodial parents who fail to co-operate fully with the CSA may face an 'interim maintenance assessment', which means they will have to pay more maintenance than the ordinary claim. This may happen if the non-custodial parent does not give sufficient information about his own or his new partner's earnings. If a non-custodial parent does not pay his due, the CSA may charge interest of arrears, or make a 'deduction from earnings' order. Among other sanctions, the CSA is also allowed to seek a liability order and to confiscate goods in lieu of payment. The ultimate sanction will be imprisonment, which may be ordered by the magistrates' court where there has been 'wilful refusal and culpable neglect' on the part of the absent parent.

Norway

Up to 1989, maintenance payments in Norway were determined and administered by the chief administrative officers of the counties (*fylkesmannen*), or by the courts in cases where maintenance came up as one of many questions during legal divorce settlements. The legal framework allowed for unlimited discretion, as there were no guidelines for maintenance assessment. The discretion-based system made the process of determination ineffective and time-consuming, which, as the number of divorces and births out of wedlock increased, imposed an unbearable workload on the *fylkesmann*. This problem came up during the work on the Act on Parents and Children, which was passed by the Storting in 1981. The Law Commission, which was appointed in 1975, discussed guiding rules for determination of maintenance, but decided against them as they feared this would make the process too inflexible (BFD 1996). However, a new Law Committee was appointed in 1980 to deal with the question of how to make maintenance demands more effective, and this commission was later asked to look into the question of standard guidelines for determining maintenance. The guidelines suggested by this Commission came into force, with some modifications, in 1989. Effective 1 October 1992 the responsibility for maintenance determination, forwarding and reclaiming was transferred from the *fylkesmann* to the National Insurance Administration. A separate agency, the Maintenance Contribution Collecting Agency, was established to deal with forwarding and reclaiming, while the local National Insurance offices are responsible for maintenance determination.

The formula for determining maintenance in Norway is considerably simpler than its British counterpart. As a main rule, maintenance is determined as a percentage of the non-custodial parent's gross income: 11% for one child, 18% for two children, 24% for three children, and 28% for four or more children. When the National Insurance offices determine maintenance, these rates will be used. Maintenance is to be split equally between the children: if the absent parent has two children, but only pays maintenance for one of them, the maintenance claim will be (18% ÷ 2) 9% of his income. In this way, children with a new partner are accounted for - but step-children are not included. Parents are free to make private agreements in which they may apply higher rates than the official percentages. However, if they wish to apply lower percentage rates, the amount paid should not be lower than the advanced amount (see below). Child maintenance is taxable income for the custodial parent, and tax deductible for the absent parent. All absent parents are liable to pay maintenance, but using the Agency is mandatory only in cases where the custodial parent is in receipt of transitional allowance. Still, approximately 90% of all maintenance cases are settled and administered by the National Insurance (BFD 1996). The majority of those have obviously applied to the NI voluntarily, probably due to the fact that maintenance is not advanced unless the case is mediated by the Maintenance Contribution Collecting Agency.

If the custodial parent wishes, she may apply for 'advance maintenance'. This is a fixed amount, currently NOK 1,020 per month (1996/97). This is forwarded by the Maintenance Contribution Collecting Agency, which in turn reclaims the money from the absent parent. This secures the custodial parent a base income, whether or not the non-custodial parent is paying his due. In this way, the problem of insecurity generated by lack of payments in the UK is largely avoided. Advance maintenance is paid even in cases where the father or his whereabouts are unknown. By December 1995, advance maintenance was paid to approximately 5,900 children whose paternity was not established (RTV 1996). This amounts to 3.8% of all children in receipt of advance maintenance.

Maintenance is determined by discretion in a number of cases: when the child is 18 years or older, if information is missing, if one of the parents lives abroad, and in cases of shared custody, among others. Where the absent parent's income is so low that maintenance for one child (11% of his income) would be less than the advanced amount, maintenance will also be determined by discretion. This is also the case where the absent parent's income is lower than 180 times the advanced amount, while the custodial parent's income is higher than 360 times this amount.

There is no minimum nor maximum maintenance level in Norway. The advanced amount of NOK 1,020 is often referred to as the 'minimum maintenance', but this is not strictly true. This amount will always be received by the custodial parent (she only needs to apply), but it will not necessarily be paid by the absent parent. If his ability to pay is very low, maintenance may be determined at zero. In such cases, the state will provide the difference between maintenance paid and maintenance received. The state will also, through the system of advance maintenance, pay the entire sum if the father is unknown. On the other hand, if the mother is in receipt of transitional allowance, this will be co-ordinated with her maintenance. The advanced amount is disregarded, but of all payments exceeding this amount, 70% is claimed by the National Insurance Scheme. As for the better-off parents, the maximum maintenance settled by the Agency is five times the advanced amount. Still, parents are free to make private agreements on higher amounts - there is no upper limit.

Non-payment of maintenance is an issue between the non-custodial parent and the Maintenance Contribution Collecting Agency. Parents may reach private agreements, but if problems such as non-payment occur, either party is free to apply to the National Insurance to take responsibility. The Maintenance Contribution Collecting Agency has ways to collect unpaid maintenance, usually by making deductions of earnings orders. Unpaid maintenance is registered as debt to the National Insurance Administration. By January 1996, this debt had reached NOK 2.8 billion. This is mostly (87%) debt to the National Insurance; the rest is in arrears to private households (BFD 1996).

Norway and Britain compared

The central characteristics of the Norwegian and British child support schemes are summed up in Table 3.2.1.

It is clear from the table and the above description that despite the apparent similarities, the two countries have established widely different systems: different in terms of the pressures, incentives and insecurities they present the two parents with, in terms of distribution of resources, and in terms of state responsibilities. Which of the two schemes will require absent parents to pay more depends on the number of children and the absent parent's income. An example is shown in Table 3.2.2 for a separated couple with two young children, for different levels of the absent parent's income.

When comparing the two countries, it appears that fathers with low and high incomes end up paying fairly similar percentages of their incomes. The lowest-earning absent parents in Norway pay an estimated 22.2% of net income, compared to the British 18.4%; however, as noted in note 3 to the table, this case is not entirely realistic as payments would probably be reduced due to low income. The highest-earning absent parent in Norway pays slightly less than his British counterpart, as a percentage of both gross and net income. The biggest differences are found for average incomes, at which level British fathers pay 30% of their net income - the maximum - and 22% of gross income, while the corresponding percentages for Norwegians are 23.6% and 18%. In both countries, the lone parents gain nothing from the lowest-earning absent parent. This is also the case in Britain for average earnings. In Norway, this is because the lowest payment is lower than the advanced amount (the estimated 'zero' in the table). In Britain, payments lower than the mother's Income Support are clawed back as compensation for the IS she receives. However, payments above this threshold are kept by the custodial parent. This is the case for the lone parent with the highest-earning ex-partner, who retains 25% of his payments. In Norway, taxation on the margins is very high for lone parents on transitional allowance. This is because of the co-ordination of higher maintenance payments with the transitional allowance, and also because of the special taxation rules for this group. 'Gain to lone parent' is defined as her increase in disposable income, and the '% of child support retained' gives this amount as a percentage of his actual payment. Hence a crucial difference between the two countries is that British lone mothers, once off Income Support, may enjoy a rapid increase in living standards. Norwegian lone mothers, on the other hand, have very little to gain from increased maintenance payments as long as they are in receipt of transitional allowance. They start off with a higher disposable income, but unless they start working for pay, their incomes are not going to increase significantly because of the maintenance they receive.

'Savings to government' are far higher in Britain than in Norway. This is partly because the Norwegian government indirectly subsidises maintenance payments, even at the highest incomes, by allowing them to be deducted from taxes. Because a lone parent on transitional allowance has a very low ability to pay tax, her tax increase in no way makes up for the absent parent's tax savings: this difference is 'lost' to the government. If we had included an example with a working mother, this would look different. Furthermore, when the absent parent has low earnings, the government subsidises the maintenance directly by providing the difference between his payments and her receipt. This is why 'savings to government' is negative for the lowest-earning absent parent: he pays less than she receives, but he still gets the tax deduction - and her income is below the tax threshold. For the two other earnings levels, savings to government are positive, yet very low compared to their British counterpart.

Two models of child support: 'children's rights' or 'father's duties'

The fundamental role of parents towards their children is rarely contested. In both Norway and Britain, parents have the primary responsibility for their own children - being unmarried or divorced does not alter this. But what does this fundamental role entail when the parents are not living together, when 'the parents' have become 'the mother' and 'the father' and live separate lives? What, in these cases, is the role of the parents, and what is the role of the state?

In some cases, unmarried mothers may not want any further involvement with the father of the child, and refuse to name him to the authorities. In other cases, the father is known, but financially unable to keep up provision for his child. A third possibility is that the father is known and financially relatively well off, but for some reason unwilling to provide for children of a previous relationship. How should states handle such threats to the fundamental principle of parental responsibility for provision? As noted in the introduction, there are two possible starting points for dealing with this question: focussing on the 'child's right', or focussing on the 'father's duty'.

Table 3.2.1 Child maintenance in Norway and Britain, 1996

	Norway	Britain
Varies with marital status	NO	NO
Mother required to name father	NO	YES
May be advanced	YES	NO
Minimum payment	NO*	YES
Taxable	YES	NO
Taken into account for social security payments	YES	YES
- disregard	YES	NO
Element of spouse maintenance	NO	YES
Deductions for seeing children	NO*[a]	YES[b]
CP's income taken into account	NO[c]	YES
Reductions for		
- own children in new family	YES	YES
- stepchildren	NO	YES[d]

a   Unless 50/50 sharing of care, in which cases maintenance is determined by discretion.
b   More than 104 nights a year.
c   Not unless the custodial parent's income is very high, while the absent parent's income is significantly lower.
d   Allowed for in protected level of income.
*   Proposed change in the Government discussion paper (Høringsnotat) of 5. September 1996.

Table 3.2.2 Child support in Britain and Norway, 1996*

	Britain			Norway [a]		
	0.5 AME	1 AME	1.5 AME	0.5 AME [b]	1 AME	1.5 AME
Gross income	748	1495	2243	887	1775	2662
Income tax	-91	-271	-450	101	286	593
Social security	-54	-129	-176	69	138	208
Net income	603	1095	1617	717	1351	1862
Exempt income	381	381	381	-	-	-
Assessable income	222	714	1236	-	-	-
Maintenance bill	333	333	333	-	-	-
Maintenance paid	111	329 [c]	447	160	319	479
Income after tax and child support	492	776	1170	557	1031	1382
Cost to absent parent						
% of gross income	14.8	22	20	18.0	18.0	18.0
% of net income	18.4	30	27.6	22.2	23.6	25.7
Gain to lone parent [d]	0	0	114	-	16	8
% of child support retained	0	0	25.5	-	5 [e]	8
Incl. forwarded amount	-	-	-	125	74	50
Lone mother's disposable income	445	445	559	1029	1045	1067
Savings to government [f]	111	329	333	-85	12	106

* The table is inspired by Millar and Whiteford 1993, Table 2. Thanks to Charlotte Koren at NOVA (Norwegian Social Research) for helping to compute the Norwegian table.
a   Average incomes in the industrial sector.
b   For incomes this low, maintenance will usually be determined by discretion. Hence the estimated amount merely serves as an illustration.
c   Reduced according to the rule that no-one shall pay more than 30% of their net income in child maintenance.
d   Estimated as the increase in disposable income as maintenance payments increase. '% of child support retained' is this amount as a percentage of the sum the absent parent pays.
e   Retained above the guaranteed level.
f   Estimated as [(the amount he pays - the amount she receives)+(her tax increase - his tax decrease)]. The state guaranteed minimum is taken as the 'zero' of the Norwegian system. The negative tax paid in cash at the lowest income level is excluded from the equation, as this tax deduction is part of the support available to all parents.

All estimates as GBP. Exchange rate Q2 1996:10.02 (OECD 1997).
Separated couple with two children under 11; lone parent in receipt of Income Support in the UK, transitional allowance in Norway, absent parent single, earning average male earnings (AME), housing costs £173 per month.

In Norway, the concept of children's rights is relatively well developed. According to Therborn (1993), Norway and Sweden were the first countries to introduce explicit legal formulations of equal parental obligations and of the best interest of the child as a paramount principle, for instance in custody legislation. Further, Norway was the first country to establish equality between children of married and non-married parents with regard to paternity and inheritance. Even by 1990s standards, the protection of children's rights is particularly strong in Norway. Norwegian children have their own ombudsman, and the children's right is the basic principle in the Act on Children and Parents, as illustrated by §30 in this Act, which establishes 'the contents of parental responsibility': 'The child is entitled to care and consideration from those who have parental responsibility. They have a right and a duty to make decisions on behalf of the child... Parental responsibility should be exercised from the child's interests and needs. Those who have parental responsibility are obliged to give the child a sound upbringing and maintenance. They shall make sure the child is given an education according to its skills and abilities. The child must not be subject to violence or in other ways be treated in a way that threatens or hurts its physical or mental health'.

The view of children as citizens with rights of their own is mirrored in the maintenance legislation. First of all, all children who are not living with both parents are entitled to 'a certain minimum maintenance payment from the government' every month - that is, the advance maintenance. The advance payment is to be regained from the absent parent - this, however, is a matter between the absent parent and the Maintenance Contribution Collecting Agency. That the father is unwilling to pay is not accepted in Norway. But by advancing a certain amount, the state makes sure his unwillingness does not affect the child in any substantial way. Further, if the father is unable to pay due to lack of resources, or if he is unknown, the state will bear the entire costs of the maintenance payment. In this context the fact that mothers are not legally required to name the father should be highlighted. The legislation allows fathers to be 'unknown' without weakening the rights of the mother or the child. In Norway, it is therefore quite clear what happens if the parents for some reason fail to provide for their children: the state steps into the parent's place to ensure that the child's individual right to maintenance is not jeopardised. The child's right takes priority over the possible need to improve the parent's behaviour.

The British legislation has a different starting point. The White Paper *Children Come First* was a direct result of the now famous speech given by Margaret Thatcher in 1990, in which she said 'When one of the parents not only walks away from marriage but neither maintains nor shows any interest in the child, an enormous unfair burden is placed on the other... No father should be able to escape from his responsibility and that is why the Government is looking at ways of strengthening the system for tracing absent fathers and making the arrangements for recovering maintenance more effective.' Hence there is no room for advance maintenance in the British system, and there is nothing the state can do if the absent parent has low ability to pay: the role of the state is limited to putting pressure on the parents to fulfil their role. Like its Norwegian counterpart, the British legislation will not accept unwillingness to pay, but neither will it accept that fathers are unknown. The state has nothing to offer the lone mother and her children if the father does not pay his due, but it can threaten the father with a number of measures to make him fulfil his parental responsibility. Hence the state does not play an independent role directly related to the under-aged citizen in need of provision - the child - but focuses on changing the parent's behaviour, if necessary forcing them to fulfil their parental obligations.

The above does not mean that the concept of children's rights is alien to the British legislation. They are, however, more developed in the Children Act 1989. This Act establishes the child's right to basic welfare provisions - to food, clothing and medical aid, to protection from harm, and to a basic education (Hoggett 1993: 24). The Act further recognises the need that may arise to take children into care if their parents are unable to care properly for them, and protects children from exploitation (sexually or in the labour market) and risk (like smoking or consumption of alcohol). Provided it has 'sufficient understanding', a child has a right to a say in any case that affects its interests, and may take his parents to court asking for a court order to be given about his upbringing (op. cit.). Still, there is relatively little correspondence between the Children Act 1989 and the Child Support Act 1991 (Fox Harding 1994). The Child Support Act is developed within a different political and legal framework - unlike Norway, where the child support legislation can not be discussed without extensive reference to the Children Act 1981.

Transfers father-mother or father-state

In discussing the role of the state v. the role of the parents with regard to provision for children, I have concentrated on the triangle parents-child-state. However, child maintenance becomes an issue only when 'the parents' are no longer a unit. Therefore, in this paragraph I would like to reformulate the triangle of relationships into mother/child-father-state. Who is seen as the main provider for the children of lone mothers: the mother herself (through employment outside the home), the father, or the state? The (often implicit) answer to this question has significant implications for the design of child maintenance schemes.

Concerning child maintenance, the legislators may focus on one of two relationships: mother-father, or father/mother-state. Focusing on the transfer of money from father to mother, whether out of concern for income in the lone-parent family or the duty of the father, means that all fathers have the same obligation. It can be seen as a matter of equality between the sexes concerning the responsibility for children: nobody should have the possibility of walking away. It can also be seen as a matter of equality between social classes: whatever the financial circumstances of the mother, the father has the same obligation to provide for his children. Focusing on the division of responsibility between the parents and the state, on the other hand, may mean that the state will not intervene in private arrangements between the parents as long as they are both independent of public transfers. Mother and father are again understood as a unit, in the sense that the distribution of resources between them is not seen as a public matter. Only when the lone-parent family becomes a burden on the public purse will there be a reason for state interference.

In Norway, the duty to pay maintenance applies to all parents not living with their children. The same rules stating the minimum applies to all: a percentage of the absent parent's income, or a sum equal to the advanced amount. However, where none of the parties are in receipt of state benefits, the parents have more freedom to make their own agreement, and they are not required to use the Maintenance Contribution Collecting Agency. After all, maintenance payments are considered as mainly a private arrangement, and it is an expressed political goal that more parents should make private agreements without involving any public body (BFD 1996). The exception is where the parents have never lived together, in which case the local office of the National Insurance takes the initiative and makes sure a satisfactory agreement is made. Whatever their previous relationship and their respective financial status, some money should always be paid from the father to the mother and their children. The exemptions to this principle are when the father is unknown or has low ability to pay, in which cases the state will 'step in' as described above.

In the UK, child support is not so much an agreement between the parents as between each of the parents and the Child Support Agency. The Agency takes the initiative by sending the appropriate forms to the parents, and in principle, all communication between the parties can be mediated by the Agency. However, this only applies to families where one of the parents is in receipt of state benefits - most often this will be the lone parent receiving Income Support or Family Credit. Where none of the parents claims benefits, they are free to decide for themselves whether or not maintenance should be paid. The state will not intervene in private affairs as long as the private affairs do not impose costs on the state budget. Further, where the lone parent is in receipt of Income Support, maintenance paid is clawed back pound for pound by the state, with no disregard. This clearly points to the British system as a system for shifting the costs between the parents and the state: where the parents are well off, the father may not be required to pay at all. Where the parents are poor and dependent on benefits, the father will certainly be obliged to pay - but the mother and the children won't see any of the money. In both cases, there is no transfer of means from father to mother.

Conclusion

Despite being established at approximately the same time, and despite the similarities in institutional design, the child support systems in Norway and the UK appear to be very different, operating on different logic. The British system was established against a background of concern for the growing number of lone parents, and particularly their increasing dependence on Income Support. The legislation appears as mainly a means to distribute the costs between the parents (her wage/his maintenance) and the state, to a far lesser degree to distribute means between the two parents. The system of clawing back maintenance pound for pound against the mother's Income Support actually prevents very effectively any flow of resources between the parents. If the mother is independent of state benefits, the government will not intervene in maintenance arrangements. If the woman chooses not to apply, again, there may be little or no redistribution of resources between the two parents. Only when the parents 'fail' to support their child by independent means and apply for benefit, will the government intervene, but not by supplying extra cash. The British authorities have nothing to offer except punitive measures - pressuring mothers to name the fathers, pressuring fathers to pay - in these situations.

The differential treatment of mothers on benefit in relation to mothers not on benefit in effect means that Britain has one law for the rich and one law for the poor. Self-supported mothers have a choice whether or not to apply for maintenance - mothers on benefit have no such choice (Wasoff and Morris 1996). Obviously, not applying to the CSA gives the parents a lot more flexibility than the rather rigid CSA formula allows. It seems unlikely that not applying for maintenance means there will be no further involvement between the two parents, nor between the absent parent and the children, although this is of course possible. Rather, a flexible private agreement allows for linking payments with the sharing of care more directly and to a higher degree than the CSA does. In private agreements, the parents may also see the initial settlement, payments or services in kind (gifts, holidays, events) and maintenance payments as united, as part of the same deal, and hence tailor their own best solution. The CSA allows for this to a very limited degree. This may be the reason why some mothers on benefit report that they do not want maintenance through the CSA, even if they would be better off financially: the application of the rigid formula would cause a breakdown in the fragile, but working, relationship they have with their children's father (Clarke, Glendinning and Craig 1994; Abbott 1996). However, unlike their better-off counterparts, poor mothers have no alternative.

Equal treatment was the starting point of the present Norwegian child support legislation: equality between children born in and out of marriage, between parents living in different parts of the country, between richer and poorer families. There is a focus on the transfer of means from the absent parent to the custodial parent: the same rules apply to all, regardless of their receipt of benefits,[6] and the rules for coordinating transitional allowance and maintenance are relatively liberal. The sharing of financial responsibility between parents and the state appears to be of lesser importance - the liberal war cry 'roll back the state' has never really won support in Norway.

Whether the child support legislation starts from a concept of 'the child's right' or 'the father's duty', it will face some problems that seem unavoidable. First, no law can be flexible enough to cover the complexity of modern family life, where families consist of 'my children - your children - our children', and where the realities change rapidly. There seems to be a trade-off between flexibility and efficiency: a scheme flexible enough to cover all the complexities of every-day family life would be ineffective and impossible to administer. Further, child support by definition imposes a continued relationship between partners who have decided they do not want to live together. The break-up of a relationship, whether married or not, is an event that is never easy and rarely happy - especially when it involves children. Child support legislation intervenes in an area characterised by insecurity, disappointment, anger and pain. By their very nature, child support arrangements will never be 'good enough'. On the other hand, most people accept that they have responsibilities for their children - financial and other - that go beyond their relationship with the other parent. Hence it seems likely that child support arrangements that are genuinely centred on the welfare of the child, without being seen as having a hidden agenda - be it the restoration of the traditional family or saving the government money - have good chances of gaining widespread acceptance.

Notes

1. I shall refer to the parent who is living in the same household as the child(ren) as the 'custodial parent', 'the parent with care' and sometimes 'the lone parent'. The parent not living in the household, who is required to pay maintenance, is referred to as the 'absent parent' - though I am aware that some find this term offensive, as 'absent' is the last thing most of those parents want to be. I sometimes refer to the 'absent parent' as 'the father' ('him'), and the custodial parent as 'the mother' ('her'). This simply reflects the most common arrangement.

2. More accurately: as a percentage of those in receipt of additional child benefit. This is paid to lone parents with children under the age of 16. It is not paid if the lone parent has a child with a new partner, or if she has been cohabiting for more than 12 of the last 18 months.

3. Seventy percent of lone mothers and 97% of lone fathers, according to the Government White Paper (1990b).

4. Income Support, Family Credit, Disabled Working Allowance or Jobseeker's Allowance.

5. Increased from 20% by autumn 1996.

6. The exemption is the fact that only where the custodial parent is in receipt of Transitional Allowance, the parents are required to use the Agency. However, this is hardly important in the present situation, when 90% of the couples in question prefer to use the Agency anyway.

References

Abbott, D. (1996) 'The Child Support Act 1991: The Lives of Parents with Care Living in Liverpool'. *Journal of Social Welfare and Family Law* 18 (1): 21-36.

Barne-og familiedepartementet (BFD) (1995) Høringsnotat med forslag til endringer ibarneloven kap. 1-6. BFD 25. oktober 1995.

Barne-og familiedepartementet (BFD) (1996) Høringsnotat. Forslag til endringer ibarnebidragsordningen etter barneloven. BFD 5. september 1996.

Bradshaw, J. and Millar, J. (1991) 'Lone Parent Families in the UK'. Social Security Research, Report no. 6. London: HMSO.

Bradshaw, J. et al. (1996) 'Policy and the Employment of Lone Parents: A Comparison of Policy in 20 Countries'. London: SPRC.

Burgoyne, C. and Millar, J. (1994) 'Enforcing Child Support Obligations: The Attitudes of Separated Fathers'. *Policy and Politics* 22 (2): 95-104.

Clarke, K., Glendinning, C. and Craig, G. (1994) *Losing Support: Children and the Child Support Act*. London: The Children's Society.

Child Support Agency (1996a) *A Guide to Child Maintenance*. CSA 2008 (April 1996).

Child Support Agency (1996b) *Quarterly Summary of Statistics, May 1996*. London: DSS.

Dennis, N. and Erdos, G. (1992) *Families Without Fatherhood*. London: Institute of Economic Affairs, Health and Welfare Unit.

Edwards, S. and Halpern, A. (1992) 'Parental Responsibility: An Instrument of Social Policy'. *Family Law* 22: 113-18.

Eekelaar, J. (1991) 'Parental Responsibility: State of Nature or Nature of the State?' *Journal of Social Welfare and Family Law* 1: 37-50.

Esping-Andersen, G. (1990) *The Three Worlds of Welfare Capitalism*. Cambridge, Polity Press.

Fox Harding, L. (1994) '"Parental Responsibility": A Dominant Theme in British Child and Family Policy for the 1990s'. *International Journal of Sociology and Social Policy* 14 (1/2).

Fox Harding, L. (1996) '"Parental Responsibility": The Reassertion of Private Patriarchy?' In Bortolaia Silva, E. (ed). *Good Enough Mothering? Feminist Perspectives on Lone Motherhood*. London: Routledge.

Garnham, A. and Knights, E. (1994) *Putting the Treasury First. The Truth About Child Support*. London: Child Poverty Action Group.

Glendinning, C., Clarke, K. and Craig, G. (1996) 'Implementing the Child Support Act'. *Journal of Social Welfare and Family Law* 18 (3): 273-289.

Government White Paper (1990a) *Children Come First: The Government's Proposals on the Maintenance of Children*. Volume 1. London: HMSO.

Government White Paper (1990b) *Children Come First: The Government's Proposals on the Maintenance of Children: The Background.* Volume 2. London: HMSO.
Government White Paper (1995) *Improving Child Support.* London: HMSO.
Hoggett, B. (1993) *Parents and Children.* London: Sweet and Maxwell.
Lewis, J. (1992) 'Gender and the Development of Welfare Regimes'. *Journal of European Social Policy* 2 (3): 159-173.
Lister, R. (1994) 'The Child Support Act: Shifting Family Financial Obligations in the United Kingdom'. *Social Politics* 1 (2): 211-22.
Lov av 8. april 1981 nr 7 om barn og foreldre (barnelova). Oslo: Grøndahl Dreyer lovdata.
Millar, J. (1994) 'Mothers or Workers? Policy Approaches to Supporting Lone Mothers in Comparative Perspective'. Paper for the conference 'Good Enough Mothering? Feminist Perspectives on Lone Motherhood', University of Leeds, 6 May 1994.
Millar, J. (1996) 'Poor Mothers and Absent Fathers: Support for Lone Parents in Comparative Perspective'. In Jones, H. and Millar, J. (eds.) *The Politics of the Family.* Aldershot: Avebury.
Millar, J. and Whiteford, P. (1993) 'Child Support in Lone-Parent Families: Policies in Australia and the UK'. *Policy and Politics* 21 (1): 59-72.
Murray, C. (1990) *The Emerging British Underclass.* London: Institute of Economic Affairs, Health and Welfare Unit.
National Association of Citizens Advice Bureaux (1994) *Child Support: One Year On.* CAB Evidence on the First Year of the Child Support Scheme. NACAB 1994.
O'Connor, J. (1993) 'Gender, Class and Citizenship in the Comparative Analysis of Welfare Regimes: Theoretical and Methodological Issues'. *British Journal of Sociology* no. 3, 1993.
OECD (1997) *Main Economic Indicators.* OECD March 1997.
Orloff, A. (1993) 'Gender and the Rights of Citizenship: The Comparative Analysis of Gender Relations and the Welfare State.' *American Sociological Review* no. 3, 1993.
Phoenix, A. (1996) 'Social Construction of Lone Motherhood: A Case of Competing Discourses'. In Bortolaia Silva, E. (ed.) *Good Enough Mothering? Feminist Perspectives on Lone Motherhood.* London: Routledge.
Rikstrygdeverket (RTV) (1995) Trygdestatistisk årbok 1995.
Rikstrygdeverket (RTV) (1996) Trygdeetatens informasjonssider.
Sainsbury, D. (ed.) (1994) *Gendering Welfare States.* London: Sage.
Social Security Committee (1993-94) *The Operation of the Child Support Act: Proposals for Change.* House of Commons 1994.
Social Security Committee (1995-96) *The Performance and Operation of the Child Support Act.* House of Commons 1996.
http://web.sol.no/trygdeetaten/aktuelt/index/html. Published 23 June 1996.
Terum, L. (1993) Stønad, samliv og sjølvforsørging. Om korleis eineforsørgarane brukar overgangsstønaden frå folketrygda . INAS-rapport 93: 1.
Therborn, G. (1993) 'The Politics of Childhood: The Rights of Children in Modern Times'. In Castles, F. (ed.) *Families of Nations. Patterns of Public Policy in Western Democracies.* Aldershot: Dartmouth.
Wasoff, F. and Morris, S. (1996) 'The Child Support Act: A Victory for Women?' In Jones, H. and Millar, J. (eds.) *The Politics of the Family.* Aldershot: Avebury.

3.3 Changes in economic well-being and income distribution in the 1980s: Different measures, different outcomes

Amy D. Crews and Richard V. Burkhauser

Most analyses of how economic well-being and income distribution changed in the United States in the 1980s and 1990s are based on comparisons of cross-sectional data.[1] (See Levy and Murnane 1992 for a review of the United States literature, and Atkinson, Rainwater, and Smeeding 1995 for a review of such studies within an international context.) Most recently, Massey (1997) and Karoly and Burtless (1995) used cross-sectional data to explore the concentration of affluence and poverty in the United States. While much can be learned from these studies, the nature of the data used limits the scope of the questions that can be answered. Cross-sectional data provide a useful way of comparing groups in a given year - e.g., workers, older people, children, those receiving social assistance transfers, those living in a given geographical location, those in the bottom or top tier of the income distribution - with similarly defined groups in another year. However, the individuals in these groups may or may not be the same. To follow the fortunes of a specific group of people in a given year over time, it is necessary to use longitudinal data. While these two alternative data sources may lead to the same conclusions, they need not do so. Here we show that cross-sectional and longitudinal comparisons of the economic well-being and income distribution of persons living in older households or in younger social assistance households in the 1980s yield dramatically different outcomes.

Data issues in measuring economic well-being

Burkhauser, Crews, and Daly (forthcoming) show how sensitive year-to-year cross-sectional comparisons of economic well-being are to the years compared, the income sharing unit chosen, and the inflation adjustment employed. While there are no formal rules for choosing comparison years for measuring changes in economic well-being, it is important to distinguish between changes due to movements up or down the business cycle from the longer-term changes that occur between two similar points in consecutive business cycles. This is especially true with respect to the 1980s, which started with the worst recession since the Great Depression but ended with seven years of uninterrupted economic growth. Here we use cross-sectional data to compare the economic well-being and income distribution of groups in the population in 1979 with similarly defined groups in 1989, the two peak years of the 1980s business cycle. We then use longitudinal data to identify members of these same groups in 1979 and follow them through 1989.[2]

Our data come from the Panel Study of Income Dynamics (PSID) and the Current Population Surveys (CPS). We use the 1980 and 1990 waves of the PSID, which provide household income information for years 1979 and 1989, respectively for both our cross-sectional and our longitudinal analyses. The PSID contains information on approximately 15,400 individuals in 1979 and 14,500 individuals in 1989. For comparative cross-sectional data, the March (1980 and 1990) CPS is used to gather information on income years 1979 and 1989. The CPS contains information on approximately 184,000 people in 1979 and 162,000 in 1989.

Although we will measure the economic well-being and position in the income distribution of individuals, most people share resources with other co-resident individuals and have access to income that does not flow directly to them. For this reason a broader unit, such as a family or a household, is used to collect information on income. But while most researchers agree that the individual is not the appropriate income sharing unit, there is less agreement about who should be included in a broader definition.

The CPS family definition, based on marriage or blood relationship, is often used as the sharing unit in the United States income distribution literature (e.g., Burtless 1996; Karoly 1996; Karoly and Burtless 1995) but the CPS household definition, based on common residence, is used in most cross-national studies (e.g., Gottschalk and Smeeding forthcoming). Atkinson, Rainwater, and Smeeding (1995) argue that using the blood or marital relationship definition rather than the less restrictive common residence definition produces a bleaker picture of the income distribution because it categorizes a larger number of individuals as single-person sharing units even when they reside and share the benefits of living with others.[3] Here we use the CPS household definition when using the CPS data. The PSID sharing-unit definition falls somewhere between the two CPS definitions in that it includes unmarried non-blood-related co-habitants in the 'family' but excludes other unmarried non-blood-related residents. For convenience of discussion, we will use the word 'household' to describe both CPS and PSID sharing units in our analysis, although the PSID definition is not exactly comparable to the CPS 'household' definition.[4]

While measures of income distribution are not affected by the cost-of-living index used, measures of economic well-being are. Boskin (1995) offers the most systematic criticism of the CPI-X index used in most measures of economic well-being and proposes alternative indices for the 1980s that are between 1 and 1.5 percentage points below the CPI-X index. While using alternative cost-of-living measures affects the magnitude of our results, they do not alter our major points. Hence, we use the CPI-X index in this paper.[5]

Sampling weights are applied throughout the analyses. In the cross-sectional analyses, the data samples for 1979 and 1989 contain all observations in the PSID and CPS samples that have non-zero sampling weights. Thus, there are individuals in the 1979 samples who are not present in the 1989 samples, and vice versa. The longitudinal sample is comprised of only those individuals who are in both the 1980 and 1990 waves of the PSID. In the longitudinal case, the sampling weights from 1989 are used in all estimations. (See Hill 1992 for a fuller discussion of the PSID weighting procedures.)

Household income is defined as the sum of all income held by individuals residing in a single dwelling, and is measured as pre-tax and post-transfer income.[6] To account for the fact that $1,000 per week provides a higher standard of living for a single-person household than it does for individuals belonging to larger households, household income is adjusted by an equivalence factor. There is no universally accepted equivalence scale, but the scale used here is one commonly used by cross-national researchers. It has an elasticity with respect to household size of 0.5.[7] In all cases, income is adjusted for household size for the year in which the income is recorded.

Defining population subgroup

To show differences between cross-sectional and longitudinal outcomes of groups, we divide the population in 1979 into three types of households. The first group we define as 'persons living in younger working households.' This group includes all persons living in households headed by an individual aged 61 or younger in which some labor earnings but no social assistance benefits are reported. Although persons living in this subgroup do not rely on social assistance, they may receive work-related social insurance such as unemployment insurance, workers' compensation, or Social Security Disability Insurance benefits.

We define the second group as 'persons living in older households.' This group includes all individuals living in a household headed by a person aged 62 or older. This category primarily captures persons living in households with a retired head who rely on social insurance and private pensions for their income support.

We define the third group as 'persons living in younger social assistance households.' This group is made up of individuals living in households that receive some form of social assistance and are headed by working-age individuals aged 61 and younger. This final group includes persons who rely on non work-related transfers for their income support.[8] While some income from these households may come from work, persons in this population are primarily dependent on non work-related benefits. Four basic programs are used for determining dependence on social assistance: Supplemental Security Income, Aid to Families with Dependent Children, Food Stamps, and General Assistance. Households that receive any one of these transfers are included in the social assistance population.[9]

In the cross-sectional analysis using either the CPS or PSID, the person's population subgroup assignment is defined in each year by the characteristics of the household in which the person lives in that year. Thus, the same individual could be included in the younger working household group in 1979 and in the older household group in 1989. For the longitudinal analysis using the PSID, a person's population subgroup assignment is defined by the household characteristic of the household in which the person lived in 1979.

The household groups we have chosen to follow are important for a number of reasons, First, in a society where work is the primary source of income, persons living in older households, whose members are predominately retired, and persons living in younger households that rely on social assistance transfers are likely to be more vulnerable over the business cycle than the majority of persons living in younger working households. Second, during the period of strong economic growth that dominated the second half of the 1980s, public expenditures on social protection as a percentage of Gross Domestic Product fell in the United States. To the extent that this decline reflects changes in the amount of social protection provided to younger social assistance and older households, the income distribution patterns between these groups and the remaining households should be different. Finally, while economic recovery is likely to raise the income of persons living in younger working households, it is less clear how it affects the well-being of persons living in younger social assistance and older households. Evaluating the experiences of each of these groups separately allows us to directly examine changes in their economic well-being over the business cycle of the 1980s.

Summary measures of economic well-being and income inequality

In Table 3.3.1 we use CPS cross-sectional data and PSID cross-sectional and longitudinal data from the two peak years of the 1980s business cycle to compare changes in economic well-being and income inequality for the entire population and our three subgroups.

Because the PSID can be used as a representative sample of the United States population in a given year as well as a longitudinal sample of that population, we expected our cross-sectional samples from the PSID and the CPS to yield similar results.[10] As can be seen in the first six columns of Table 3.3.1, this is the case with respect to the total population and each of our subgroups.

Table 3.3.1 Summary measures of household size-adjusted income inequality for persons using cross-sectional and longitudinal data

	Current Population Survey[a]			Panel Study of Income Dynamics					
				Cross-Sectional[b]			Longitudinal[c]		
	1979	1989	Percent Change	1979	1989	Percent Change	1979	1989	Percent Change
				All Persons					
90/10 Ratio	6.41	7.70		5.96	7.64		5.83	7.35	
Mean Income	20,803	23,065	10.8	23,065	25,571	10.86	23,704	26,587	12.16
Median Income	18,263	19,316	5.8	19,502	20,439	4.80	20,153	21,207	5.23
Sample Size (individuals)	184,036	162,028		15,424	15,201		11,292	11,292	
				Persons Living in Younger Working Households[d]					
90/10 Ratio	4.54	5.64		3.95	4.88		3.91	5.41	
Mean Income	22,971	25,273	10.0	26,025	29,037	11.57	26,228	29,928	14.11
Median Income	20,532	21,702	5.7	22,459	23,401	4.19	22,570	24,117	6.85
Sample Size (individuals)	133,022	115,676		10,426	10,312		8,018	8,018	
Population Proportion	72.01	71.58		73.67	71.21		77.36	77.36	
				Persons Living in Older Households[e]					
90/10 Ratio	6.93	7.12		6.63	6.83		6.84	7.00	
Mean Income	18,191	21,305	17.1	18,765	22,241	18.52	21,033	17,554	-16.54
Median Income	14,006	16,015	14.3	13,441	16,275	21.08	14,848	12,987	-12.53
Sample Size (individuals)	34,307	32,608		1,780	2,170		1,046	1,046	
Population Proportion	19.10	20.13		15.01	18.66		11.21	11.21	
				Persons Living in Younger Social Assistance Households[f]					
90/10 Ratio	7.64	9.67		5.77	6.70		5.87	9.583	
Mean Income	8,793	8,017	-8.8	8,600	6,423	-25.31	8,198	11,917	45.36
Median Income	6,218	5,158	-17.0	6,586	4,873	-26.01	6,504	9,302	43.02
Sample Size (individuals)	12,772	11,141		2,952	2,425		2,054	2,054	
Population Proportion	6.89	6.69		9.44	8.31		9.70	9.70	

a   Post-transfer, pre-tax household size-adjusted income per individual in 1989 dollars based on data from the March *Current Population Survey* (1980, 1990).
b   Post-transfer, pre-tax household size-adjusted income per individual in 1989 dollars based on data from the *Panel Study of Income Dynamics* (1980, 1990).
c   Post-transfer, pre-tax household size-adjusted income per individual in 1989 dollars based on data from the *Panel Study of Income Dynamics* (1980, 1990). Sample restricted to individuals observed in both years.
d   Individuals living in households with labor income but no social assistance income that are headed by someone aged 61 or less.
e   Individuals living in households headed by someone aged 62 or more.
f   Individuals living in households that are receiving social assistance benefits that are headed by someone aged 61 or less.

Source: Authors' calculations based on the March *Current Population Survey* (1980, 1990) and the *Panel Study of Income Dynamics* (1980, 1990).

Our cross-sectional results for the total population are similar to those of other researchers (e.g., Karoly and Burtless 1995; Karoly 1993). Average economic well-being increased between the two business cycle peak years as measured by mean or median household size-adjusted income but income inequality also grew. We use as our summary measure of income inequality the 90/10 ratio - i.e., the household size-adjusted income of the person at the 90th percentile relative to that of the person at the 10th percentile.[11] With respect to our subgroups, average economic well-being rose both for persons living in younger working households and for persons living in older households. It was only among persons living in social assistance households that average economic well-being fell. That is, the real average household size-adjusted income of persons living in social welfare households in 1989 was lower than the real average household size-adjusted income of persons living in social welfare households in 1979.

Given the qualitatively similar cross-sectional results between the two data sets, the remainder of the paper will concentrate on differences between the cross-sectional and longitudinal samples of the PSID.[12] To be included in the PSID longitudinal sample, an individual had to be observed in both 1979 and 1989; hence, the longitudinal PSID sample size in 1979 is smaller than the cross-sectional PSID 1979 sample. This reflects attrition both because of death and non response.[13]

Cross-sectional and longitudinal comparisons of the total population in 1979 and 1989 are similar. Among persons observed in 1979 and 1989, income inequality and average economic well-being rose between the two peak years of the 1980s business cycle using either cross-sectional or longitudinal data. The increase in median income in the cross-sectional comparisons was 4.80 percent. The increase in median income in the longitudinal data was 5.23 percent.

It is in the subgroup comparisons that important differences are found between the cross-sectional and longitudinal views of household size-adjusted income. When the same people are followed over the period in the younger working household group, their average real household size-adjusted income is shown to rise at a somewhat higher rate - from 1979 to 1989, median income in the longitudinal sample rose by 6.85 percent while median income in the cross-sectional sample increased by only 4.19 percent. But these relatively small differences in the magnitude of growth pale before the change in both size and direction of the growth observed in the other two subgroups. It is these dramatic differences that make it important for analysts to make clear which questions cross-sectional and panel data are being called upon to answer.

Using the cross-sectional data we find that the median household size-adjusted income of persons living in older households in 1989 is 21.08 percent higher than that of persons living in such households in 1979. But when we actually follow the fate of persons living in older households in 1979, we find a drop of 12.53 percent in their median income rather than a substantial increase. Changes in the cross-sectional population due to the entry of new cohorts and the exit of old ones masks the fate of aging older people. It is the entry of higher income 'new' old that is driving the improvements in cross-sectional comparisons of the average economic well-being of persons living in older households.

The contrast between cross-sectional and longitudinal views of persons living in younger social assistance households is equally stark. While the median household size-adjusted income of persons living in social welfare assistance households in 1989 is 26.01 percent lower than that of such persons in 1979, the actual fate of the 1979 cohort of social welfare assistance households is much brighter. The real household size-adjusted median income of persons living in social welfare assistance households in 1979 rose by 43.02 percent over the two peak years of the 1980s business cycle. In this case the much improved economic outcomes of social welfare recipients who exited the program over the decade is masked by cross-sectional comparisons which include a mixture of new recipients and those who remained on the program.

How the distribution of income changed between 1979 and 1989: Cross-sectional versus panel views

Traditional summary measures of income inequality - such as the 90/10 ratio or the Gini, Thiel, and coefficient of variation indices - are well established methods for summarizing inequality in an income distribution. (See Atkinson 1983 for a discussion of these measures.) By design, however, these measures summarize an entire distribution with one value. Because few distributions with known properties can be completely described by one parameter, however, the use of these summary indices produces an incomplete view of the underlying distribution of interest.

Kernel density estimation is an elegant alternative to using traditional summary statistics to measure income inequality. It provides a picture of the entire income distribution in terms of the income density function, from which we can observe the distribution's location, spread and modality simultaneously. It can also capture absolute increases in income levels via shifts in the density function to the right. Hence, it can show that increases in inequality can arise from a variety of types of changes in the shape of the density function. One type, a 'squashing down' in the middle combined with a 'stretching' at each end is typically discussed in the literature (see for example, Danziger and Gottschalk 1995, Figure 5.1, p. 99). But this is only one possibility, as our data will show. Changes in modality are also revealed by changes in 'clumping' at different points along the income scale.

Lorenz curves also provide a picture of the income distribution, but they only provide information about spread and offer nothing about the other two characteristics. Moreover, one can use the density function estimates to derive nonparametric estimates of distribution functions, standard summary indices, and Lorenz curves, if required. For these reasons we use kernel density estimation here to evaluate how the income distribution changed in the United States during the 1980s for the entire population and our subgroups.

In their simplest forms, kernel estimators are smoothed histograms. Data in a neighborhood around a point are used to estimate the distribution of a variable of interest (e.g., income) over a population. However, while histograms restrict observations to any one neighborhood group, kernel estimators theoretically allow an observation to be included in an infinite number of neighborhood groups, which results in a smoothing of the distribution shape. In practice, an observation is included in a finite number of groups, where the number of groups is equal to the sample size. The idea underlying kernel density estimation is a viewing window that slides over the data; the estimate of the density depends on the number of observations that fall within the window as it passes along the income scale.

In all estimates, weighted adaptive bandwidth kernel estimators are used with the Epanechnikov kernel function. Kernel estimators are well established in the statistics and econometrics literatures; an excellent reference on kernel estimators is Silverman (1986). The specifics of the methodology employed here may be found in Burkhauser, Crews, Daly, and Jenkins (1996a).

Changes in the income distribution

The results of our kernel density estimations using PSID data are shown in the Appendix. Appendix Figure 1.4A.1a shows the kernel density estimates for the entire cross-sectional PSID data sample for the years 1979 and 1989. The line marked 'A' denotes the income at which the population density for the 1979 income distribution first rises above the density for the 1989 income distribution. This occurs at $5,850, which is approximately 93 percent of $6,311, the poverty line for a single-person household in 1989. The line denoted by 'B' marks the income at which the 1989 density again becomes taller than the 1979 density. Line B is at $33,250 or approximately five times the poverty line for a single-person household in 1989. These two lines capture the 'middle' of the income distribution for the total population.[14] In Appendix Figure 1.4A.1b, which shows the estimates for the longitudinal PSID data sample, lines A and B occur at $8,700 and $33,730, respectively.

The definitions of the left and right intersection points denoted by A and B in the two samples represent the income boundaries of the drop in middle mass of the entire population over the two peaks of the 1980s business cycle. For each sample we use these intersection points to discuss our subgroups. We do this regardless of where the particular subgroup densities may intersect, since these subgroups are part of the whole population. Appendix Table 1.4A.1 shows how the mass in each distribution is divided across the intersection points of the 1979 and 1989 data in both the PSID cross-sectional sample and the PSID longitudinal sample.[15]

Table 3.3.2 reports the change in the middle mass between 1979 and 1989 using both the cross-sectional and panel sample of the PSID for all people and for the subgroups discussed in Table 3.3.1. As was the case in Table 3.3.1, there are no substantial differences in the results for the overall population. In the cross-sectional sample the middle mass fell by 6.51 percentage points over the decade with 66.82 percent shifting to the right (becoming richer) and 33.18 percent shifting to the left (becoming poorer). Using the panel data, we find that 88.95 percent of the mass shifted to the right and 11.05 percent shifted to the left. Also, similar to Table 3.3.1, results for the subgroup of persons living in younger working households is not greatly changed by using the panel data. The vast majority of the drop in the middle goes to the right - 83.81 percent in the cross-sectional sample and 89.61 percent in the panel sample. The kernel density estimates for this subpopulation are shown in Appendix Figures 1.4A.2a and 1.4A.2b.

Table 3.3.2 Cross-sectional versus longitudinal views of distributional shifts over the peak-to-peak business cycle years of the 1980s

Population Groups	Segments of the Income Distribution	Cross-Sectional Data	Longitudinal Data[a]
All Persons	Change in middle density mass	-6.51	-5.52
	(Percentage shifted left)	33.18	11.05
	(Percentage shifted right)	66.82	88.95
	Change in left density mass	2.16	0.61
	Change in right density mass	4.35	4.91
Persons in worker households	Change in middle density mass	-7.97	-7.22
	(Percentage shifted left)	16.19	10.39
	(Percentage shifted right)	83.81	89.61
	Change in left density mass	1.29	0.75
	Change in right density mass	6.68	6.47
Persons in older households	Change in middle density mass	-0.21	1.21
	(Percentage shifted left)	(b)	269.42
	(Percentage shifted right)	1,028.57	(b)
	Change in left density mass	-1.95	3.26
	Change in right density mass	2.16	-4.46
Persons in social assistance households	Change in middle density mass	-16.85	0.76
	(Percentage shifted left)	100.71	(b)
	(Percentage shifted right)	(b)	306.58
	Change in left density mass	16.97	-3.09
	Change in right density mass	-0.12	2.33

a Sample restricted to observations of the same persons in both years.
b No mass from the middle shifted into this tail; rather, mass from this tail shifted into the middle.
Source: Authors' calculations based on the *Panel Study of Income Dynamics* (1980, 1990). All calculations are based on pre-tax post-transfer household size-adjusted income per individual in 1989 dollars.

It is in the comparisons of subgroups of persons in older households and in social assistance households that the differences between the two samples are dramatic. The cross-sectional view of the income distribution of persons living in older households captured in Appendix Figure 1.4A.3a shows the large drop in middle mass slid entirely to the right and was accompanied by a loss in density mass from the left tail. Appendix Figure 1.4A.3b, using longitudinal data, shows quite a different result. When the cohort of people living in older households in 1979 is followed over ten years their income distribution shifts to the left with all of the loss in the middle mass moving leftward. In 1989 the density mass peaks just above the poverty line and just below the left intersection line A with a second smaller mode at about $18,500. This figure also shows a loss in the density mass in the right tail. As reported in Table 3.3.2, the gain in density mass in the left tail is 2.7 times the loss in the middle mass; thus, more than half of the gain in mass below line A came from the right tail.

The contrast in outcomes between the cross-sectional and longitudinal data sample is equally stark for people living in younger social assistance households in 1979. The cross-sectional data comparison in Appendix Figure 1.4A.4a captures a clear shift to the left in the entire distribution. All drops in middle mass go leftward. Appendix Figure 1.4A.4b shows the outcome is dramatically different when viewed longitudinally. There is a substantial drop in mass in the left tail, a slight increase in middle mass, and a substantial increase in the right tail mass found in 1989 for those who were on social assistance in 1979. Cross-sectional and longitudinal data track two very different distributional movements for this subgroup.[16]

Conclusion

Cross-sectional views of economic well-being and income distribution have dominated the recent literature on the changing distribution of income in the United States. The analyses in this study confirm the results found by others. Household size-adjusted income inequality increased substantially over the decade of the 1980s, with the greatest gains going to individuals living in households that had connections to the labor market or who were headed by someone aged 62 or older. Individuals living in households that depended on social assistance programs saw their economic well-being decline over the decade. However, conclusions about the appropriate policy responses based on these estimates may overlook how these policies may affect individuals over time.

Little difference was found in how the income distribution changed for the overall population when longitudinal rather than cross-sectional data was used. Similarly, longitudinal estimates for the younger working household group were similar to the cross-sectional results. However, large differences were found for the two subgroups most vulnerable to changes in economic policies. When individuals living in households headed by someone aged 62 or older in 1979 were followed, it was shown that they experienced substantial losses in their economic well-being over the decade. Thus, those living in households headed by someone aged 72 or older in 1989 were much worse off at the end of the 1980s than they were in 1979. The differences are equally striking for persons living in households receiving social assistance. Cross-sectional comparisons show that people living in younger social assistance households in 1989 are considerably worse off than those who lived in such households in 1979. However, when people living in a younger social assistance household in 1979 are followed over ten years, their economic well-being is found to dramatically improve.

In creating pictures of the 1980s it is important to set the lens appropriately. For instance, using cross-sectional comparisons of older persons as evidence that across-the-board cuts in social security benefits are less harmful to older people than they would have been in previous decades, because the average income of older people has risen, would clearly miss the fact that while new cohorts of older people are economically better off than previous cohorts, income falls as one ages and the 1980s did not change this reality. Likewise, declines in the economic well-being of those on social assistance programs in the 1980s should not be used to suggest that people who were on social assistance at the beginning of the 1980s became worse off over the decade.

Notes

1. For exceptions, see the recent literature on economic mobility based on longitudinal data, e.g., Duncan, Boisjoly, and Smeeding (1996), Burkhauser and Poupore (1997), Burkhauser, Holtz-Eakin, and Rhody (forthcoming).

2. While all our analyses compare peak-to-peak business cycle years, we do not believe our results are sensitive to alternative choices of appropriately paired years. In Burkhauser, Crews, Daly, and Jenkins (1996a), we find similar cross-sectional results for peak-to-peak and trough-to-trough (1982 to 1992) years using CPS data.

3. Burkhauser, Crews, Daly, and Jenkins (1996a) verify this claim using data from the CPS. While they found qualitatively similar overall results using the two definitions, the proportion of individuals in the lower tail of the distribution was larger using the CPS family-based definition.

4. We also assume that household members equally share household income during the period they are together. Jenkins (1991) makes a strong case for studying the within-household distribution of income. Lazear and Michael (1988) attempt to do so with respect to adults and children in a given household.

5. Burkhauser, Crews, and Daly (forthcoming) show the effect of using the CPI-X index rather than one which does not over-adjust for inflation on the 'cross-over' point - the percentile at which income in period $t + x$ is first equal to income in period t - in across year cross-sectional economic well-being comparisons.

6. The PSID provides information on the money value of Food Stamps and the rental value of the house of home owners but these data are not available in the CPS. For consistency, we do not include the cash value of Food Stamps or the rental value of the house of homeowners in our PSID income measure.

7. Equivalence scales contain assumptions about the returns to shared living. Many equivalence scales, even complicated ones, can be approximated well by a single parameter scale (see Buhmann, Rainwater, Schmaus, and Smeeding 1988). An equivalence scale with an elasticity with respect to household size of 1 (the per capita scale) implies no economies of scale. An elasticity of 0 (i.e., with no adjustments to household income) implies an infinite number of individuals can live equally well with a given household income as a single-person household with that income. An elasticity of 0.5 (the square-root scale) assumes that the true economies of scale lie directly between these two extremes. See Burkhauser, Smeeding, and Merz (1996) for a discussion of the sensitivity of different equivalence scales in cross-national comparisons. The household elasticity implicit in the United States Bureau of the Census poverty scale is 0.56 (Buhmann et al. 1988). While most poverty studies in the United States use the Census poverty scale, it has been severely criticized (see, for example, Citro and Michael 1995). Others who also use the square-root equivalence scale are Burkhauser, Crews, and Daly (forthcoming), Burkhauser, Crews, Daly, and Jenkins (1996a, 1996b), Karoly and Burtless (1995), and Atkinson, Rainwater, and Smeeding (1995).

8. There is a fourth residual group which consists of individuals living in households that do not receive social assistance benefits or labor income. These individuals are included in all analyses for the total population but are omitted from all subpopulation analyses.

9. While it is usual to classify these programs as social assistance programs and programs like Social Security Old-Age and Survivors Insurance as social insurance, in fact, for the vast majority of current older persons, the present discounted value of their social security benefits greatly exceeds what could have been purchased by their

contribution and that of their employer's. For a fuller discussion of these points, see Burkhauser and Warlick (1981) and Steuerle and Bakija (1994).

10. The quality of the PSID data on income is quite high. Several studies have attempted to compare different income components in the PSID with other data sets. The Unicon Research Corporation was commissioned by the National Science Foundation to conduct comparisons of the descriptive characteristics of individuals who had been lost and those remaining in the panel. Becketti et al. (1988) find that while there were statistically significant differences in the empirical distributions of observed characteristics between the PSID and CPS, most were of no practical significance. For some variables, particularly education and income, there was some reason to believe the reports in the PSID may be more accurate than those in the CPS.

    Duncan and Hill (1989) compare various transfer-income sources for the PSID with national aggregates in 1980: AFDC; SSI; Old-Age, Survivors, and Disability Insurance; and other social welfare programs. The PSID aggregates equal 91.8 percent of the official aggregates. This is a major improvement over the 1979 CPS counts. Gottschalk and Moffitt (1992) look at labor earnings and hourly wage rate distributions of 2,500 white men aged 16 to 59 during the years 1970 through 1980 in both the PSID and the CPS. They find considerable conformity in age, education, marital status, and levels of weeks worked. Regression analysis of the earnings and wage distribution over the period shows similar directions of change in between-education group levels as well as in within-group dispersion. The magnitudes differ somewhat, however.

    Fitzgerald, Gottschalk, and Moffitt (1994) find the PSID sample was roughly consistent with the CPS in 1968 and has remained so through 1989 for male heads, wives, and female heads. However, as a rule, the PSID finds higher earnings than does the CPS. One reason for this may be a 'success bias' in panel studies. However, this discrepancy has not worsened over time.

11. In previous work, using cross-sectional data from the CPS, we have found similar results using other measures of income inequality - Gini coefficient, Thiel (0), Thiel (1). See Burkhauser, Crews, Daly, and Jenkins (1996a).

12. Results from analyses using the CPS may be found in Burkhauser, Crews, Daly, and Jenkins (1996a, 1996b). The former study uses the CPS family definition as the income-sharing unit rather than then CPS household definition, but includes analyses using the three population subgroups. The latter study uses the CPS household definition but does not do the subgroup analyses. The results are similar to those presented here for the PSID cross-sectional data.

13. Despite the fact that our PSID longitudinal subsample in 1979 is restricted to those who are still in the sample in 1989, there is little difference between the average economic well-being and the 90/10 ratio of that sample and those of the full 1979 PSID cross-sectional sample.

14. Any definition of middle income is arbitrary. The definition of the middle using the left and right intersection of two densities is appealing in this case only because it creates a visual image of the middle, and it allows for an examination of the symmetry with which the mass contained in the middle shifts into the two tails. (See Danziger and Gottschalk 1995, p. 99, for a discussion of the symmetry property with respect to the disappearing middle class hypothesis.) Our purpose here is not to make a political judgement about the boundaries of the middle class but rather to provide some insight into how the distribution of income changed in the 1980s and how the use of cross-sectional versus panel data to measure this change can influence the observed outcome.

15. Burkhauser, Crews, Daly, and Jenkins (1996a) use cross-sectional data from the CPS and the Family Expenditure Survey of the United Kingdom to show that the middle mass of the distribution in both the United States and the United Kingdom declined during the 1980s but that the vast majority of that mass shifted to the right.

16. These longitudinal differences may be due to effects of policy changes, macroeconomic influences, or a statistical factor, in particular that the 1979 sample consists of people who were receiving means-tested social assistance. Because of regression to the mean such a group of people would tend to have larger incomes in 1989 regardless of other factors. This paper does not attempt to allocate the changes to these effects.

References

Atkinson, Anthony B. (1983) *The Economics of Inequality*, 2nd edition. Oxford: Oxford University Press.
Atkinson, Anthony B., Rainwater, Lee, and Smeeding, Timothy M. (1995) *Income Distribution in OECD Countries: The Evidence from the Luxembourg Income Study (LIS)*, Social Policy Studies No. 18. Paris: OECD, October.
Becketti, Sean, Gould, William, Lillard, Lee, and Welch, Finis (1988) 'Attrition from the PSID,' *Journal of Labor Economics*, 6: 472-492.
Boskin, Michael (1995) 'Toward a More Accurate Measure of the Cost of Living.' Interim Report to the Senate Finance Committee, Advisory Commission to Study the Consumer Price Index, Washington, DC, September 15.
Buhmann, Bridget, Rainwater, Lee, G. Schmaus, and Timothy M. Smeeding. (1988) 'Equivalence Scales, Well-Being, Inequality, and Poverty: Sensitivity Estimates across Ten Countries Using the Luxembourg Income Study Database,' *The Review of Income and Wealth*, 34 (June): 115-142.
Burkhauser, Richard V., Amy D. Crews, and Mary C. Daly. (Forthcoming) 'Recounting Winners and Losers in the 1980s: A Critique of Income Distribution Measurement Methodology,' *Economic Letters*.
Burkhauser, Richard V., Amy D. Crews, Mary C. Daly, and Stephen P. Jenkins. (1996a) *Income Mobility and the Middle Class*, AEI Studies on Understanding Economic Inequality. Washington, DC: The AEI Press.

Burkhauser, Richard V., Amy D. Crews, Mary C. Daly, and Stephen P. Jenkins. (1996b) 'Testing the Significance of Income Distribution Changes over the 1980s Business Cycle: A Cross-National Comparison.' Unpublished working paper, Center for Policy Research, The Maxwell School. Syracuse, NY: Syracuse University.

Burkhauser, Richard V., Douglas Holtz-Eakin, and Stephen Rhody. (Forthcoming) 'Labor Earnings Mobility and Inequality in the United States and Germany During the 1980s,' *International Economic Review.*

Burkhauser, Richard V. and John G. Poupore. (1997) 'A Cross-National Comparison of Permanent Inequality in the United States and Germany,' *Review of Economics and Statistics,* 79(1) (February 1997): 10-17.

Burkhauser, Richard V., Timothy M. Smeeding, and Joachim Merz. (1996) 'Relative Inequality and Poverty in Germany and the United States Using Alternative Equivalency Scales,' *The Review of Income and Wealth,* 42(4) (December): 381-400.

Burtless, Gary. (1996) 'Trends in the Level and Distribution of U.S. Living Standards, 1973-1993,' *Eastern Economic Journal,* 22(3) (Summer): 271-90.

Citro, Connie F. and Robert T. Michael. (1995) *Measuring Poverty: A New Approach.* Washington, DC: National Academy Press.

Danziger, Sheldon and Peter Gottschalk. (1995) *America Unequal.* Cambridge, MA: Harvard University Press.

Duncan, Greg J. and Daniel Hill. (1989) 'Assessing the Quality of Household Panel Survey Data: The Case of the Panel Study of Income Dynamics,' *Journal of Business and Statistics,* 7(4): 441-452.

Duncan, Greg J., Johanne Boisjoly, and Timothy M. Smeeding. (1996) 'Economic Mobility of Young Workers in the 1970s and 1980s,' *Demography,* 33(4) (November): 497-510.

Fitzgerald, John, Peter Gottschalk, and Robert Moffitt. (1994) 'A Study of Sample Attrition in the Michigan Panel Study of Income Dynamics.' Prepared for the conference on Non-response in Panels, Washington, DC, February 24-25.

Gottschalk, Peter and Robert Moffitt. (1992) 'Earnings and Wage Distributions in the NLS, CPS and PSID. Part I of Final Report to the U.S. Department of Labor, Earnings Mobility and Earnings Inequality in the United States.

Gottschalk, Peter and Timothy M. Smeeding. (Forthcoming) 'Cross-National Comparisons of Earnings and Income Inequality,' *Journal of Economic Literature.*

Hill, Martha S. (1992) *The Panel Study of Income Dynamics: A User's Guide.* Beverly Hills: Sage Publications.

Jenkins, Stephen P. (1991) 'Poverty Measurement and the Within-Household Distribution,' ESRC Agenda for Action, *Journal of Social Policy,* 27: 457-483.

Karoly, Lynn A. (1993) 'The Trend in Inequality among Families, Individuals, and Workers in the United States: A Twenty-Five Year Perspective.' In Sheldon Danziger and Peter Gottschalk (eds.), *Uneven Tides: Rising Inequality in America.* New York: Russell Sage Foundation.

Karoly, Lynn A. (1996) 'Anatomy of the U.S. Income Distribution: Two Decades of Change,' *Oxford Review of Economic Policy,* 12(1) (Spring): 76-95.

Karoly, Lynn A. and Gary Burtless. (1995) 'Demographic Changes, Rising Earnings Inequality, and the Distribution of Measured Well-Being, 1959-1989,' *Demography,* 32(3) (August): 379-406.

Lazear, Edward P. and Robert T. Michael. (1988) 'Allocation of Income Within the Household.' Chicago and London: University of Chicago Press.

Levy, Frank and Richard Murnane. (1992) 'U.S. Earnings Levels and Earnings Inequality: A Review of Recent Trends and Proposed Explanations,' *Journal of Economic Literature*, 30: 1333-1381.

Massey, Douglas S. (1997) 'The Age of Extremes: Concentrated Affluence and Poverty in the Twenty-First Century,' *Demography*, 33(4) (November): 395-412.

Silverman, Bernard W. (1986) *Density Estimation for Statistics and Data Analysis*. London: Chapman and Hall.

Appendix

Table 1.4A.1 Percentage of individuals living in each income-to-needs group, by population subgroup and year

Population Groups	Income to Needs	Cross-Sectional		Longitudinal [a]	
		1979	1989	1979	1989
All Persons	Less than left intersection [b]	6.99	9.15	5.67	6.28
	Between left and right intersection [c]	74.68	68.17	75.48	69.96
	Left intersection to poverty line [d]	1.47	1.03	7.88	8.98
	Poverty line to right intersection	73.21	67.13	67.60	60.98
	Greater than right intersection	18.33	22.68	18.85	23.76
Persons in worker households	Less than left intersection [b]	1.30	2.59	3.22	3.97
	Between left and right intersection [c]	76.50	69.53	74.79	67.57
	Left intersection to poverty line [d]	0.61	0.49	1.95	4.62
	Poverty line to right intersection	75.89	69.05	72.84	62.95
	Greater than right intersection	22.20	27.88	21.99	28.46
Persons in older households	Less than left intersection [b]	12.02	10.07	11.75	15.01
	Between left and right intersection [c]	75.54	75.33	72.83	74.04
	Left intersection to poverty line [d]	2.62	1.81	12.07	18.65
	Poverty line to right intersection	72.93	73.52	60.76	55.38
	Greater than right intersection	12.44	14.60	15.41	10.95
Persons in social assistance households	Less than left intersection [b]	41.12	58.09	16.37	13.28
	Between left and right intersection [c]	58.37	41.52	83.32	84.08
	Left intersection to poverty line [d]	6.08	4.14	48.30	32.26
	Poverty line to right intersection	52.29	37.38	35.02	51.81
	Greater than right intersection	0.51	0.39	0.31	2.64

[a] Sample restricted to observations of the same persons in both years.
[b] Left intersection occurs at $5,850 in the cross-sectional data and $8,700 in the longitudinal data.
[c] The right intersection occurs at $33,250 in the cross-sectional data and $33,750 in the longitudinal data.
[d] The poverty line for a single-person household is at $6,311 in 1989 dollars.

Source: Authors' calculations based on the *Panel Study of Income Dynamics* (1980, 1990). All calculations are based on pre-tax post-transfer household size-adjusted income per individual in 1989 dollars.

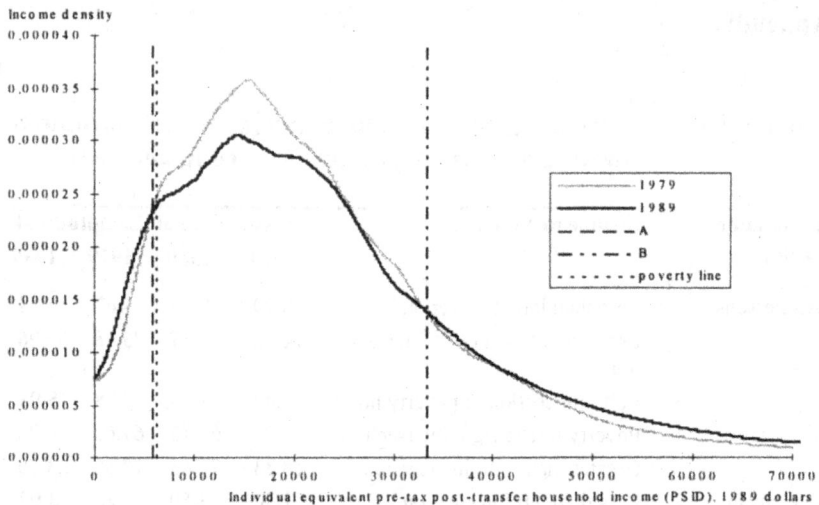

Figure 1.4A.1a The income distribution of the United States in 1979 and 1989: cross-sectional data (total population)

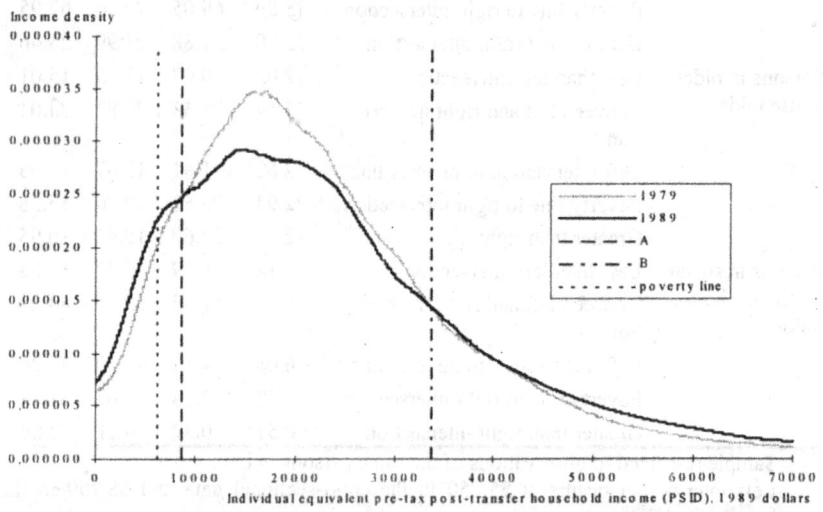

Figure 1.4A.1b The income distribution of the United States in 1979 and 1989: panel data (total population)

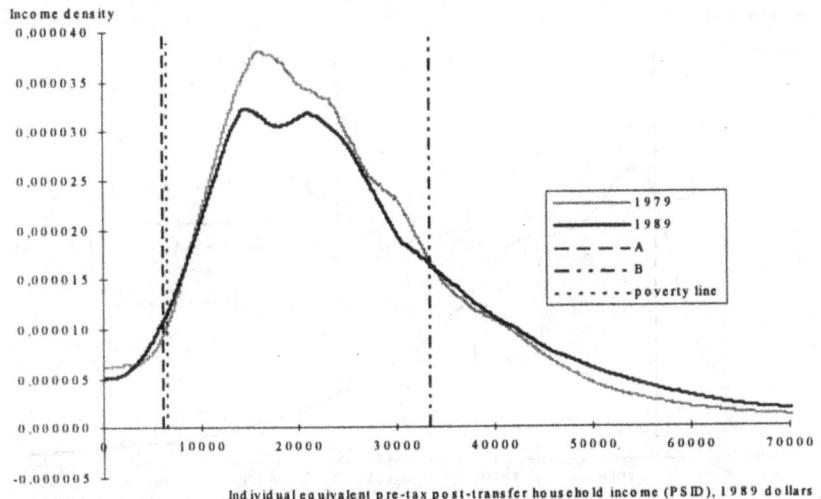

Figure 1.4A.2a   The income distribution of the United States in 1979 and 1989: cross-sectional data (persons in younger worker households)

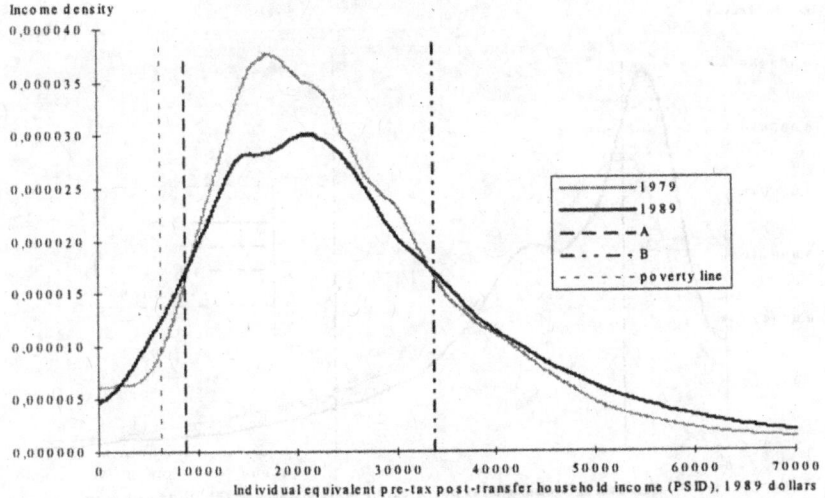

Figure 1.4A.2b   The income distribution of the United States in 1979 and 1989: panel data (persons in younger worker households)

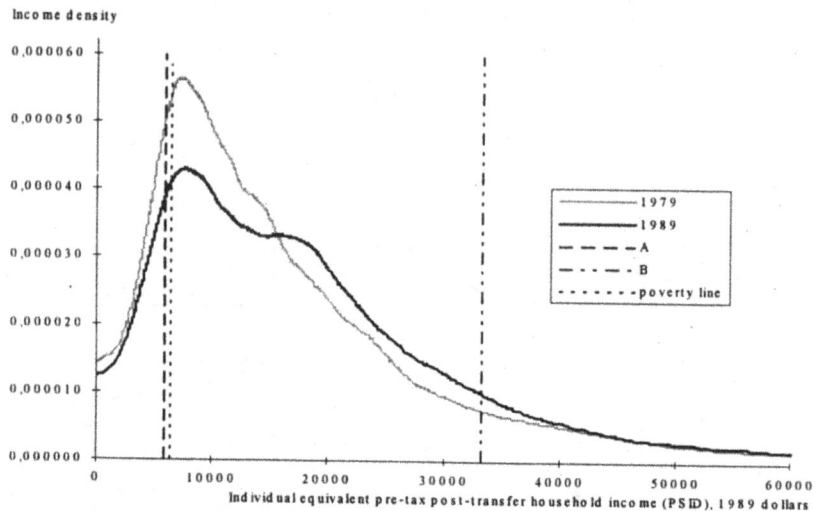

Figure 1.4A.3a The income distribution of the United States in 1979 and 1989: cross-sectional data (persons in older households)

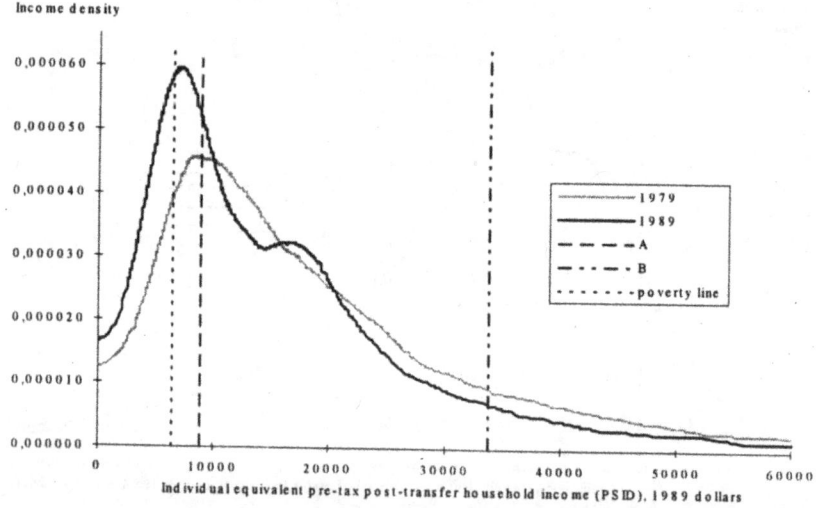

Figure 1.4A.3b The income distribution of the United States in 1979 and 1989: panel data (persons in older households)

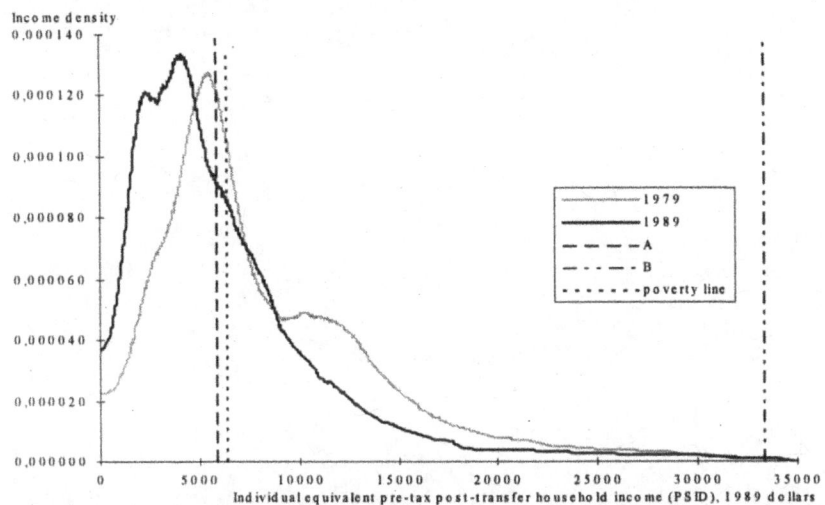

Figure 1.4A.4a The income distribution of the United States in 1979 and 1989: cross-sectional data (persons in social assistance households)

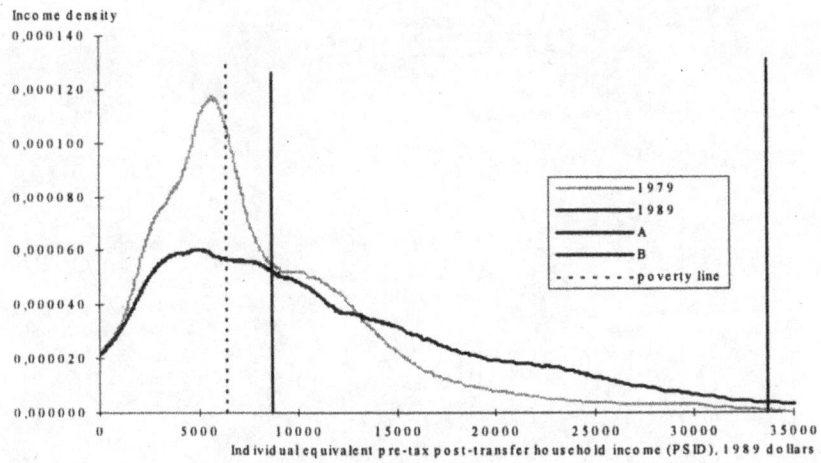

Figure 1.4A.4b The income distribution of the United States in 1979 and 1989: panel data (persons in social assistance households)

PART 4

PRIVATIZATION OF SOCIAL INSURANCE

4.1 Dimensions of privatisation: The Swedish welfare state in transition

Tor E. Eriksen and Lars Söderström

Introduction

All societies take measures to protect individuals from the consequences of inadequate earnings due to lack of working ability (childhood, old age, sickness, etc.), lack of working opportunities (un-employment), or simply bad luck, for example failure of crop due to weather conditions.

Protective measures could be public or private, collective or individual. The main organisational forms of social protection are depicted in the following triangle:

The civil society includes churches and friendly societies of all sorts, and, of course, ordinary families, all representing private organisations of a collective nature. The market is usually understood as a set of mutually beneficial contracts.

By privatisation we mean a transfer of responsibility from the public domain to the private domain, collective as well as individual.

Many private protective measures are regulated by law. For example, marriage laws regulate the relationship between spouses, parents and children, etc. Another example is that people engaged in certain activities, such as car driving, are required to carry some sort of liability insurance. With respect to such cases, privatisation would take the form of deregulation, allowing individuals more discretionary power.

A radical form of privatisation is to move protective measures from public to private administration, but otherwise keep them intact. A typical example would be that some kind of liability insurance, presently in the social insurance scheme, was put under the administration of private insurance companies. In Sweden, a possible candidate for such a privatisation would be the work injury compensation scheme. The corresponding schemes in Denmark, Finland and Norway are already under private administration.

In the context of sickness benefits, another example would be that employers are requested to provide sick pay during, for example, the four first weeks of sickness. The administration of the provision of sickness benefits is then partly privatised.

There are many other forms of privatisation. A switch from grants to loans in the student support system is an example of how the nature of benefits may be changed in a way that implies increased private responsibility. The social assistance scheme is another candidate for this kind of transformation (allowing for an opportunity to write off debts in certain cases).

In this context one could also think of changes in the size of benefits. Lower compensation levels in the social insurance system force people to look for private complements, individually or collectively. A topic of crucial importance is how the reduction of public benefits is being brought about. For example, in the case of sickness benefits one can choose between a lower compensation ratio, say 65% instead of 90%, and a longer waiting period, say 14 days instead of 1 day. The private solution will look much different in these alternatives. Finding a private insurance policy that covers the difference between a 90 and 65% compensation may turn out to be more difficult than to find a private insurance policy that gives a 90% compensation from the 2nd to the 14th day.

In the case of benefits in kind, like health care, a similar privatisation would be to introduce or increase user charges, either as a fixed deductible charge or in proportion to the amount of services used. Once again, it would be of crucial importance how this is done; private insurance will more easily fill in certain gaps than others. The sum of all social protective measures, private as well as public, would probably be very different if one introduced user charges of one sort or the other.

Moreover, in the case of benefits in kind, a privatisation could take the form of a switch from public to private production. For example, health care could be provided by private instead of publicly employed GPs or/and private instead of public hospitals. There are several ways to bring about this kind of privatisation. One possibility is to have certain activities contracted out to private entrepreneurs, for example nursing homes. Another possibility is to give the individuals concerned a voucher to pay for private services of a particular kind. Transportation would be a typical example. Instead of having public buses, etc., individuals might be given a voucher to pay for transportation by private taxis.

Finally, social protection under public administration may be financed in a private rather than public fashion. Social insurance schemes are typically financed out of general taxation or a particular earmarked tax, for example a pay-roll tax. A form of privatisation would be to replace this type of financing with mandatory actuarial insurance premiums. The protective measures in question would then be financed in accordance with the Benefit principle.

We will now give some examples of recent privatisation of the Swedish social protection system. It has not been our aim to achieve a comprehensive description of what has happened, or is about to happen, in Sweden. We simply wish to choose some examples in order to highlight what can be described as variants of privatisation. The examples we choose are dental insurance, sickness allowance insurance, widow's pension and the new pension system

Background

There has been a considerable privatisation of previously public services in Sweden in recent years, especially at the municipal level. This has included such disparate activities as rubbish collection, child supervision and compulsory schooling. At the national level it has included dissolving state monopolies and introducing competition. Examples include the railways, telephone system and the post office. Even state control of the sale of alcohol has been questioned.

The aim of changing the social insurance system has to a certain extent been to reduce the state's budget deficit. Governments have chosen to unburden the budget through lower levels of compensation, longer qualifying periods, etc., or a transfer of administration into private hands. Another motivating factor has been to make this transfer as efficient as possible. By increasing the amount of excess insurance and the amount of social checks involved when administration is transferred from state organs to private employers, governments have chosen to restrain presumed benefit abuse.

A further reason is that it has not been thought possible to achieve necessary improvements in quality in the public system. One example is the abolition of the widow's pension. Adapting the old pension system to achieve equal treatment of men and women would have meant an increase in costs. This was avoided by abolishing the widow's pension, although interim measures were introduced.

Many years of debate about the Swedish welfare model were crowned with an analysis of the questions given by the economic commission headed by professor Assar Lindbeck. The commission had been asked to propose alternatives for a positive development of Swedish business and society. The commission presented its proposals and information in 1993.[1]

At the social-political level it was proposed, among other things, that social insurance be removed from the state budget, and even from the public sector eventually, and that a statutory limit would be set for the amount of compulsory and voluntary insurance, including the pension insurance, etc., agreed by employers and employees during wage negotiations.

The commission argued that Sweden should avoid moving from a state system to a compulsory corporate system. It was thought that such a form of privatisation would not bring necessary improvements in efficiency, and would entail clear risks. One risk that was outlined was that the formation of funds that occurs in private insurance arrangements, under trade union management for example, could lead to excessive concentration of power within business life.

The commission's proposals - if implemented at their most radical - would mean a far-reaching privatisation of the Swedish social insurance system with state regulation of maximum benefit levels.

The larger picture

The cost and financing of the Swedish social insurance system is presented in table 4.1.1. The figures are for the 1995/96 budget year which covered 18 months. It is very clear that social insurance operates at a surplus. To a certain extent, however, this is an optical illusion, because the table includes continuous financing (pay as you go) and consolidation/funding in order to cover future payments.

Health and parenthood insurance show large surpluses, but contributions from the insured will be increased for these areas. This can be seen as an example of how governments view specially destined contributions as general tax revenues.

The cost of the basic pension includes payments by the National Government Employee Salaries and Pensions Board totalling SEK 13,420 million. The table's other costs of SEK 439,786 million agrees with the costs in the income statement's transferral section, but has been grouped here with consideration to financing.

Health insurance charges, basic pension charges and general contributions from the insured to health insurance and basic pensions, are given as the source of funding. Only the net cost after deductions for received charges are reported as state subsidies. For the basic pension, the entire basic pension charge is shown for financing of other basic pension benefits, i.e. mainly old age pension. Basic pension charges finance around 72% of basic pensions, when disability pensions are excluded.

The surplus for health and parenthood insurance in the budget year was around SEK (Swedish Krone) 27 billion. As in previous years, this sum was transferred to the state budget. It should be noted that the surplus in health and parenthood insurance exceeds the cost of disability pensions within the basic pension provision.

Figures for interest and fund holdings within supplementary pensions are approximate, based on preliminary information and the National Social Insurance Board's calculations. Supplementary pensions provide a surplus overall when interest from AP Funds are included.

Table 4.1.1 Social insurance finances, budget year 1995/96, in SEK billion

	Cost	Financing					Accumulated surplus
		Contributions	State grant	Interest	Other	Surplus	
Child benefit, advance payments, etc	43,141						
Health and parenthood benefit	73,173	100,351				27,178	44,144
Work injuries insurance	9,651	13,969	212	98	142	4,770	-15,242
Basic pension							
- disability pension	20,504		20,504			0	
- other	86,285	62,040	24,245			0	
Supplementary pension		125,426		82,000		32,562	597,000
- disability pension	33,420						
- other	141,444						
Premium reserve (new pensions)		15,196		1,367		16,563	20,457
Housing supplement, pensioners	14,959		14,657		302	0	
Partial pension	2,805	2,114		1,246		555	5,321
Support to the handicapped, etc,, periodisations	27,824	39	24,964	151	1,396	-1,274	-2,830
Total	453,206	319,135	125,549	84,862	4,014	80,354	648,850

Source: National Social Insurance Board (RFV), Annual report of the social insurance budget year 1995/96, p 10.

Work injuries insurance now provides a surplus and the accumulated debt is being gradually paid off. During the year the deficit has been cut by around SEK 5 billion.

In total, social insurance has yielded a surplus of around SEK 80 billion during the 18 months of the 1995/96 budget year.

The table also includes compulsory savings. Payments are already being made to the, not yet finalised, premium reserve share of the general pension system. This interim fund, which will amount to more than SEK 20 billion, will be managed at a later date by the AP Funds or by private fund managers approved by state inspectors, all in accordance with the wishes of the individual saver.

The following chapters report some examples of reforms which, according to our broad definition, can be characterised as privatisation.

The question that is asked is whether the reforms can be seen as examples of ideological restructuring of social insurance.

Dental insurance - a retreat

The first proposal for universal dental insurance was made in 1964. It was proposed that dental insurance be included in universal health insurance.[2] The proposal did not lead to a government bill. Sweden did not set up universal, although separate, dental insurance until 1974. The aim was to 'provide access to good dental care at a reasonable cost for the general public'.[3] Provisions were made for both private and public dental care.

Dental insurance was for adults. Free dental care within the public system was given to children up to age 16 (later 19).[4]

Dental insurance was clearly focussed on preventive care, but the first years of the system were largely spent on repairs. Patients with a large accumulation of dental problems had to queue to receive treatment and tensions arose between private dentists and dentists in the public system. The public system had difficulties in recruiting dentists. Dental fees were set in such a way that they were competitively neutral (choice of dentist) and did not affect choice of treatment.[5]

Over the years the focus on preventive dental care has diminished and the system now accounts for a much smaller part of the patient's cost for dental repairs. The overall cost development for dental insurance is shown in table 4.1.2. Table 4.1.3 shows how much patients pay for different types of treatment. As the table shows, there has been a large amount of privatisation to the extent that dental patients are paying a larger share of the total cost.

Table 4.1.2 The costs of dental insurance, SEK billions. Current prices

Year	1991	1992	1993	1994	1995
Cost	4.2	4.0	3.5	3.4	2.4

Source: National Social Insurance Board.

The large cost reduction for dental insurance is primarily due to increased excess payments in the system, see table 4.1.3. Other factors affecting cost developments were identified in the National Social Insurance Board's comments on the reduction.[6]

The ongoing cost reduction is probably also due to tighter economic conditions for many house-holds in Sweden, which among other things results in reduced demand for dental care. Increases in excess charges strengthen this effect. The care that is in demand is also, according to our studies, of a simpler and less costly nature.

It is an open question whether dental insurance will be completely abolished except for certain exposed groups. The changes already made to the system have mainly concerned its financing, with patient protection against high charges being cut considerably.

There are hardly any suitable private alternatives to universal dental insurance. The opportunity for private individuals to purchase private dental insurance is closely linked to the health of the person's teeth. The insurance offered on the private market is dependent on the insured person having a healthy set of teeth. Premiums are usually age differentiated and the insured person must pay a relatively high excess charge.

Table 4.1.3 Costs of treatment (SEK) and patient's share (%) for various types of treatment. Current prices

Treatment	1974		1984		1996	
	Cost	Patient share	Cost	Patient share	Cost	Patient share
Examination [a]	109	39	254	60	345	100
Less serious care [b]	265	49	621	60	1,231	85
Bridgework 1 [c]	1,722	43	4,014	77	5,672	83
Dentures [d]	1,098	25	2,866	56	8,424	68
Bridgework 2 [e]	10,300	27	24,012	60	36,388	69

a Standard examination.
b One triple-layer amalgam filling on the molar and two single-layer plastic-composite fillings on front teeth.
c Bridgework comprising three stages of which one suspended in metal-ceramic.
d Full set of dentures (usually both jaws) including examination and x-ray.
e 10-stage bridge in metal-ceramic with 4 suspended stages on one jaw and a 6-stage bridgework with two suspended stages in the other jaw and partial dentures there as well. Begins with examination, x-ray of entire mouth and 2 hours' preventive care.

Private dental insurance has the same characteristics as risk insurance and does not correspond with the social-political objectives of dental insurance. Furthermore, the changes in the system emphasise the differences in attitudes towards medicine and dentistry. It seems as though dentistry is being considered primarily as an aesthetic activity.

Sickness allowance insurance

The cost of health insurance increased throughout the 1980s. The number of people with a disability pension, or a disability lasting more than a year, increased up until 1994.

Table 4.1.4 Number of people with disability pension or disability lasting more than one year. Thousands

Year	Number
1980	311
1990	436
1994	458 turning point

Source: National Social Insurance Board.

Table 4.1.5 Costs for sickness allowance, work injury benefit and disability/temporary disability pension. SEK million. 1995 prices

Year	1980	1985	1990	1991	1992	1993	1994	1995
Sickness allowance	32,230	29,730	43,899	35,747	21,963	18,752	19,402	19,514
Work injury	3,151	3,240	12,471	13,107	13,208	11,932	8,204	6,857
Disability/temporary disability pension	25,270	28,289	33,489	33,732	35,933	36,431	38,067	37,367
Total	60,651	61,259	88,859	82,586	71,104	67,115	65,673	63,738

Source: National Social Insurance Board.

Cost developments for sickness allowance, work injury benefit and disability pension including temporary disability pension during 1980-95, are presented in table 4.1.5.

The large changes in the cost of sickness allowance starting in 1990, work injury benefit starting in 1993 and the recent fall in costs for disability pension (including temporary disability pension) are linked to a series of reforms that have affected compensation levels, the division of responsibility between the social services and employers, and a tightening of the allocation criteria within disability pensions.

The list below summarises these reforms:

Date	Change
1 March 1991	Compensation level reduced from 90% to 65% during the first three days of each period of sickness and to 80% for the period up to the 90th day.
1 January 1992	Employer to pay sickness compensation during the first 14 days of each sickness. Employer to gain responsibility for identifying the rehabilitation needs of the employee. Co-ordination period for work injury benefit and sickness allowance increased from 90 to 180 days. Social insurance offices to gain responsibility for co-ordinating rehabilitation.
1 January 1993	Tighter definition of work injury.
1 April 1993	One day qualification for sickness allowance and work injury benefit. Rehabilitation allowance of 100% for rehabilitation oriented towards working life (under 1 year).
1 July 1993	Right to work-injury benefit abolished in principle. Compensation level reduced from 80 to 75% for people with a sickness period that lasted 365 days during the previous 15 months. Compensation level of 80% for medical rehabilitation, organised by a doctor as part of an approved rehabilitation plan.

1 January 1995   New contribution from the insuree, 3.95%, to health insurance

1 July 1996   Compensation level within sickness allowance insurance set at 75%.

1 January 1997   Employer's responsibility for sick pay extended to 28 days.
Small businesses can continue, within certain limits, to sign agreements with social insurance offices concerning voluntary insurance against high sick pay costs.

Reforms within sickness allowance insurance concern changes in benefit levels and the introduction of excess charges in the form of qualification days. The most interesting aspect in terms of principle is the introduction of contributions from the insured person and a sick pay period. The sick pay period means that the employer has become the health insurance provider for the first month of the employee's sickness.

Since the state regulates benefit levels during the sick pay period, the economic protection of the insured person is not affected in principle, only the equalisation of risks that the state offers the company within the framework for sickness allowance insurance.[7] However, in a recent decision by the Labour Court it was stated that the addition to sickness allowance of 10 percentage points, which both sides of the labour market have agreed to, need not be paid out during the extension of the employer insurance period.

The pension system's survivor's insurance

It was seen to be necessary to reform the survivor's insurance within the pension system to make it equal for men and women. The findings of the pensions commission[8] included a proposal for a new survivor's insurance. It would be centred on children's pension, not favour either gender, and be better directed towards the needs of the surviving adult. Widow's pension would be abolished.

The government produced a bill[9] based on the proposal but then retracted it when it failed to attract sufficient support in parliament. The reason given was that such a wide-scale reform required much greater parliamentary support.[10]

The pension drafting committee produced an interim report in 1987[11] in which they proposed a reform of survivor's benefits within national insurance which was very similar to the earlier proposal by the pensions commission. The proposal was that widow's pension would be abolished and be replaced by a survivor's pension that would be the same for men and women. The pension would be based on need to a certain extent, and only serve as support during a brief re-orientation period - while the survivor was looking for work and moving into a smaller home. It was re-commend-ed that the pension for surviving children would be strengthened. The insurance was reformed in accordance with the proposal.

Table 4.1.6 Estimated costs for 1989-2030 for child and widow pension according to existing legislation. Base sum SEK 23, 300. Costs in SEK million

Benefit	1989	1990	1995	2000	2010	2020	2030
Widow's pension							
Basic pension	1,373	1,369	1,422	1,562	1,684	1,590	1,600
Supplementary pension	5,612	5,813	6,949	7,910	10,541	12,042	12,302
Total	6,985	7,182	8,371	9,472	12,225	13,632	13,902
Child pension							
Basic pension	198	198	198	198	198	198	198
Supplementary pension	380	380	380	380	380	380	380
Total	578	578	578	578	578	578	578
Total, existing rules							
Basic pension	1,571	1,567	1,620	1,760	1,882	1,788	1,798
Supplementary pension	5,992	6,193	7,329	8,290	10,921	12,422	12,682
Total	7,563	7,760	8,949	10,050	12,803	14,210	14,480

Source: Table 4.19 i SOU 1987:55.

In a special comment[12] the reasons for abolishing widow's pension were analysed. The comment notes that the strong emphasis on the need for re-orientation support had hidden the fact that most women who become widows do so at an age when they already are, or soon will be, eligible for old age pension. The needs of young widows and children were thus only part of the problem. The argument that just widow's pensions would be assessed according to need - 'widow's pension is paid to women irrespective of their need for it and of the economic consequences of their husband's death' - has little logic and relevance because the same argument could be applied to the old age pension.

The strongest argument for reforming survivor's pension was the need to counteract expected cost increases. The size of these is indicated in the calculations reported in the drafting committee's report, see table 4.1.6.

It is hard to judge the extent to which a lowering of state protection for survivors has led to people taking out private insurance. There are no reliable statistics about private insurance based on gender. The fact that total pension savings has increased, however, is shown in tables 4.1.7-4.1.10. In general there has been strong growth in the private insurance market during the 1990s. The Financial Supervisory Authority's figures show that women in general have less insurance than men.

Table 4.1.7 Direct individual life insurance with basic compensation. Tax category P

Category	1993	1994	1995
First insured men	766,633	1,283,155	1,059,613
First insured women	663,453	1,125,057	928,808

Source: Financial Supervisory Authority.

Table 4.1.8 Fund insurance. Tax category P

Category	1993	1994	1995
First insured men	75,215	99,311	111,730
First insured women	66,077	85,394	93,918

Source: Financial Supervisory Authority.

The reform of the pension system's survivor protection meant that the equality aspects were covered by asking people who wanted widow's or widower's pension to look to the private market. Insurance companies offer well developed insurance packages in this field, although with greatly different premiums, for which the insured person is not taken in their existing condition, as with the previous national insurance, but must undergo a medical check-up.

Table 4.1.9 Life insurance companies. Income and costs for direct insurance, 1980, 1985, 1990, 1994 and 1995. SEK million

	1980	1985	1990	1994	1995
income from premiums	10,980	24,900	42,302	48,757	50,179
individual insurance	2,893	10,209	21,575	16,340	18,290
life insurance	2,800	9,960	20,863	15,614	15,425
sickness and accident insurance	93	249	712	728	865
labour market insurance	7,455	13,575	18,036	28,703	30,346
occupational pension insurance	5,287	10,849	14,871	26,267	27,889
group life insurance (TGL)	713	1,070	1,887	1,861	1,846
group health insurance (AGS)	1,387	1,524	1,123	123	53
severance pay insurance (AGB)	68	315	155	452	558
other group insurance	632	1,023	2,691	3,714	3,543
group pension insurance	-	-	-	430	399
group life insurance	551	1,629	2,488	3,072	2,975
group sick & accident insurance	81	104	203	212	169

Source: Financial Supervisory Authority.

Table 4.1.10 Percentage who save for pensions and average saved amount (SEK per month)

	1993		1994	
	%	amount	%	amount
Women	23	570	27	600
Men	20	810	22	820

Source: Postens Privatekonomi AB.

The new pension system - the premium reserve share

In 1960 Sweden started a twin track general pensions system. In addition to the basic pension, which was the same for everyone, there would be a supplementary pension based on previous earned income. Both parts are pay as you go.

The Swedish pension system is currently being reformed. The aim is that the entire pension shall be proportional to a person's earned income throughout their life. Previously, the pension was calculated from average income over the best 15 years of earnings. Because people will be guaranteed a certain minimum level of pension in the new system, and this level will be quite high, the new system will have the characteristics of a basic pension complemented with an income-based supplementary pension.

The reformed system will have two parts. Of a total charge of 18.5% of total salary, 2 percentage points will be allocated to a premium reserve fund. The rest, 16.5 percentage points, will be used to pay for a pay-as-you-go pension system.

In 1994 a special investigator was asked by the government to look into a premium reserve system within the general pension framework and make a proposal as to how such a system could be formulated.[13] To a certain extent the investigator went outside his remit and proposed compulsory savings during the period in work instead of an insurance:

The management of capital during the income-earning period would be carried out in a pure savings system without insurance. The insurance function would then have importance for the individual only at the time of entering retirement. Management of the savings would be done in special security funds until the individual saver enters retirement. At that date the money would be used to sign a pension insurance with a state insurer.[14]

World Bank multi-pillar pension system:

Mandatory public pillar	Mandatory private pillar	Voluntary savings pillar

'Poverty alleviation function' ⇐ ⇒ 'Savings function'

The investigator's proposal is reminiscent of the proposal for a pensions system made by the World Bank.[15]

That the insurance should be managed by the state agrees, among other things, with the equalisation of risk that was chosen. The reform thus means changes in all three areas of influence: regulation, administration/production and financing.

Questions about the form of the insurance, the terms for the state insurer and capital management remain unsolved.

Final comments

The reforms mentioned within national insurance cover regulation, administration/production and financing. A certain amount of responsibility has been transferred from social insurance to the insured individual (survivor's pension) or the employer (sick pay). Levels of excess charges have risen through the extension of qualifying periods (sickness allowance) and increased patient charges (dental insurance). Costs have been passed from the state budget to employers and municipalities, and people have been given lower compensation levels and stricter testing of the right to benefit (work injury and sickness allowance insurance). However, the state has retained its regulation of benefit levels.

In the case of the premium reserve share of the planned pension system, the insured individual has been given greater choice among fund managers, but the state remains as insurer.

Additional parts of national insurance will be reformed in the near future and planned changes within sickness and work injury insurance can entail further changes in the distribution of responsibility between the state, employers and individual citizens.

Even though the main driving force behind these reforms has been the need to cleanse public finances, we can note a certain interest in private solutions for the social welfare system. The changes can therefore be expected to survive when the current economic problems have been mastered. The future will reveal if this is true. What we are now witnessing could only be an interlude in the development of the Swedish welfare state.

Notes

1. SOU 1993: 16 New conditions for economics and politics.

2. SOU 1965:4.

3. SOU 1972:81.

4. The background to the 1974 reform was that several surveys had shown that dental status was a class matter. It was considered that the reasons for this were that it was too expensive to go to the dentist. The timing for introducing dental insurance was suitable because private dentists were short of patients and could be expected to join the new system. On the government side there was also seen to be a positive benefit in the fact that with dentists linked to the system they would be more directly a part of the tax system.

5. In a special feature about insurance in the dentist's journal (1974:11), the chairman of the association of dentists (page 653) wrote that some county councils right at the start refused to accept charges that were competitively neutral. The background was that, among other things, councils had decided to reduce charges generally by 20%. The leading article in the same journal argued that the trend of people moving from public to private treatment was a long term trend of increased privatisation of dental care (page 619). It was also reported that the board of directors of the Federation of County Councils had interpreted the same trend as proof that private treatment had become far too profitable (page 620).

6. National Social Insurance Board. Annual Report for the social insurance 1995/96 budget year, page 36.

7. Note that the state provides insurance for small businesses which can be seen as a re-insurance.

8. SOU 1981:61.

9. Prop 1983/84:73.

10. See Parliamentary report 1988:9 page 4.

11. SOU 1987:55.

12. SOU 1987:55 special comment by Tor Eriksen, pages 393-396.

13. Directive 1994:96.

14. SOU 1996:83 General pension savings, page 37.

15. Averting the old age crisis. Policies to protect the old and promote growth. The World Bank 1994.

4.2 Privatization of retirement income

John A. Turner and David Rajnes

In 1981, Chile privatized its social security system, replacing its traditional pay-as-you-go system of numerous schemes for separate occupations with a single privately managed individual account system. The apparent success of the Chilean system has inspired other countries to consider similar reforms. The influence of Chile's retirement income system has been greatest in Latin America because of geographic proximity, shared language, and cultural ties, and in part because of a similar history of problems in managing traditional social security systems,. Some countries in Central and Eastern Europe, such as Hungary and Kazakstan, however, have indicated they will enact similar reforms.

Privatization concepts

Privatization as a general term refers to the replacement of a government function by the private sector. Privatization of the production of goods and services is appealing because the powerful forces of competition may bring about efficient production. In the private market, goods and services are produced, sold, and improved with less coercion and control than when done by government.

Privatization of retirement income often means the replacement of government-managed social security by plans with private sector management and private sector investments. This definition is sometimes expanded to include mandatory occupational or individual plans that supplement social security benefits by private sector arrangements. Mandatory supplements may substitute for increases in social security benefits, and in that sense replace benefits that would have been provided by government.

While the management of investments in a funded social security system is the most important aspect of social security privatization, it is only one of several retirement income functions that can be privatized. Each of the following functions can be privatized: record keeping concerning the accounts of beneficiaries, the choice of fund managers, receipt of contributions and disbursement to fund managers, the management of the investment of funds, disbursement of benefits, and the insurance of promised benefits in defined benefit and defined contribution system.

The government investing social security assets in the private sector could also be considered a form of partial privatization. This has been done through Provident Funds in a number of countries, such as Indonesia, and through traditional defined benefit social insurance schemes in a few countries, such as Canada and Japan.

There is not one generally accepted definition of privatization. While there is widespread agreement that replacement of a government function by the private sector is privatization, there are grey areas as to what constitutes privatization. A few examples of the issues involved in defining privatization of retirement income systems are discussed here. In all cases, however, the important question is not the definitional question whether the policy is good policy.

When the Chilean individual account pension system was first established, it was largely invested in government debt that was used by the government to finance the liabilities of the old social security system. It was thus initially not much different in the assets backing it than the system it replaced. This type of investment pattern of moving gradually from investment in government bonds to investment in the private sector allows for a gradual transition from a non-privatized to a privatized system.

All privatized social security systems maintain some government involvement, and sometimes the involvement is extensive. The Chilean system incorporates a number of government guarantees, and thus is not a pure privatized system. By comparison, the voluntary private pension systems in a number of countries involve no contingent liabilities to government and thus as a component of a retirement income system may be considered to be more thoroughly privatized than the Chilean system.

The question of what constitutes privatization is related to the question of the role of the government in providing retirement income. A distinction can be drawn between the privatization of retirement income and the privatization of social security. A measure of privatization of retirement income that focuses more on outcomes than on the transformation of governmental institutions is the percentage of retirement income provided by social security.

The Thrift Savings Plan for federal government employees in the United States provides another example of issues involved in clarifying what is privatization. The Thrift Savings Plan is a retirement savings program where the individual government worker can choose within limits the amount to contribute and the assets in which the contributions are invested. The federal government contracts with private sector investment management companies to handle the investments. The government handles the administrative record keeping, the choice of investment managers, and the menu of possible investments, but the investments are selected from the menu by workers and the management of investments is handled in the private sector. Thus, some functions of this plan have been privatized while others remain in government control.

Along these lines, participants in the Central Provident Fund in Singapore have the option to transfer funds from their government managed individual retirement account into a special account in which the investment decisions are made by the individual account holder. Over time, the range of permissible investments has grown. Since 1978, investing in stocks on the Singapore stock exchange, bonds, gold and shares of mutual funds have been allowed. Since 1994, purchase of foreign equities and bonds listed on regional exchanges has also been allowed.

In some countries, private pensions predate the social security scheme and thus do not replace social security. Contracting out in the United Kingdom, where workers are not required to participate in the earnings-related part of social security if they participate in another plan that is at least as generous, was established in part so that the British earnings-related social security benefit scheme would not replace preexisting occupational plans. In all countries, private sector alternatives to social security interact through the political process with the social security system, and through this process affect the size of social security.

In some countries, not all workers participate in the privatized system. In Japan, only workers in firms meeting minimum size qualifications can participate in the contracting out system. In the Netherlands and Denmark, occupational pensions are mandatory not by law but through wage agreements that have the force of law for workers in most industries.

Reasons for privatization

Countries have indicated a number of reasons for privatizing their social security systems. Many of the reasons for privatizing social security are similar to reasons for privatizing other government enterprises (Van der Hoeven and Sziraczki 1997). Nonetheless, considerable controversy exists over many of the reasons.

1. In many countries the current social security system relies on large subsides by the state because contributions are insufficient to finance outlays. Privatization has occurred to reduce the government deficit and to reduce the size of government.
2. Some countries have been unable to adequately manage defined benefit systems and feel that defined contribution systems would be easier to manage, both politically as well as financially. Privatization has been motivated by the poor quality of services provided by government social security institutions. Competition in private sector management is thought to be more efficient and lead to better services than monopolistic management by government.
3. Some pay-as-you-go schemes are inequitable in their distribution of benefits. For example, since most Latin American countries rely heavily on indirect taxation, the poor contribute disproportionately to the funding of benefits they probably will not receive (Lacey 1996). Another aspect of equity is equity across generations in taxes paid and benefits received.
4. Countries see social security pension reform as a possible means of raising domestic savings, correcting economic distortions in labour markets presumably caused by traditional pay-as-you-go (PAYG) schemes, and reducing contribution evasion.
5. Demographic changes that are raising the retirement system dependency rate (the ratio of beneficiaries to covered workers) are making pay-as-you-go social security systems more expensive. The decline in the population growth rate and the growth rate of real wages has reduced the implicit rate of return on social security, making market rates of return relatively more attractive.

6. Some people favour privatization as a way of increasing the range of individual choice and as a move towards greater private sector reliance as an aspect of economic liberalization. Privatization is desired because it gives individuals greater responsibility for their retirement income. Privatization is seen as a way of developing private sector enterprises--money managers and insurance companies. It is part of the process of creating a competitive market economy.
7. For some the desire for privatization is due to a general distrust of government--the government cannot be trusted as a financial institution.
8. Privatization is sometimes seen as a way of encouraging the development of capital markets in countries with poorly developed capital markets. Privatization may be seen to be feasible in countries that formerly had poorly developed capital markets but whose capital markets have developed to the point where they could provide adequate investment opportunities.
9. In some countries, privatization may be popular currently because of the strength of financial markets. Historically, stocks in the United States, for example, have averaged about a 6 to 7 percent real rate of return. Over the past decade, the average annual real rate of return has exceeded 11 percent. From October 1990 April 1997, the Standard & Poor's 500 index did not experience a decline as large as 10 percent. In comparison, over the period 1950 to 1990, the index declined by at least 10 percent every year and a half on average. It declined by 20 percent every six and a half years on average (T. Rowe Price 1997). With the strength of capital markets in recent years, with high average rates of return and reduced volatility, privatization is seen as providing higher benefits for the same level of contributions.
10. The privatization of social security may be used to assist in the privatization of state assets. State assets can be sold or given to the privatized social security system.

The ease with which a country can establish a privatized system depends on aspects of the existing system. The greater is the relative size of the group currently receiving benefits, the more costly it is to continue paying for those benefits while starting a new system. In general, the greater is the unfunded liability of the existing system, the greater is the difficulty in making the transition to a privatized system.

Sometimes privatization issues are confused with funding and investment issues. Privatization is generally thought to require funding, but France has mandatory privatized occupational pension schemes that use pay-as-you-go financing.

Some of the advantages sought from privatization can equally well be gained from changes in traditional social security systems that do not involve privatization. For example, some of the gains attributed to privatization are due to funding with investment in capital markets. Traditional systems could be reformed to permit such funding, although care is needed to assure that the process of choosing investments does not become politicized or subject to favoritism..

Privatization does not always save the government money. In the United Kingdom, because of incentives provided for workers to opt out of social security, privatization has been a sizable net expense for the government.

Preconditions for privatization

Four preconditions are essential for establishing a privatized retirement income system--(1) a well-defined set of property rights and (2) the legal environment to enforce them; complemented by (3) at least a rudimentary capital market and (4) local expertise with the ability to regulate private providers (Valdes-Prieto 1993). For pension systems that provide annuity benefits, an additional precondition is required: (5) local expertise that can design and operate sophisticated insurance contracts. Each of these preconditions require development of institutions and training of skilled technicians to operate them.

Without well-defined property rights established through laws and regulations there can be no private sector and thus no privatization option available to state pension provision. Without a competent enforcement mechanism to ensure property rights, individuals would not be able to claim funds designated in their names. Moreover, in instances where the government may want to compensate workers for past contributions into an existing system, a reliable property rights framework allows workers to claim accrued rights associated with the existing state schemes.

Rudimentary capital markets, at a minimum a developed banking system, provide an outlet for private sector investments as well as an incentive for private savings to accumulate. Similarly, a liberalized economic environment characterized by minimal state interference in market operations, can assist the privatization of a retirement income system.

Actors

A number of actors and institutions are involved in the privatization of social security.

Workers are required to save funds for retirement and to acquire insurance for covering invalidity and survivorship risks. The risks workers bear change when a pension system is privatized. As the variety of choices required of employees in privatized pension systems increases--from the initial contact with the privatized pension system (competing fund managers), during the working years (investments), and to the termination of active working life (option for a phased withdrawal versus annuity)--risk rises to the individual.

Firms may be required to withhold employee contributions to a mandatory privatized system and may be required to contribute an additional percentage of employee wages toward their future retirement. Firms also may considering the contracting-out option by establishing a plan that replaces part of social security.

Pensioners generally have left the labor force and thus the real value of their future benefits is susceptible to inflationary changes.

Pension fund management companies manage individual fund accounts, investing the proceeds. Where a phased withdrawal form of retirement income is chosen, pension companies handle the process. Pension fund activities must conform to standards promulgated by a supervisory framework established by the state. For example, investment restrictions may set limits on the amount of portfolio permitted in certain economic sectors or types of financial instruments. Additional guidelines may force companies to meet the pension fund industry standard for profitability by mandating that additional capital reserves be set aside in the event of poor future performance.

Insurance companies contract with pension fund companies to provide a range of pension investment options and to provide disability and survivors benefits. The long-term nature of the savings flow, along with the re-insurance activities, promote a sizable investment pool.

Government operates a framework to supervise private pension activities. This policy may take the form of guidance, for example, fiduciary guidelines, or amount to a formidable array of strict standards designed to minimize fraud and avoid excessive risk-taking. Licensing and supervision over permissible investments by pension fund companies are just two of the latter areas of state involvement. Beyond typical social safety net programs, the state may assume contingent liabilities in the form of guarantees. Some of the more common guarantees provided by the state include benefits indexation, establishing a floor for minimum pensions at some poverty level or wage standard, and insurance against pension fund bankruptcy. In Chile, insurance companies are insured by the government, since annuities are guaranteed, at a discount, should an insurance company bankrupt.

Forms of privatization

There are two main dimensions to privatization of social security: 1) Social security can be completely replaced or it can be partially replaced or supplemented, and 2) participation in the privatized social security can be voluntary or mandatory. As indicated earlier, when privatization is partial, several functions can either be privatized or left as a responsibility of the government. In reality, even when replacement is considered to be full, some functions remain as state responsibilities. Four categories are defined by the intersection of those two dimensions. In each of the following four categories, benefits can be provided either by defined benefit or defined contribution plans.

Mandatory full privatization The most significant form of pension privatization occurs when the public pension system is fully replaced by a privately-managed system of pension funds. This is complete mandatory privatization.

In this case, the system comprises several groups. There are workers with their mandatory contributions. Firms will be involved to the extent they pay a portion of the mandated contribution or become involved in checkoff of the wage. Pension fund management companies, insurance companies, and government regulators together form the financial framework within which savings flow and are eventually invested. The state role is redefined as regulator of the private sector framework.

Chile has for all new labour force entrants completely replaced its pay-as-you-go social security system with a privately managed defined contribution system with mandatory participation for all new private sector employees. There are no defined benefit examples of mandatory full privatization.

Voluntary full privatization With voluntary full privatization, workers choose whether to participate in a public sector or private sector system. The private sector system has features similar to a mandatory fully privatized system. Parallel privatized pension systems are created when the pension law permits competition between the public system and the private sector. Both types of schemes are earnings-related.

Colombia and Peru provide defined contribution examples. There are no defined benefit examples.

Mandatory partial privatization. Mandatory partial privatization occurs when employers or employees are required to contribute to privately managed retirement funds as well as to government managed social security. They can be required by law or they can be required by collectively bargained wage agreements having the force of law. Mandatory individual supplementary accounts are another form of mandatory partial privatization. Legislation specifies minimum provisions relating to amounts needed to be contributed periodically. The mandated occupational or individual plans form the second tier of the pension system, while the first tier tends to be at least partially redistributive.

In Switzerland and France, private pensions are mandatory for basically all workers, while in the Netherlands and Denmark they are mandatory for most workers. In Switzerland, the plans can be either defined contribution or defined benefit. In the Netherlands, they are defined benefit. Australia has an income tested first tier complemented by a mandatory defined contribution scheme. It is counted as a mandatory partial scheme because the income test is structured so that about 80 percent of Australian retirees receive benefits from it. If eventually reliance on the income tested benefit is greatly reduced, as expected, Australia will become, like Chile, a mandatory fully privatized system.

Sweden has a mandatory defined contribution system with a contribution rate of 2 percent. Presumably in order to meet the Maastricht requirements concerning government budget deficits, the Swedish government is currently managing the system so that its surpluses reduce the overall government budget deficit. It is expected that this scheme will be transferred to private sector management after the deadline for meeting the Maastricht requirements has passed. At that point, Sweden will be categorized as having a mandatory partially privatized scheme.

Latvia is in the process of establishing a mandatory defined contribution scheme that will supplement a pay-as-you-go scheme. When the mandatory defined contribution scheme is in place, Latvia will be categorized as having a mandatory partially privatized system. Poland is discussing a pension reform proposal that would introduce mandatory private pension funds.

Voluntary partial privatization In contracting out, voluntary partial privatization occurs. The government acts in its legal capacity to authorize terms and conditions permitting a private sector agent to contract with individual citizens in voluntarily replacing a portion of their national retirement plan.[1] In general, a firm or individual opts to negotiate with an approved third party providing a comparable benefits plan that substitutes for the government plan. In exchange, the firm or individual makes a reduced mandatory contribution to the government scheme. For that firm or individual, the private sector option is presumably chosen if it minimizes long-run costs for providing a desired level of benefits, given consideration of risks. The government's long-run pension liabilities are reduced when the private sector alternative is chosen, although the extent of liability reduction depends on whether the government offers benefit guarantees or inducements to opt out of the government plan.

In the United Kingdom, all workers may voluntarily withdraw from the earnings-related part of social security but are required to remain in the basic flat rate part of social security. Contracting out can occur either through defined benefit or defined contribution plans. In Japan, a similar option is available through defined benefit plans but it is not open to all workers. Argentina and Uruguay using defined contribution plans also allow voluntary choice of the state run scheme or a private scheme for part of social security provision.

When participation is voluntary, the government must give careful thought to the incentive structure for opting out of social security. The government may make the privatized and nonprivatized systems equivalent, providing no incentives or disincentives for opting out. It can alternatively offer incentives or disincentives for opting out. In Japan, the government has attempted to make the choice of opting out neutral while in the United Kingdom the government at great expense has encouraged opting out. Similar choices for workers and decisions for governments concerning incentives arise in the situation of mandatory privatization when workers who have participated in the old system have the option of transferring to the new system.

The Government's role in a privatized system

Countries have thus pursued several routes for privatizing social security. In all of them, however, the state remains responsible for providing minimum antipoverty benefits. In many of them, the state provides a minimum benefit either to all retired workers and dependents or to those whose benefits fall below a certain level. It sometimes provides other guarantees such as a minimum relative rate of return guarantee in the Chilean system. In all privatized social security systems, the government continues to play a role as a regulator of the system.

Concerns about privatization

Risks

One of the concerns about a funded individual account system is that the system will be structured so that workers will be allowed to withdraw their money before retirement. It may be politically difficult to prevent workers from withdrawing part of their funds for preretirement needs. Such a feature reduces the income available to workers in retirement.

A further concern is who should decide the investment portfolio in an individual account defined contribution system. In systems where the accounts are provided on an individual basis, the individual usually is responsible for choosing from a limited menu of alternatives. Related to the issue of who should decide the investment mix are the issues of what should be the government regulations concerning the investment mix and what would be the optimal portfolio for a pension fund to hold.

When given discretion in deciding, issues arise as to whether individuals have sufficient information about investments to make wise decisions. Traditional employer-managed pension plans in the United States on average outperform employee-managed pension accounts by 150 to 200 basis points (1.5 to 2.0 percentage points) a year. For a 35 year old, a 200 basis point difference translates into a 50 percent smaller pension starting at age 65 (American Academy of Actuaries 1996). Thus, individual management of an individual account plan can have a large effect on ultimate retirement benefits.

There is a cost in resources expended on obtaining financial information when each individual is responsible for making investment decisions related to his or her pension account. The government may have a responsibility to provide financial information to workers to assist them in making wise investment decisions.

Survivors and disability benefits are usually provided through social security systems in conjunction with old age benefits. Issues arise as to how these benefits should be provided in a privatized social security system. In Chile, they are provided by the investment management firms purchasing life and disability coverage for workers from private life insurance companies. Government regulation limits the variation in options that life insurance companies can provide. In the privatized retirement income system in Kazakstan, survivors and disability benefits are provided by the government.

A further issue is how are cost-of-living adjustments to be provided to retirees. In Chile, cost-of-living indexing is possible because the government provides indexed bonds in which private financial institutions can invest to provide indexed benefits. Indexed bonds are also available in the United Kingdom and the United States, but in nearly all other countries, indexed bonds are not available.

An important design issue relates to the bearing of financial risks. In a defined benefit system, the sponsoring organization bears the financial risks. In a defined contribution system, the risks are generally borne by the individual. The Chilean system modifies this arrangement by guaranteeing a minimum rate of return relative to the rate of return received by other investment management companies. This shifts some of the risk to the investment management companies and ultimately to the government.

A further design issue is who controls the voting of stock proxies. Generally, that is controlled by the fund manager even though the individual worker or retiree is the owner of the shares.

Administrative costs may be high with privatization. Private firms have advertising and marketing costs and in general are unable to realize the economies of scale realized by national social insurance institutions. Administrative costs may also be high in part because of the frequent switching of funds by affiliates.

Contribution evasion in privatized systems may be a further concern, especially for low income workers. Many low income workers who are required to contribute may fail to do so.

Financing the transition

When pay-as-you-go social security is privatized, the need remains to finance the payment of social security benefits that have been accrued under the old system. In effect, future generations of workers will need to finance their own retirement through the privatized system and at the same time continue to pay for the existing program for their elders. The difficulty of financing the transition a factor impeding some countries from privatizing their social security systems.

It is unclear how a large investment of social security funds in the economy would affect the stock market or the economy. It depends in part on the availability of investment opportunities. The new capital could spur productive capacity. If it does not, however, it could push up stock market prices without leading to economic growth. Government financing through social security funds that were formerly invested in government stocks musts either be replaced by another form of government financing or government expenditures must be reduced. Increased government borrowing could crowd out private investment and lead to higher interest rates. However, social security investment could offset the money leaving the market to finance government debt, leaving net stock market investment unchanged.

Conclusions

Many countries have privatized part of their social security systems and the trend is toward more countries adopting such reforms. There is a wide range of options for privatizing social security. The main variants are that it can be full or partial replacement of government provision of benefits and it can be mandatory or voluntary.

Note

1. In the United Kingdom and Japan this replacement has focused on the earnings-related portion only.

References

American Academy of Actuaries' Committee on Social Insurance (1996) 'Privatizing Social Security.' *Contingencies* 8 (July/August): 24-30.

Lacey, Robert (1996) 'Pension Reform in Latin America: Current and Future Challenges and the Role of the World Bank', *Economic Notes* 5, May.

Van der Hoeven, Rolph and Sziraczki, Gyorgy (1997) *Lessons from Privatization: Labour Issues in Developing and Transitional Countries*, Geneva: International Labour Office.

Table 4.2.1 Privatized social security systems (including mandatory occupational systems)

Type of Privatization	Countries			
	Defined Contribution	Defined Benefit	Both	Hybrid
Full Mandatory	Bolivia Chile Kazakstan Mexico			
Full Voluntary	Colombia Peru			
Partial Mandatory	Denmark Australia Finland Hungary Ivory Coast Poland Uruguay	Netherlands Latvia Sweden	Switzerland	France
Partial Voluntary	Argentina Greece Mauritius	Japan	United Kingdom	

4.3 Privatization of social insurance and welfare state efficiency: Evidence from the Netherlands and the United States

Leo J.M. Aarts and Philip R. de Jong

Introduction

During the 1970s and 1980s public expenditures on social protection have soared in most OECD-countries. Although some of the increase is induced by changing demographics, certainly part of it is due to inadequacies in the legal and institutional design of the national social insurance systems. Some countries clearly have done better than others in absorbing the structural changes in the economy brought about by the oil-crises of the 1970s, the acceleration of technological change in the 1980s and the globalization of national economies. Under such circumstances business looks for ways to adjust the work force to the new economic conditions and employees, especially older workers, look for shelter against the increasing productivity demands which they feel they can no longer meet. How successfull they are in finding protection depends on the legal and institutional design of the national social insurance systems. Dutch experiences with sickness benefit and disability insurance programs show that the combination of high replacement rates (relative to other compensation schemes), vaguely stated eligibility criteria and unaccountable program administrators induced a massive demand for sickness and disability benefits. While disability benefit volumes increased in most welfare states, the Netherlands experienced the largest disability program growth by far, thus illustrating the importance of the institutional setting in which social insurance programs operate.

In this paper we present a simple framework for the efficiency analysis of mandatory social insurance. In section 2 we will show that the net gain from social insurance hinges not only on the certainty that it can provide where private insurance markets fail, but also on the incentive structure implied by the administrative design and its impact on the size of the moral hazard component. In section 3 we evaluate the latest policy measures that were taken to curb spending on sickness and disability benefits in the Netherlands within this framework. In section 4 the importance of institutional design is further illustrated in a discussion of divergent experiences in the delivery of Workers' Compensation in the United States. Section 5 concludes.

The efficiency of social insurance; a simple framework

Demand and supply of insurance

Most people value certainty and look for possibility to avoid the risks they are exposed to. Insurance markets thrive on risk aversion. Since they value certainty risk-averse individuals are willing to pay an insurance premium that exceeds their expected losses. How much value they place on certainty depends on the depth of their aversion and on the size of expected loss.

Take the case of a person whose utility function of income is given in Figure 4.3.1 and who earns a monthly income of either 5,000 or 1,000. Each outcome occurs with a probability of 0.5. The expected income $\hat{Y}$, and the expected loss $\hat{L}$ are:

$$\hat{Y} = 0.5 \times 1{,}000 + 0.5 \times 5{,}000 = 3{,}000 \tag{1}$$

$$\hat{L} = 0.5 \times 4{,}000 + 0.5 \times 0 = 2{,}000 \tag{2}$$

As indicated in Figure 4.3.1 this person derives a utility value of 100 from an income of 5,000, while an income of 1,000 yields a utility level of 30. So his expected utility, equals:

$$\hat{U} = 0.5 \times 30 + 0.5 \times 100 = 65 \tag{3}$$

This person can reach a utility of 65 in two different ways. First, by exposing himself to the risk of income loss he reaches an expected utility as calculated in eq. (3). Second, the utility of 65 may result from a situation without income risk. The fixed income yielding a utility value that equals the expected utility level is indicated by Y*. From Figure 4.3.1 it can be read that Y* equals 2,400. The example-person is indifferent between receiving a certain income of 2,400 and the uncertainty of getting either 1,000 or 5,000 guilders, each with a 50% probability.

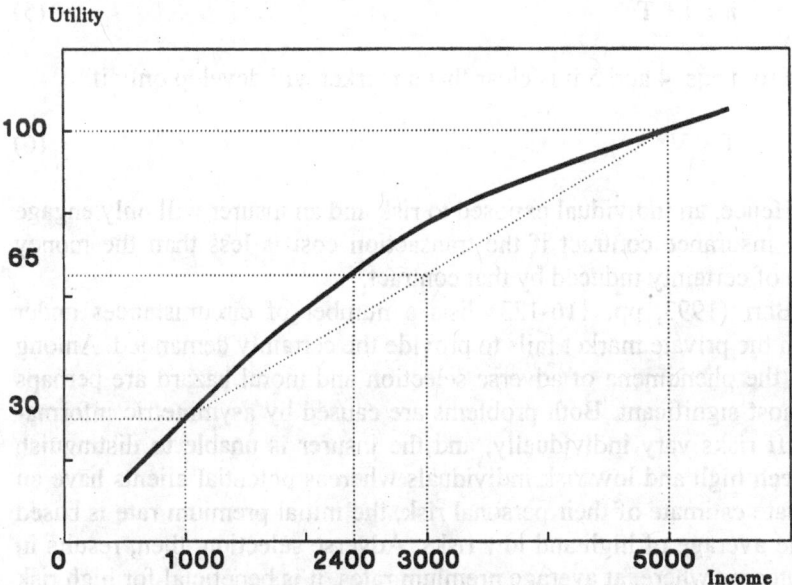

Figure 4.3.1   Utility function of a risk-averse individual

The positive difference between the expected income $\hat{Y}$ and the certain income Y* indicates the amount of money this person is willing to pay (at most) to avoid uncertainty. We call this the money value of certainty V [see e.g. Barr (1993, p.113)]. To avoid the probability of a loss of 4,000, he would be willing to pay an insurance premium, π, that exceeds the expected loss by 600 guilders at most.

Clearly, there will be positive individual demand for insurance if:

$$\pi < \hat{L} + V \tag{4}$$

On the supply side, insurance policies will be offered only if the premium is high enough to cover the carrier's cost; not only the cost of transfers to policyholders who suffer losses but also the transaction costs involved in running the insurance bussiness, for example the costs associated with the distribution of policies and the management of claims. Private insurance carriers will only supply insurance policies if the insurance premium at least covers the expected loss plus the transaction costs per policy:

$$\pi \geq \hat{L} + T \tag{5}$$

From eqs. 4 and 5 it is clear that a market will develop only if

$$T \leq V \tag{6}$$

Hence, an individual exposed to risk and an insurer will only engage in an insurance contract if the transaction cost is less than the money value of certainty induced by that contract.

Barr (1993, pp. 116-123) lists a number of circumstances under which the private market fails to provide the certainty demanded. Among these the phenomena of adverse selection and moral hazard are perhaps the most significant. Both problems are caused by asymmetric information. If risks vary individually, and the insurer is unable to distinguish between high and low risk individuals whereas potential clients have an accurate estimate of their personal risk, the initial premium rate is based on the average of high and low risks. Adverse selection, then, results in an outcome where, at average premium rates, it is beneficial for high risk people to buy full coverage whereas low risk people may decide not to take (full) insurance.

Moral hazard occurs if insurance coverage induces an increase of the expected loss by changing the risk behavior of the insured. The difference between the expected values of post- and pre-insurance losses ($\hat{L}_t - \hat{L}_0$) is defined as the moral hazard component.

As a consequence of moral hazard a risk-averse person will be either *over*-insured or *under*-insured. He will be over-insured when he buys coverage for losses that would not have occurred without insurance. However, the individual may also decide to buy no insurance at all. This would be his decision if $\pi (=\hat{L}_t + T) > \hat{L}_0 + V$, or if $\hat{L}_t - \hat{L}_0 > V - T$. In words, under-insurance will occur if the size of the moral hazard component exceeds the net gains of insurance.

Some efficiency implications of mandatory social insurance

Adverse selection and moral hazard cause market inefficiencies that most governments seek to correct by introducing a mandatory social insurance systems.

Under mandatory social insurance, the insurance contracts are specified by law. It is not uncommon to finance social insurance by a uniform contribution rate. More often than not the financing of social insurance involves a redistributive mechanism implying cross-subsidies from low to high risk policyholders. In our simple model we assume a flat rate social insurance premium calculated to cover average expected loss ($\hat{L}_m$) plus the cost (per policy) of program administration. Therefore π equals $\hat{L}_m + T$.

Compared to the alternative situation where there is no market for insurance, the individual gains from social insurance if the maximum premium he is willing to pay ($\hat{L} + V$) exceeds the mandatory contribution rate π. The size of his gain equals:

$$(\hat{L} + V) - (\hat{L}_m + T) \qquad (7)$$

Hence, the utility gain an individual obtains from mandatory social insurance is high if his risk is relatively high, if he has a strong preference for certainty, and if the administrative cost per policy is low.

From eq. (7) it also appears that some individuals would be better off without social insurance. The introduction of social insurance, therefore, is unlikely to yield Pareto efficiency. Whether or not social insurance yields a net welfare gain for the entire population can be calculated by simply adding the individual gains and losses. Since the sum of expected individual losses ($\hat{L}_T$) equals the sum of the average losses, the size of the welfare gain can be expressed as the difference of the aggregate money value of certainty and the total administrative cost:

$$V_T - T_T \qquad (8)$$

Moral hazard

Eq. (8) is valid only if we can assume that the risk behaviour of the mandatorily covered individuals is not affected by the insurance. This may be a plausible assumption in the cases of social insurance programs covering old age, it is unlikely to hold for most of the other socially insured income-risks. The endogeneity of income risks covered by social welfare programmes is well documented in a plethora of studies confirming the incentive effects of such programmes with respect to the risk behaviours of both covered workers and their employers. If indeed coverage induces a behavioral response by the insured the sum total of covered expected losses ($\hat{L}_{c,T}$) will exceed the sum total of expected losses prior to social insurance coverage ($\hat{L}_{0,T}$). The difference between the post- and pre-insurance expected values of total losses is defined as the moral hazard component of the insurance program. Evidently, the moral hazard component reduces the overall welfare gains. For social insurance programs containing a moral hazard component the size of the welfare gain equals:

$$V_T - T_T - (\hat{L}_{c,T} - \hat{L}_{0,T}) \tag{9}$$

Mandatory social insurance yields a net welfare gain if the difference between the aggregate money value of certainty and the aggregate cost of program administration exceeds the aggregate moral hazard component. The size of the welfare gain depends on the aggregate money value of certainty, the total administrative costs and the size of the moral hazard component.

Trade-offs between moral hazard, the value of certainty and administrative cost

With the exception perhaps of old age insurance, social insurance schemes typically cover risks that contain a potentially large moral hazard component. The prevalence of moral hazard is indeed one of the very reasons of the existence of social insurance.

The moral hazard component can be controlled in two ways: one is to mitigate the behavioral response of the insured by introducing coinsurance, the other is to try and reduce the moral hazard by intensive monitoring of the insured and the claims they file. Either way involves welfare losses. Co-insurance obviously reduces the value of certainty V_T, since the individuals at risk no longer get full coverage, whereas intensive monitoring increases the cost associated with the provision and administration of the insurance T_T.

In social insurance, the extent of coverage (or its complement: the level of co-insurance) is the outcome of a political process which is layed down in the law. Here, we will not go into the question of how to set this legal standard. Instead, we focus on the trade-off between administrative (monitoring) costs and the size of the moral hazard component.

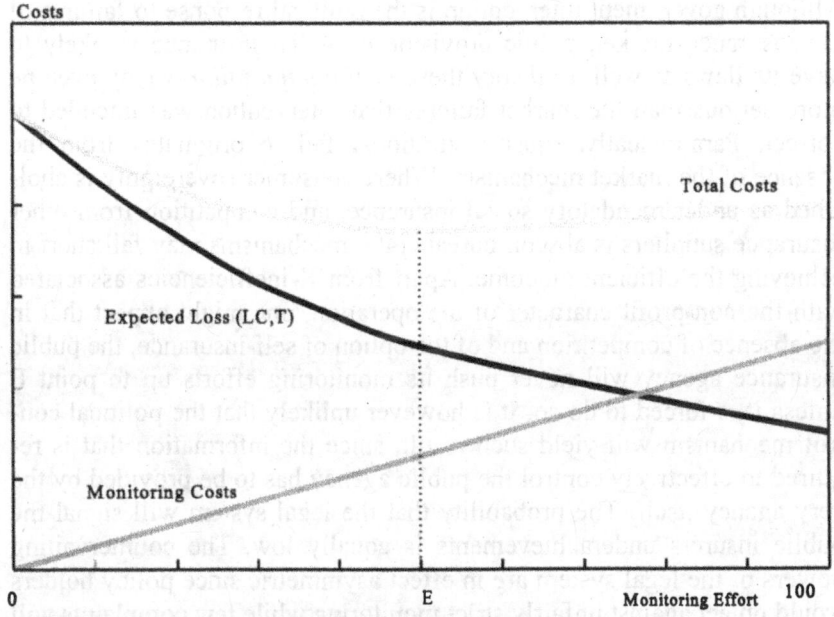

Figure 4.3.2   **Efficient monitoring effort**

Given the extent of coverage then, the size of the moral hazard component depends on the level of monitoring activities and of course their efficacy. Health care insurance may be more easy to monitor than for instance disability insurance, which in turn will be less difficult than unemployment insurance.

Figure 4.3.2 shows how the monitoring effort, measured on a scale from 0% to 100%, relates to the expected value of total covered losses $\hat{L}_{c,T}$ to monitoring costs and to total costs. We assume that monitoring costs increase proportionally with the monitoring effort and that the marginal returns of monitoring (reflected in the reduction of the moral hazard component) are decreasing. The efficient level of monitoring is in point E where the sum of monitoring costs and the expected value of covered losses reaches its minimum. Given the politically determined extent of coverage, the marginal cost of monitoring will exceed the marginal benefits in terms of moral hazard reduction beyond this point.

Public social insurance; suboptimal monitoring effort

Although government intervention is the political response to failures of the insurance market, public provision of social insurance is likely to have its flaws as well. In theory these *institutional failures* may even be more serious than the market failures that intervention was intended to correct. Paradoxically, most institutional failure originates from the absence of the market mechanism. Where consumer sovereignty is abolished as under mandatory social insurance, and competition from other insurance suppliers is absent, bureaucratic mechanisms may fall short in achieving the efficient outcome. Apart from X-inefficiencies associated with the non-profit character of the operation, one might expect that in the absence of competition and of the option of self-insurance, the public insurance agency will never push its monitoring efforts up to point E unless it is forced to do so. It is however unlikely that the political control mechanism will yield such result, since the information that is required to effectively control the public agency has to be provided by the very agency itself. The probability that the legal system will signal the public insurers underachievements is equally low. The countervailing powers of the legal system are in effect asymmetric since policy holders would object against unfairly strict monitoring while few complaints will be filed against lax monitoring practices.

In sum, we would like to argue that the public agency providing mandatory social insurance will put too little effort in monitoring the insured. As a consequence the moral hazard component will be greater than the size that is necessary to realize the full potential welfare gain expressed in eq.(9).

Public social insurance in the absence of moral hazard

The aforementioned drawback of publicly provided mandatory social insurance seriously affects the efficiency of insurance schemes that cover the risk of harmfull events that can be manipulated by the insured and from which they derive 'secundary gains', e.g. in the form of leisure as is the case in unemployment insurance [see Barr (1993)].

Not all risks typically covered by mandatory social insurance are like that however. Mandatory social old age insurance for instance does not suffer under the moral hazard phenomenon. Most people would like to live a long and healthy life irrespective of insurance coverage. And while some people would change their behavior to increase life expectancy in response to availability of old age insurance benefits, this would hardly be counted as a welfare loss. On the contrary, if anything people are encouraged to lead healthy lives and to refrain from activities that may induce an untimely death. Apparently the moral hazard component in old age insurance, if there is any, is considered to contribute positively to welfare.

If moral hazard is not considered a loss, or if it simply does not occur, the failure to efficiently contain the phenomenon has become irrelevant. Under such circumstances the net welfare gains of mandatory social insurance equals the balance of the aggregated value of certainty and the total of administrative costs (see eq. 8).

Given the chosen level of certainty, minimizing administrative costs yields maximal aggregate gains. Administrative costs are defined as all costs associated with the provision of the insurance other than compensation expenditures. We see three reasons why the administrative costs of mandatory social insurance are low relative to that of private insurance. First, the 'contracting costs' of social insurance are very low. Since insurance is mandatory its distribution does not require costly marketing, advertizing and selling. Furthermore, as the policy conditions are legally determined, social insurance avoids the cost of drawing tailor made contracts. A second cost advantage is derived from the scale of operations in social insurance. The social insurer can spread the fixed costs over the complete 'market', whereas private insurers share the market with their competitors. Finally, the capital cost of the public social insurer tend to be lower than that of a private carriers due to the risk compensation the latter has to pay to capital providers.

The relative cost advantage of social insurance is illustrated in Table 4.3.1 where we compare the administrative costs of mandatory social old age insurance with those of semi-mandatory pension funds, of private old age group-insurance and of private individual pensions in the Netherlands in 1993.

Table 4.3.1 Administrative cost of Dutch old age pensions; percentage of total premiums (1993)

Mandatory Social Insurance (AOW)	1.2%
Semi-mandatory Pension Funds:	
-Branche Specific Funds	5.8%
-Firm Specific Funds	4.4%
Private Pension Insurance:	
-Group Insurance	7.2%
-Individual Insurance	21.1%

Sources: Financiële verslagen Verzekeringskamer, Verzekeringskamer 1995, Sociale Nota 1996, Ministerie van SZW 1995.

By far the least costly is the administration of mandatory social old age insurance. It takes 1.2% of total premiums to administer this program. The semi-mandatory pension funds rank second in this table. Their administration accounts for 4.4% and 5.8% of total premiums in firm and branch specific funds respectively. If a firm specific pension fund exists, participation is mandatory for all employees. In branches with a branch specific pension fund participation is mandatory for all employees in the branch. Firm and branch specific pension funds are governed by employer and employee representatives. Private insurance contracts involve the highest administrative costs. Whereas the administrative costs for private group insurance, typically covering groups of employees on an voluntary basis, are relatively modest (7.2%), individual old age insurance appears to be expensive: running this business requires 21.1% of total premiums.

Apparently the administrative cost of old age insurance decreases with the number of participants in the insurance contracts. Mandatory insurance is less costly than semi-mandatory pensions. In turn, the cost of these pension funds are lower than that of voluntary group insurance. Far the most expensive are the individual contracts. If mandatory social old age insurance would be as costly to administer as private individual old age insurance, the total expenditures under this scheme would rise by 25% to Dfl 40 bn (6.8% of GDP in 1993). These figures suggest that the Dutch mandatory and semi-mandatory pension system induces substantial welfare gains indeed. It is only fair to add however, that the gains of heavily standardized insurance contracts should be weighed against the losses in terms of consumer sovereignty. Of course it is hard to strike the balance. It is reassuring however to observe that while most people would prefer their suits to be tailor made, they are perfectly willing to settle for off-the-peg.

Case I: The Dutch sickness and disability insurance

The Dutch disease

Over the past 25 years, most of the OECD countries have seen substantial declines in older male labor force participation as well as considerable increases in the availability and generosity of disability, and other early retirement, benefits. The concurrence of these tendencies suggests that disability programs have been generally used to achieve more general social policy goals, such as low (youth) unemployment.

On closer comparison, however, the age-specific trends in the number of disability beneficiaries show significant cross-national differences. To contain unemployment, the Netherlands clearly chose the income maintenance option, even for those under 45. Other countries, such as Sweden and Germany, largely opted for employment security for ailing workers under 60 and restoration of their earnings capacities where possible. Part of the German excess labor supply was captured by relaxing benefit eligibility criteria, both for disabled and able-bodied workers over 60.

International data (e.g. in Aarts et al. (1996), or Einerhand at al. (1995)) highlight the unique position of the Netherlands. For those younger than 60, the number of disability prevalence rates - *i.e.*, disability beneficiaries per 1,000 workers - have been about three times as high as other countries during the 1980s. Furthermore, the average Dutch beneficiary age is 49, which compares to 57 in Sweden and Germany. As one can plausibly assume that the Dutch do not have significantly poorer health statuses and job conditions than other European populations, the difference must be sought in the way disability benefits are being allocated.

The Dutch social insurance system

Sickness benefits When a Dutch worker is unable to perform his or her job because of illness or injury, irrespective of its cause, he or she is entitled to sickness benefits. Sickness benefits replace 70 percent of gross wage earnings but collective bargaining agreements between employers and employees stipulate that sickness benefits be supplemented to the level of net earnings. Sickness benefits end after 12 months. They are not means-tested.

Disability benefits Under the Dutch ruling any illness or injury entitles an insured person to a disability benefit after a mandatory waiting period of 12 months. While other OECD countries distinguish people with disabilities by whether the impairment occurred on the job or elsewhere, only the *consequence* of impairment is relevant for the Dutch disability insurance program.

Compensation for loss of earning capacity due to long-term, or permanent disablement is provided by a two-tier disability insurance program. The first tier is universal, with eligibility being based on citizenship. These national disability insurance programs typically offer flat rate benefits that are, of course, earnings tested but are not tested for other household means. They target those handicapped congenitally, or in early childhood, and provide benefits from age 18 onwards. These basic benefits also cover self-employed people.

Eligibility for a supplement is restricted to labor force participants. These second-tier benefits are based on age and wage earnings. Previously, coverage did not depend on age, or any other count of insurance coverage years. This meant that every member of the population at risk was fully covered. When found fully (80-100 percent, see below) disabled the statutory replacement rate was equal to that of Sickness benefits, *i.e.*, 70 percent of before-tax earnings, with a cap on covered earnings of about $ 35,000 per annum.

By definition, eligibility for disability pensions is based on some measure of (residual) capacity or productivity. The Dutch disability program is unique in that it distinguishes seven disability categories ranging from less-than-15 percent, 15-25 percent disabled, and so on to

80-100 percent disabled. So, the minimum degree of disability yielding entitlement to benefits is 15 percent.

The degree of disablement is assessed by consideration of the worker's residual earning capacity. The degree of disablement, then, is the complement of the residual earning capacity and defines the benefit level. Prior to the reforms of 1993, only jobs that were compatible with one's training and work history could be taken into consideration in assessing residual capacity.

Administration Until recently (March 1997) the Dutch disability plan differed from other national programs, not only because it has no separate work injury scheme and has a more elaborate system of partial benefits, but also because its social insurance programs (disability and unemployment insurance, and sickness benefits) were run by autonomous public agencies which lack direct governmental (political) control. These 'Industrial Insurance Associations' represented different branches of industry. Membership in one of these Associations was obligatory for every employer, and each firm was assigned to one of the Associations by law. This means that each Association held a, legally protected, sectoral monopoly. The Associations were managed by representatives of employers' organizations and trade unions, and had discretion to develop autonomous benefit award and rehabilitation policies without having to bear the fiscal consequences of their policy choices, as disability and unemployment insurance expenditures are funded by nationally uniform, pay-as-you-go contribution rates. Therefore, the administrative autonomy that the legislator allowed two major interest groups - employers' organizations and trade unions - was not balanced by financial responsibilities.

Hidden unemployment Workers with disabilities have a higher-than-average sensitivity to cyclical downswings. Independent of the operation of disability programs, they are among the first to be made redundant. Both American and European studies show a significant relationship between labor market conditions and disability program participation rates. These studies do not explain the extent to which there may be severely disabled individuals hidden among workers in boom periods or (mildly disabled) unemployed persons hidden among disability benefit recipients in slack periods.

As discussed, European workers who lose their jobs are usually covered by earnings-related unemployment insurance. Unemployment insurance entitlements are of limited duration, and followed by flat-rate, means-tested social assistance. Improper use of disability benefits as a more generous, and less stigmatizing, alternative to unemployment benefits was quite common in the 1975-1990 period. It provided employers with a flexible instrument to reduce the labor force at will and kept official unemployment rates low.

Until 1987, the Dutch law explicitly recognized the difficulties impaired workers may have in finding commensurate employment by prescribing that the benefit adjudicators should take account of poor labor market opportunities. The administrative interpretation of this so-called 'labor market consideration' was so liberal as to award a full benefit to almost anyone who passed the low threshold of a 15 percent reduction in earnings capacity. The autonomy allowed to employers' organizations and trade unions in the administration of the disability insurance program was used to suit their common interest in a lenient award policy because they could shift the financial burden of such a policy to national funds that spread the pay-as-you-go contribution rates equally over all employees. As a result, the share of unemployed (or 'socially disabled') among disability insurance beneficiaries, applying the pre-1993 eligibility standards, is estimated to be 40 percent. The fact that the abolition of this legal provision could not halt the growth in the prevalence of disability transfer payment recipients induced further amendments from 1993 onwards.

In addition to cash compensation, Dutch disability insurance offers in-kind provisions covering job accommodation and training costs to promote redeployment of impaired workers. As a consequence of the lenient award policy, spending in this area is minimal. In 1993, spending on provisions in kind under the Dutch disability insurance program amounted to 0.8 billion guilders. Only 20 million (2.5 percent of provisions expenditures, about 0.1 percent of total disability expenditures) was used for vocational rehabilitation and workplace adjustment. The rest was spent on provisions for general daily activities (mobility, dwelling, etc.). The amount is extremely low simply because very few claims are filed. On a per-capita basis Germany, for instance, spends 42 times more than the Netherlands does on vocational rehabilitation.

Evaluation The disparity between the Dutch disability program experience and that of the other countries may be largely explained by differences in incentive structures. Some of these incentives are intended and reflect national preferences. For instance, a strong preference for prevention and rehabilitation, in countries like Germany and Sweden, has induced legislators to mandate rehabilitation for all workers with functional limitations, except for those over 60 and for the severely disabled. This policy is supported by a quota system in Germany, and by wage subsidies and employment programs in Sweden. Such policies give a clear signal to the insured population that eligibility for disability transfer benefits is based on complete, and irreparable, loss of earning capacity. A similar signal is issued by the United States' Social Security Disability Insurance (SSDI) program requirement of an, often uncovered, waiting period of five months without *any* gainful activity due to severe disablement which is meant to deter applications for a disability benefit.

Until the reforms of 1993, such clear signals were missing in the Netherlands. In terms of the framework set out in the previous Section, none of the parties involved in the use and management of sickness and disability benefit programs were confronted with the costs of excessive use and excessive leniency. A wealth of data, both aggregate program statistics and results of micro-research, attest to the substantial amount of moral hazard present in these two health-related income maintenance programs. To mention a few additional figures:

- In 1995, that is after the reforms that will be discussed below, disability benefit recipients still constituted 13 percent of the work force, and 8 percent of the working age population. Disability benefit expenditures are 3.5 percent of GDP. These are, by far, the largest disability benefit volume and spendings among OECD countries.
- Apart from the general difficulties in translating clear-cut limitations in terms of loss of earning capacity most disability benefits used to be awarded on the basis of subjective health complaints which often contain a substantial behavioral element. At the end of 1995 there were 860,000 disability beneficiaries; 30 percent of the awards were based on psychic problems, and 29 percent on diseases of the musculo-skeletal system. These two diagnostic groups are likely to contain a large number of difficult to substantiate complaints. Moreover, 12 percent had their awards based on unclear, or unknown, symptoms. As a comparison, only 7 percent is based on diseases of the cardiovascular system.

- In Aarts and De Jong (1992, Chapter 10), we focussed on behavioral responses to the disability program. We confirmed the notion that the probability of disability program entry is determined both by medical and non-medical factors. The disability indicators reflect the medical-sociological definition of disablement and, therefore, incorporate the influence of both the nature and severity of impairment and the strenuousness of job requirements. The measurement of functional limitations was based on objective assessments by social insurance doctors and vocational experts.

  Employment opportunities and income and leisure considerations also appear to have remarkably powerful impacts on individual disability program risk. Specifically, a person with vocational characteristics that reduce the likelihood of reemployment is much more likely to enroll in the disability program. Economic factors underlie the voluntary retirement character of the disability program.

  The probability of disability program entry was shown to also depend on the views and preferences of the other two agents involved – the employers and the gatekeepers of the program. The estimation of a structural model revealed the relative impacts of self-perceptions and gatekeepers' ratings of disability on the probability of a worker entering the disability system. The views of the treating physicians appeared to be very influential in the worker's self-perceptions of the extent of disablement. Self-ratings and gatekeepers' ratings were found to be equally important in determining the disability program incidence. In their determinations, the disability gatekeepers seem to add age to their medical data as a proxy for labor market opportunities. The main conclusion that emerged from this study was that 'for lack of a manageable disability standard, disability insurance enrollment is largely at the discretion of individual employees and their employers' (p.354).

- The predominance of informal rules and procedures in the administrative system that prevailed before the 1993 reforms was further confirmed by two empirical studies in the field of sickness and disability. Van der Veen (1990) studied the behavior of street-level bureaucrats involved in assessing disability benefit eligibility and concluded that formal disability assessment procedures continued to leave ample discretion to the program gatekeepers despite the 1987 reforms. The program gatekeepers appeared to apply their own informal criteria to reach a decision on benefit eligibility. They weighed heavily how much they felt the applicant 'deserved' and 'needed' the benefit. In their professional attitude they showed an inclination to minimize the number of exclusion errors and to give applicants the benefit of the doubt.

- Van Eck (1990) studied the decision making process of social insurance doctors in monitoring sickness benefits claims and reached similar conclusions. When functional limitations are hard to measure (*e.g.*, mental limitations), social insurance doctors cannot 'hide' behind rules and formal tests. They must rely on personal judgement. Claimants who realize that their acceptance depends on the doctor's subjective judgment hold the doctor personally responsible for the entitlement decision. Since the doctor, who largely relies on information provided by the claimant, is inclined to give the claimant the benefit of the doubt, a negotiating process starts in which the claimant may effectively bias the doctor's decision.

These data strongly suggest that the presence of a relatively generous, and leniently administered, system of sickness and disability benefits has elicited behavioral reactions by the three major interest groups (employees, employers, and administrators) that, in the absence of such insurance systems, would have been quite different. In other words, the Dutch sickness and disability programs contain a substantial moral hazard component.

Without an analytic framework in which the extent of moral hazard can be identified and measured we can only use international data to give a guesstimate. In Aarts *et al.* (1996) we compare the Dutch disability prevalence rates with those in Germany, and find that a well managed disability program as in Germany yields a disability volume of one third of that in the Netherlands. Taking the difference between the Netherlands and Germany as a proxy of the size moral hazard component in the Dutch Sickness Benefits and Disability Insurance programs, we arrive at an estimate of *two-thirds* of benefit outlays. In 1990, the benefit expenditures under both these programs were about Dfl. 30 billion, or 6 percent of GDP implying that reduction of moral hazard to the German standard could save as much as 4 percent of GDP.

Disability insurance reforms

Greying of the labor force was forecast to produce an increase of 50 to 80 percent of the volumes under these runaway sickness and disability benefit systems over the coming 25 years, if both the programs and the administrative practices would have remained unaltered. Under fiscal and demographic pressures government changed both programs.

Since August 1993, disability is more strictly defined. Residual capacity is now defined by the earnings flowing from any job commensurate with one's residual capabilities as a percentage of predisability usual earnings. As a consequence, the Dutch definition of full, 80-100 percent, disablement now resembles the eligibility standard that prevails under the United States SSDI program. Not only has the definition of suitable work been broadened, the medical definition of disability has also been tightened: under the new ruling, the causal relationship between impairment and disablement has to be objectively assessable.

As of 1994, the disability status of all beneficiaries who then were younger than 45 is being reviewed according to these new standards. The reviews affect about 30 percent of the 1995 beneficiary volume and are scheduled to be completed by 1998. In 1994 and 1995, 91,500 beneficiaries younger than 40 have been reviewed; 29 percent of those reviewed had their benefits terminated, and 16 percent were reclassified in a lower disability category, and saw their benefits reduced accordingly. From a sample taken at the end of 1995 we can learn that, one year after the reviews, 23 percent of those who had suffered a loss of benefit income had increased their work effort. More specifically, among those 54 percent who were not in paid employment at the time of the review, 30 percent held a job one year later. Most of the others were still dependent on some form of transfer income. These outcomes show that the reviews have been successful in reducing the beneficiary volume, but less so in increasing the work effort of those who had a full award before they were reexamined using the stricter rules.

As part of the reforms of 1993, the amount and entitlement period of earnings-related disability benefits are now dependent on age to simulate a contribution years requirement. Under the new benefit calculation system, which became effective under the same Act as the stricter eligibility standards, the disability benefit period is cut in two parts: a short-term wage-related benefit, with the previously existing 70 percent replacement ratio, followed by a benefit with a lower replacement ratio.

Both the duration of the wage-related benefit period, and the replacement ratio thereafter depend on one's age at the onset of disablement. During the follow-up period, a fully disabled beneficiary receives a base amount of 70 percent of the minimum wage *plus* a supplement depending on age at onset. For beneficiaries with residual earning capacities, these lower replacement rates are adjusted in accordance with their degree of disability.

The new benefit rules meant a sharp break from a quarter century of disability entitlement to wage-related benefits of unlimited duration. Age now serves as a proxy for work history, or 'insurance years' introducing a quasi-pension element into the disability system. The reduction in government provided disability insurance has spurred a lively market in which private insurers are competing with corporate and industry pension funds to cover the gap between the old system, with a statutory replacement rate of 70 percent, and the new calculation scheme with age-dependent replacement rates. Private coverage of these supplements is capital funded and financed by premiums that are differentiated according to risk at the level of individual workers or firms. Specific firms and even complete branches of industry signed collective bargaining agreements that readjust the gap between the old and new replacement rate so that 85 percent of all employees are covered by such gap insurance.

As of 1998, experience rating will be introduced under the public disability insurance scheme. Moreover, firms may opt out of the public insurance system for the first five years of their disability benefit payment liability.

Privatization of sickness benefits An additional form of privatization was first introduced in 1994, when employers were mandated to cover the first six weeks of sick pay themselves, and to contract with a private provider of occupational health services. These services monitor sick spells, advise firms on the nature and extent of the health risks to which their manpower is exposed, and on how to reduce these risks.

In March 1996, the Sickness Benefit Act was abolished altogether, and employers' responsibility for coverage of sick pay was extended to a maximum of 12 months, after which Disability Insurance takes over. Under the Civil law, firms are obliged to replace 70 percent of earnings lost to sickness. They may choose freely whether they want to bear their sick pay risk themselves or have (part of) it covered by a private insurer.

This is a remarkable change. A fully regulated monopoly market on which firms were assigned by law to 'their' public Insurance Association, and to which private insurers had no access, has been transformed into a deregulated one on which private insurers freely bid for contracts with firms that seek to insure their sick pay liabilities.

Changing the administration In the debate on disability policy the focus gradually shifted toward the program administrators. In 1993, a multi-party parliamentary committee investigated the operations of the Insurance Associations, with special attention to the administration of the disability insurance scheme. A vast number of current and former administrators, civil servants, and political responsibles were publicly interrogated by the committee. The picture that emerged from the nightly televised summaries was devastating for the image of the Insurance Associations. What most suspected, and what had already been shown by research, was now publicly confirmed. The committee's report created broad political support for drastic changes regarding, in particular, the dominant, and autonomous, position of the trade unions and employers' representatives in the management of social insurances.

As a consequence, the 13 public Insurance Associations that were responsible for the administration of the Disability and Unemployment Insurances were abolished in March 1997. Traditionally, or under pressure of their pending abolishment, all of the Insurance Associations had already delegated their administrative tasks to four Administrative Offices. These Offices are private parties which are expected to compete for contracts with individual firms, or groups of firms if they prefer a joint contract. From 2000, this social insurance administration market will be open to new entrants.

Reform results Evidence that the new rules are biting is that during 1994, benefit terminations due to recovery, *i.e.*, being found fit for generally accepted work, increased by about 40 percent. The stricter regime has also affected the incidence of new disability awards. Among the total population at risk, awards dropped by 25 percent in 1994. Employees were also affected by the sickness benefit system, which increased employers' interest in strict management of absenteeism. Days lost to sickness also dropped by 15 percent in 1994. While the disability benefit cuts have been offset to some degree by collective bargaining, supplements above the 70 percent replacement level have mostly been abolished. Therefore, the decrease in awards may well be the combined result of increased stringency of the gatekeeper and lower application rates.

A smaller number of awards and a steep increase of benefit terminations resulted in a 2 percent decrease of the private employee disability insurance beneficiary population in 1994. This was the first year in the history of Dutch disability policy in which the beneficiary population actually fell from the previous year. In 1995 the number of beneficiaries dropped even steeper, by 6 percent.

Case II: US Workers' compensation

Introduction

US Workers' Compensation is a social insurance program providing cash benefits, medical care, and rehabilitation services to workers disabled by work-related injuries or diseases. Distinctive from most other social insurance programs in the United States, workers' compensation programs are operated at the state rather than at the federal level. In addition, it is the only social program that involves extensive use of private insurance carriers (Thomason and Burton, 1993).

Workers' compensation covered 96 million workers and paid $43 billion in benefits in 1993. In terms of benefits paid it is only somewhat smaller than the combined total of the two federal programs that cover non work-related disability, Social Security Disability Insurance and Supplemental Security Income, which was $55 billion in 1993. Between 1975 and 1993 benefit expenditures in constant dollars grew by 250 percent. This increase is partially explained by the expanded coverage of workers' compensation statutes and more liberal cash benefits.

Except in Texas and New Jersey, employers have to buy workers' compensation insurance to cover their personnel. By this mandatory insurance the liability of employers is limited to the policy rules laid down in the workers' compensation statute of the state in which an employer operates. On the one hand, providing coverage under the State Workers' Compensation Act protects employers from additional claims by injured employees under tort law. It is said to act as the 'exclusive remedy'. On the other hand, every work-related disease or injury is covered, irrespective of its cause. This 'no-fault' approach means that an employee does not have to prove the employer's liability. Although both Texas and New Jersey are 'non-mandatory' states only in Texas employers can be found that opt out of the workers' compensation statute.

Each state can choose its own mode of insuring workers' compensation. In 28 states the provision of workers' compensation is completely left to the private market. Private insurance companies compete with each other and with self-insured firms on the workers' compensation market. Fourteen states are 'competitive state fund' states as they have a state fund competing with private carriers and the self-insured. Then there are six 'exclusive state fund' states where the state fund holds a legally protected monopoly. In four of these states, however, self-insurance is allowed. And, finally, Texas and New Jersey are non-mandatory states.

Characteristics of the workers' compensation market

The interstate diversity of workers' compensation insurance modes can be seen as a natural experiment in private provision of social insurance. Exclusive state funds are similar to the way in which European welfare states use to organize their social insurances. Competitive markets for social insurance in Europe have recently been introduced (for instance, to insure sickness benefits in the Netherlands, see section 3), or are being studied as an alternative to the traditional collective funds that hold a monopoly.

Two general characteristics of workers' compensation markets strike European observers as pertinent to the privatization discussion. First, while social insurances in Europe mostly are financed through uniform, pay-as-you-go, contribution rates, workers' compensation plans differentiate premiums by 500, or more, risk groups which are defined by industry and profession. In a competetive setting this detailed set of basic premiums will be further refined to take account of the risk experience of a firm. The extent of experience rating usually depends on firm size.

Not only private carriers use differentiated, and experience rated, premiums, the state funds, whether competitive or exclusive, do so too. Moreover, all market participants - whether private or public - use the same funding method, *i.e.*, prefunding. Prefunding means that premiums are calculated such that the annual total premium sum of a carrier is sufficient to cover the discounted value of the expected benefit streams of those who have come to suffer a work-related injury or disease in the current year. This creates a level playing field for all the participants in a workers' compensation market.

The second relevant feature of well functioning workers' compensation markets is a substantial involvement of the state. The state does not only define the basic policy standards (entitlements, replacement rates, et cetera) by legislative action, its workers' compensation agency also monitors the operation of the program, or actively participates in the market through a state fund.

State agencies may promote efficient outcomes of privately run workers' compensation systems in two ways. First, they can improve the quality of market outcomes:

1. by providing actuarial data to new insurers so that they have easy access to the market;
2. by publishing the products and prices offered by competing carriers so that the market is as transparent as possible and firms can make informed choices;
3. by establishing a residual market to which firms that cannot find a reasonable contract on the competitive market can be assigned. These firms may be new, or may have a bad risk history. Residual market premiums are set by the state agency. Naturally, they are lower than the commercial ones, and the ensuing losses are borne by the private carriers participating in the competitive market, proportional to their market shares.

The operation of a residual market, secondary to a competitive one but yet financed by the participants in the commercial market, has several advantages. It introduces compulsory acceptance of all firms but only at the aggregate level. Through the residual market the private carriers can collectively guarantee that every firm can meet the obligation to provide its personnel with workers' compensation coverage. If each separate insurer would be obliged to accept any firm that seeks insurance the market would not work properly.

A second advantage is that the premiums charged in the residual market effectively act as a ceiling for the competitive rates so that competitive rates do not have to be regulated. This also means that a crucial task for the state agency is to calculate the residual market rates as actuarially fair as possible. If, for instance for reasons of solidarity with difficult to insure firms, the rates are set too low the losses that usually are financed as a surcharge on the competitive

rates increase. As the experience in some states shows these blown up competitive rates fuel a dynamic mechanism by which the residual market explodes and the competitive market dwindles;
4. by establishing a competitive state fund that may help to contain the residual market as it can act as a 'soft' insurer. Crucial, however, is that the state fund also calculates actuarial rates.

The second way in which a state agency can promote efficiency is by implementing rules that reduce transaction costs, specifically litigation costs. Transparency of a workers' compensation statute, and appeals' procedures that induce settlement at an early stage have proven very effective. Crude calculations in Aarts and De Jong (1996) show that litigation costs vary from 4 percent of total program expenditures in Wisconsin to 20 percent in New Jersey. This variation can be explained by the extent to which state agencies are involved in the design and operation of appeal procedures.

Evaluation

The workers' compensation experience shows that the possibility to self-insure is crucial to contain moral hazard. Whether workers' compensation is provided through a competitive market, or through an exclusive state fund, the fact that firms have the option to self-insure if the premiums offered are too high relative to the risks covered forces private carriers as well as state funds to maintain efficient levels of monitoring effort.

As one would expect research shows that moral hazard is not completely eliminated. Butler (1994) reviews 18 papers in which a positive relation between benefit increases and claim frequency and severity is found. This positive effect is the balance of two opposite behavioral reactions: As benefits increase, employers attempt to reduce their (insurance) costs by providing safer workplaces, by selecting workers who have a good health record, or by fighting claims in court. Employees, on the other hand, take less precautions or file more, and more severe, claims. Apparently, the employee (moral hazard) effect dominates. Butler reports an average elasticity of 0.6 of claims with respect to benefit increases. If this result is combined with other results on moral hazard under workers' compensation a 'guesstimate' of 10 percent is obtained.

This relatively low figure should be set against the transaction costs of having social insurance provided by a competitive market. Aggregate operating costs of private insurers and state funds are, respectively, 25 and 12 percent of premiums (Aarts and De Jong, 1996, p.51). This difference is due to the fact that state funds have no marketing and selling costs and, furthermore, are not taxed.

Conclusions

The politically defined extent of coverage determines the aggregate value of certainty people get from mandatory social insurance. Given the value of certainty the aggregate efficiency gain depends on transaction costs and the size of the moral hazard component. Transaction costs are composed of monitoring and other delivery costs. If the risk covered is not liable to moral hazard, such as in old age insurance, provision by a public monopoly has a clear cost advantage over private provision. However, in the presence of moral hazard a public monopoly tends to maintain an inefficiently low level of monitoring effort. Under such conditions, privatization of social insurance may push total (moral hazard *plus* monitoring) cost towards its minimum.

The United States experience with provision of workers' compensation shows that efficiency can be enhanced by introducing competition. This can be done either by exposing a state monopoly fund to the competitive pressure of self insurance, or by provision through a competitive insurance market. In the first option monitoring costs are forced to their efficient level while maintaining the delivery cost advantages of a public monopoly. In the second option the state may manage the market in a way that reduces the delivery costs inherent to private provision. This requires provision of actuarial and product information to the market parties, and close monitoring of claim management.

In Section 3, we mentioned that benefit expenditures under the Dutch Sickness Benefits and Disability Insurance schemes totalled 6 percent of GDP, in 1990. Using the comparable German benefit outlays to indicate the efficient size of the moral hazard component we arrived at an estimate of 4 percent of GDP as the reduction necessary to reach the efficient level of Dutch sickness and disability benefit outlays. However, such a reduction would induce an increase in administration (monitoring) costs. In 1990, administration costs amounted to Dfl. 1 billion, or 0.2

percent of Dutch GDP. In Section 4, we reported that in the U.S. Workers Compensation market private insurers spend about 25 percent of premiums on administration costs. This percentage can be used as an estimate of the administrative cost at the efficient level of moral hazard in a privatized system. A reduction of Dutch benefit expenditures (or premiums which equal expenditures under a PAYG system) to their presumedly efficient level of 2 percent of GDP would, therefore, involve administration costs of 25 percent of premiums - or 0.5 percent of GDP.

Summing up, a reduction of Dutch sickness and disability benefit outlays to their presumedly efficient level of 2 percent of GDP would require an increase in administrative effort from 0.2 to 0.5 percent of GDP. Or, in nominal terms, a Dfl. 1.5 billion investment in increased monitoring effort would obtain a Dfl. 20 billion reduction in sickness and disability transfers.

Although it is early to draw firm conclusions, indications are that the recent changes in the Dutch sickness and disability schemes have caused a significant decrease in benefit recipiency. The drop in sickness benefit claims is entirely due to privatization. While coverage was left unaltered monitoring effort increased by making firms financially responsible for the provision of benefits. The disability volume decreased after eligibility standards were tightened, replacement rates were reduced, and the insurance administration offices were privatized. As a result of the disability program changes the moral hazard component is likely to have decreased. It is too early to tell if this is the result of a reduction in certainty, or an increase in monitoring effort, or both.

References

Aarts, L.J.M., and De Jong, Ph.R. (1992), *Economic Aspects of Disability Behavior*, Amsterdam-New York: North-Holland Publishing Cy.

Aarts, L.J.M., and De Jong, Ph.R. (1996), *Private voorziening van sociale zekerheid in de praktijk. Een emprirische studie naar de verdeling van private en publieke verantwoordelijkheden in de verzekering van het risico van beroepsgebonden arbeidsongeschiktheid in de Verenigde Staten*, COSZ/Ministerie van Sociale Zaken en Werkgelegenheid, Den Haag: VUGA.

Aarts, L.J.M., Burkhauser, R.V., and De Jong, Ph.R. (1996), *Curing the Dutch Disease. An International Perspective on Disability Policy Reform*, Aldershot, U.K.: Avebury.

Barr, N. (1993), *The Economics of Welfare State*, 2nd Edition, London: Weidenfeld & Nicholson.

Butler, Richard J. (1994), 'Safety Incentives in Workers' Compensation', in John F. Burton, Timothy P. Schmidle, *1995 Workers' Compensation Year Book*, Horsham (PA), pp.I-82-91.

Einerhand, M.G.K., Knol, G., Prins, R. and Veerman, T.J. (1995), *Sickness and Invalidity Arrangements. Facts and Figures from Six European Countries*, The Hague: Ministry of Social Affairs and Employment.

Thomason, Terry, and Burton, John F., Jr. (1993) 'Economic Effects of Workers' Compensation in the United States: Private Insurance and the Administration of Compensation Claims', *Journal of Labor Economics*, pp. S1-S37.

Van der Veen, R.J. (1990), *De sociale grenzen van beleid*, Stenfert Kroese: Leiden.

Van Eck, M.A.A. (1990), *Het beslissingsproces van de medische functie van het GAK*, doctoral dissertation, Amsterdam.

PART 5

HEALTH CARE

5.1 Cautionary lessons from the West: What (not) to learn from other countries' experiences in the financing and delivery of health care

Theodore R. Marmor and Kieke G.H. Okma

Introduction

The western welfare state was initially created, among other aims, to remedy the most glaring defects of industrial capitalism. There is a large literature about its development, its origins and its cross-national dispersal in the twentieth century, and, at the close of this century, about its future. Nothing like that range of literature exists about the cross-national development of health financing or about the contemporary spread of ideas about how to reform the costly and controversial public programs for redistributing and rationalizing medical care in modern democracies.

This paper discusses the lessons to be learned from the experiences of western democracies with universalistic health insurance and medical care programs The first section addresses general issues in what we have termed cross-border learning. The second section addresses the issues raised by how western health insurance systems developed over time. Origins, expansion, and retrenchment - these are the categories in which we review the most broadly accepted generalizations. The third section elaborates how the systems reveal common underlying principles but diverging institutional forms and administrative arrangements. The fourth section turns from developmental generalizations to the claims one may justifiably make about the contemporary structures of medical care in western democracies. After reviewing a case study of importation of policy ideas in section five, we finally address promises and pitfalls of trying to draw lessons from these experiences for non-western nations.

The process of cross-border learning

The last years have seen a rapid growth in what might be called the 'cross-border learning industry' in social policies.[1] As there is no realistic laboratory for experiments in major welfare state programs, nations understandably turn to the experiences of others when seeking solutions for their policy problems. Indeed, one of the main purposes of many conferences is to explore what nations can learn from the experience of other welfare states. And so, this discussion starts with some commentary on the very concept of cross-border learning. We offer seven general observations.

First, we want to emphasize the important differences between 'learning about' and 'learning from' another country (Marmor, 1995). The first expression refers to acquiring knowledge about program facts and actual developments - in our case, in the financing and delivery of medical care. The second refers to the use of that knowledge across borders: what lessons can we draw from the experience of another country that may be useful to the policy making in one's own country?

Second, there are obvious but often neglected differences between comparing similar systems and comparing quite different ones. The first comparison set may be helpful in the design of specific policy measures; whereas the second type of comparison may add to our understanding of the few structural elements found in almost all medical care systems.

Third, the rapid recent growth in the 'cross-border learning industry' not only prompts the question of why, but why *now*? The international dissemination of policy ideas seems to be linked to a number of unarguable developments over the past two decades. First, the financing of medical care has everywhere become a major financial component of the budgets of mature welfare states. (Marmor, 1995). When fiscal strain arises - especially from prolonged recession - policy scrutiny (not simply incremental budgeting) is the predictable result. Secondly, mature welfare states, as Rudolf Klein argued in the late 1980s, under almost all circumstances come to have less capacity for bold fiscal expansion in new areas (Klein 1988). This means managing existing programs (in new ways perhaps, but in changing economic circumstances) necessarily assumes a larger share of the public agenda. Thirdly, there is what might be termed the wearing out (perhaps wearing down) of the post-war consensus about the welfare state. By that we mean the effects of more than two decades of fretfulness about the affordability, desirability, and governability of the welfare state.[2]

In such a context, new ideas seem warranted. Yet, there is much ill-advised 'cross-border shopping'; often, foreign ideas match poorly with the specific conditions in the home country. There seems to be too little focus on the applicability of the imported ideas. Policy making, after all, is not only a search for promising ideas, but also for ways ideas match local conditions. Lesson-drawing should include learning from one's own past (as well as learning from other policy sectors). Yet new ideas often disseminate fast just because they are 'new': 'No one wants to be caught wearing yesterday's ideas' (Klein, 1995a).

Fourth, the shaping and results of public policies are obviously affected by organized interest groups. In medical care, there are an extraordinary number of stakeholders, including central and regional governments, advisory bodies, professional associations, organizations of institutions and consumer groups. In each country, they are grouped differently, with different roles and functions. Together, they constitute the 'institutional heritage' in any nation's medica policy arena (Björkman and Okma, 1997). For example, in Germany and The Netherlands the major interest groups in social policies are represented in advisory bodies, which are regarded as integral parts of consensual decision making. By contrast, the same participants in the US mostly act as lobby groups. Fifth, policy making is hardly a purely rationalistic process. It is embedded in conflicting values and norms, and meets practical implementation impediments. The outcomes of policy making are not only influenced by interest groups, but also by public opinion and the media. Even when there is substantial evidence of the effectiveness of certain types of policy measures, that evidence may be ignored or underutilized. Evidence does not necessarily change minds. So the questions are: what evidence forms the basis for policy making? Are there universal lessons to be learned from health reforms and health policies elsewhere? Why does such evidence lead to contentious interpretation? And in what cases is information used as 'warfare ammunition'? (Tuohy 1996; Pfaff, 1996).

Sixth, (health) policy making always involves explicit and implicit trade-offs. Well-known examples include the trade-off between efficiency and fairness; cost containment versus quality improvement; cost containment versus consumer choice; professional autonomy versus the need for planning medical services; professional autonomy versus democratic control; different levels of budget trade-offs; and the choice of 'big bang' versus incremental policies. The balancing of all these (real or perceived) trade-offs requires knowledge and understanding of the policy context in particular nations. This context includes broader societal ideas and ideologies; the degree of public acceptance of state authority and public support for government measures; power relations between government and other stakeholders; and the institutional heritage in any particular policy arena.

Seventh, health policies in Western European (and other) countries reveal many common pressures, a number of similar principles, and some similar policy reactions and measures, But they also include dissimilar institutions and patterns of interest group representation in the policy debates. Most developmental adjustments take place within the framework of existing institutions. There are only rare cases of radical reforms of the institutional setting, usually in extraordinary circumstances such as post-war reconstruction or deep economic recession (Klein, 1995b).

In most cases, the pressure to control public spending has been the most important factor triggering recent health reforms. The reforms often follow quite similar principles. Many aim to modify the role of the state in public life and to reduce public spending. Many claim to increase the efficiency of publicly funded services by changing the financial incentives facing the providers and consumers of these services. Medical financing policies affect the distribution of income as well. Changes in payment structure or freezing providers' fees may curtail the incomes of medical professionals and others; budgeting hospitals and other health care institutions may reduce the income of managers and personnel; delisting services from the coverage of social health insurance affects both providers' and consumers' incomes; introducing copayments or increasing out of pocket payments may affect lower income groups more than others; the introduction of flat rate premiums as substitutes for income-related contributions implies a shift from higher income to lower income groups. Such measures evoke strong opposition. Indeed, the policy debates and policy outcomes of the last two decades show that retrenchment is more difficult than expansion of social (health) insurance and welfare programs (Pierson, 1994).

Based on the above observations, we might conclude that there is convergence in international rhetoric. But this convergence obscures the fact that there is considerable divergence in actual experience. It is therefore necessary to unpack, to unravel and to disaggregate the issues, and to clearly define the concepts used. Learning from the experience of other nations is a far more difficult task than the growth and speedup of international commentary would suggest. Indeed, there is an extraordinary imbalance between the magnitude of the information flows - from CNN to the fax, from international consulting firms to conferences - and the capacity to learn useful lessons from them. The very speedup of communication *about* developments abroad may actually reduce the likelihood of defensible, cross-national learning.

The next section of this paper describes some of the main features of origins and program development of the current medical care systems in OECD member states to illustrate the similarity in underlying principles, but the wide variety in institutional forms and administrative arrangements.

Principles and program development of current medical care systems

Welfare state development and health insurance

In many Western European countries, the collective arrangements of the modern welfare states for the funding and provision of medical care have origins tracing back to the Middle Ages when churches, monasteries and local governments set up hospitals as asylums for the poor, the elderly, the sick, and the mentally ill (Starr, 1982; De Swaan, 1988). The medieval guilds supported their members or members' widows in case of illness or death. In Britain, the 18th century Poor Laws required local communities to support the poor. After the industrial revolution, 18th century friendly societies and 19th century labor unions acted as mutual support groups in providing income protection to their members. Churches, local communities and charities continued to provide some medical care and other social services.

The first explicit social legislation passed during the last quarter of the 19th century. This started with government regulation of labor conditions, regulation of the position of medical professionals, and public health measures aimed at protecting the public from contagous disease. In 1883, the German politician Otto Von Bismarck introduced mandatory sickness fund membership for wage earners. In the first half of the 20th century, extensive debate about the need for social protection led in time to broader acceptance of the basic social insurance principle of welfare state arrangements.[3] The growing awareness of the need to deal with income insecurity was fueled by labor unrest, and by reformers wanting to compensate for the ravages of industrial capitalism. There was pressure to strengthen the role of the state in expanding and organizing solidarity which hitherto had been limited to certain population groups only (e.g. members of sickness funds). This extended role of the state entailed a power shift from organized consumers to the state, and next, to providers. It encouraged interest groups to organize themselves. In reaction to the powerful position of sickness funds, providers of medical care created (or fortified) their interest associations (Abel-Smith in OECD 1996). For instance, in The Netherlands, medical professionals, the hospital federation and the association of apothecaries joined the health policy arena in the beginning of the century (Okma, 1997). In particular, this debate focused on the issues of mandatory contracting of services by the sickness funds and the administration of the health insurance. The providers claimed positions on the board of the funds, and wanted mandatory contracting; the labor unions opposed these claims. The dispute led to a deadlock which was only solved when the German occupational forces introduced the 'sickness fund degree' in 1941, with mandatory sickness fund participation for all lower wage earners, and with mandatory contracting of hospitals and medical professionals by the funds.

In spite of the development of income protection schemes for the working population based on the insurance principle, the role of the state in poverty alleviation remained largely residual, with emphasis on family support and private charity. There was a lively international exchange of ideas and principles. Labor unions and employers' associations exchanged views in international conferences; international organizations such as ILO presented reports on the new developments. Several countries commissioned expert advisory committees to study developments abroad.

Post-war expansion towards universalism[4]

After the Second World War most if not all Western European states developed more comprehensive welfare states based on widening solidarity and social insurance principles. In the extraordinary circumstances of the post-war reconstruction -- and fresh memories of the devastating effects of the pre-war economic crises -- there was wide public support for the principle of universal of near-universal social insurance as systemic solutions for major income risks. The premise of such development was the universalization of income protection (Klein, 1995b).

Moreover, favorable economic conditions allowed for the creation of general (and sometimes generous) income protection schemes for the working population, and other groups as well. There was a steady -- if not always gradual -- expansion of the range of risks for which there was collective protection: unemployment, old age/retirement, sickness, and its expenses, disability, motherhood, large families.

Second, there was a continuous expansion of the populations covered. The arrangements included both universal and specific schemes. Population-wide schemes included general old age pensions, invalidity benefits, universal health insurance, child allowances, and universal welfare support. The specific schemes focused on certain population groups (defined by employment status, age or otherwise) or certain functions. The latter included public funding for hospital or school construction, school milk, mother and child care, urban housing, rental subsidies, and education subsidies.

The development of social health insurance largely followed the general welfare state development. But there were also some country-specific elements, in particular in the mix of funding and in administrative arrangements. As mentioned before, both the funding and the provision of social health insurance had roots in earlier non-statal mutual support arrangements. The medical care arena is populated with more organized interest groups than other areas of social security. These groups have specific interests and power positions. They seek to influence the shaping and outcome of health policies, often claiming to represent consumer interests. The very character of decision-making in health care gives the medical professionals a dominant position (Arrow, 1963; Schut, 1995). Thus, even while health insurance may be seen as integral part of social security, the policy context, and the groups involved in the policy arena have distinguishing characteristics.

The OECD member countries mostly opted for one of two dominant patterns of program expansion of health insurance and administration: (a) the Bismarckian model (introduced in Germany, and adopted by The Netherlands, Austria, France, Belgium, and Japan); and (b) the Beveridge model (first introduced by the UK and USSR, followed by the Scandinavian countries, New Zealand, Australia, Canada, as well as parts of US social policy). These two basic models are characterized by a series of distinguishing features:

- **eligibility**: citizenship (all citizens) or employment (workers and their families) as the main eligibility criterion;
- **universalism**: universalistic welfare state programs versus expanded welfare state coverage by the aggregation of discrete programs;
- **public administration**: administration by government or by intermediary work-related institutions;
- **channelling the funding**: contributions levied through general taxation or earmarked taxes, versus income-related contributions and employers' contributions;
- **contracting**: public officials managing money and contract negotiations versus publicly controlled decentralized inter-mediary organizations.

Some countries developed hybrid models, combining elements from both models. For example, in Germany and The Netherlands, mandatory health insurance is not extended to all income earners. Self-employed and higher income groups may take out voluntary private health insurance. Remarkably, both countries show very low rates of non-insurance. Both countries have a separate population-wide social insurance for long term care. Thus in actual practice, the two countries have realized universal health insurance. In the UK, everyone is covered under the National Health Service, but increasing numbers of citizens - some ten percent by recent estimates - opt for additional voluntary insurance (expecting better quality or more rapid treatment). In France, the majority of the sickness fund members have taken out additional private insurance to cover the risk of co-payments.

Retrenchment

The post-war decades brought economic prosperity and expansion. In Europe, there was high economic growth, low unemployment and high population growth. In the mid-1970s, all three factors changed rather suddenly. The two oil crises led to economic stagnation and high (and persistent) levels of unemployment. Demographic extrapolations had not foreseen the rather sudden drop in population growth, accelerating the aging of the populations. These factors combined added to the rapid growth of public spending, while the shrinking taxation base threatened to cause sharp rises in contributions rates for social insurance. Secondly, ideological conflict fueled the debate on the future of the welfare state. Welfare economists, critical philosophers and both left wing and right wing critics expressed growing dissatisfaction with the dominant (and, some of them claimed, largely ineffective) role of the state (Marmor, Mashaw, and Harvey, 1990). Some proposed drastic reductions in the benefit levels of social security, and a shift from public to private funding. There seemed to be convergence among critics, and a growing consensus about the need to reduce the role of the state; to redirect the system to encourage greater efficiency; to focus services to specific groups; and to increase the responsibility of the individual citizen. There was, however, little unanimity about the way these changes should take place. In the end, retrenchment efforts did not seem to have much effect (Altenstetter and Haywood, 1991). But there was wide consensus in the need to control public spending, and this included (mostly publicly funded) health care as well.

Paul Pierson provides an in-depth analysis of the processes of retrenchment under the Reagan and Thatcher administrations of the US and the UK (Pierson, 1996). Both administrations explicitly formulated retrenchment policies, aimed at curtailing social welfare programs. But in the end, they only had limited success in actually doing so. Expanding entitlements is, politically speaking, easier than curtailing them. The consequences of expanding benefits are spread over all participants in the welfare schemes and thus cause only marginal increases in costs, whereas the sometimes large benefits are usually concentrated on specific population groups. By contrast retrenchment, such as the delisting of services or the shift from public to private funding, only brings marginal benefits (a slight decrease in contribution rates) but very visible and concentrated costs. Often, the targeted groups are well-organized, with good access to the media and to the political arena. Secondly, the very expansion of welfare state arrangements has created its own constituencies. This means not only the direct beneficiaries, but also the civil servants and others involved in the administration and the provision of these services. They all have a stake in maintaining or expanding, rather than cost control or contraction of their programs.

Pierson's findings - though limited to the Anglo-American comparison - are of interest to the general student of welfare state development.

He shows strong public support for collective financing of health insurance. In spite of a general shift towards political conservatism, the Reagan and Thatcher administrations were not very successful in realizing their retrenchment policies in medical care. (It is worth noting that this was true for a unitary political system [Britain] and a fragmented one [the US], both led by leaders popular in the early 1980s). Pierson also emphasizes the distinction between 'programmatic retrenchment' and 'systemic retrenchment'. The first refers to direct reductions in public spending for certain programs, the second to measures which affect spending levels in the longer term. In several OECD member states, retrenchment policies were initially focused on the first category, but then shifted towards the latter. These included measures such as the abolishment of indexed entitlements and efforts to limit growth in future funding.

One can observe a wide range of retrenchment efforts in most if not all OECD countries. Fiscal pressures and political consensus on the need to restrain public spending understandably fueled retrenchment debates in medical care. Several countries commissioned expert advisory committees to address the issues of rationing and prioritization (Stockholm Conference, 1996). Others critically reviewed the scope of benefits, and started to delist certain services such as cosmetic surgery, out of hospital drugs or dental care for adults. The Dutch Dunning Committee, for example, suggested criteria for reducing the coverage of the social health insurance (Dunning Committee, 1991). In other cases, there were newly sharpened eligibility criteria, and independent assessment centers for inpatient and ambulatory care. Some countries raised (formal or informal) access barriers. The debates paid increasing attention to (implicit or explicit) rationing, and several countries introduced or raised copayments (Klein, Day, and Redmayne, 1996).

But in the end, there was (seemingly) very little substantial retrenchment, nor any real overturn of the existing medical care systems. The welfare state debates affected health policy struggles, but the outcomes suggest that there was more rhetoric than reality (Altenstetter and Haywood, 1991). At the same time, it should be noted that these processes have not yet ended, and that some retrenchment measures may only take effect in the longer term. If grand change has not marked the cost control experience of western democracies, continuous talk of reform has. Here is where it is worth reviewing the very categories within which we evaluate medical care arrangements for cross-border learning.

System elements

There are four elements that define the basic structure of any medical care system: the administrative arrangements; the funding mechanisms; the range of services (or income risks) covered; and the financial conditions or access barriers. These four elements are central to any comparison of different systems and to efforts to assess the effects of policy measures on existing medical care services.

Administrative structures

Administrative structures include the way in which interest groups and governments share responsibilities in the operation of social policies generally. Some Western European countries have long traditions of corporalist arrangements (Wilson,1990). In such countries, there is 'arms-length legislation,' and decentralized decision-making power. This may also include collective bargaining for labor conditions. Other countries have developed a dominant role of (central or regional) governments while there are only few which moslt rely on the market for the allocation of funding or the administration of health care and health insurance.

Funding

OECD reports distinguish five major funding sources for health care: general taxation, social security contributions, income-related contributions for social health insurance, flat rate premiums for private health insurance, out of pocket payments (OECD, 1992; OECD, 1994). General taxation and social health insurance are the two main funding sources, but each country has its own particular mix of financing streams. These entail a variety of funding channels: Treasury; Health department; social health insurance agencies; specialized agencies channeling employers' contributions and wage deductions by employers; private health insurance;[5] and health services which charge direct payments by health care consumers. Each of these funding channels is empowered with specific administrative and financial responsibilities. And as the funding structure largely determines the distribution of decision-making power over allocation, it also implies the power to shift insurance risks from the one actor to another, e.g. by setting budgets for insurance agencies, budgets for hospitals and institutions, or by introducing other financial incentives. Within the regulatory framework of social health insurance, there are different contracting models (OECD, 1992; OECD, 1994). The National Health Service in the UK and other countries originally assumed that most providers of health services would be government employees. When this model met with too much resistance, the British government decided to nationalize hospitals, but to maintain the independent status of general practitioners as self-employed professionals (Klein, 1995). The status of hospitals has been partially reversed and most if not all now have gained the status as independent trusts. Other European countries show a mixed pattern of ownership and management of health care services. In Canada, almost all providers are non-statal institutions and self-employed professionals, but there is substantive government regulation and public financing.

Coverage

In most countries, health insurance started out with insurance for hospital care and the services of medical doctors. Next, other services followed, such as pharmaceuticals, physiotherapy, psychiatry, and related social services. In the end, most OECD member states have similar coverage of the basic social (and private) health insurance schemes. But there still remain substantial differences in the coverage of health insurance, and in the borderlines between medical care and (other) social services. Some schemes include ambulatory and in-patient psychiatric care, pharmaceuticals, home care, health spas, preventive check-ups, vaccinations, and pap smears in the mandatory health insurance. Other schemes exclude such services.

Several countries (Germany, Finland, Sweden, The Netherlands, the state of Oregon in the United States, Canada, New Zealand and others) set up committees to reassess the present insurance coverage, and to advise on possibilities for delisting (Stockholm Conference on Priorities, 1996). Like other retrenchment measures, delisting of health care services from social health insurance has been very contentious. Facing strong opposition, not many countries have actually delisted many services apart from some well known examples such as cosmetic surgery or dental care.

Financial conditions

The dominant social insurance character of health insurance has not led to a total ban of additional payments in most OECD nations. (Canada is an exception to the general rule). Most universalistic plans have incorporated user charges and some other financial access barriers. These are sometimes income-related (which means that both contributions and actual entitlements to health care services may be income-related), and in some cases, there is a stop-loss provision or an income-related ceiling to the aggregate of user charges. Many OECD debates over the past two decades have emphasized the 'need' to decrease public funding for health care by limiting coverage of social health insurance and by increasing user fees.

How to draw lessons from other countries

In the national and international commentary on contemporary medicine, all four of the above features - administrative structures, funding, coverage, and financial conditions - are the subjects of vigorous debate. The challenge for scholars and policy makers, however, is not merely to evaluate the claims made, but to understand how the policy lessons of one country can be reasonably extended to another. What are the rules of defensible conduct here and are they followed? The truth is that, whatever the appearances, most policy debates in most countries are (and will likely remain) parochial affairs. They address national problems, emphasize historical and contemporary national developments in the particular domain (pensions, health care finance, transportation), and embody conflicting visions of what policies the particular country should adopt. Only rarely are the experiences of other nations - and the lessons they embody - seriously and systematically considered. When cross-national evidence is employed in such parochial struggles, its use is typically that of policy warfare, not policy understanding and careful lesson-drawing (Tuohy, 1996; Pfaff, 1996).

The reasons for this are almost too obvious to cite. Policy makers are busy with day-to-day pressures. Practical concerns incline them, if they take the time for comparative inquiry, to pay more attention to what appears (not) to work, not academic reasons for what is and is not transferable and why. Policy debaters - whether politicians, policy analysts or interest group representatives - are in struggles, not in seminars. Like lawyers, they seek victory, not illumination. For that purpose, compelling stories, whether well-substantiated or not, are more useful than careful conclusions. Interest groups, as their label suggest, have material and symbolic stakes in policy outcomes, not reputations for intellectual precision to protect.[6] And, one must add, there are not that many knowledgeable critics at home, of ideas about 'solutions' abroad, a further inducement to misuse information once the will is there.

In this context, the central issues that all countries face are, first, how to learn effectively from the cross-national experience and, second, how to learn about the process of policy change itself. If the point of making cross-national comparisons is to draw instrumental lessons for one's own political system, there is no difference in the intellectual requirements between substantive and procedural lesson-drawing. The argument, elaborated elsewhere, is this. There are two possible bases for drawing strong policy lessons from the experience of others. Crudely put, one is what can be learned from quite similar collectivities. If conditions are broadly comparable - economically, politically, culturally - one can be reasonably confident that a particular policy is possible, that it might well be implementable, and that, roughly speaking, the results in country A are likely to be similar to the consequences in your system. In short, policy transplantability and structural similarity are closely linked. (The Scandinavian nations, to the outsider, appear to provide many instances of this process.) But, with this form of learning comes constraints. The most promising, appealing and compelling policy 'answers' may, for instance, lie elsewhere, in a very different sort of society. What to do? Nothing necessarily, we would argue, but understanding that to be the case and to be cautious in just importing such answers as a solution to national problems. This conclusion is, of course, is another way of saying that learning about other national experiences is not the same as learning from them.

There is, however, another form of lesson-drawing that is rare, but powerful. This second form consists of generalizations from the widest variety of cases – as opposed to a 'similar system' or 'dissimilar system' analytic design. If a policy generalization holds over many divergent cases, some powerful factor is at work, something policy makers and administrators ignore at their (and their constituents') peril. The logic is straightforward: if Q follows from policy Z in countries A to T, why should nation R believe its experience will be totally different? Just as the most similar design narrows the range of findings, so too does the most different design narrow the scope. But in the latter instance the narrowing is not of countries, but the likelihood there will some important transplantable generalizations. One example is that the costs of implementing new policies are always much larger than those estimated by their advocates. Another - perhaps a corollary - is that policy makers and policy analysts typically promise too much, ultimately generating, in turn, anger and disappointment. Still another is that wholesale transformation of the ways doctors are paid - a familiar yearning of health policy analysts - is almost never a practical option. If accepted, this last cross-national lesson has obvious practical importance for payment policy debates.

A case study: managed competition and Britain's National Health Service

The increased flow of cross-national claims, as noted earlier in health policy provides new reasons to reconsider the promise and pitfalls of cross-national policy 'learning.' In the context of fiscal strain, new ideas about restraining health inflation have a ready audience. During the 1980s there was a growing set of confident claims, particularly in the United States, about what reforming the 'health care market' through competitive policies might offer. The international spread of those ideas - especially the United States export to Britain - constitutes a case study of intellectual transfers in a contemporary context of economic constraint and increasingly rapid communication. This intellectual impact is an example of British importation of - and action partly on the basis of - a set of ideas unproved in the United States.[7]

The story, complex in detail, is quite simple in outline. A purely Thatcherite model for reforming the British NHS would have been to turn it into a national insurance scheme, to get rid of state ownership of medical facilities, and to encourage the purchase of private health insurance as either a substitute for state provision or as 'topping up' of what was on offer by the national scheme. But when the government's 'think tank' put forward such an approach in 1982 as one among several options for containing public spending, this provoked an extraordinary outburst which convinced Thatcher that this approach was politically undoable.[8] What followed instead was a series of reviews of the NHS and the serious consideration of radical changes within its internal structure. The Thatcher government conceded the major principle that medical care ought to be a right of citizenship, free at point of service to everyone. But beyond that it announced without prior consultation or Parliamentary debate the creation of 'internal markets' within the NHS, a model substantially affected by the thinking of pro-market American health economists in general and Alain Enthoven in particular.

The Enthoven contribution came in two forms. The dissemination of his writings from a narrow audience of health economists to a wider one of political activists was the preliminary element; Enthoven got invitations from British groups and exposed them to the same set of ideas he had promoted for nearly two decades in the United States.[9] But he found an opportunity far more effective than the normal process of lecturing, writing, and consulting. He produced for The Economist a lenghty treatise on reform of the NHS through the expansion of what he and others called 'internal markets.' Accepting that it was politically impossible to change the basic entitlement of the NHS, Enthoven pushed nonetheless for the incorporation of competitive conditions within the NHS. Accepting that Britain had controlled overall expenditures in health care, Enthoven brought his familiar litany of complaints about medicine practiced without the benefits of controlled (or 'managed') competition. Echoing critical rhetoric about unresponsive governments and monopolistic professionals, Enthoven, like many health economics counterparts in the United States, thought that reconstituted and regulated markets could properly reform British medicine. He is reported to be unhappy with the resulting adaptation of his ideas, but cannot complain that they went unnoticed.

Neither the validity nor the vitality of Enthoven's pro-market ideas in health care was central, it turned out, to the ease of its reception. In fact, the striking thing is the British adoption, without effective challenge, of ideas that were largely untested in the United States and, to the extent they have been, proved terribly disappointing. This was an instance of almost pure theory being transplanted across an ocean, contextless and lacking critical evaluation as well as evidence of its efficiency.

What this case illustrates is that ideas do not travel well because they are good or bad, clever or dumb. Ideas are elements in policy warfare whose take-up is determined not by their intrinsic validity but by the local setting - its culture, institutions and contemporary moods, demands and political circumstances. Were the quality of evidence supporting a national experiment in internal markets the test for acceptance, Alain Enthoven would have been sent back for more preliminary evidence of the workability of his ideas.

The demand for new ideas

The spread of 'managed competition' ideas from the United States to Britain is but one aspect of a much wider phenomenon. Other nations - like Australia, France, New Zealand, The Netherlands or Sweden - gave attention to this class of reform notions. And the critical scrutiny in those instances was no more searching than that revealed by our case study. What is going on? The answer, bluntly put, is that policy making is not truth-seeking and one needs to pay attention to the character of political demands to explain what gets attention. We have made the case so far that merchants of ideas market 'quick fixes' to apparently gullible politicians and policy makers. Even if true, the question remains: why are the policy makers interested?

The demand for fresh ideas about how to rationalize the finance, delivery and management of health services is not all that difficult to explain. Fiscal and budgetary pressures on governments everywhere increased tremendously with the slowdown of economic growth, high unemployment, and persistent rises in the share of national income allocated to health care through much of the 1960s and 1970s. The pressures in health care have some basis in demography. For example, the aging of Europe's population is now being matched by the rapid increase of Japan's old; North America's aging population is catching up with that in Germany, which means that nearly eighteen percent of the population will be over 65 years of age by 2020. The elderly typically use more health services than the working population and so there is no surprise that increased numbers of elderly means more consultations, service demands, and the like.[10] It is also the case that many services have little or no proof of cost-effectiveness, and there is good evidence of both over-use *and* under-use interventions.[11]

When this is combined with the understandable efforts of provider groups to maintain their incomes and employment, the stage is set for persistent demands for more funds in the health sector. The combined effects of supply factors, demographic and technological change - the persistent innovation in what health services can be provided - create largely unevaluated and emotional demands for increased funding. And that in turn increases the demand by policy makers for policies which might deflect - and/or diminish - the flow of funding requests. The introduction of competition in health care - and market devices generally - seemed to promise rapid relief.

There is more to the receptiveness issue than simple ideological convergence, however. Cost containment crises (real or perceived) enhance gullibility in the policy making community and create market opportunities for quick fixes. Everywhere in the OECD world during the 1970s and 1980s there were public finance strains - crises to those who had to cut the rate of increase in health and other budgets after long experience with what Rudolf Klein has called the growth state. Just as budget feasts are sources of innovation, so are budget famines. Additionally, the past two decades have witnessed a rapid spread of business marketing and public relations practices into government. Modern health care systems are getting used to reorganization plans every few years, all accompanied by the hype and hyperbole of modern management consultants.

More generally, management consultants - and their counterparts in international accounting firms - now market their 'products' with the enthusiasm of religious converts. The spread of business schools and executive education internationally is at work here as well. Sometimes this process is mediated by important policy figures with experience in business, a tolerance for managerial and market reform ideas, and the capacity to shepherd ideas into policies.[12]

The point to be made here, however, is that the proliferation of new ideas - whether mediated or not - is a process far speedier and internationalized than in the formative years of the welfare state. The revolution in travel and communication means that ideas in New York can be communicated the next day to television and newspaper audiences in London (and in Stockholm, Paris, Bonn or The Hague). Geographically, the range has become even wider than that: there is now advocacy of 'managed care' in Eastern Europe, Africa, and Asia. Alas, the internationalization of social policy ideas has brought little in the way of cross border evaluation, skepticism, and reliable knowledge.[13] As we illustrated in the case of managed competition, the transplanted model was largely theoretical with little if any evidence that bore on its workability - at home or abroad.

This need not mean ideas from one national setting are irrelevant to the policy world of others. But it does mean that evidence, argument, and cross-examination is particularly required when the justification for policy innovation is abstract, drawn from other national experience, or simply derived from models in other fields.

For example, the there is wide agreement among health care experts who have studied international evidence seriously[14] that single-pipe funding of health services is both less wasteful administratively and more conducive to controlling costs. The fact that this proposition was not understood at the moment in the United States Congress during 1992-94 is irrelevant to its truthfulness and crucially relevant to the barriers facing cross-border learning. What remains striking in much of the international policy talk is the indifference to evidence, evaluation, and plausible argument.[15]

Counterpoints

Quite apart from the substantive and political issues that influence the effectiveness of cross-border learning, countries show diverging capacities, which may vary over time, to act flexibly and in response to changing circumstances and changing problems, both existing and emerging. There are different patterns of system learning, and these seem to be linked to the institutional policy environment. Some countries have shown a large degree of 'successful pragmatism,' partly based on rational fact finding and learning from experience, and partly on effective consensus. Examples of such successful pragmatism may be found in countries like Sweden, Norway, Denmark, or The Netherlands. Examples of countries where rigidity appears to prevent timely changes, and in the end, forcing abrupt adjustments are Germany, with institutional rigidities, and France and the UK with ideological rigidities. Italy provides an example of unsuccessful chaos because of lack of strength of governments to negotiate and to implement policy changes in an orderly manner. Japan provides an example of some successful policy changes based on systematic comparison and flexible system adjustments, for example, in health insurance or mother and child care.

In Asia, there are several interesting examples of policy learning and policy adjustment. Japan and Korea have adopted the Bismarck model of sickness fund insurance, but have also adjusted this system to the requirements of their own policy context. By extending this model to include the whole population, Japan avoided the access problems of certain high-risk groups to the private insurance market. Taiwan also has a degree of the Bismarckian system. That country now faces new challenges in the process of transforming its regime into a modern industrial democracy state. Industrialization also caused rapid changes in the labor force because of the new labor market participation by women, and the necessity for new and skilled workers. Additionally, these changes will lead to increased demands on labor conditions and social insurance. Thailand is going through a similar process of modernization; its government has made systematic efforts to study the social legislation of other countries. After extensive international comparison and policy debate, Singapore has introduced a mandatory pension scheme and health insurance which combines extensive government regularion and safenet provisions with individual savings accounts to be administered under centralized state control.

The experience with cross-border learning suggests that the use of international examples has the capacity both to confuse and to illuminate. In many cases, the former have predominated. There is reason to believe, however, that East Asian nations, used to borrowing and adapting, will make better use of Western experience than has been the case within the West itself.

Notes

1. See e.g. Ditchley House Conferences 1992, 1993, and 1994; the Four Country Conferences on Health Policies and Health Reforms in The Netherlands (1995), in Canada (1996) and in Germany (1997).

2. The bulk of this ideological struggle took place, of course, within national borders, free from the spread of 'foreign' ideas. To the extent similar arguments arose cross-nationally, as Kieke Okma has noted, mostly they represented 'parallel development.' But, there are striking contemporary examples of the explicit international transfer and highlighting of welfare state commentary. Some of this takes place through think tanks networks; some takes place through media campaigns on behalf of particular figures; and, of course, some takes place through academic exchanges and official meetings.

3. There are, in general, four basic principles of social welfare programs; the 'behaviorist,' the 'residualist,' the 'social insurance,' and the 'populist egalitarian' principles. (Marmor, Mashaw and Harvey, 1990:23). In the development of the modern welfare states, all four have played a role. The first half of this century saw a shift in emphasis from residualist role of the state into the direction of the social insurance principle, but the residualist principle has not disappeared. It even seems to be gaining ground in recent retrenchment debates, where universal entitlements are curtailed and, access to services is limited by means and income testing. Further, the behaviorist principle (also advocated by the Beveridge Committee in 1943) stresses the need for the welfare recipient to take an active role in trying to return to work as quickly as possible. In several countries, recent health care reforms stress the importance of health services in the reintegration of incapacitated and ill workers, thus emphasizing behavioral changes. Finally, 'healthy policy advocates' seem to favor a redistribution of the determinants affecting health, thus taking a somewhat populist egalitarian view.

4. It is important to note that the term 'universal' may be taken in a literal sense, that is applicable to all (legal) residents of a country; but it may also refer to arrangements which have no legal base to enforce population-wide membership but which do, in actual practice, reach the same goal. Examples of such (near-) universalism are Germany and The Netherlands, where substantial parts of the population do not fall under the mandatory health insurance but where government regulation and informal agreements between government private health insurance have created virtual universalism.

5. It is interesting to note that income-related contributions became only relevant after the Second World War because of the expanding membership including middle income groups. The new technologies introduced since the early 1960s increased the possibility of heroic medical interventions with very high costs, thus necessitating the inclusion of middle income groups into exisiting insurance schemes. As participants no longer had roughly the same incomes, the contributory system had to convert the (community rated) flat rate premiums into some kind of income-related charges.

6. The political fight over the Clinton health plan vividly illustrates these generalizations. The number of interest groups with a stake in the plan's fate – given the nearly one-trillion dollar medical economy – was enormous; there were more than 8,000 registered lobbyists alone in Washington and thousands more trying to influence the outcome under some other label. The estimates of expenditures on the battle are in the hundreds of millions; one trade association, The Pharmaceutical Manufacturer's Association, spent $7 million on 'public relations' by 1993. The most noted effort was that of the Health Insurance Association of America, who produced the infamous Harry and Louise ad. Washington was awash in interest group activities during the health care reform battle of 1993-94, but the character, impact, and meaning of those activities are far from clear.

7. In his comments on an earlier draft of this paper Julian Le Grand observes that the general disenchantment with state provision in the U.K. provided a fertile ground for the reception of market ideas; the general quasi-market drive did not stop in health care but also included other areas such as education.

8. One of the factors that made it unusable was the work of Gordon McLachlan at the Nuffield Provincial Hospitals Trust. His networking and use of the McLachlan-Maynard book on health reform had substantial impact.

9. Interestingly, it was Gordon McLachlan and the Nuffield Trust again who brought Enthoven to the United Kingdom and published Enthoven's treatise on 'gridlock' in the NHS.

10. However, OECD studies show that aging is but one (and not the most important one) of the factors explaining the growth of health expenditure; other causes are the capacity of institutions; the number of health professionals; rising income levels and rising public expectations (Oxley and MacFarlan, 1995).

11. See the work of Robert Brook et.al., *Health Policy*, circa 1991 and elsewhere.

12. The late Sir Roy Griffiths was an example of such a figure in health policy during the Thatcher years. Griffiths, it should be emphasized, was also a significant force for sanity. In particular, his work limited some of the excesses contemplated by the Thatcher government in 1988-89. Briefed by his friends, Griffiths helped to move Thatcher away from changes in finance to private health insurance. He was also quite critical of what we have called management 'quick fixes.' We are indebted to Rudolf Klein for alerting us to the likely significance of international consultants in the spread of market-type reforms in health care. Personal communication, Spring, 1994.

13. The portrait we have painted is reinforced by some of the work of the World Bank, USAID and Project Hope bodies in Africa, the former Soviet empire, and elsewhere. The 1993 World Development Report on health care also pressed for market reforms in health care and health insurances. For a discussion of this, see Lou Opit's review of this Report (Opit 1994). The real nature of this problem is that half-baked ideas (i.e. theoretically attractive but not substantiated by evidence) are marketed not only by disciples but by international agencies with formidable power to influence policy makers. The same is true for some of the 'healthy public policy' campaigns of World Health Organization WHO. So the point is the transfer of such policy ideas, regardless its ideological hue.

14. The range of experts who have made this claim is very large and their writings very extensive. Such a bibliography would include work of the following: Robert Evans, Morris Barer, Greg Stoddart, and Carolyn Tuohy in Canada; Alan Maynard, Rudolf Klein, and Tony Cuyler in Britain; Jean de Kervasduoe and Gerard de Pouvoirville in France; Noaki Ikegami in Japan; Jeff Richardson, Peter Botsman, and John Deeble in Australia; and numerous others. In the United States, such a view is commonplace

among those outside the world of mainstream economists. See, for example, Reinhardt 1989; and US GAO 1991.

15. To extend the argument, note the spectacle of American salesmen of market reforms in health care going to Eastern and central Europe to peddle their model of balance among cost, quality and access. Using the United States as a model of sustainable balance in this regard is rather like going to a brothel to study chastity.

References

Altenstetter, C. and Haywood, S.C. (1991) *Comparative Health Policy and the New Right. From Rhetoric to Reality*, Hong Kong: Macmillan.
Arrow, K.J. (1963) 'Uncertainty and the welfare economics of medical care', *American Economic Review*, 1963(5):941-973.
Björkman, J.W. and Okma, K.G.H. (1997) 'Restructuring Health Care Systems in The Netherlands: The Institutional Heritage of Dutch Health Policy Reforms', *Health Policy, National Schemes and Globalization*, Björkman, J.W. and Altenstetter, C. (eds), London: MacMillan.
De Swaan, A. (1988) *In Care of the State. Health Care, Education and Welfare in Europe and the USA in the Modern Era*, Oxford: Polity Press.
Ditchley House Conferences (1992, 1993, 1994) *Summary of the Chairman*, Oxfordshire: Ditchley House Foundation.
Dunning Committee (1991) *Kiezen en delen. Rapport van de Commissie Keuzen in de Zorg*, Rijswijk: Ministerie van Welzijn, Volksgezondheid en Cultuur.
Four Country Conference on Health Care Reforms and Health Care Policies in The United States, Canada, Germany and The Netherlands (Conference reports), Amsterdam, 1995; Montebello, 1996; Boppard, Germany 1997.
Klein, R. and O'Higgins, M. 'Defusing the Crisis of the Welfare State: A New Interpretation', in Marmor and Mashaw, (eds.) *Social Security Beyond the Rhetoric of Crisis*, (Princeton, N.J.: Princeton University Press, 1988), esp. pp. 219-224.
Klein, R. (1995a) 'Learning From Others: Shall the Last be the First Markets', *Conference Report of the Four Country Conference on Health Care Reforms and Health Care Policies in The United States, Canada, Germany and The Netherlands*, Amsterdam 1995.
Klein, R. (1995b) *The New Politics of the National Health Service*, (3rd ed), Harlow, Essex: Longman.
Klein, R., Day, P. and Redmayne, S. (1996) *Managing Scarcity. Priority Setting and Rationing in the National Health Service*, Buckingham: Open University Press.
Marmor, T.R., Mashaw, J.L. and Harvey, P.L. (eds) (1992) *America's Misunderstood Welfare State. Persisting Myths, Enduring Realities*, Basic Books.
Marmor, T.R. (1994) *Understanding Health Care Reform*, New Haven: Yale University Press.
Marmor, T.R. (1995), *The Politics of Medical Care Re-Form in Mature Welfare States: Fact, Fiction, and Faction*, Paper prepared for the Four Country Conference, Amsterdam, February 23-25, 1995.

OECD (1992), *The Reform of Health Care. A Comparative of Seven OECD Countries*, Health Reform Studies nr 2, Paris: Organization for Economic Cooperation and Development.

OECD (1994) *The Reform of Health Care. A Review of Seventeen OECD Countries*, Health Reform Studies nr 5, Paris: Organization for Economic Cooperation and Development.

OECD (1996) *Economic Studies*, Paris: Organization for Economic Cooperation and Development.

Okma, G.H. (1997) *Studies on Dutch Health Politics, Policies, and Law*, (Ph.D. thesis, University of Utrecht) Rijswijk.

Opit, L., The World Bank, 'World Development Report 1993 Investing in Health', *Health Economics*, Vol.3:127-131 (1994)

Oxley, H. and MacFarlan, M. (1995) 'Health Care Reform: Controlling Spending and Increasing Efficiency', *OECD Economic Studies*, No. 24, Paris: OECD.

Pfaff, M. (1996) *An overview paper prepared for the Four-Country Conference on Health Reforms and Health Policies*, Montebello, Quebec, May 16-18, 1996.

Pierson, P. (1994) *Dismantling the Welfare State? Reagan, Thatcher and the Politics of Retrenchment*, New York: Cambridge University Press.

Reinhardt, U. 'Health Care Spending and American Competitiveness', *Health Affairs*, 8(4): 5-21, 1989.

Schut, F.T. (1995) *Competition in the Dutch Health Care System*, (Dissertation) Rotterdam.

Starr, P. (1982) *The Social Transformation of American Medicine*, Basic Books.

Stockholm Conference on Priorities (1996) The First International Conference on Priorities in Health Care, Stockholm, Sweden, October 13-16, 1996.

Tuohy, C.H. (1996), *Health Reform, Health Policy 2000. Canada in Comparative Perspective*, paper prepared for the Four Country Conference on Health Reforms and Health Policies, Montebello, Quebec, May 16-18, 1996.

US GAO (1991) US General Accounting Office, *Canadian Health Insurance Lessons for the United States*, US Government Printing Office, Washington, DC, 1991.

Wilson, G.K. (1990) Interest Groups, *Comparative Politics*, (Basil Blackwell, ed) Cambridge, MA.

World Bank. (1993) 'Investing in Health', *World Development Report 1993*. Washington, DC: The World Bank.

5.2 Inter-generational equity: The concept of a 'fair innings'

Alan Williams

Introduction

In public policy-making a balance has to be struck between the well-being of the elderly and the well-being of the non-elderly. Some public provisions predominantly benefit the old (such as health care and pensions) and it has consequently tended to be on those subjects that the explicit discussion of inter-generational equity has been concentrated. But the issue is more pervasive than this. The choice of the minimum rate of return required on any public sector investment is an expression of the balance we wish to strike between improving the well-being of current generations versus improving the well-being of future generations, and since the current older generation will not be around to enjoy these future benefits, this social time preference rate is one of the many elements in public policy-making that has a bearing on Inter-generational equity.

But I want to set aside social time preference in this discussion, and concentrate on the implications for Inter-generational equity of the widespread desire in social policy to reduce inequalities. The particular inequality I am going to concentrate on initially is inequality in people's lifetime experience of health. I am going to assume that equity would be improved if (some) such inequalities were reduced. It turns out that this has some rather strong implications for the terms on which the elderly should be allowed to gain access to health care. I will then speculate as to whether this way of thinking about Inter-generational equity in health care could be applied more broadly to Inter-generational equity across a broader spectrum of public services. This is the part of the paper where my own thoughts are least well developed, and it will not be difficult to persuade me that the 'fair innings' concept (which I will explain more fully shortly) does not travel well, across geographical frontiers or across public services (you will have a much harder job convincing me that it is not relevant to health care). But I plan to start with the World Bank, and the approach to equity (with respect to the Global Burden of Disease) which they have embraced, inspired by Chris Murray and Alan Lopez.[1]

Global equity in health

The great advantage of the Murray/Lopez approach is that they have a carefully articulated system which raises, and confronts, far more of the thorny issues in this field than any other approach that I have come across. Because their whole thrust is quantitative, they cannot take refuge in vague rhetorical gestures when the going gets tough, but have to take the bull by the horns, say what they have decided to do, and then work it through. Although I shall criticise them shortly for failing to realise the implications of one such openly declared position, this was an aberration (though an important one in the present context).

Their task was to estimate the Global Burden of Disease.[2] They do this, in short, by taking each main disease in turn and estimating the number of years of life lost through that disease, and the amount of disability caused by that disease amongst those suffering from it. These two elements (loss of length of life and loss of quality of life) are added together using the concept of the DALY (disability-adjusted life year) as the common unit. The year of a person's age at which DALYs are lost is taken into account, because it is held that a person's social value varies with their age, and in calculating the global burden of disease an explicit formula is used to generate these ageweights. It is graphed in Figure 5.2.1. A 3% discount rate is then applied to reflect the different time profiles of 'burden' associated with different diseases. The burdens are aggregated across populations, resulting in an estimate of the Global Burden of disease, which can be disaggregated by disease, or region, or age or sex, or (later, as the work proceeds) by risk factor, etc. It has already generated many thick tomes full of numbers, with more to come. But here I want to concentrate on just 2 elements in the way these numbers are generated, that are of special interest in the context of intergenerational equity.[3]

It should be noted that the age-weights in Figure 5.2.1 are not equity weights. They are an abstract representation of the observation that when in their middle years people are of more value to a society than when in their earlier and later years. This annual incremental value is not just derived from people's participation in what might normally be regarded as 'economic activity', but also in child-rearing, nursing sick relatives, homemaking and other forms of 'household production'. The detail is suspect (for instance I doubt whether countries with very low birth rates would assign a social value of 0 to newborns, nor rich countries regard the social value of the elderly in the same way as a very poor country might) but since some such 'efficiency' notion based on social worth underlies much health care policy in most countries, the general principle seems to be right.

In my view, the same cannot be said for the way in which the 'years of life lost' are calculated. These are not the actual extra life years likely to be enjoyed by the sufferers from a disease if it were eradicated, but instead the notional extra life years they would have enjoyed if they had belonged to a community enjoying the longest life expectancy yet attained by a significant human sub-population (namely, one with a life expectancy at birth of about 80 years). Murray's reason for adopting this 'ideal standard' is that he wishes to avoid concluding that:

> the death of a 40 year-old woman in Kigali contributes less to the global burden of disease than the death of a 40 year-old woman in Paris because the expectation of life at age 40 is lower in Rwanda than in France. Equivalent health outcomes would be a greater burden in richer communities than in poorer communities.[4]

This compensatory procedure appears, prima facie, to be very praiseworthy from a humanitarian viewpoint, but there are two big snags about it. The first is that by incorporating this notional element into the very calculations themselves, rather than bringing them to bear later as a social judgement about equity, we have volumes of data which purport to be factual (estimates of the global burden of disease) but which are actually fictional. The fictional bit is one person's rough and ready adjustment of actuarial tables to generate data which he hopes will induce policymakers to act in such a way as to bring about an outcome which he likes better than what would have happened if he had presented them with the 'factual' data. The second is that if the specific implications of this particular actuarial adjustment are followed through, they indicate that Murray's ideal standard seems far from ideal from the viewpoint of Inter-generational equity. This I will explain.

Pretending that someone has a life expectancy of 80 years when in fact it is only 40 years, is tantamount to giving a equity weight of 2 to each year of that person's actual life expectancy. Table 5.2.1 indicates the impact of the Murray assumption in different circumstances.

Table 5.2.1 Overall effect: equity weight implicitly attached to a year of life lost

Actual Life Expectancy (a)	40	50	60	70	80
Notional Life Expectancy (b)	80	80	80	80	80
Implied equity weight (b/a)	2.0	1.6	1.3	1.1	1.0

Suppose we took three different communities. There is a rich one where life expectancy at birth is 80 years. There is a middle income country where life expectancy at birth is only 65 years. And there is a poor one in which life expectancy at birth is only 50 years. We know that the implied equity weight attached by Murray to a newborn in each of these three countries is 1 (80/80), 1.23 (80/65), and 1.6 (80/50) respectively. But not all years of life lost are lost by newborns, so Murray applies the same principle across all age-bands. As in the quotation above, the life expectancy of 40 year olds can similarly be compared across the communities (using the rich, low mortality, community always as the notional baseline). The result is then the rather surprising one shown in Figure 2. The main oddity here is that on equity grounds the people who actually survive the hardships that kill most people in their respective communities are regarded as deserving of a higher equity weight than those with the poorer prospects earlier in life.[5] I cannot believe that this is what Murray intends, nor what most users of the global burden of disease approach would wish to see incorporated in the data they are handling.

The fair innings concept

I would like to start from a different standpoint, which centres on people's supposed entitlement to a 'fair innings'. The concept of a 'fair innings' reflects the feeling that everyone is entitled to some 'normal' span of health (usually expressed in terms of life years, eg 'three score years and ten'). The implication is that anyone failing to achieve this has in some sense been cheated, whilst anyone getting more than this is 'living on borrowed time'. It has been expounded in John Harris's book *The Value of Life*, Routledge & Kegan Paul, London, 1985, where it appears on pages 91-94. He seems to have some difficulty in accepting it, however, as may be gained from the following passage:

> What the fair innings argument needs to do is to capture and express in a workable form the truth that while it is always a misfortune to die when one wants to go on living, it is not a tragedy to die in old age; but it is on the other hand both a tragedy and a misfortune to be cut off prematurely.

Without telling us what are the key distinctions between a 'misfortune' (a person's judgement about themselves?) and a 'tragedy' (a social judgement that separates one misfortune from another?), he ends up accepting 'a reasonable form of the fair innings argument' as being one in which 'people who had achieved old age or who were closely approaching it would not have their lives further prolonged when this could only be achieved at the cost of the lives of those who were not nearing old age'.

It is upon this piece of homespun philosophy that I propose to build in what follows.

It is worth noting four important characteristics of the 'fair innings'. First of all, it is a notion of equity that is outcome based, not process-based or resource-based. Secondly, it is about a person's whole life-time experience, not about their state at any particular point in time. Thirdly, it reflects an aversion to inequality. And fourthly, it is quantifiable, and even in common parlance it has strong numerical connotations. Death at 25 is viewed very differently from death at 85, and age at death is the key variable which is most often focussed upon. In my view, age at death should be no more than a first approximation, however, because the quality of a person's life is important as well as its length, (as indicated in the World Bank approach by the use of disability-adjusted life years, and not just life years, to measure the burden of disease). But for simplicity's sake I will continue to work with life years here.[6]

To apply this to Murray's situation requires us first to take a step back and look at a simplified example in which there are only two communities, the richest and the poorest of those used in my illustrations above. In Figure 3, life expectancy at birth in the poor country (50 years) is measured on the horizontal axis, and life expectancy at birth in the rich country (80 years) is measured on the vertical axis. The point in space where these coincide is marked 'Actual'. The diagonal line from the origin represents the locus of points at which the two communities would have identical life expectancy at birth. Murray appears to wish this to be at 80, but this is wildly ambitious, so perhaps it would be better to start more modestly. If we were to split the difference between 50 and 80, it may be that our egalitarian wishes would be satisfied if we could have everyone equal at 65 (as marked on the diagram). But suppose these egalitarian ambitions were put to a more severe test, and policy-makers were asked what sacrifice in overall average life expectancy they would regard as worth making in the interests of fairness. In the diagram I have supposed that these policy-makers would be prepared to sacrifice 2 years overall to eliminate a difference of 30 (which is a very weak degree of aversion to inequality). That is to say, in effect, that social welfare (or, in Murray's context, 'Global Welfare') is the same whether we are at the 'Actual' situation or at 'Equal at 63', and I have drawn a social welfare contour ('FI=63') accordingly.[7] Note that the (negative) gradient of this social welfare contour at the 'Actual' situation is 1.6, which is the rate at which it would be necessary to increase life expectancy in the rich country in order to compensate for a unit reduction in life expectancy in the poor community. The slope of this tangent is, in fact, the equity weight emerging from the fair innings approach in this situation. It is no accident that it takes precisely the value of the implied equity weight that Murray's method assigned to a newborn in the poor community, because I have fiddled the figures so as to bring this about. But my 'equity weight' was derived from an explicit trade-off between efficiency (maximising average life expectancy) and equity (making its distribution more equal) elicited from policy-makers. In principle it would also be up to them to determine the 'fair innings', which in this case I took to be 63 years.

If it is safe to assume that people's aversion to inequality (ie the degree of curvature of the social welfare contours) would not vary much if we adopted more ambitious targets, such as setting a fair innings at 70 or even 80, we could explore the implications of doing that too, though they may not be attainable globally in the near future. In Figure 4 I have done this for a fair innings set at 70, and then estimated the equity weights that would be generated in each of the three communities considered earlier. At birth the weights are about 1.4 in the poor community, just over 1 in the middle one, and less than .9 in the rich one. But for those people who survive, their prospects of reaching the fair innings steadily improve. Even in the poorest community, by the age of 45 the balance has tipped in their favour. In the middle income country it happens much sooner, because life expectancy improves markedly for those who survive the first 5 years. But what I want you to note is the contrast between these age profiles and those in figure 2 earlier. The Fair Innings equity weights clearly favour the young over the old, because the old have either already had a 'fair innings', or stand a much better chance of getting one than their younger fellow citizens. So the desire to reduce inequalities in lifetime experience of health implies discrimination against the elderly.

The nature of this discrimination needs some careful elaboration. The equity weights do not fall to zero, so old people are never totally excluded from consideration. An age weight of .5 would mean that we limit the amount we are willing to spend to provide (say) an extra year of healthy life for that person to half of what we would be prepared to spend for that same benefit for a 'standard' person (ie one with a weight of 1). This approach has two advantages. First, we only spend on things that actually improve health, and the more they improve health the more we are prepared to spend on them. This is because of the outcome orientation of the fair innings approach. Second, the 'high priority' groups do not have access to a bottomless purse, because the extra weight is finite and fixed, and things will still be denied if the (equity-weighted) cost-benefit ratio is not good enough. So what we see here is a gentle tightening of the criteria as people approach and pass the selected 'fair innings'. It does not imply that for those under the age of 70 nothing is refused, but after 70 nothing is offered, which is what some people seem to think age discrimination is all about.

Generalisability

Some years ago I wrote a short tongue-in-cheek essay called '.....makes a man healthy, wealthy and wise!'[8] Those of you familiar with the relevant folklore will know that it is being 'Early to bed and early to rise....' which generates this amazing contribution to human well-being, though that was not the message in my essay, nor the principle on which I actually conduct my personal life. The message in my essay was that human well-being depends on people's capacity to accumulate and deploy the three human capital assets of health, wealth and wisdom. I explored the problems of diversifying one's portfolio, of asset switching, and the dangers of low levels of investment. It is to those ideas that I now wish to return.

In the preceding discussion I have implicitly assumed that health was the primary (indeed the sole) source of human welfare. If I had to choose a single indicator of human welfare I would indeed choose quality-adjusted life expectancy, where the quality-adjustment would pick up the 5 basic elements in the EuroQol Measure of health-related quality-of-life (mobility, self-care, usual activities, pain/discomfort, anxiety/depression).[9] But people's ability to participate in the life of their community depends also upon their knowledge and skills and attitudes (which I lump together as 'wisdom'), and upon their access to real resources, public or private ('wealth'). Like many others, I would like to be able to devise some general (value) index which brought together a specific index of health (quality-adjusted life expectancy?), a specific index of wealth (the present value of lifetime income in the broad definition, plus the present value of access to public resources?) and a specific index of 'wisdom' (which would have to include literacy and numeracy, but also practical knowledge of how society works and what it offers). The problem is that quantification has not proceeded far with respect to even rather crude notions of what I am 'wisdom'. The value weights required within such an index would probably be even more difficult to elicit and deploy than the value weights in QALYs. But if the concept were considered important enough, the measurements could be approximated initially and improved on later. They couldn't be much more problematic than Murray's method of calculating the Global Burden of Disease![10]

If some such 'level of living' index were available to us, what I would like to discuss is whether it be appropriate to apply the 'fair innings' concept to it, so as to generate a common set of equity weights to be applied across a wide range of social policies? In principle it would seem very attractive to do so. Looking back at paragraph 9, the properties there listed still seem just as desirable here, namely having a concept which is outcome based, which takes a person's whole life-time as the unit of observation, which reflects aversion to inequality, and which is quantifiable. It seems to me that the fair innings concept applied to people's lifetime expectation of well-being in the three domains I have outlined would fulfil Sen's desire for a measure which would indicate a person's 'capabilities',[11] which could then be compared (for fair innings purposes) either with their own fellow-citizens or with some broader reference group, with equity weights calculated accordingly. Being broader than any one domain of well-being, it would inevitably raise the issue of whether the improvement of educational facilities would be a more cost-effective way of reducing lifetime inequalities in well-being that improving health care, and whether the relief of poverty might not be better than either. It would also enable us to discuss the extent to which deprivation in one domain might be compensated, in the interests of fairness, by favourable treatment in another domain. And it would highlight the particular injustices associated with multiple deprivation, where particular subsets of the population have poor health, no wealth, and very limited literacy, numeracy or useful knowledge and skills. These wider equity weights would focus on the whole situation, and should overrule the specific ones generated by the piecemeal approach in which we tend to look at health alone (like me) or wealth alone (like most social security research).

I have also been speculating as to whether, in this broader field, the fair innings argument would generate equity weights which discriminate against the old. If a community has undergone a sudden transition from very low levels of well-being to very high ones (as has happened in Japan, for instance), and many of the improvements have not been accessible to the older members of the society, then it may be that the lifetime prospects of the old remain lower than the lifetime prospects of the young, and the equity weights would tilt the other way. This cohort effect is of course present in the health field, where, in most countries, successive generations have enjoyed better health than their parents' generation did, but these changes have been gradual enough not to have a dramatic effect on the equity weights that I have calculated so far. But with a broader range of considerations to take into account, it may well be that in the countries 'in transition' in Central and Eastern Europe the elderly are less likely to get a fair innings than the younger members of those communities, so that Inter-generational equity will require equity weights favouring the old over the young.

Conclusion

I first encountered the fair innings as a serious philosophical concept about 10 years ago, but only in the past couple of years have I realised its potential as a guide to empirical work concerning the reduction of inequalities in social policy generally, and in health care in particular. It is a very simple idea, but it gets us into deep water rather quickly. With whom do we feel sufficient solidarity to share a common notion of a fair innings? In health terms, do smokers have a right to the same 'fair innings' as non-smokers, and do men have a right to the same fair innings as women? Do the women of Rwanda have a right to the same fair innings as the women of France? Who should make these decisions? How should they be implemented, and by whom? But these thorny issues would be present whatever equity concept we adopted, and because the 'fair innings' notion is much closer to popular ways of thinking than many philosophical notions of distributive justice, it stands a better chance of being thought through with wide participation than most others do.

Here its quantifiability is also very important. On the whole, debates about equity are not cast in quantitative terms. Much more typical is philosophical argument designed to persuade the reader in principle to adopt or abandon a particular position, such arguments often being conducted around illustrative case studies, which present problems to be resolved, but which are usually inconclusive. This is because ethical principles are 'essentially contestable', by which is meant that 'there are competing conceptions of justice, all of which have respectable arguments in their favour.'[12] Most commentators observe that such principles inevitably conflict with each other, and none 'trumps' the others, so that no principle is absolute. In the presence of such unanimity about the relativity of ethical values, it is the more surprising that there has been almost no attempt to establish empirical trade-offs. Only with some quantification will it be possible to devise rules that can be applied in a consistent manner with a reasonable chance of checking on performance (ie holding people accountable). At present, although reassurance is frequently offered that equity considerations have been taken into account, there is no way of establishing what principles were brought to bear, or what influence they actually had upon the outcomes. Judging by the persistence of health inequalities, and the almost universal agreement that they are deplorable, it is tempting to conclude that the rhetoric is not matched by any real commitment to do anything effective. Quantification thus has potential for clarification, for performance measurement, for accountability, and for policy analysis and reappraisal. The quest for greater quantification of equity considerations seems worth pursuing on those grounds alone, despite the hostility it is likely to engender from those who mistakenly equate precision with lack of humanity.

Annexe

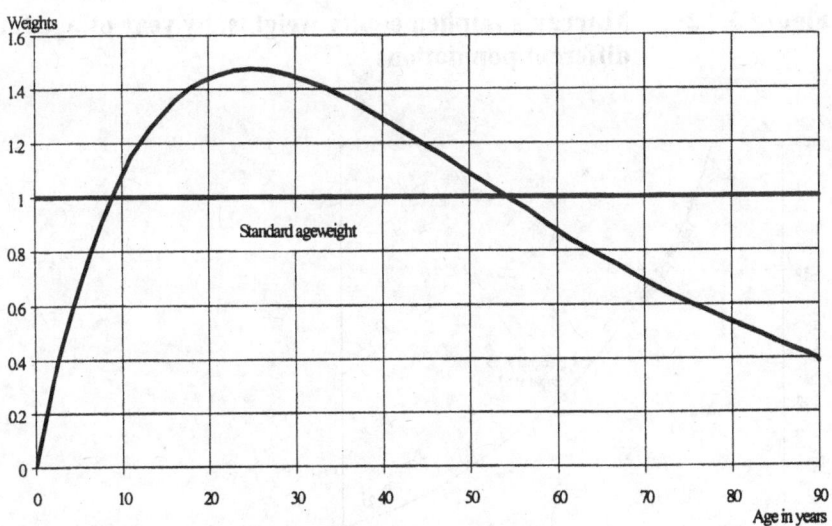

Figure 5.2.1   Relative value of a year of life
Source: World development report 1993.

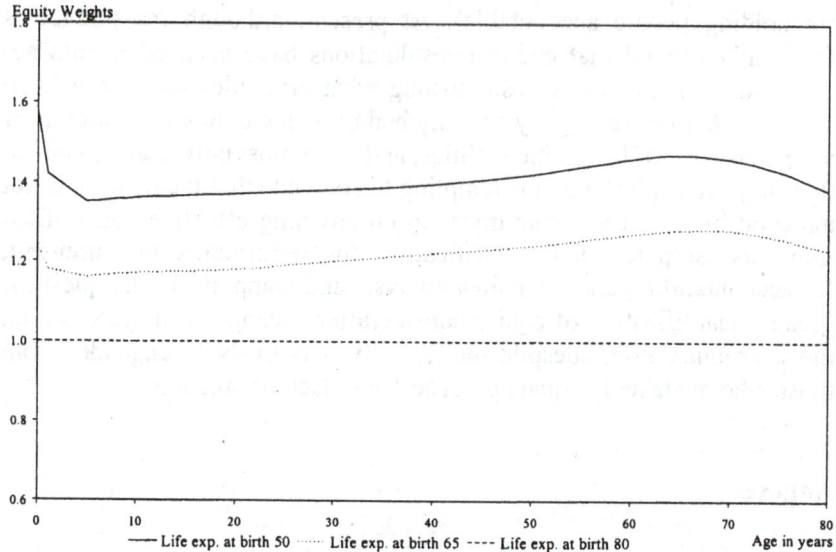

Figure 5.2.2 Murray's implied equity weights, by year of age for different populations

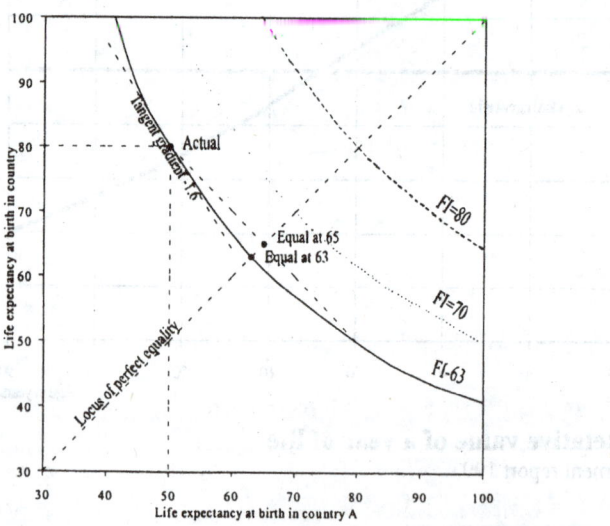

Figure 5.2.3 Social welfare contours by fair innings when inequality aversion low (r = 0.1)

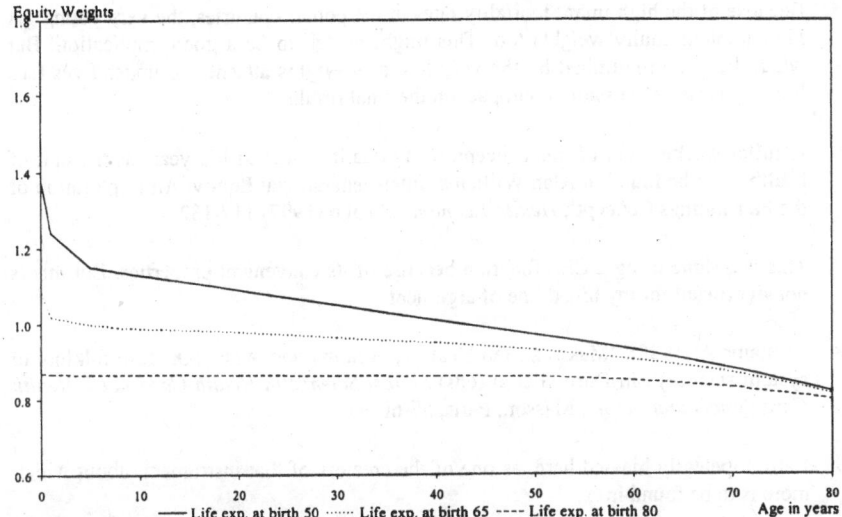

Figure 5.2.4   Equity weights if fair innings = 70 years

Notes

1. See *World Development Report 1993* (Oxford University press for the World Bank, 1993) and Murray CJ 'Rethinking DALYs' in Murray CJL & Lopez A (eds) *The Global Burden of Disease Vol I*, Harvard Univ Press for WHO and the World Bank, 1996.

2. The fact that I do not consider this task a particularly useful one is not germane at this point. My reservations were neatly summarised in the following: 'the total "costs of illness" can only indicate the benefits of treatment options if an intervention is capable of totally eradicating or entirely preventing the disease in question... The most pertinent questions facing policymakers usually relate to scale: ... by how much should an existing programme be expanded or contracted? The answer to this question requires a marginal analysis which compares the expected change in benefits with the cost of the intervention which brings that change about.'
Shiell AK et al 'Cost of Illness Studies: An Aid to Decisionmaking?' Health Policy 8 1987 pp 317-323.

3. I shall ignore the discount rate issue, since all I wish to say on that matter I said in my opening paragraph.

4. Murray CJL 'Rethinking DALYs' in Murray & Lopez (eds) *The Global Burden of Disease* p. 14.

5. Because of the high infant mortality rates in the poorer countries, the very young get high implied equity weights too. This might be felt to be a good implication. But when these are multiplied by the very low age-weights attached to under fives (see Figure 1) this has virtually no impact on the final results.

6. A fuller working out of this concept, using quality-adjusted life years as the unit of health, is to be found in Alan Williams 'Inter-generational Equity: An Exploration of the Fair Innings Concept', *Health Economics* Vol 6 (1997) 117-132.

7. This was done using a CES function because of its convenient properties. But this is not significant for my broad line of argument.

8. Williams A (1988). 'Makes a Man Healthy, Wealthy and Wise! (Or from folklore to system science)'. In Duru G et al (eds) *System Science in Health Care Vol 2 Health Care System and Actors*, Masson, Paris, 57-60.

9. I am hopelessly biassed here, as one of the creators of that instrument, about which more is to be found in ....

10. I have spared you details of how he derives value weights for the disability and suffering caused by disease world-wide!

11. For a more detailed account of this notion, see Chadwick R - 'Justice in Priority-Setting', in *Rationing in Action*, BMJ Publishing Group, 1993, who cites Gallie WB 'Essentially Contested Concepts' *Proceedings of the Aristotelian Society* 1955-6, 56, 169-198.

List of contributors

Leo J.M. Aarts
　E.M. Meyers Institute for Research on Law,
　Associate Professor,
　Department of Economics, Faculty of Law,
　Leiden University, The Netherlands.

A.B. Atkinson
　Warden of Nuffield College,
　University of Oxford, UK.

Richard V. Burkhauser
　Professor of Economics,
　Center for Policy Research,
　Syracuse University, NY, U.S.A.

Amy D. Crews
　Associate Professor,
　Center for Policy Research,
　Syracuse University, NY, U.S.A.

Tor E. Eriksen
　Director Social Insurance Office of Värmland,
　Karlstad, Sweden.
　Extraordinary Professor of Social Sciences,
　University of Goteborg, Sweden.

Peter Flora
  Professor of Sociology,
  Faculty of Social Sciences,
  University of Mannheim, Germany.

Barry L. Friedman
  Professor of Economics,
  Brandeis University, Boston, Mass., U.S.A.

Robert H. Haveman
  Director of LaFollette Institute of Public Affairs,
  Professor of Economics,
  University of Wisconsin, Madison, Wisc., U.S.A.

Karen C. Holden
  Associate Director of LaFollette Institute of Public Affairs,
  Professor of Consumer Science and Public Affairs
  University of Wisconsin, Madison, Wisc., U.S.A.

Philip R. de Jong
  Professor of Economics of Social Security,
  Erasmus University, Rotterdam, The Netherlands, and
  Associate professor of Economics, Faculty of Law,
  E.M. Meyers Institute for Research on Law,
  Leiden University, The Netherlands.

Jun-Young Kim
  Professor of Economics,
  Department of Economics,
  Sung Kyun Kwan University,
  Seoul, Republic of Korea.

Julian Le Grand
  Professor of Social Policy and Administration,
  Department of Social Policy and Administration,
  London School of Economics and Political Science, UK.

Timothy McBride
    Institute for Research on Poverty,
    University of Wisconsin, Madison, Wisc., U.S.A.

Theodore R. Marmor
    Professor of Public Policy and Management,
    Institute for Organization and Management,
    Yale University, Newhaven, Conn., U.S.A.

Kieke G.H. Okma
    Senior Political Advisor to the
    Minister of Health, Welfare and Sport,
    Rijswijk, The Netherlands.

Einar Overbye
    NOVA, Norwegian Social Research Institute,
    Oslo, Norway.

Christopher Prinz
    Senior Researcher,
    European Center for Social Welfare Policy and Research,
    Vienna, Austria

Joseph F. Quinn
    Professor of Economics,
    Department of Economics,
    Boston College,
    Chestnutt Hill, Mass., U.S.A.

David Rajnes
    Consultant,
    Washington, DC, U.S.A.

Martin Rein
    Professor of Social Studies and Planning,
    Department of Urban Studies and Planning,
    Massachusetts Institute of Technology,
    Cambridge, Mass., U.S.A.

Anne Skevik
    NOVA, Norwegian Social Research Institute,
    Oslo, Norway.

Timothy M. Smeeding
    Professor of Economics,
    Maxwell School,
    Center for Policy Research,
    Syracuse University,
    Syracuse, NY, U.S.A.

Lars Söderström
    Professor of Economics,
    University of Lund,
    Sweden.

John A. Turner
    Senior Advisor,
    International Labour Office,
    Geneva, Switzerland.

Alan Williams
    Emeritus Professor of Economics,
    University of York, UK

Amy Wolaver
    Institute for Research on Poverty,
    University of Wisconsin, Madison, Wisc., U.S.A.

Barbara L. Wolfe
    Director, Institute for Research on Poverty,
    Professor of Economics and Preventive Medicine,
    University of Wisconsin, Madison, Wisc, U.S.A.

Cathleen D. Zick
    Professor of Family and Consumer Studies,
    University of Utah, Salt Lake City, Utah, U.S.A.